Contents

Acknowledgments   ix

Introduction: Sympathy and Orientalism   1

1. Marco Polo's Fabulous Imperial Connections   27

2. Jesuit Channels between Europe and Asia   74

3. A Genealogy of Cosmopolitan Reading   114

4. News of the Ming Dynasty's Collapse   155

5. Vondel's Tragic Chinese Emperor   177

6. Wieland's Secret History of Cosmopolitanism   196

7. Adam Smith and the Chinese Earthquake   220

8. Goethe Reads the Jesuits   243

9. Chinese-German Pairings   269

10. World Literature and Goethe's Chinese Poetry   296

Bibliography   355

Index   381

ACKNOWLEDGMENTS

I am first indebted to Eric Hayot, whose friendship and generosity supported this project from the start, to On-Cho Ng for sharing his knowledge and encouragement, to Shuang Shen for sending me to China more than once, to Ana Carolina Hosne for sharing her research, to Chris Long for his digital humanities support, to Walter Demel for his scholarly friendship, and to Gita Dharampal-Frick for her kindness and intellectual inspiration. I was very much aided by insights from Birgit Tautz and Ronnie Hsia, who first turned me on to the Jesuits. For hosting me on illuminating visits to Nanjing University, I am grateful to Trace Chen, Cong Cong, Leil Dongxue, Andong Lu, Yuhan Peng, Zhengdong Tang, and Xiang Zhou. Members of the German Studies Association Seminar on Asia-German provided insightful comments on drafts of the book chapters. For inviting me to present early versions of the book, I also thank Willi Goetschel at the University of Toronto, Aaron Jaffe at Louisville University, Venkat Mani at the University of Wisconsin, Carl Niekerk at the University of Illinois, Cecilia Novero at the University of Otago, Joseph O'Neil at the University of Kentucky, Qinna Shen at Bryn Mawr College, and Chunjie Zhang at the University of California.

The book would never have been written without a fellowship at the University of Heidelberg's Cluster of Excellence Asia and Europe in a Global Context, led by Barbara Mittler and Axel Michaels. A fellowship from the Penn State University Center for Humanities and Information allowed me to work with media theorists. My work was aided through a three-year grant to the Penn State Department of Asian Studies from the Henry Luce Foundation. The invitation to teach at the Institute of Advanced Studies in Humanities and Social Studies in Nanjing University was invaluable.

CHINESE SYMPATHIES

Introduction

Sympathy and Orientalism

How do people grow to care about distant strangers? How do they overcome their own fear and ignorance to recognize affinities between themselves and foreigners far away? Can societies move beyond the cautious hospitality sometimes offered stranded transients to acknowledge full-fledged kinship? What beliefs encourage inherently suspicious people to drop their guard against aliens? What personal traits and cultural norms did Europeans perceive in Asians to be similar to their own? How did the intellectual regimes justifying sympathy shift in the face of internal critiques? Does sympathy for others persist even when the rationales for such a feeling change?

This book examines how Europeans first came to identify with Chinese figures to such an extent that they could readily discover similarities between themselves and East Asians. The establishment of seventeenth- and eighteenth-century information channels through transoceanic trade allowed missionary letters, theological treatises,

imperial histories, tragic dramas, moral philosophies, literary translations, and poetic cycles to portray correspondences between China
and Europe. A succession of intellectual regimes, each professing
to have no immediate alliance with any other—Jesuit missionaries, baroque encyclopedists, Enlightenment moralists, world literature translators—managed to refine textually mediated emotions
to such an extent that they all could assert that the Chinese were
fundamentally no different than themselves.

Early modern European sympathies for Chinese culture existed in
a double sense of the word—as emotional responses to another person's condition (real or imaginary) and as unseen influences exerted
between two bodies over a great distance. Both forms of sympathy
depend on some form of communication. The discovery of an intellectual affinity requires a prior mediating connection that allows the
correspondence to seem plausible. Whereas ancient cosmological beliefs in sympathetic relations presumed the existence of elemental media that allowed transmissions between planets and bodies on earth,
the eighteenth century's moral psychology of sympathies depended
upon the conveyances provided by scriptural and visual images.[1] The
ability of informed Europeans to identify with people in China, based
solely on their reading of missionary and travelers' reports, constituted the utmost test of David Hume's observation: "No quality of
human nature is more remarkable, both in itself and its consequences,
than that propensity we have to sympathize with others and to receive by communication their inclinations and sentiments."[2]

Before it became a word to designate shared emotions, sympathy was understood as an unseen cosmological affinity between two
separate bodies. Johann Heinrich Zedler's *Grosses vollständiges
Universal-Lexicon aller Wissenschaften und Künste* (Universal lex-
icon of all sciences and arts) provides a definition from the early
Enlightenment: "In natural philosophy a hidden accordance of two
bodies and inclinations, the one to the other. . . . Philosophers of na-

---

1. For an expanded, environmental definition of media, see John Durham Peters, *The Marvelous Clouds: Toward a Philosophy of Elemental Media* (Chicago:
University of Chicago Press, 2015).
2. David Hume, *A Treatise of Human Nature* (New York: Barnes and Noble,
2005), 244.

ture have provided countless examples of such sympathies in the wide world and have found them between certain plants, metals, stones, and the like." Saturn for example is supposed to have an influence on lions, pigs, asses, cats, rabbits, ostriches, cranes, ravens, owls, moles, toads, scorpions, flies, bugs, and other creatures that swarm about at night. A second meaning lies in medicine whereby one body part that is not diseased suffers along with another part that is, or whereby a cure has no visible cause for its unseen healing ability. Finally, a third definition addresses moral reason in the sense that sympathy describes the agreement and affection two bodies have toward one another, so that two people with the same natural character (choleric, sanguine) will also often share the same tastes or manner of speaking.[3]

Sympathy for Chinese culture has often been classified as Sinophilia, whereas disdain has been labeled Sinophobic. Curiously the latter term does not refer to a fear of China or of Chinese people invading or migrating so much as a liberal contempt for the place as a backward monarchy mired in archaic conventions. In either case, an unseen, difficult to define relationality exceeding ordinary bounds is called forth when characterizing Europeans relations to Chinese culture. Not confining themselves to silk, porcelain, and other commodities, historians have also turned to terms such as "fashion" or "enthusiasm" to characterize European motivations to understand or emulate Chinese culture. *Chinese Sympathies* invokes an older epistemology of resemblances as it appears in twenty-first century affect theory, which focuses on "visceral forces beneath, alongside, or generally *other than* conscious knowing, vital forces insisting beyond emotions."[4] Another alternative to the Sinophobia/philia model would

---

3. Johann Heinrich Zedler, *Grosses vollständiges Universal-Lexicon aller Wissenschaften und Künste* (Leipzig: Zedler, 1732–1754; online edition available at https://www.zedler-lexikon.de/index.html?c=startseite&l=de), 41:744: "In der Natur-lehre eine verborgene Uebereinstimmung zweyer Cörper und Neigung des einen zu dem andern. . . . Von solcher Sympathie geben die Naturkündiger unzählbare Exempel in der grossen Welt, und finden sie zwischen den Planeten und gewissen Gewächsen, Metallen, Steinen, u.d.g."

4. Gregory J. Seigworth and Melissa Gregg, "An Inventory of Shimmers," in *The Affect Theory Reader*, ed. Melissa Gregg and Gregory J. Seigworth (Durham, NC: Duke University Press, 2010), 1 (emphasis in original).

be to recollect the almost metaphysical sense of curiosity Europeans took in East Asia as an exotic location. In general, the presumption remains that some additional explanation needs to be provided to account for European interest in China. The attraction, along with its inevitable reversal, is never considered self-evident.

The layered meanings of "sympathy" in emotional and corporeal terms converges with erotic attraction. Enlightenment writers preserved some of the older cosmological resonances of the word when they wrote about desire. Thus, for example, Christoph Wieland described the emergence of sexuality as "a secret sympathy, which arises from the equal, harmonious condition of the bodies and spirits, whispering softly to the young lad and blossoming maiden that they were made for each other."[5] While Wieland portrays erotic sympathy in mutual terms, sentimental literature also recognized one-sided expressions of sympathy, without waiting for confirmation. As communications networks were slow to deliver responses to correspondence, the recipient's initial burst of emotion was itself sufficiently interesting. Sympathies in the eighteenth century no longer had to hang together with a cosmological order. The Renaissance formation of sympathy approached inclinations, actions, and states of mind from outside the subject as exterior forces rather than grounding them in a hidden interiority.[6] Personal affinities could be characterized as driven by an other. The cosmological understanding of sympathy was replaced slowly over the course of the early modern period and into the late eighteenth century by an internalized, subjective feeling, which appeared in its earliest form as personalized, Christian compassion and then became an individualized moral feeling and eventually an uncontrollable desire. The question of whether feelings emerge from within or outside the person con-

5. Christoph Martin Wieland, *Gesicht von einer Welt unschuldiger Menschen*, vol. 29 of *Sämmtliche Werke* (Leipzig: Göschen, 1857), 86. "Eine geheime Sympathie, die aus einer gleichgestimmten Beschaffenheit der Leiber und Gemüther entsteht, lispelt mit sanfter Stimme dem Jüngling und dem aufblühenden Mädchen ein, daß sie für einander geschaffen sind."
6. Leo Spitzer, "Classical and Christian Ideas of World Harmony: Prolegomena to an Interpretation of the Word 'Stimmung,'" *Traditio* 2 (1944): 409–64, 3 (1945): 307–65.

stitutes thereby an indeterminacy between thought and action—the zone of affect theory. One literary representation of this undecidable moment appears in both classical Chinese poetry as *yi jing* (idea-scape) and in German Romanticism as the aesthetics of *Stimmung* (mood or atmosphere).[7]

Sympathies require mediation, either through communication or some unseen cosmological force. The collective quality of emotions becomes more obvious when personal statements are understood as manifestations of media dynamics. This book argues that early modern affects about Asia were conditioned by the operation of information channels that sent and received news from abroad. Specifically, the ability to feel sympathy for distant people depends upon communication networks running between different locations. This book examines in particular how information channels create sympathy between people separated by great distances. While compassion is often described as a natural emotion, it requires training in how to generate and direct itself. Additionally, it usually comes into being within an informed and concerned community, which may well be distributed across wide spaces. How is it that modern readers can feel an emotional connection with distant people solely because they have read a news report about them? The history of European caring often begins with examples of crisis and suffering, wherein safe and untroubled humans developed the capacity to care about unseen, unknown victims, but eventually the emotional capacity to identify with strangers extended further, so that Europeans learned to care even about daily life on the other side of the world.

How did the history of reading media prepare people to think with foreigners, to share their perspectives, rather than rejecting them? This book focuses on early modern connections between China and Europe, but it serves as a prelude to the more modern question of how people care about distant suffering. Why are written reports about the oppression of ethnic minorities, the plight of

---

7. Louis Luixi Meng, "Idea-scape (*yijing*): Understanding Imagery in the Chinese Poetic Tradition," *Comparative Literature: East & West* 23.1 (2015): 29–48; David Wellbery, "Stimmung," in *Aesthetische Grundbegriffe*, ed. Karlheinz Barck, Martin Fontius, Dieter Schlenstedt, Burkhart Steinwachs, and Friedrich Wolzettel (Stuttgart: Metzler, 2010), 5:703–33.

refugees, and the destruction wrought by plagues, earthquakes and other disasters received with attention and care? Rather than stress all the reasons why sympathy is short-lived and politically ineffective, I want to examine how Europeans first learned to care at all. I will show that this focus on suffering is but the first stage in a more elaborate history whereby readers, some of them admittedly exceptional intellectuals, learned to identify with foreigners even when they were not victims, but rather were simply living only somewhat dramatic lives. The ultimate goal of my argument is to show how contemporary cosmopolitanism emerged out of a Christian and then Enlightenment morality of sympathy. In literary terms, I seek to show how both secular and Christian cosmopolitanism fostered the identificatory reading strategies underlying Goethe's world literature.

If we read Foucault's description of Renaissance sympathies, we recognize that his epistemology of analogies is itself built upon an analogy with communication technologies. "Sympathy can traverse the vastest spaces in an instant; it falls like a thunderbolt from the distant planet upon the man ruled by that planet; on the other hand, it can be brought into being by a simple contact."[8] Foucault continues: "It excites the things of the world to movement and can draw even the most distant of them together." Then a few pages later Foucault makes the analogy explicit: "Sympathy creates communication between our bodies and the heavens, and transmits the movement of the planets to the affairs of men."[9] You do not need to be a hardboiled German media theorist to ask whether in fact it is communication that creates sympathies, not the other way around. The ability to draw analogies, to perceive parallels or even just similarities, requires communication. It is not enough for missionaries to posit similarities between Christianity and Buddhism or Confucianism; they must also be in a position to do so. Transportation and communication facilitate sympathetic identifications, though they by no means guarantee them.

---

8.   Michel Foucault, *The Order of Things: An Archeology of Human Sciences* (New York: Vintage 1973), 23.
9.   Foucault, *The Order of Things*, 27–28.

Sympathy for China takes several routes. Initially it is directed towards the figure of the emperor and his supporting administrative culture. German intellectuals who perceived an idealized similarity between themselves and China came to adopt the notion that they too served as mandarins—poets, philosophers, but crucially also state administrators. In the Holy Roman Empire, the nexus between intellectuals and bureaucrats was not nearly as established as in China; thus German identifications with China included a certain utopian wishfulness. The first practitioners of this comparison were the Jesuit missionaries who quickly conformed themselves to the Chinese imperial administration so as to walk, talk, and write as though they were mandarins. The Jesuits' adaptation of Catholic teaching to the Confucian elite, referred to as "accommodation," set a standard that was followed in Germany by philosophers such as Leibniz and Wolff, princes such as August the Strong, and eventually poets such as Goethe.

Chinese Sympathies offers an analogy about analogical thinking with its claim that not only did the first missionaries perceive fundamental similarities between early Confucian texts and Christian revelation, but that the first European translators also discovered correspondences between Chinese fiction and European novels. For almost two centuries, Jesuit missionaries asserted their primacy as interpreters of Chinese culture based on their access to the ruling elite. No other European organization could claim to know how the inner circles of power operated in China. Europeans living within absolute monarchies understood that gaining admittance to the imperial palace and the houses of the administrative elite was a rare privilege. Mastery of Mandarin was central to the Jesuit's exclusive position, and European scholars often complained that the missionaries made little effort share their skills by publishing linguistic books. Their privileged position was challenged only with the appearance of Chinese novels translated by English and French scholars who had learned the necessary languages on their own. Translators relied heavily on Jesuit treatises to explain the society depicted in scholar-beauty romances, but they also argued that reading fiction written for native Chinese allowed Europeans insight into domestic settings and emotional dramas that Catholic priests would never have witnessed or recounted. By 1800 reading translated novels was plausibly a more secure form of knowledge about Chinese manners than relying solely on reports from travelers. Chinese novels were not written for Europeans; they did not address the Western gaze; they showed no knowledge of their own strangeness. The earliest examples of Goethe's world literary readings in Persian, Chinese, and Serbian literature all shared that they were not written for the European cultural elite. They had come into being autonomously within parallel cultures that were not yet conditioned by the market forces that would later draw them together.

Inevitably though, any understanding of a translated novel depended on the information provided by Jesuit reports, so in the end they could not completely split away from the missionary information store. The techniques required to make translated novels intelligible to Europeans had also already been developed over the century of missionary writing. The ability to identify with foreign figures and to visualize scenes imaginatively, even though they included wholly unfamiliar elements, had already been taught to Catholic readers of Asian missives. The Catholic recipient of the missionary letter was not merely receiving information from a distant confidant, but rather was participating in a mutual relationship between sender and receiver as members of the global church. The missionary depended on the faithful to hear his message; his position within the community was defined not just by his possessing more knowledge, but also by sharing a common worldview with his audience back home. Missionaries frequently referred to themselves as belonging to a collective modeled on the life of Francis Xavier, founder of the Jesuit mission in Asia. This communal bond between souls connected by correspondences, epistolary and spiritual, served as a model for later sentimental forms of cosmopolitanism. The "rise of the novel" allowed these older, identificatory modes of reading to be readjusted for the sake of a secular relationship to the text. The image of the Asian martyr, suffering an inexpressibly painful death for the sake of his or her newly adopted Christian faith, was the starting point for a second, at first exclusively Catholic, identification. Here the strangers were made familiar through the shared Christian faith and then elevated to figures of veneration through a death that replicates Christ's crucifixion. While rejecting martyrdom as theological fanaticism, Enlightenment moral philosophy turned the cultic figure into a more abstract victim—the tortured brother and the earthquake victim. If the Catholic world saw martyrs as witnesses to unwavering faith, the Enlightenment recast martyrs as victims succumbing to state oppression—a vision that still inspires political sympathies. From the beginning of Catholic globalism, the sight and thought of distant physical suffering was supposed to lift the barriers that separated Europeans from Asians. The legend of Spanish cruelty in the Americas, the exploitation of South Asians by Dutch and English merchants, and the suffering of the African slave also relied on psychological techniques and formal representations first elaborated in the late medieval church. Strikingly, such images of intense suffering elicited little sympathy within China itself. Confucian administrators would not have venerated images of executed prisoners, for they would have been seen as rebels or tricksters. Jesuits refrained from showing pictures of Christ's crucifixion or martyrs within China—a visual strategy that ultimately led to accusations that the mission was suppressing more than just the most central image in Christianity, but also its defining theological moment.[10]

Sympathies fluctuate. Moods are ever changing. Enlightenment philosophers well understood that an ethics based on sympathy was likely to be unstable, to wax and wane in its concern for others, in the intensity of its commitments. Accordingly, this book posits a model of mobilization and circulation, wherein knowledge about China lies dormant in German libraries for long stretches, forgotten, unrecognizable to most people who stumble across it, only to be mobilized, rediscovered, and brought back into circulation at striking moments of inspiration. My work provides a series of close readings concentrating on Jesuit missionary reports about China, baroque martyr dramas and compilations about Chinese converts, Adam Smith's sentimental thought experiment about China, and

---

10. *China und Europa: Chinaverständnis und Chinamode im 17. und 18. Jahrhundert, Ausstellung vom 16. September bis 11. November 1973 im Schloß Charlottenburg, Berlin* (Berlin: Verwaltung der Staatlichen Schlösser und Gärten, 1973), 132.

Goethe's espousal of Chinese literature as a source for world literature. These diverse texts converged as stimulants for Goethe's idea of world literature and his late poetic cycle "Chinesisch-Deutsche Jahres- und Tageszeiten" ("Chinese-German Book of Hours and Seasons")—probably the first German literary text with an Asian-German title intended to provoke nationalist Romantics. World literature, as Goethe proposes and as we shall examine in chapter 10, is driven by an inclination to recognize resemblances among disparate texts. As David Damrosch suggests, Goethe practiced an intensive mode of reading across an extensive range of literary texts by concentrating on analogies rather than on differences.[11] His attention was drawn to metaphors that translate between cultures, for suggesting underlying similarities.[12] Given that "analogy is nothing other than the deep love that binds together things that are remote, seemingly diverse or inimical,"[13] such epiphanies could obviously be based on a misunderstanding or misperception, so that the perceived similarity is technically incorrect even as it produces a complex comparison. Misunderstandings often emerge from the aspiration to communicate what has not yet been fully understood. The recognition of similarities between divergent cultures is often so suffused with utopian desires that it seems unintelligible to those who do not share these feelings. Jesuit accommodation in China—with all its misreadings of Confucianism—provides an early example of the search for resemblances between literary texts and traditions, a tendency that also guided Goethe's interpretation of foreign literature. He was not interested in organizing knowledge so much as stimulating his own ability to write poetry. Rather than positing and applying an overarching concept of humanity and po-

---

11. David Damrosch, *What Is World Literature?* (Princeton, NJ: Princeton University Press, 2003), 297–300.

12. "But the greatest thing by far is to have a command of metaphor. This alone cannot be imparted by another; it is the mark of genius, for to make good metaphors implies an eye for resemblances" (Aristotle, *Aristotle's Theory of Poetry and Fine Art*, trans S. H. Butcher [New York: Dover, 1951], 87 [1459a]).

13. Filippo Marinetti, "Technical Manifesto of Futurist Literature," in *Futurism: An Anthology*, ed., Lawrence Rainey, Christine Poggi, and Laura Wittman (New Haven, CT: Yale University Press, 2009), 120.

etry, his readings were focused on detecting resemblances between his own writing and that of others. To the extent that these similarities were then understood as reflecting a larger unity, Goethe did share in the premodern presumption of an organic wholeness to human existence. He was more concerned with how texts overlapped and intersected than in the application of an abstract concept to diverse forms of writing. These similarities could come into being without having to assert some complex causal connection between them, yet their recognition was greatly enhanced by the increased circulation of texts through expanding international media circuits.

Goethe's advocacy of world literature was motivated in part by the recognition that the translation of narratives provided a more subtle insight into the foreign society than the compilation of information. The novel's implicit bond between narrator and audience allowed Europeans to enter into private Chinese spaces that missionaries, merchants, and explorers could never reach. By reading translated novels, Europeans were eavesdropping on conversations and events to which they would otherwise never be privy and were allowed thereby to recognize similarities hidden behind exterior differences. Translation seemed to lift the linguistic barrier that confined Chinese-European mediation to a handful of learned missionaries during the early modern period.

World literature incorporates several readerly intentions that in isolation seem antithetical to one another. The inclination to approach writing about foreign countries with sympathy for the settings, characters, and events stands at odds with the drive to garner autonomous units of information that can be placed in a systematic relation to other information gathered from different sources. Nevertheless, the reading practices of world literature emerged from these early attempts to isolate information about foreign cultures. From the European reception of Marco Polo and Mandeville to the very first Portuguese seafarers' reports, humanist readers in Europe sought to isolate truthful and then later useful information from the narrative within which it was embedded. As this distinction became more explicit, the category of fiction, as an invented narrative with no immediate, direct correspondence to existing reality, also came into existence. While Jürgen Osterhammel is quite correct in arguing that Enlightenment writing about China became increasingly focused on information as distinct from fables, he simplifies the relationship between the two terms. Well into the eighteenth century, most Europeans learned about China through Jesuit dramas, Italian operas, tea cups and porcelain miniatures, and long-winded baroque novels brimming with summary reports. The desire to learn about China was described as curiosity, not science. The seventeenth century saw different strategies for distinguishing between piety, edification, curiosity, learning, and entertainment. Jesuit reports from Asia were written with a clear understanding that their accounts would be compiled, revised, and republished into school dramas, sermons, prayers, meditations, and scholarly collections. While scientific information in the sense that moderns recognize was included in all these genres, Jesuits considered it completely within keeping of their primary mission to integrate piety with scholarship. As trained humanists, Jesuit writers were well versed in the methods and models of ancient historians and naturalists, yet the Enlightenment drive to isolate information from a larger context that included personal and communal salvation was antithetical to their purpose. Individual missionaries in China such as Martino Martini or Nicoló Longobardo might have written in a concise, informative style that echoed Thucydides or Herodotus, but they were always concerned to demonstrate how the Christian God was guiding the Jesuit mission. Martini provided a remarkably clear account of the Ming dynasty's fall, but he insisted on explaining this cataclysm as divine justice because the last emperor had refused to convert to Christianity. The theological interpretation implicit within his matter of fact narrative was revised and made more explicit for European audiences in Joost van den Vondel's tragic drama, *Zungchin*. The difference between observing and converting China emerges in seventeenth-century Jesuit reports, but these tendencies were stitched back together as those texts were revised and recirculated in Europe. Not until the eighteenth century, when scientific disciplines such as geography defined themselves as distinct from imperial, commercial, or theological regimes, was information perceived as a distinct entity that existed apart from the individuals and institutions engaged in its collection. Information was not merely about some object; through its circulation in diverse networks, information became valuable as a thing that some people possessed and others lacked.

The discourse positing an autonomous world literature develops as forms of representing China become differentiated during and after the Enlightenment. For most of the sixteenth and seventeenth century, the scholarly or Protestant inclination to isolate scientific knowledge about China required a critical examination of Catholic missionary writing, as well as the introduction of new genres. For well over a century, the first Jesuit missionaries translated Confucian philosophical texts into Latin. Chinese dramas and narratives were excluded from their long-term translation projects. The many dramas Europeans saw about China were actually adapted from missionary narratives; they were not written by the Chinese for their own purposes. Historical scholarship has focused on what the Jesuits brought back from China, but just as important was the long list of objects and texts that the missionaries silently excluded from their transfer project. The formal qualities of Chinese art became visible to Europeans indirectly through the trade in textiles and porcelain, without any substantial Jesuit commentary. Stories and plays written by Chinese for their own audiences were not accessible to Europeans until the eighteenth century.

As I discuss in chapter 10 the first Chinese fictional narratives were translated by merchants living in Canton as part of their own language learning efforts. While Jesuits taught themselves Mandarin by translating Confucian classics, English and Portuguese traders tried their hand at poetry, drama, and narrative fiction. These translators still saw domestic literature as means of understanding Chinese culture in ways that the missionaries did not. Chinese stories had the advantage of depicting household scenes that had previously been outside the interest or purview of Jesuit missionaries. How did the Chinese get married? The question was better answered in a narrative written by a Chinese author for Chinese readers than by a European missionary or merchant. Initially, literature was another data source for curious Europeans. The missionary drive to organize all representations of China within the final aim of converting the emperor and his subjects to Christianity was being replaced by a more mercantile desire to understand how the Chinese think and act. The Jesuits of course did not fail to have a response to later translations: Who better to describe China, a learned Christian priest or a profit-seeking merchant?

In the midst of these debates, certain continuities still held fast. The first translations of novels retained explicit parallels between literature and information, in that the narratives are interspersed with countless footnotes offering the European reader ethnographic explanations of every detail. If a character rides a horse or holds a dish, the early translations include a footnote to an earlier Jesuit report about domestic animals or porcelain. This encyclopedic approach to novels followed the earlier baroque tendency to compile knowledge in narrative form. The shift toward treating Chinese writings solely in aesthetic terms first appeared, predictably enough, in Weimar. In their correspondences about China and in their incomplete revisions of translated fiction, Goethe and Schiller did not treat Chinese literature as just another means of conveying ethnographic knowledge. Instead they focused on the internal forms of Chinese literature—anything from the moral character of a literary figure to the poetic mood of a natural landscape. These they perceived as distinctly Chinese, yet comparable to European fiction. Their motives were quite writerly. Goethe and Schiller read Chinese as well as Persian and Indian literature because they were looking for good material to adapt for their own writing. Their search to appropriate Asian literature focused on the translatability of aesthetic and ethical forms—the dramatic tension underlying a plot, the natural harmonies of a poem, the metaphysics implied by an event.

World literature emerged when Europeans attribute aesthetic autonomy to writing in other cultures. Readers such as Goethe presumed that foreign texts were fictions with a double-sided relationship to their own society—that the work constructed representations according to its own rules that were distinct from external reality and yet reflected the pressures and expectations regulating the society within which the text was first written. World literature constitutes itself as a second order reflection upon foreign texts. In projecting this wider framework on to foreign writing, readers presume that all imaginary writing is itself implicitly engaged in reflection about the conditions that determine its own existence. A desire to under-stand, though not necessarily a drive to gather information, moti-vates this reading of foreign writing. Chinese novels were expected to reveal insights to foreigners even as their depictions address other members of the mandarin and merchant classes. Chapter 10 eluci-dates how Goethe extends just such an interpretation to the first European translations of Chinese fiction. His recognition of analo-gies between Chinese and European novels was not only focused on characters and social scenes, but also included a shared poetic inde-terminacy in representing nature. As he isolated aesthetic qualities in Chinese romances, Goethe translated, or reinscribed, them into his own lyric poetry. The Chinese novels he read encourage such pas-sages between genres, for like German novels around 1800, their prose narrative is often interrupted and analyzed self-reflectively by inserted poems.

The ongoing interest in China in the early modern period de-pended more upon the persistence of the Jesuit mission there than on any other European drive. Likewise, the end of European affir-mations of Chinese society had more to do with the suppression of the Society of Jesus than with the supposed trivialization of high Chinese culture in courtly luxuries. Even within the period of Je-suit mediation between China and Europe (1582–1773), the flow of information varied dramatically. The Jesuits were remarkable for how each new generation of missionaries in China integrated its own reports with the previous ones, yet intellectuals in Protestant Europe often felt that acquisition of new knowledge about China was still a hodge-podge process, so that scholars and publishers were often compelled to recycle older, already established stories.

Sympathy may not suffice to establish a consistent and universal moral principle. Furthermore, it is open to self-interested manipu-lation. Yet the absence of sympathy, in the face of obvious reasons for it, is worse, a sign of real trouble and cruelty. From *Don Quix-ote* onward sympathetic readers have been mocked for their naïveté even as they have become a locus of fascination. Expanding the range of sympathy for Europeans does not mean that all people within that space are treated morally, but it does include them, for better or worse, as subjects of moral judgment. Sympathy is hardly

sufficient for moral action. For Adam Smith, the feeling served as
the foundation of morality, yet he also insisted that secondary judgments of the critical spectator were necessary for producing stable
moral evaluations.

This book traces the moral emotions emerging from and reinforcing the perception that Europe and China shared important parallels,
in terms ranging from compassion-pity-sympathy-identification to
later formulations such as empathy-solidarity-cathexis-authoritarian
adoration. The French, German, and English traditions have formulated an entire range of philosophical emotions.[14] Likewise an array
of skeptics emerged: Spinoza, Mandeville, Kant, Nietzsche, Brecht. In
the early modern period, these feelings did not unfold in a linear
sequence with one replacing the other; rather, they emerged peri-
odically only to disappear again, with silences in between. While
emotional responses to distant Chinese figures appeared in distinctly
different forms, these were not necessarily the same as the sequence
of emotional responses that audiences undergo during the course of a
performance or reading. Hans Robert Jauß postulates that the reader
or viewer of an aesthetic work experiences fluctuating disposi-
tions toward a fictional character. "Astonishment, admiration, being
shaken or touched, sympathetic tears and laughter, or estrangement
constitute the scale of such primary levels of aesthetic experience
which the performance or the reading of a text brings with it. The
spectator or reader may enter into these states but also disengage
himself at any moment, take up the attitude of aesthetic reflection,
and start in on his own interpretation which presupposes a further,
retrospective or prospective distancing."[15] The important point in
both historical and individual processes remains the inherent muta-
bility of sympathetic responses. Many different types of writing about
China elicited identificatory responses. While aesthetic works were
prominent, in the seventeenth century they were by no means distinct
from religion. Furthermore, any number of travelogues, letters, trea-

---

14. Sigrid Weigel, "The Heterogeneity of Empathy: An Archeology of Multiple Meanings and Epistemic Implications," in *Empathy*, ed. Vanessa Lux and Sigrid Weigel, 1–23 (London: Palgrave MacMillan, 2017).

15. Hans Robert Jauß, *Aesthetic Experience and Literary Hermeneutics*,
trans. Michael Shaw (Minneapolis: University of Minnesota Press, 1982), 153.

tises, and histories offered opportunities for seeing the Chinese as similar to Europeans. China was not a constant presence in European discourses, but when curiosity led to a new rush of interest, old emotions were revived and revised to conform with new discourses. Sentimental moral sympathy may have shared qualities with Catholic compassion for Chinese and Japanese martyrs, but these emotions were articulated within fundamentally different metaphysical and epistemological frameworks. The object of these emotions shifted continuously, in that "China" was represented variously, depending on the medium, in terms of singular Christian martyrs, the emperor, the Confucian canon, the populace as a whole, the administrative elite, or by a few select literary characters, with considerable overlap in each case.

The historical examples presented in *Chinese Sympathies* show how subjects imagine their own relations within an extended information network. How does an individual perceive emotional relationships over distance and through media without ever having direct sensory contact with the object of their interest? What medial techniques enable, compel, and lure the subject to invest emotional interest in information that lacks any immediate embodiment? Why do people care about the humans that are not present, about whom they can only read or see in images? This book looks at the long-distance identifications that reading and viewing enable. How do Europeans transform news about foreigners into a personal concern for them? The genealogy of cosmopolitan interest in strangers in distance places moves from martyr dramas to world literature. How do information networks reconfigure subjective feelings? How does reading realign emotional investments beyond the individual's immediate environment? Do long-distance information networks simply broaden the range for the narcissistic subject to discover even more distant confirmations of itself, or does the extension of identification also transform the subject? Do expanding networks allow the recipient to assume different subject positions within a expanded range of identities? How can readers in Central Europe imagine that they are like a Buddhist monk in China? If we use spatial metaphors such as the horizon of expectations, then Chinese characters seemed to hover at the edge and even just beyond, at the farthest extreme, positioned where they were both fascinating and a test for identification over a long distance. The sense of distance was itself an effect of weak and fluctuating media channels between the two societies. As media channels grew more stable into the eighteenth century, China seemed not as far away, while the South Pacific islands became the new boundary marking the "impossibly far away."

Most every study of baroque and Enlightenment representations of Asia ponders the question of its own relation to nineteenth-century colonialism. It is a mistake for German eighteenth-century scholars to imagine that their field remains immune from the dynamics of orientalism. The logistical aspirations and apparatuses of the early modern church preceded, enabled, and were later absorbed into colonial empires. Prior to the late nineteenth-century, when the German Reich took an active interest in colonization, German Enlightenment thinkers refined methodologies and techniques for interpreting Asian texts, including those that sought to understand them from an "inside" vantagepoint.[16] Edward Said unambiguously sees eighteenth-century "sympathetic identification" that exceeds comparative study as a cultural formation that preceded orientalism. He cites Herder's *Ideas on the Philosophy of Human History* as the pivotal work that calls on readers to engage Asian texts with *Einfühlung* (empathy) in order to recognize "the hidden elements of kinship between himself and the Orient."[17] Herder was by no means alone. Many German thinkers sought to find an underlying unity that joined East and West, whether it was a biblical origin as a lost tribe, or a scriptural origin in which Chinese characters were derived from hieroglyphs, or Leibniz's and Wolff's hunch that Christians and Confucians shared a rational natural theology, or Lessing's family genealogy that related the three monotheisms to each other, or Goethe's universal sense for poetry, or Friedrich Schlegel's insistence on a linguistic unity. As this book will show, early modern orientalism displayed different forms of sympathetic identification: first, a moment of fascination and fear regarding the Chinese

---

16. Edward Said, *Orientalism* (New York: Vintage, 1979), 19.
17. Said, *Orientalism*, 118.

emperor as possessing and exceeding the qualities of Western monarchy, coupled with pity for the suffering Asian as victim. These extremes could be combined, as Walter Benjamin showed for the baroque drama, where absolute power and total abjection were often presented as different aspects of the same figure. Yet outside the theater they were more often isolated into ideal types. Each of these figures of sympathy was valued differently by Europeans depending on how they viewed monarchs or martyrs, as persons to venerate, admire, despise, or pity. These judgments were inevitably caught up with internal European conflicts over politics and religion that defined the limits of identification generally, whether across cultures or within them. For example, the Enlightenment's critique of Asian despotism had more to do with fears about European absolute monarchy than with the power structure of distant kingdoms.

Aside from Said's claim that "sympathetic Orientalism" lays the foundation for later more aggressive structures, we should not forget that advocates for early modern trade between Europe and China were already trying out the ideological terms that would later define nineteenth-century colonialism. Even if these mercantile discourses appear in minor, adumbrated forms, it would be a mistake to draw an absolute distinction between early modern approaches to the Orient and full-fledged, "technical colonialism." Well before colonialism became established, some of its basic ideas were in circulation. Already deep in the seventeenth century, Dutch and English East India traders were eager for China to open its ports to free trade. The 1655–1657 Dutch Embassy China urged the emperor to engage in "onderlingen Koophandel"—a term that the English translated as "free and mutual commerce."[18] By all accounts, the Chinese court understood commerce as the exchange of gifts with foreigners who arrived at regular intervals to pay homage to the emperor. Any economic relationship outside such ceremonies was

---

18.   John Nieuhof, *Het Gezantschap der Neêrlandtsche Oost-Indische Compagnie aan den Grooten Taratarischen Cham, den tegenwoordigen Keizer van China* (Amsterdam: Jacob van Meurs, 1665), 4; John Nieuhoff, *An Embassy sent by the East India Company of the United Provinces to the Grand Tartar Cham or Emperor of China*, trans. John Ogilby (London: John Macock, 1669), 3.

viewed with suspicion. The Dutch, and later the English, notions of free trade were clearly thus a challenge to imperial channels of exchange, which remained firmly in operation under Kangxi and Qianlong emperors. Even Immanuel Kant, who was no great admirer of Asian practices, considered it prudent for Japanese and Chinese rulers not to offer hospitality to all Europeans who arrived on their shores. While there is no comparison between seventeenth-century merchants' appeals and British strategies in the Opium Wars, the possibilities were apparent to all long before they became historical reality. The Dutch blamed Jesuits advising the emperor for the rejection of their trade proposal. At stake was the European reliance upon the imperial center for access to China in general. Even without such input, it would have been clear that the Dutch proposal sought to circumvent imperial channels in commerce. The Jesuits held a privileged access to the imperial circles while the Dutch and English had no entrée. "Free trade" became a slogan for the nineteenth-century British, but in the early modern era, it simply signified a failed attempt to bypass inter-imperial relations. Before orientalism, Asian-European relations involved a more symmetrical monarchical balance of power. Missionaries were more concerned with conversion than trade. Catholic priests near the emperor counseled against offering entry to Protestant merchants. No European courtiers questioned the authority of the emperor in Beijing; rather they saw his office as a confirmation of their own monarchical order. *Chinese Sympathies* concentrates on these multiple, imperial and missionary channels between China and Europe in establishing diplomatic, religious, scholarly, and emotional bonds. Ultimately my approach to the early modern period seeks to demonstrate that Michel Foucault's genealogy of early modern discourses confirms Walter Benjamin's claim that the baroque has a vital relevance for the modern era.[19] This book concentrates on the particular example of the baroque fascination with China and its transformations (*Funkstionswandel*) during the eighteenth century. While I eschew Benjamin's faith in origins as revealing

---

19. Peter Bürger, *Theorie der Avant-Garde* (Frankfurt: Suhrkamp, 1982), 114n20.

essential truths, I also insist that genealogies are not defined by epistemic ruptures so much as slowly shifting continuities. In particular, seventeenth-century formulations of a cosmological sympathy between Asia and Europe were secularized as moral psychology within the Enlightenment and then popped back up again, almost full-fledged, as subjective speculations in German Romanticism and idealist *Naturphilosophie.*

In summary, the book's genealogical argument, leading up to the final, tenth chapter on world literature and Chinese novels, runs as follows. In the first chapter, I explain how Marco Polo was the first European to establish a recognized allegiance with the Emperor of China. His travel memoir set the model for centuries of later readers who imagined an ideal relationship with a parallel civilization, but one in which all things were grander and more intelligent. Polo's *Travels* also underscores the interdependence of Chinese sympathies and logistical networks of travel and communication between the two ends of the continent. Polo's writing commences my long history of information channels and their ability to sustain intercultural affinities. Generations of German writers wrote oriental fables based on Polo's narrative. Christoph Wieland and Franz Kafka offer examples of how Polo's account was incorporated through the modern trope that the Habsburg Empire was the China of Europe.

Chapter 2 explains how starting in the late sixteenth century, Jesuit missionaries in China and Japan began to send reports about those kingdoms to Europe. They circulated widely in scholarly, aristocratic, ecclesiastical, and lay formats. With the establishment of Asian Catholic institutions, German Catholics were first encouraged to pray for the success of missionaries in East Asia. They concentrated their spiritual efforts in support of prominent figures such as Francis Xavier, who was soon canonized, and then on the other missionaries who sent back letters reporting on their work to convert Chinese and Japanese to Christianity. Increasingly Catholics in Europe received stories about Asian converts who displayed pious steadfastness in the face of heathen rulers who demanded that they renounce their new faith. Missionaries provided the most reliable information about Asia. The report of one missionary, Antonio Almeida, reveals the transformation Europeans underwent as they gave up their own identities to learn the local language and manners, to become, in their own understanding, Chinese.

Chapter 3 explains that Catholic information channels formed a spiritual circuit to strengthen the resolve of all participants: missionaries sent letters to Europeans who in return sent their prayers beseeching God's support for the missionaries and their converts. Catholics in Europe were strengthened in their resolve by the example of the faithful working far off in the distance. The church defined itself in global terms. As Catholics read about Chinese and Japanese converts, they were encouraged to consider not just the narrow plot of events but also the wider context within which these stories took place. Curiosity about Asia was encouraged. Readers were supposed to feel compassion for individual missionaries and martyrs by meditating on the society within which their suffering and passion occurred. This method of paying attention to historical details in order to foster a more complete spiritual union with the distant pious figure emerged from late medieval monastic techniques of contemplating the life of Christ. This meditative attentiveness was extended in the seventeenth century to all matters related to the Jesuit mission in Asia. Pious Europeans were encouraged to emulate the examples of Asian missionaries and converts. Many did so enthusiastically.

All the chapters dealing with the Jesuit missionaries emphasize how they tried to integrate themselves in imperial administrative circles by accommodating Christian teachings to their interpretation of the earliest Confucian writings. This attempt to reconcile the two religions implicitly followed the medieval church adaptation of Greek philosophy. Unlike Christian confrontations with Islam and Judaism, Jesuits did not try to refute Confucianism; instead they sought to distribute their own writings within Confucian channels of communication, thereby reinforcing the compatibility between them.

Chapter 4 analyzes Martino Martini's account of the Ming dynasty's defeat by Manchu invaders from the north. His work is more than just a missionary report in that it provided a political history of Asia through a range of figures in whom Europeans could take an interest. Martini's history recapitulates the broader larger Jesuit tendency to describe China as an ideal moral society in which the emperor and his magistrates professed an ancient teaching that shared an original understanding of the divine similar to Christianity. The emperor played a central role in this new appreciation for Chinese society as he was also the object of Jesuit efforts to convert the country. Particular emperors were represented as sympathetic to Christian teaching, perhaps even almost ready to convert.

Chapter 5 explicates one of the first European plays written about a Chinese emperor, Joost van den Vondel's tragic drama, *Zungchin*. As Europeans began to write tragic dramas based on reading missionary reports, the Chinese emperor and the Christian converts around him became the focus of audience identification. Rather than present the emperor as a stereotypical hostile pagan ruler, the play depicts him as a well-intentioned but weak monarch who failed to convert to Christianity. Writers and dramaturges tried to bring plays about China into line with their understanding of Aristotle's account of tragedy. Within philosophical circles, Chinese figures such as Confucius were identified as near saints, comparable to leading moral figures in the Western tradition.

Contrary to church teachings, radical Enlightenment thinkers adapted Jesuit accounts of Chinese thought and politics to claim that a nation could be ethical and civilized while ruled by atheists. Rationalist thinkers revised Christian forms of compassion by eliminating the attention to martyrs, who held steadfast to dogma. Enlightenment writers sought to extend audience sympathies to all include all virtuous individuals, regardless of their religion.

Chapter 6 uses the writings of Christoph Wieland to show how friendship rather than martyrdom became the basis for a new mode of identification. Sympathizing with a foreigner as a potential friend constituted a secular parallel to Christian compassion grounded in faith. By the middle of the eighteenth century, missionary reports from Asia were treated with increased skepticism because the Jesuits were increasingly criticized for their political positions in Europe. In an effort to detach from church teachings, Enlightenment moralists removed all references to martyrs in their dramatical writings, preferring instead to extend the range of tragic identification to include more ordinary people. This chapter explains further how the Enlightenment mobilized the ideal of friendship as an emotional framework for interpreting foreign texts and information. The chapter supports the book's larger argument about how the missionary channels that inspired Catholic connections to Asia were replaced by sentimental identifications that enabled world literature. Wieland's cosmopolitan sentimentalism elaborates the aesthetic preconditions for Goethe's claim that Chinese novels belong to world literature. Wieland's invention of the term *Weltliteratur* reflects the eighteenth century's awareness that postal systems not only created new forms of writing but also brought translated texts into circulation within Europe.

Chapter 7 builds on the thesis that sentimental cosmopolitanism was an international movement built on global communication channels by focusing closely on an important passage in Adam Smith's *Theory of Moral Sentiments* in which he asks: How would a European respond to news of a cataclysmic earthquake in China? His choice was not random for Smith had read the major eighteenth-century sources of information on China and had come see the kingdom as a parallel civilization, whose economic success challenged the universality of his theories on free trade. His query raised the central concern of a morality based on sympathy: Do feelings of compassion extend over great distances to include foreigners? Smith contemplated the response on a European-wide level, not merely as a British concern. Smith's thought experiment constituted a nonreligious, psychological adaptation of the compassion Christians were supposed to feel at the sight of the suffering martyr. While Jesuit missionaries deployed images of Chinese martyrs to mobilize Catholic identification with Asian converts, Smith offered an Enlightenment adaptation in which Chinese suffering was caused by a natural event rather than a pagan tyrant. He also made two implicit points: first, that the communication channels between Asia and Europe were so steady that it was plausible for such news to reach an ordinary person, and second, that sentimental feelings were readily extended to China based on the older martyr model. His affirming the possibility that Europeans could feel meaningful sympathy for Chinese earthquake victims sets up the later possibility of world literature. In this sense Smith's thought experiment is a forerunner of Goethe's world literature idea. When Goethe told Jo-hann Peter Eckermann that the age of world literature was approaching because international channels of communication within Europe and the world had revived after the end of the Napoleonic Wars, he was referring to the media condition described in Smith's media-sympathy postulation.

The cosmopolitan possibility that sympathetic bonds could develop between people throughout the world and at different times in history became an increasingly common assumption among sentimental readers. Accordingly, sympathy for Chinese people grew independent of religion. Asian works of fiction that shared similarities with European genres were slowly being translated into German, French, and English, allowing educated readers to compare foreign figures in these works with other more familiar literary characters and themselves.

Chapters 8 and 9 analyze Goethe's assertion that the basic positions taken during a sixteenth-century Jesuit disputation with a Buddhist monk in Nanjing were analogous to the epistemological debates in Weimar between Kantians and Idealists. What happens in China happens in Germany, too. Added to the philosophical nuance of Goethe's comparison was that he cautiously disguised his own identification with the Buddhist position because of the emerging atheism controversy involving accusations made against Fichte's teaching in Jena. Goethe's inclination to perceive analogies between philosophy in China and in Germany anticipates his later comments about the similarities between Chinese and European novels that served as the basis for his pronouncements about *Weltliteratur*. A careful reading of Goethe's and Schiller's correspondence shows that as a heretical thinker, Goethe was inclined to identify with the Buddhist disregard for Christian theism, even as he cautiously avoided entering into yet another Enlightenment debate over religion.

At the end of this genealogy, my book will have demonstrated how Germans first came to discover similarities between themselves and East Asians to such an extent that they could identify with the Chinese. Such sympathies manifested themselves in a wide range of genres, each with its own intended purpose and manner of addressing readers. All of them depended upon the sporadic flow of news from Asia provided by missionaries communicating through trading vessels. Long after the Jesuits' initial goal of converting China by accommodating Christianity to Confucian teaching had been supplanted, the belief that the two cultures shared fundamental similarities continued to guide European perceptions of East Asia. Although world literature and Enlightenment cosmopolitanism were radically opposed to theological creeds, these idealized networks repurposed many of the intercultural strategies and presumptions deployed by missionaries. Without the global Catholic Church, world literature would never have emerged as it did.

1

Marco Polo's Fabulous Imperial Connections

From the very earliest, travel writers have felt the need to secure their credibility with readers. For adventurers it has always been important that their stories were believed. The farther the journey and the stranger the location, the more authors struggled to establish the plausibility of their narrative. If distance and unfamiliarity were inversely related to the likelihood that a travelogue would be believed, they were also directly connected to the audience's eagerness to enjoy the tale. All narratives are caught in the paradox that the more an author insists on the truth of his tale, the more readers question its veracity. At every stage, the accuracy of one traveler's account is measured against previous texts. The possibility of a text's fictionality creeps through all early travel literature. From the first, thoughtful readers struggled with how to treat the possibility that an emotionally engaging travel narrative did not correspond to the lived reality of foreign places. To sooth these contradictions, travel literature was required to balance the urge to narrate a compelling epic with accurate and insightful description of the strange peoples and places encountered along the way.[1]

As much as European writing about China suffered under the suspicion that the stories told about the Middle Kingdom were invented, readers never wanted the stories to end. Any examination of relations between China and Europe must also include the history of credibility and how it was established. The history of information, goods, and people flowing between cultures also includes a nuanced record of how plausibility was asserted or denied. Did this person really travel to China? Are his stories to be believed? How was this silk spun? Where was this tea cup manufactured? The notion of authenticity became important only in the mid-eighteenth century. Before that, institutional authority and rhetorical strategies were more likely to determine whether a traveler's tale was considered believable. In the face of the uncertainty almost any travel narrative creates, comparing one travel text with another became the stay-at-home scholar's best method for detecting exaggerations.

Very early on, in the first Italian compilations of travel writing, this comparative approach tried to test the truthfulness of a description and plausibility of a narrative by reading one text against another. Thus, an empirical problem was addressed philologically. In writings about China, fables were intertwined with history from the earliest. As fiction came to be distinct from ethnographic and geographic description and the genres separated, truthfulness was nevertheless evenly distributed among all of them. Later readers recognized that fictional writing often conveyed more insight into a society's hidden structures than a traveler's hastily composed observations. By the end of the eighteenth century, fables and romances from Asia were recognized as privileged sources of information. The challenge for Europeans was to find means of negotiating through a foreign story's strangeness to recognize basic similarities. Marco Polo's *Travels* was the first attempt at such a mediation.

---

1. Peter Uwe Hohendahl, "Zum Erzählproblem des utopischen Romans im 18. Jahrhundert," in *Gestaltungsgeschichte und Gesellschaftsgeschichte*, ed. Helmut Kreuzer and Katie Hamburger (Stuttgart: Metzler, 1969), 79–114.

Well into the nineteenth century, Marco Polo's work served as the baseline for determining what stories and descriptions were within the realm of the possible.[2] Giovanni Botero, for example, in his 1589 comparative study of world governments defends his own description of China: "These things I here deliver ought to be not thought by any man to be incredible. For (thanks that Marco Polo in his relations affirmeth far greater things) these things I speak are in these days approved to be most true by the intelligences we do receive continually both by secular and religious persons, as also by all the nations of the Portuguese."[3] Still, a critical reader might wonder if Botero's reliance on *parekbase*, an author's direct address to the reader, undermined precisely what he sought to accomplish—acceptance. The first-person narration invited the reader to judge the author's character as if the text were a person. Although many of the first books about sea journeys were cobbled together from the recollections of ships' crews by scribes who had never left home, these texts adopted a single authorial voice. When Arnold Montanus compiled an illustrated volume about Dutch embassies to the Japanese shogun, he arranged at least four separate seamen's journals into a single line of observation, with the presumption that readers were more likely to accept the truthfulness of one voice rather than a string of recollections.[4]

Although Marco Polo's *Travels* has often been challenged as filled with exaggerations, it remains the first book to read for Europeans curious about the China.[5] Its lingering authority may stem from the

---

2. Folker E. Reichert, "Marco Polos Buch. Lesarten des Fremden," In *Fiktion des Fremden. Erkundung kultureller Grenzen in Literatur und Publizistik*, ed. Dietrich Harth (Frankfurt: Fiscehr, 1994), 180–202.

3. Giovanni Botero, *The Reason of State*, trans P. J. and D. P. Waley (New Haven, CT: Yale University Press, 1956), 266.

4. Arnold Montanus, *Denckwürdige Gesandtschafften der Ost-Indischen Gesellschaft in den Vereinigten Niederländern an unterschiedliche Keyser von Japan* (Amsterdam: Jacob Meurs, 1669); Reinier H. Hesselink, "Memorable Embassies: The Secret History of Arnoldus Montanus' *Gedenkwaerdige Gesantschappen*," *Quaerando* 32.1 (2002): 99–123.

5. For a recent summary of these doubts, see Kim A. Phillips, *Before Orientalism: Asian Peoples and Cultures in European Travel Writing, 1245–1510* (Philadelphia: University of Pennsylvania Press, 2014), 54–60.

narrative's muted tone, a surprising quality given the remarkable events it recounts. Polo's book conveys the practicality of a merchant's handbook. While he justifies his traveling to China with the possibility that the Mongols might be converted to Christianity and brought into an alliance against Islam, there is little indication within the many chapters that he and his companions put much effort into this plan. Polo characterizes the religious practices in the many cities along his route as so many forms of idolatry and maintains a consistent antipathy for Islam, but he does not try to incorporate them all into a single Christian tale of salvation. In the end, Polo shows a practical appreciation for the Mongol policy of allowing subjugated nations their religion so long as they obey and pay taxes. The khan himself appears at least curious about Christianity, yet over the course of its episodic movement, the travelogue eventually settles on the material wealth and military prowess of Kublai Khan as its center of interest.[6] While Polo includes a handful of stories about magic and sorcerers, they do not come close to the wild fantasies of John Mandeville's *Travels*, Europe's other popular medieval romance about the East. Time and again the splendor and extravagance of Kublai Khan's court are shown to be the true marvel in Polo's narrative.

Marco Polo initiates a European tradition of understanding China and its culture that focuses on the emperor and his administrative elite. What appears in Polo's story as a successful feudal relationship becomes the myth that justifies European approaches to China. Even though the physical boundaries, religions, languages, and populations of China were unfamiliar to Europeans, the basic presumption from the start was that China has a single emperor, who rules completely and unopposed over this territory. Thus if knowledge of China was to have any security, it inevitably had to be routed through imperial channels. Whatever ambiguities prevailed within China, Europeans oriented their diplomacy, com-

---

6. Hermann H. Wetzel, "Marco Polos *Milione* zwischen Beschreibung und Erzählen," In *Beiträge zur sprachlichen, literarischem und kulturellen Vielfalt in den Philologien: Festschrift für Rupprecht Rohr*, ed. Gabriele Birken-Silveman and Gerda Rössler (Stuttgart: Franz Steiner Verlag, 1992), 533.

merce, and discourses around the figure of the emperor.[7] In setting up this paradigm, medieval and early modern travelers were hardly inventing a new understanding of China; rather, they were following Confucian protocols and ideology. Nevertheless, a tone of implicit inter-imperial competition between China and a variety of European monarchies generated a succession of strategic and symbolic comparisons that would last until the end of World War One.[8] Sanjay Subrahmanyam refers to the synchronic "transfer of imperial models and notions, in the sense of movement across a group of competing empires."[9] As a merchant, Polo could barely disguise how pleased he was to have entered into the service of such a supremely wealthy and powerful master. He was particularly proud of his ability to inform and entertain the khan with his observations about the people he encountered along his journeys. Polo could show Europeans that he attended the emperor of China and that his connection was direct and personal, and in the process he set a very high standard of what it meant for a traveler to successfully reach China. Like a good merchant working both ends of the supply chain, Polo could offer up his experiences moving across Asia at both ends of the journey. Kublai Khan was no different than any European reader. He was also curious to know more about foreign lands, and Marco Polo could offer him stories just as well. The emperor was both the center of the story and the perfect audience. Most importantly, the emperor stood as the ancient, stable ontological and political center of China, suggesting a coherence and continuity that Europeans thought they had lost with the demise of the Romans. The impression left upon Western readers about the unquestioned centrality of the emperor's authority was considerable. Throughout this book, I will show that European

---

7. Ge Zhaoguang, *What Is China? Territory, Ethnicity, Culture and History*, trans. Michael Gibbs Hill (Cambridge, MA: Harvard University Press, 2018).

8. My understanding of the concept derives from Laura Doyle, "Inter-Imperiality," *Interventions: International Journal of Postcolonial Studies* 16.2 (2014): 159–196.

9. Sanjay Subrahmanyam, "Holding the World in Balance: The Connected Histories of the Iberian Overseas Empires, 1500–1640," *American Historical Review* 112.5 (2007): 1360.

identification with China was routed through the figure of the emperor and his Confucian administration. This imperial identification was most visible in European courts as they formulated complex rituals of conspicuous consumption, drawn from accounts of the entertainments, festivities, and hunting expeditions undertaken in the Mongol courts, but it extended much farther into the most complex corners German intellectual philosophy and poetry.[10]

So obvious was Polo's delight in the millions of gold coins collected for the khan's court that early Italian readers teasingly referred to the *Travels* as *Il Milione*.[11] Giovanni Battista Ramusio, the translator and compiler of first-hand travel writing, explained the tendency for readers to wonder about Polo's numbers: "And because in the continual repetitions of the story which he gave more and more often when speaking of the magnificence of the Great Khan, he stated that his revenues were from ten to fifteen millions in gold, and in the same way in speaking of many other riches of those countries he spoke always in terms of millions, they gave him as a nickname, Messer Marco Millioni."[12] Polo's nickname points to the suspicions that arise when a description's scale reaches unfamiliar heights—just how vast was the wealth, territory, and population of Kublai Khan's empire? In his lectures on China and world history, Hegel underscored how Polo's text presented Europeans with a scale that they considered fabulous at first, only to later learn from other travelers that it was accurate: "In the thirteenth century, a Venetian, Marco Polo, was the first to explore China. Still, his conclusions were considered to be fables. Later everything he stated about its expanse and size was fully confirmed."[13]

10. Phillips, *Before Orientalism*, 65, 169.

11. As with all matters in Polo scholarship, this nickname has been much debated. See Marina Münkler, *Erfahrung des Fremden, Die Beschreibung Ostasiens in den Augenzeugenberichten des 13. Und 14. Jahrhunderts* (Berlin: Akademie Verlag, 2000), 123.

12. Quoted in Henry H. Hart, *Marco Polo: Venetian Adventurer* (Norman: Oklahoma University Press, 1967), 251.

13. Georg Wilhelm Friedrich Hegel, *Vorlesungen über die Philosophie der Geschichte*, ed. Eva Moldenhauer and Karl Markus Michel (Frankfurt: Suhrkamp, 1986), 12:149.

Augmenting the European reader's concern about the accuracy of Polo's measurements was the all-too-familiar tendency for storytellers to exaggerate. After all, Polo's manuscript was recounted orally during his imprisonment in a Genoese prison, written down by his fellow inmate—a classic setting for storytellers to pass the time by embellishing their past. In the vague border between fiction and truth, readers might expect a traveler to exaggerate, but they would hope he did not lie completely about ever having made the journey. Not only did one have to travel for years to reach China from Italy, but the entire trip involved scalar quantities far greater than anything in Europe: farther distances, more people, denser cities, overwhelming armies, fabulous levels of concentrated wealth were just some of the topics in which the scale of Asian social units exceeded the levels familiar to Europeans. Given the differences, it was easy for readers to conclude that Polo had simply gone from description to fantasy. The doubts about Polo reveal the scalar limits of early modern European imaginations. Up until the nineteenth century, the average European traveling by foot could cover no more than twenty-five miles in a day; a rider in a hurry might reach thirty to forty miles so long as the horse held out. The range of Europeans' geographical identities did not extend out to the breadths Polo claimed to have traversed.

For a Venetian, it was quite understandable that Polo organized much of his travel by concentrating on cities and the spaces in between them. The territories between cities are described often in terms of the time required to traverse them. Eventually, in his narrative of his initial journey to the khan's court, Polo replaces his sequential recitation of cities and provinces through which he passed with a general description of the Mongol messenger relay system, thereby suggesting that his travel was sped up or at least facilitated by being taken up by the imperial couriers. Early on in his narrative, geographical description gives way to postal logistics. "I do not propose to enumerate the provinces at this stage, as I shall be giving a full account of them later in the book. Let us turn now to the system of post-horses by which the Great Khan sends his dispatches."[14] Suddenly, the mode of

---

14. Marco Polo, *The Travels of Marco Polo*, trans. Ronald Latham (London: Penguin, 1958), 150.

transportation has become more interesting than the places through which one travels. Given the narrative drive to reach the khan's court, it comes as no surprise that Polo shows a particular fascination with the Mongolian postal system, which sends riders and runners between stations—many of them located in regions with sparse settlements. For modern scholars, Polo's detailed description of Yuan administrative-geographic structures reinforces his claim to have made the journey.[15]

The possibility that political agents could have different scalar allegiances was well understood in feudalism. The Holy Roman Empire consisted of dispersed territories. Sovereignty was rarely concentrated in a single unified territory. A lord would have obligations scattered across the map, to kings, bishops, larger territories in his immediate proximity and then to distant rulers who never showed themselves. Proximity was important in the face of so many relations, because rulers exercised power by being in a particular location—hence the many itinerate kings. From Charlemagne on, the emperor above the alps could expect trouble when he went off to Italy, for his absence allowed the Saxons, the Hanoverians, and the Bavarians, among others, the time and space to rebel. Empires generally require logistical networks that allow information, troops, and goods to travel across dispersed spaces. In Polo's narrative cities within the empire exist as nodes in one or more networks. His view of Asia as a series of centers reflects his commercial attitude.[16] His networked string of spatial connections also reveals a strategy for empires to regulate their diverse populations by linking them together "as webs or networks with diverse morphologies, connect-

---

15. Hans Ulrich Vogel, *Marco Polo Was in China: New Evidence from Currencies, Salts and Revenues* (Leiden: Brill, 2013), 7.

16. "Towns and cities can be regarded as nodal points in a series of networks, which belong to several different categories. At the highest level, we may identify: international trading networks by water; international trading networks by land; major communications routes between administrative centres; major communications routes between religious centres; routes between educational centres" (Alex Cowan, "Nodes, Networks and Hinterlands," in *Cultural Exchange in Early Modern Europe*, ed. Donatella Calabi and Stephen Turk Christensen [Cambridge: Cambridge University Press, 2007], 2:29).

ing people and events in one node to others near and far."[17] How China maintained such systems was a central question well before Mongol rule.[18] Marco Polo was the first European to answer how such vast empire could be held together.

The single most imposing fact China impressed upon the first European visitors was its continued existence as a coherent empire, composed of diverse populations and languages stretched across very large territories. Whether this image was completely accurate may be open to debate, but medieval and post-Reformation Europe had no political entity on its scale and antiquity. China's expansiveness impressed Jesuit missionaries longing for a reunified Christianity, just as it had stirred Marco Polo, a city-state native. For classically trained humanists, the obvious comparison was with the Roman Empire. China's imperial coherence impressed Leibniz, as well as many European princes eager to acquire a similar grandeur. The Jesuit plan for converting China to Christianity focused on the institutions that made empire possible—the administration, the exam system, the imperial court, the overarching official language, the print culture, the information networks. Having recognized the mechanisms by which the Chinese empire operated, the Jesuits often felt relieved of the task of preaching to the populace.[19] They were often accused of having an elitist orientation but in the case of China, the example of the Roman Empire's conversion from the emperor Constantine on downward seemed most apt. Early visitors to China were compelled to ask: What makes empire possible? How does it hold itself together? Why to people obey? The 1644 defeat of the Ming dynasty struck European readers as a stunning event, and they wrote a string of texts about the collapse and the subsequent violent reformulation of the unified empire under the Manchu invaders. With the reign of the Kangxi emperor, only the third

17. Patsy Healey, "Relational Complexity and the Imaginative Power of Strategic Spatial Planning," *European Planning Studies*, 14.4 (May 2006): 526.

18. Hilde de Weerdt, *Information, Territory, and Networks: The Crisis and Maintenance of Empire in Song China* (Cambridge, MA: Harvard University Press, 2015).

19. David Porter, *Ideographia: The Chinese Cipher in Early Modern Europe* (Stanford, CA: Stanford University Press, 2001), 79.

in the new Qing dynasty, China seemed to have restored its imperial order. The aura of China's structured civilization lasted well into
the nineteenth century. When Napoleon smashed the Holy Roman
Empire, Goethe thought to flee to China.

A long tradition of Western commentary on China juxtaposes the
regulation of space and the passage of time. China is perceived as
having organized the geography of its empire, though at the expense
of temporal advancement. In writing about China in *The Order of
Things*, Michel Foucault reiterates the fables about China as an idealized space: "In our dreamworld, is not China precisely this privileged *site* of *space*? In our traditional imagery, the Chinese culture
is the most meticulous, the most rigidly ordered, the most deaf to
temporal events, most attached to the pure delineation of space; we
think of it as a civilization of dikes and dams beneath the eternal
face of the sky; we see it, spread and frozen, over the entire surface
of a continent surrounded by walls."[20] Foucault reveals that the orientalist fantasy of China is grounded in a European projection
about its spatial organization.[21] By reaching back to Marco Polo,
Foucault identifies a critical apparatus to examine writing about
China. He isolates the conceptualization of space and its administrative regulation as central to Europe's fascination with China as
a government that rules over vast area and many peoples.

We can critically examine this fable by using Foucault's own theoretical remarks on space, for they help explain what drives Marco
Polo's concerns as a travel writer. In his Berlin lecture "Of Other
Spaces" Foucault explains that when a new space or site is delin-
eated, this new discovery immediately raises the need for information.[22] Who lives in the space? How are the sites within related to
one another? Do they form a constellation? Are they linked together
in a series? When Marco Polo describes Central Asia as an expansive space, extending farther than anyone in Europe had hitherto

20. Michel Foucault, *The Order of Things: An Archeology of the Human Sciences* (New York: Vintage, 1973), xix (emphasis in the original).
21. Zhang Longxi, "The Myth of the Other: China in the Eyes of the West,"
Critical Inquiry 15.1 (1988): 108–31.
22. Michel Foucault, "Of Other Spaces," trans. Jay Miskowiec, *Diacritics*
16.1 (1986): 22–27.

imagined, he also feels compelled to explain what kind of humans fill it. He becomes a rudimentary demographer, obliged to classify the population within this enormous territory. Information was just as important for medieval Europeans as it is today. They too sought to classify and organize people by types, to understand their movements, and, most importantly for Polo, to learn about their logistical infrastructure. Polo like Foucault keeps coming back to the problems of traffic when representing Asian spaces. By understanding China, Asia, or the Mongol Empire as a network of cities with long distances in between, he also answers the question of how these sites relate to each other—in other words, how movement between them is defined.

The rigors and technologies of travel have long been functioned as tropes in attesting the authenticity of any travelogue. Late medieval and early modern travel literature could not help but foreground the strange and wonderous means, such as magic carpets, used to move between Europe and Asia. If industrial media technologies seek to hide the methods of transmission so that messages can more effectively convey their illusion of immediacy,[23] early modern missives and commodities proudly bore the scars of their transportation. Almost every travelogue written after the Portuguese rounded the southern cape of Africa to make their way to India devoted its opening pages to the trials of such a long ocean voyage. Recounting its misery and boredom was a basic step for any traveler seeking to establish his creditability as someone who had indeed visited Asia. While Europeans marveled at the nautical feat, we should not forget that Marco Polo's journey over land was a wonder in itself. Crossing territories may not have required the same technological advances as Portuguese vessels and navigation techniques, but it would still have demanded previously unheard of political and logistical coordination. For the medieval reader, the Mongol system of sending messengers from the Chinese imperial capital out across the entire length of the empire and back again,

---

23. Anthony Enns, "Introduction: The Media Philosophy of Sybille Krämer," in Sybille Krämer, *Medium, Messenger, Transmission: An Approach to Media Philosophy*, trans. Anthony Enns (Amsterdam: University of Amsterdam Press, 2015) 15.

all within a measurably short period of time, would certainly have counted as one of the wonders of Asia. The Mongol postal system was curious enough so that John Mandeville borrowed two different versions of how it operated in his fabulous narrative. A fifteenth-century manuscript of Polo's *Livre des merveilles du monde*, now at the Bibliotheque Nationale de France, includes an illustration of the mythical king of the Nestorian Christians, Prester John, receiving messengers from Genghis Khan, bearing a request for the hand of his daughter in marriage.[24] As Polo tells the story, Genghis was a vassal of the Christian king, so that when the rising Mongol ruler asked for the marriage alliance, Priester John was quite offended that his underling would dare make such a request indirectly, by sending his marriage proposal through messengers, rather than appearing in person as a subordinate. After his proposal is rejected, Genghis Khan then appears with his full army to vanquish Priester John, reinforcing the notion that Marco Polo is far more interested in recounting Mongol power than in discovering lost Christian civilizations in Asia. The French manuscript offers an illustration focused solely on the postal system's operation in which the grandson, Kublai Khan, is shown sending and receiving his messengers.[25]

Once the reader has discovered the logistical organization of Marc Polo's narrative, the cities he has been describing on his route, one after the other, appear themselves as little more than stages along the postal route, arranged in a series of circuits that ultimately arrive at Kublai Khan's court. According to Polo's description—and there are many sources that corroborate his impressions—Mongol messengers could carry a message or item over 200 miles in a single day.[26] Messengers who set out along a highway could find a posting station with fresh horses after twenty-five miles. These hostels were well kept, with spacious lodgings and beds, comfortable

24. Umberto Eco created his own compilation of bibliographic wonders in *The Book of Legendary Lands*, trans. Alastair McEwen (New York: Rizzoli, 2013), 103.

25. Marco Polo, *Devisement du monde ou Livre des Merveilles Récit de voyage* (1410–1412) (Paris: Bibliotheque national de France, Manuscripts, Fr. 2810 fol. 1). https://gallica.bnf.fr/ark:/12148/btv1b52000858n/f9.planchecontact.

26. Norbert Ohler, *The Medieval Traveller*, trans. Caroline Hillier (Woodbridge, Suffolk: Boydell, 1989), 101.

enough for a visiting king, Polo claims. As many as 400 horses were stabled there, so the messenger could always find a ready replacement. Polo asserted that this system extended throughout the Mongol empire, leading him to conclude that the ability to send messages and travel along these routes "is surely the highest privilege and the greatest resource ever enjoyed by any man on earth, king or emperor or what you will."[27] While Polo makes clear that the Mongol postal system was intended solely for Kublai Khan, he also allows the reader to presume that he was himself able to move through these networks while in the Khan's service. In Marshall McLuhan's terms, the postal system was in effect an extension of Khan's human powers: "The personal and social consequences of any medium— that is, of any extension of ourselves—result from the new scale that is introduced into our affairs by each extension of ourselves, or by any new technology."[28] Understood in this way, the postal riders introduced an entirely new scale of coverage extending throughout not only China but much of Central Asia.

Polo well understood that the speed and discipline of the horse relay within the Mongol Empire allowed them to rule over widely dispersed territories. "When the need arises for the Great Khan to receive immediate tidings by mounted messenger, as of the rebellion of a subject country or of one of his barons or any matter that may concern him deeply, I assure you that the messengers ride 200 miles in a day, sometimes even 250."[29] Polo's account of traveling along the Mongol postal system thus illustrates how the vast empire was administered. The relays allow officials and merchants to move through space without stopping at the older boundaries that differentiated territories before they were overwhelmed by the Mongols. Likewise, travelers could pass through territories unrestrained by internal economic or political arrangements. Postal systems produce space, or, more precisely, geographical knowledge, by connecting places that would otherwise be isolated from one another;

27. Marco Polo, *Travels*, 151.
28. Marshall McLuhan, *Understanding Media: The Extensions of Man* (Cambridge, MA: MIT Press, 1994), 7.
29. Marco Polo, *Travels*, 154.

they create the potential for relationships between the inhabitants of the various stopping points. Unlike magic carpet rides, postal routes allow for the possibility of repeated journeys, so that any number of different relationships can be sustained over time. Initially, this new geographical knowledge is organized sequentially because it emerges from travel. Only after the journey's end, and after Polo's narrative has been read repeatedly, does his diachronic geography become classified into a static picture of spatial relations.

Given that space is organized in terms of the journey's linear movement, it is always important to consider the prepositions used to describe the passage. In Polo's account, Europe is just the starting point for his journey. Unlike eighteenth-century explorers, he does not dwell on his departure from his home for long, so that his narrative quickly becomes a trip *toward* the Great Khan's court, rather than a journey *from* Europe. Enlightenment travel literature is often keenly aware of its separation from Europe. In his lecture on universal history, Schiller defines the passage away from Europe as a regression backward to the earlier stages of human civilization. Medieval and early modern accounts of travel to China do not assume this attitude. Instead, regardless of how many varieties of human communities encountered along the way, the goal of any trip to China is to approach the imperial seat. Polo's sense that he was travelling *toward* China rather than away from Europe lasted for centuries. Even when in their haughtiest heights, European descriptions of journeys to China at some point refer to themselves as progressions *toward* the emperor's court. The only question seems to be how far into the trip this orientation takes over. Polo's narration implies that the Mongol postal system sped up the journey, even though he makes clear that he was not immediately privy to its benefits and had to wait until he was formally in the khan's service to actually ride along its routes.

The logistical operations that enable travel and are written into many travelogues serve to enhance their credibility. Hence any narration of an extraordinary journey requires extensive description of the means by which travel was even possible at all. To this day, scholars judge the authenticity of travel reports by the difficulties they recount in moving from place to place.[30] Coupled with the attention to transportation is the awareness that a destination is fundamentally transformed by the mechanisms that allow it to be reached. The Mongol conquest both transformed China and made it approachable. Just how inaccessible China was remained a topic of speculation for centuries. With each new avenue of access, the kingdom became a more plausible object of knowledge. Marco Polo's fascination with the logistics of the postal system reveals an awareness of the interdependence of time and space with each other—a familiar concern for any merchant engaged in long-distance trade and communications. Thus the movement of Mongol messengers constitutes an early point of reflection about media links between Europe and China. The postal network organizes space while tracking temporal sequences. The standard perceptions of the time it takes to move over a distance are dramatically upended by the systematic organization of Mongolian riders. Not only does the postal system reinforce the terrifying image of the Mongolian military; it also aggrandizes the emperor for possessing such an apparatus at his personal command. Asia may seem impossibly large to the ordinary pilgrim, but it becomes a manageable entity within the Mongol communications network. The possibility that information could be distributed at previously unheard of speeds reinforced the important ideological assertion that China was organized into a single coherent political entity, as opposed to being fragmented into many unrelated, singular places. Half a millennium later, the story of the Pony Express in the American West recounted much the same relay system of riders and horses. By discussing the Mongol post, Polo was lending credibility to his narrative, for a fundamental question almost every reader would have raised was: How could he have even made the journey, there and back? In order to convince

---

30. Thus, Hartmut Walravens can conclude: "Padre Schrecks Reisebriefe geben einen authentischen Eindruck von den Schwierigkeiten Anfang des 17. Jahrhunderts, nach China zu gelangen und im Lande zu leben" (Hartmut Walravens, *China Illustrata: Das europäische Chinaverständnis im Spiegel des 16. bis 18. Jahrhunderts* [Wolfenbüttel: Herzon August Bibliothek, 1987], 11).

anyone that he had traveled the vast distance to China, Polo had to explain the means by which such a journey was possible. By focusing on the conditions that made travel possible, his attention and the reader's were thus shifted away from providing rich descriptions of particular locations to the logistics of movement. The procedure of travel became an important component in itself. Since all travelogues are obliged to explain the manner in which one moves from place to place, they introduce a technological awareness of the conditions that make geographical knowledge possible. With a similar eye on what makes the projection of military power and the accumulation of knowledge over long distances possible, science studies overlaps with traditional naval history by focusing on the construction and sailing techniques of the Portuguese carrack.[31]

Like Marco Polo, the sixteenth-century Jesuits were impressed with internal Chinese communication networks. Integrating the missionary message into the postal networks used by the empire's elite required that they switch away from preaching, the preferred manner of Christian proselytizing, to writing in a manner familiar to mandarins. Once the Jesuit mission's leader, Matteo Ricci, and his colleagues began composing and translating Christian and humanist works into the court language, their China mission wound up having two simultaneous and antithetical media strategies: to communicate across the oceans in a manner that reinforced European support and to address the Chinese elite in familiar terms.[32] As great as the distances were that the missionaries had traveled across the Indian Ocean, Ricci quickly recognized that their message would need to reach much farther into the intimate spaces of Chinese society. Within the first years, he concluded that the mediation provided by the printed page within China's administrative channels was far more effective than itinerate sermons in overcoming the barriers placed on the missionary.

31. Bruno Latour, *Science in Action: How to Follow Scientists and Engineers through Society* (Cambridge, MA: Harvard University Press, 1987), 221–23.

32. *China und Europa: Chinaverständnis und Chinamode im 17. und 18. Jahrhundert, Ausstellung vom 16. September bis 11. November 1973 im Schloß Charlottenburg, Berlin* (Berlin: Verwaltung der Staatlichen Schlösser und Gärten, 1973), 145.

Polo's fixation on logistics carried on into the age of sea voyages. When the Dutch East India Company sent an embassy to the emperor in 1655 to plead its case for opening trade relations, it sent ships from Batavia and then traveled slowly on Chinese barges up the river and canal network from Canton to Beijing. The official publication of the embassy, illustrated by Jan Nieuhof, represents Chinese cities seen from along the water route so picturesquely that they almost appear Dutch. Yet when the members of the embassy finally disembark from the canal boats so that they can approach Beijing by land, Nieuhof makes sure to offer his readers a reminder of the Mongol, in this case Manchu, postal riders. Off in the corner of his Beijing city scape, as the figures closest to the spectator, Nieuhof includes two military riders, coming and going to and from the Forbidden City, presumably with important dispatches. (See figure 1 and, for more detail, figure 2.)

Information relays have a long history in China. Already during the Song dynasty, communication networks had begun to join provincial officials within an imperial network that circulated gazettes, official documents, and military reports. As these missives moved between administrators, they were evaluated and commented upon, so that the magistrates developed relationships across the postal system as well as to the center.[33] Later, Mongol rulers adopted the established administrative regimes, including the promotion of lower Han officials and expansion of existing postal networks. Just how deeply these deliveries were integrated into the life of mandarins we will see in chapter 10 when we analyze the Ming/Qing romances that Goethe read.

Polo's focus on the Mongol post raises larger questions about the importance of information networks within China, particularly among administrators, and then an even broader comparison between Chinese and European networks. To what extent do the similarities between the networks allow or encourage the application of concepts such as the public sphere to describe the complex relations between the imperial court and provincial administrators? While

---

33. Hilde de Weerdt, Chu Ming-Kin, and Ho Hou-leong, "Chinese Empires in Comparative Perspective: A Digital Approach," *Verge: Studies in Global Asias* 2.2 (Fall 2016): 58–69.

Figure 1. View of Beijing as Dutch embassy arrives. Source: Joan Nieuhof, *Het Gezantschap der Neêrlandtsche Oost-Indische Compagnie aan den Grooten Taratarischen Cham, den tegenwoordigen Keizer van China* (Amsterdam: Jacob van Meurs, 1665).

Figure 2. Detail of Beijing view showing postal horsemen coming and going.

seventeenth-century news of every variety circulated through Europe in handwritten newspapers, in China the much older system of governmental news was distributed via administrative gazettes, called *Dibao*. Originally intended solely for imperial magistrates, during the Ming dynasty they began to be read by a larger audience. These dispatches would draw the attention of any local business or official interested in news from the imperial court. As they read such dispatches, scholars debated their implications and thereby created a network among themselves as well as to the imperial capital.[34] Chinese novels incorporated these mail relays into their plots so that court intrigues and marriage proposals would fail or succeed depending on the timely arrival of the messenger.

Modern Europeans have often followed Polo's interest in the Chinese mail systems—always with an implicit reference back to Europe. Enlightenment historians already noted that the Mongols had a postal system well before any existed in Europe: "It seems that the Emperor Cublay established postal delivery in his empire long before it was known in Europe."[35] Nineteenth-century commentaries were less worried about the antiquity of the Chinese system than its efficiency. In a review of the third Chinese romance translated into a European language, *The Two Fair Cousins* (*Les deux cousines*), the Tory politician David Wedderburn commented somewhat haughtily: "Postal arrangements in China at the period of our romance appear to have been defective, and considerable confusion arises from letters, generally sent by a special messenger, not being forwarded or duly delivered."[36] We know that fiction is never an accurate depiction of a postal system, for letters always arrive just at the moment when the story requires it, especially if they are very late. As any reader of novels knows, delayed letters can hide bad news or unfavorable instructions, thereby allowing new friendships to blossom. While he points to

---

34. Hung-tai Wang, "Information Media, Social Imagination, and Public Society during the Ming and Qing Dynasties," *Frontiers of History in China* 5.2 (2010): 180.

35. Johann Wilhelm von Archenholtz, ed., "Fragmente aus der Reisegeschichte des Marco Polo, eines berühmten Reisenden des dreyzehnten Jahrhunderts," in *Literatur- und Völkerkunde*, (Dessau und Leipzig, 1783), 3:102.

36. David Wedderburn, "The Two Fair Cousins, A Chinese Romance," *The Fortnightly* 24 (1878): 507.

similarities between Chinese and English narratives, Wedderburn may have been a little over eager to find fault with Chinese civilization. The larger point is that modern Europeans have long followed Marco Polo's fixation on Chinese postal networks. A decade after the Second World War and in the midst of occupied Germany, the sinologist Peter Olbricht reflected on the importance of logistics in a global war: the Mongol information network set an example for modern industrial forces: "Trailing behind their armies, postal routes pulled all of Asia together into one unified net. The organizational measures by the Mongols were extraordinary and, in this regard, should be considered an accomplishment in its own right, even if one must consider that the Mongols used the models and experiences of their conquered lands, especially from Persia and China for their own innovation."[37]

Contemporary German media theory has also begun to focus on the courier as figure that helps understand the operation of media channels. Without directly addressing Mongol riders, Sybille Krämer states: "The messenger . . . represents a primal scene of media transmission."[38] The emissary's vantage point makes it clear that much communication is unidirectional without any opportunity for dialogue. For Krämer, the messenger's trajectory shows that most communication follows a transmission model of sender and receiver, in which the letter carrier has no influence on the content of the message he bears. The messenger does not operate autonomously, but rather serves an external authority—in Polo's example, Kublai Khan. The postal system is not a separate machine unto itself, but rather a privileged instrument of sovereign power.

Delay in Kafka's Media Fable

While outside observers from Polo to Olbricht were struck by how swiftly and securely the information chain operated, functionaries

---

37. Peter Olbricht, *Das Postwesen in China unter der Mongolenherrschaft im 13. Und 14. Jahrhundert* (Wiesbaden: Harrassowitz, 1954), 39.
38. Sybille Krämer, *Medium, Messenger, Transmission: An Approach to Media Philosophy*, trans. Anthony Enns (Amsterdam: University of Amsterdam Press, 2015), 19.

within a network were more apt to recognize the many small ways in which the delivery sequence never reached beyond the many courtyards of the imperial palace. In his fable "An Imperial Message," Franz Kafka breaks down the stages that a courier had to pass through into a differential calculus of delay before he is able to reach the horse-relay system.[39] The German term for "message," *Botschaft*, has a religious connotation indicating much more than mere communication but invoking divine revelation, thereby reinforcing the notion that the emperor is himself almost a deity. True to Claude Shannon's model of communication, the actual content of the emperor's message remains unknown. The parable depicts a courier's movement between communication nodes as part of the transmission circuit: sender, receiver, interference.[40] The recipient knows his position even though the message has not yet been delivered, because he recognizes the existence of the channel between the emperor and himself, perhaps because other communications have already explained that an important message is on its way.

As Wolf Kittler notes, both the parable and the narrator's knowledge of the message's intended delivery travel faster than the courier.[41] Within literary terms, the parable itself can be understood as a *Botschaft*. "Most of Kafka's stories and novels have to do with messages that move along long paths toward the intended recipient(s) from a hidden position or person, and that originate from some ultimate, obscure, distant authority, whether divine, legal, bureaucratic,

---

39. An array of brilliant essays and books has been written on Kafka and China, some dealing directly with the importance of media relations across space: Weiyan Meng, *Kafka und China* (Munich: iudicum verlag, 1986); Michael Wood, "Kafka's China and the Parable of Parables," *Philosophy and Literature* 20.2 (1996): 325–37; Rolf J. Goebel, *Constructing China: Kafka's Orientalist Discourse* (Columbia, SC: Camden House, 1997); John Zilcosky, *Kafka's Travels: Exoticism, Colonialism, and the Traffic Writing* (New York: Palgrave, 2003); Christopher Bush, *Ideographic Modernisms* (Oxford: Oxford University Press, 2010).

40. John M. Kopper, "Building Walls and Jumping over Them: Constructions in Franz Kafka's 'Beim Bau der chinesischen Mauer,'" *MLN* 98.3 (1983): 351–65.

41. Wolf Kittler, *Der Turmbau zu Babel und das Schweigen der Sirenen, Über das Reden, das Schweigen, die Stimme und die Schrift in vier Texten von Franz Kafka* (Erlangen: Palm und Enke, 1985), 47, 49.

or regal."[42] When Friedrich Kittler wrote that "so many of Kafka's texts deal with the materiality of channels of information," he singled out the "Imperial Message" as concentrating on "delay."[43] The intended recipient in Kafka's imperial message professes loyalty while he awaits the message that may never arrive, but this delay allows him to daydream at his window without interruption. Kafka probably read Marco Polo's step-by-step explanation of the Mongol courier system. If Polo praised Kublai Khan for possessing the most efficient postal system in the world in order to establish the credibility of his claim to have traveled through China, Kafka offered a calculus of delay in the form of a fable that inverts the imperial bureaucracy's claim to efficiency.[44] Kafka's parable reverses the direction and redefines the fictional status of Polo's supposedly accurate description of Khan's courier system. The farther the messenger moves away from the emperor, the less likely he will reach the intended recipient. In Kafka's narrative, in which the emperor functions as the sender, the political logic insists that that the emperor cares about his subjects so much that he sends them his last personal message. Within the logic of both Polo's late medieval and Kafka's modern communication circuit, the delay of a message becomes just as important to its recipient as its arrival. Once a message has entered into a delivery system, the optimism of the closed system indicates that it has either "arrived" or is "en route." "Delay" refers to a temporary condition in the present tense indicating ongoing travel, rather than the present perfect "failure" or "loss" of the message. Kafka has the recipient sitting by his window daydreaming while waiting for the message to arrive, his passivity heightened by the window that frames his detached observation of the world in which the emperor's messenger is riding. The thin spatial barrier created by this one architectural detail reiterates the layered alienation produced by the emperor's many courtyards, as if daydreaming were a little like dying. Within a system of communi-

---

42.   Barbara E. Galli, "Introduction: Translation Is a Mode of Holiness," *Cultural Writings of Franz Rosenzweig* (Syracuse, NY: Syracuse University Press, 2000), 15.

43.   Friedrich A. Kittler, *Discourse Networks 1800/1900*, trans. Michael Meteer and Chris Cullens (Stanford, CA: Stanford University Press, 1990), 338.

44.   Weiyan Meng, *Kafka und China*, 80.

cation that presumes delivery, the absence of a letter, or its significant delay, grants the recipient a temporary freedom. In the strict
logic of the postal network, delay allows for the play of imagination until the message arrives. So long as the message cannot be
tracked, the recipient's thoughts are free to move beyond the parameters of the administrative.

In *The Poetics of Space*, Gaston Bachelard observes that different orders of space—in his example, the interior and exterior of a
bourgeois house—are by no means symmetrical balanced. Even
though the volume of interior spaces is much smaller than the vastness outside the house, the perception of space developed by the secluded mind is far more immense than the consciousness of exterior
realms. "Immensity is within ourselves. It is attached to a sort of
expansion of being that life curbs and caution arrests, but which
starts again when we are alone. As soon as we become motionless,
we are elsewhere; we are dreaming in a world that is immense."[45]
With a similar juxtaposition of spatial regimes, Kafka matches the
fabled territory of China up to the subjective expanse created while
dreaming. While Polo values the postal system for its efficiency, Kafka's fable shows that the stricter and more efficient the relations
within an information network are, the more important delay becomes, for it offers the patient subaltern time. While Polo insists on
the efficiency of travel along Mongol messenger routes to eliminate
any suspicion that his trip to the Khan is fabulous, Kafka reintroduces the contented happiness of the fable by concentrating on those
moments when the imperial logistics grind to a halt. The disruptions
inherent in any logistical relay system (noise, rerouting) can become
a mechanism for imagination; the potentials of fantasy substitute
for the delivery of information.

Kafka's parable acquires an additional connotation, given the
common nineteenth-century trope comparing Austria-Hungary to
China. The story's form suggests a parallel between the two empires. The absence of specific historic details lends the story an ontological quality, as if it were a reduction of the many stories known
about the emperor, while at the same time it is addressed personally

---

45.   Gaston Bachelard, *The Poetics of Space* (Boston: Beacon, 1994), 184.

to the reader. The double move that maintains the detached center of existence while also extending a personalized address was an important mode of interpellation, one that was necessary to shore up monarchical authority in a democratizing Europe. With the same double move as the Christian deity, emperors stood above the fray of ordinary politics, even as they expressed their personalized concern for the needs of their subjects. Within the eroding crises of modern society, this ability for imperial power to define both center and periphery was increasingly unstable, both in China and Europe. Kafka suggests a parallel between empires, in which the old monarchical comparisons between the Chinese and European rulers has become unstable. Whereas seventeenth-century absolutist rulers reveled in their similarities with the Chinese emperor, Kafka's parable suggests that this ideology is fading fast.

If Polo had compared a Habsburg ruler with the khan, the comparison would have been understood as flattering. In 1273, two years after Marco set off from Venice with his father and uncle, Rudolf I of Habsburg was elected King of the Romans, thereby starting the imperial lineage that lasted until the end of World War One. Franz Josef, Austria's longest reigning monarch, died one year before Kafka wrote "An Imperial Message," and the dynasty came to an end two years later. The Habsburg monarchy was one of the few institutions that spanned the 600 years between Marco Polo and Franz Kafka. The comparison with China was common currency in nineteenth-century complaints about Austria's lack of modernity, its adherence to Catholic tradition, and it archaic ceremonial distinctions. Of course, it must be added that Kafka was writing at a moment when emperors were generally losing their mandate: the last Qing ruler abdicated in 1912, the czar was executed in 1917, and the kaiser would soon leave Berlin for exile in the Netherlands.

The analogy between China and Austria emerged shortly after the collapse of the Holy Roman Empire; it can be traced back to Ludwig Börne's 1818 essay, "Shy Comments. About Austria and Prussia," in which he celebrates Prussia for the speed and dynamism of its reform movement. While Börne deploys a string of metaphors to denounce the Habsburgs, who represent the last pure monarchy in Europe—in other words without any constitutional restraints—it was his one-line insult—"Austria is the European China, a still standing, out-grown state"—that stuck.[46] If Enlightenment intellectuals mobilized the image of Asiatic despotism against Louis XIV, Börne revived a less threatening, more ossified version against the Habsburgs to claim they have been fully superseded by more agile states. Once set in motion, the analogy would be repeated throughout the next century. In a 1827 letter, Goethe made a point of defending the intellectual culture "in the Austrian states, which we so like to represent as Europe's China."[47] Goethe was not so much affirming Börne's comparison as acknowledging that many have adopted it. Karl Marx updated Börne's analogy to the post-revolutionary situation in 1853, when he compared the allowances China made after the first Opium War with Austria's initial response to the revolutionary demands of 1848: "Such language as this, and such concessions we remember to have heard from Austria, the China of Germany, in 1848."[48] In the prologue to *Ideographic Modernisms*, Christopher Bush argues against the presumption that references to China in Kafka are actually representations of something else.[49] The absence of a specific historical setting for the "Imperial Message," the possibility that the story could just as well be about the Austro-Hungarian Empire as any other, need not exclude the serious possibility that Kafka was writing within a long lineage of European descriptions of China initiated by Marco Polo. The double possibility that the parable is about China and Europe reflects the inevitable comparisons that all European discourse on China contains. To understand China beyond its distant strangeness is to recognize its similarity. The emphasis on postal delivery only underscores the potential for some fundamental interchange between the two orders.

46. Ludwig Börne, "Schüchterne Bemerkunge. Über Oestreich und Preußen," in *Gesammelte Schriften*, 3rd ed. (Stuttgart: Fr. Brodhag'sche Buchhandlung, 1840), part 2, 63.

47. Johann Wolfgang Goethe, Letter to Nees von Esenback, September 6, 1827, in *Goethes Werke* (Weimar: Hermann Böhlaus Nachfolger, 1887–1919), sect. 4, 43:51. Henceforth cited as WA, with section number preceding volume and page.

48. Karl Marx, "Revolution in China and in Europe," *On Colonialism* (Moscow: Foreign Languages Publishing, 1960), 17.

49. Bush, *Ideographic Modernisms*.

Despite the initial political use of the comparison to critique Austria's lack of democratic modernization, Kafka does not apply the analogy ideologically so much as write from within its terms. Kafka's parable incorporates the spatial relations from earlier European literary texts that draw parallels between Europe and China. The short version of the parable published in 1919 does not directly refer to China, while the tale's inclusion in the longer story of "The Great Wall of China" places it within a narrative context that explicitly explains Chinese bureaucracy. As Kafka adapts details from Polo's description of Chinese bureaucracy and logistics, the reader wonders whether he is not also describing Austrian imperial operations. By lifting the short parable "An Imperial Message" out from the larger report on the construction of the Great Wall, Kafka also removes all geopolitical references that would allow the reader to situate the story in China or Europe. This ambiguity also alerts the reader to the possibility that European and Asian emperors may operate within similar administrative constraints and possibilities. By allowing us to indulge in the similarities between Chinese and Austrian emperors, the text reinforces the idea that imperial states share certain structural features.[50] Indeed, the courier's inability to escape the confines of the court is reminiscent of eighteenth-century novels depicting the failings of aristocratic courts. The physical separation between the emperor at the center of his crowded court and the reader-recipient in his provincial abode is typical of both of European Enlightenment and sentimental fiction, as well as sixteenth-century Chinese romances that depict scholar-magistrates who retire from the imperial court but nevertheless receive news regularly. In considering possible antecedents to "An Imperial Message" we should not exclude actual Chinese novels that had been translated into European languages, such as *The Two Fair Cousins* (*Les deux cousines*), known in German as *Die beyde Basen*. But even as they were reading this Chinese novel, its similarities with European novels were already obvious to Goethe and the sinologist Abel Rémusat.

---

50. Ann Laura Stoler and Carole McGranahan, "Introduction: Refiguring Imperial Terrains," in *Imperial Formations*, ed. Ann Laura Stoler and Carole McGranahan (Santa Fe, NM: School for Advanced Research Press, 2007), 5.

Already in the eighteenth century, the comparison between China and Austria seemed apt. One prominent example from the Weimar literary scene laid out much the same scenarios as "An Imperial Message." Christoph Martin Wieland's 1772 mock oriental tale, *Der goldne Spiegel, oder Die Könige von Schechian* (The golden mirror, or the king of Scheschian), opens with a warning to the Chinese emperor, who issues commands that never quite reach his subjects beyond the capital city. Already in the eighteenth century, Wieland was implicitly positing an affinity between European and Chinese imperiality. Following the example of *A Thousand and One Nights*, *Der goldne Spiegel* offers a well-wrapped package of narrative frames and stories within stories, purporting to provide a history of Scheschian, a fictitious Asian empire. The migration of the novel's inner narrative is marked by its many retranslations, a common premodern practice. That is, the book purports to derive from a Chinese translation from the original Schechian language (now extinct), which was then translated again from the Chinese into Latin by a Jesuit priest, only for Wieland to provide the last translation into German. The chain of re-renderings of a lost text from an extinct society is so dizzying that all ideas of authenticity fall away. The Chinese translator in fact speculates that the original is really a collection of passages from an ancient chronicle intended to teach princes how to rule. The main story line is told for the shah of Indostan who has difficulty sleeping, so his favorite concubine and the court philosopher begin to narrate the history of this imaginary, fallen empire. In terms of genre, the novel is certainly akin to early modern narratives intended to educate princes. Wieland describes Scheschian in terms that make its similarity to the Holy Roman Empire clear, and most commentators agree that the intended, ideal reader was emperor Joseph II of Austria.[51] Rather than criticizing

---

51. Matt Erlin, *Necessary Luxuries: German Literature and the World of Goods, 1770–1815* (Ithaca, NY: Cornell University Press, 2014), 100–34; W. Daniel Wilson, "Intellekt und Herrschaft. Wielands Goldner Spiegel, Joseph II, und das Ideal eines kritischen Mäzenats im aufgeklärten Absolutismus," *MLN* 99.3 (1984): 479–502; Walter Benjamin, "Christoph Martin Wieland: Zum zweihundersten Jahrestag seiner Geburt," in *Gesammelte Schriften*, ed. Rolf Tiedemann and Hermann Schweppenhäuser (Frankfurt: Suhrkamp, 1985), vol. 2.1, 395–406.

the Enlightenment emperor bent upon reform, Wieland sought to teach him. The intended effect failed—Wieland never received an appointment in Vienna. However he was called by the Duchess Anna Amalia to Weimar to serve as the tutor to her young prince, the future Duke Karl August. Far from offering clear principles of statecraft, Wieland gives vent to his skeptical views on absolute monarchy.[52]

The novel commences with the Chinese translator's opening dedication to the Chinese emperor in which he explains the fundamental problem with absolutist courts—in flattering terms: the emperor issues commands for the well-being of his subjects, but his servants and courtiers delay and distort them so that they never come to pass. Thus, the Chinese translator declares: "Your majesty's strongest desire is to make your people happy. This is the one goal of your tireless efforts; it is the object of all your councils, the content of your laws and commands, the soul of the praiseworthy enterprises you begin and execute."[53] Then he explains, in terms anticipating Kafka's parable, how the many layers of administration prevent the emperor's commands from being fulfilled:

> Yet how unhappy would you perhaps become, if you learned how far behind your wishes their execution remains, despite all your efforts! The innumerable crowd of your servants, divided up into the many classes, orders, and types that you need in order to dispense your power, for humanity sets limits to even for the most limitless of monarchs, the need in all matters to rely on instruments for your well-meaning actions, makes you—now please don't be shocked by an unpleasant yet restorative truth—makes you the most dependent of all inhabitants within your immeasurable kingdom.[54]

Unlike Montesquieu, Wieland does not grant his imaginary Asian despot unlimited power over his subjects. Instead he shows the futility of such a position. Much in the same manner as Marshall McLuhan, the emperor overestimates his powers when he believes that his messengers are extensions of his own authority. All such authority is

---

52. Benjamin, "Christoph Martin Wieland," 400.
53. C. M. Wieland, *Sämmtliche Werke* (Leipzig: Göschen, 1856), 7:vii.
54. Wieland, *Werke*, 7:vii–viii.

tempered by courtiers and bureaucrats who siphon off power in small amounts, so that what seems like vast capability is in fact utter dependency—a lesson for absolute bosses and modern media messengers alike.

While Kafka's narrator addresses the reader with the familiar "Du," Wieland's Chinese translator addresses the emperor with the relatively familiar "Sie"—at least by eighteenth-century standards when addressing the Chinese or Holy Roman Emperor. Both accounts juxtapose the appearance of the emperor's caring and overwhelming authority with the inability to have his commands obeyed. Wieland's speaker explains to the emperor the problem that Kafka's subject experiences from the opposite end of the communication such that Wieland's text addresses the emperor who sends the command, whereas Kafka's turns to the subject who expects to receive it. Both describe an asymptotic increase in the impossibility of the emperor's command being fulfilled, the farther the command travels and the longer it takes. Wieland is completely skeptical that an imperial order will be obeyed; Kafka leaves open the possibility of its arrival. While the Kafka passage stresses the labyrinthian architecture of the imperial palace, Wieland's text emphasizes not only the masses of people among whom the emperor's power is distributed, but also the vastness of the bureaucracy and the empire: "the wide circumference of your numberless provinces."[55]

The impression that China was a fabulous place permeated early modern European readers of travel reports. When Jesuit missionaries set out to convert China in earnest, they started sending back reports about the Middle Kingdom. Moving inland from Canton, their intention was to gain access to the imperial court.[56] As Jesuit letters and reports back home filled in the details in Marco Polo's description of China, they also faced a similarly skeptical yet fascinated readership in Europe. Even within the Church hierarchy, missionary reports from China were viewed with both wonder and circumspection. In 1655, Pope Alexander VII wrote to the Chinese

---

55. Wieland, *Werke*, 7:viii.

56. Ronnie Po-chia Hsia, *A Jesuit in the Forbidden City: Matteo Ricci 1552–1610* (Oxford: Oxford University Press, 2010).

dowager empress that her realm had long been considered a "Fab-
ulosum," which in the German translation became a "Fabel und
Mährlein."[57] The pope drew a direct parallel between Polo's long
journey across Asia and the Jesuit missionaries who now have supplanted his role in China. In both cases, the difficulty in reaching
China lent it an imaginary aura. "Your huge kingdom is fabulous,
cut off by deserts and almost infinite distances, and false religions
and worship have taken over. How could truth travel across so many
seas and wandering roads when the stars and heavens are different
and the shores are closed even to merchants who seek to trade not
in gold and precious stones, but in the pearl of conversion."[58] By
characterizing China as a land of fables, the pope was not expressing rationalist skepticism so much as referring to a familiar literary
genre that was itself regularly deployed by Catholic missionaries.
As he noted, the first fantastical feature of any story about China is
the very claim that the author visited the place. To suggest that one
could actually arrive in China was already to posit a surprising connectedness between societies that undermined the claim that one
was uniquely superior to the others. In evaluating the accusation
that China itself was a land of fable, we should allow ourselves some
dialectical nuance, so that we do not define fables merely as un-
truths, for this narrow epistemological approach overlooks the
truth in fictional narration. Far from being just outlandish distortions, idealized depictions of travel to China can be understood as
self-conscious utopias. If China appears in missionary reports as a
remarkably ordered and just society, this reflects the expectations
and desires of Europeans sent there. To remove the fabulous leaves
the prospect that China is just as ordinary and debased as Europe—a
plausible enough conclusion, so long as one wants to deny humans
any hopeful aspirations. Travels to China were particularly prone
to be accused of being fabulous, the more so if they were written

---

57. Erasmus Francisci, *Neu-polierter Geschicht- Kunst- und Sitten-Spiegel
ausländischer Völcker fürnemlich Der Sineser, Japaner, Indostaner, Javaner, Malabaren, Peguaner, Siammer, . . . und theils anderer Nationen mehr* (Nürnberg: Johann Andreae Endters and Wolfgang des Jüngern Erben, 1670), 433.

58. Athanasius Kircher, *China Illustrata*, trans. Charles Van Tuyl (Bloomington: Indiana University Press, 1987), 93.

long ago. The aversion to fabulous tales became a mainstay of En-lightenment criticism. John Locke so abhorred fables, that he skipped over the theological controversies surrounding the biblical account of Noah's arc: "Not to speak therefore of what is absolutely fabulous, or only supposititious, let us come to the first sailors famed in History; and touching those times lightly, descend to matters of more certainty and better authority."[59] Locke similarly dismissed John Mandeville's medieval travelogue and Fernão Mendes Pinto's later adventures in East Asia under the Portuguese as fabulous.[60]

It was already a convention for medieval travelogues to insisted that every word written on their pages was absolutely and com-pletely true. Thus, later reports about China had to find additional means to establish their own credibility. The Jesuits managed to surpass, and in the case of Polo, confirm earlier accounts by main-taining a long-distance network of correspondents who provided detailed information over the course of many decades. From 1582 until their suppression after 1774, the Jesuits offered the most detailed descriptions of China, yet even when the authority of their writings was established, they were also harried by the same skeptical challenges that have been brought to bear on Marco Polo's book down to the present. The missionaries understood their affinity with Polo, for they provided information to Europe-ans that reinforced his account. Martino Martini, the Jesuit who wrote learned histories and geographies of China, was keenly aware of Polo's reputation: "I hold it a duty to free that most noble patri-cian from the accusation of mendacity and from the other calum-nies to which he has been subject: the more so because his accusers who have so lightly condemned in him things they cannot under-stand are far worthier of reproof."[61] In 1667 the Jesuit compiler Athansius Kircher retold Polo's journey in his *China Illustrata* with a special emphasis on the missionary purpose of his journey.

59. John Locke, "The History of Navigation," in *The Works of John Locke* (London: Thomas Davison, 1823), 10:361.

60. Locke, "A Catalogue and Character of Most Books of Voyages and Trav-els," in *The Works of John Locke* (London: Thomas Davison, 1823), 10:538, 547.

61. Quoted in John Larner, *Marco Polo and the Discovery of the World* (New Haven: Yale University Press, 1999), 173.

Kircher wonders why Polo never mentions the Great Wall, but he concludes that Polo's Cathay corresponds directly to the China that contemporary missionaries also describe, thereby reinforcing the sense that the Jesuits were reviving Polo's mission, with a great zeal to convert, no doubt, but also with an interest to study and trade with China.[62] Ever the well-read humanists who displayed their sources, Jesuits like Kircher published about China in the lineage of Polo.[63]

Acknowledging the possibility that a reader might question the veracity of reports from China, the eighteenth-century Jesuit Jean-Baptiste Du Halde opened his own massive compilation of Jesuit letters from China by remarking on the skepticism with which the wonders Marco Polo described that were met:

> What the traveling Venetian published passed for the fruits of his imagination as it searched for excitement. Everything that he recounted about the antiquity of the monarchy, the wisdom of its laws and government, the fertility of the land, the riches of its commerce, the prodigious multitudes of its inhabitants, the gentleness and politeness of its mores, the industry that makes the arts and agriculture flourish, its good taste and ardor of its sciences, all this was taken as a pure fiction that did not even bother to observe the laws of verisimilitude.[64]

This list of China's exceptional qualities appealed to the Jesuits as well. The challenge for Du Halde was to convey much the same image of China while not losing credibility. Marco Polo's descriptions could not be confirmed by other thirteenth-century Europeans; there was no network of correspondents through which follow up questions could be answered or more elaborated information acquired. His travelogue could not be augmented with others. Not until the Jesuit mission's reports could Polo's claims be checked. The Jesuit mission came close to the system of accumulating and con-

62. Kircher, *China Illustrata*, 80–82.

63. Larner, *Marco Polo*, 173–75.

64. Johann Baptista du Halde, *Description géographique, historique, chronologique, politique, et physique de l'empire de la chine et de la tartarie chinoise* (Paris: Henri Scheurleer, 1736), 1:ix.

firming data from across the globe that Bruno Latour described in
his actor-network theory.

The memory of Marco Polo's reception, the fact that his account
seemed fabulous at first and grew credible only over time itself became part of the work's own history as well as the history of European writing about China generally.[65] In 1671, as part of his effort
to develop Berlin into a center of Chinese scholarship, Andreas Müller edited and published one of the oldest manuscripts in Berlin's
royal collection, a Latin translation of Polo's *Travels* composed by
the Dominican Franciscus Pipinus between 1315 and 1320.[66]
Goethe later read Müller's reprint in 1813 in the Weimar library,
just as he was studying China and Persia assiduously.[67] Given the
repetitive and intensive reading habits of early modern scholars, we
can hardly be surprised that 500 years after Marco Polo first set out,
China was still organized according to the tropes he introduced.[68]
Goethe, for example, continued to underscore how the Venetian's
travelogue seemed like a fable; he also suggested that this helped
explained the text's long-standing appeal. "This exceptional man
stands at the top of the list. His journey occurred in the second half
of the thirteenth century; he managed to reach the farthest points in
the East, lead us through the strangest circumstances, about which
we are filled with wonder and amazement because they seem
fabulous."[69] So familiar was the image of the merchant returned from
the Orient with precious wares tucked away in his sleeves, that

---

65. Horst von Tscharner, "China in der deutschen Dichtung des Mittelalters
und der Renaissance," *Sinica* 9 (1934): 16.

66. *China und Europa*, 125.

67. Donald Lach, "The Chinese Studies of Andreas Müller," *Journal of the
American Oriental Society*, 60 (1940): 566.

68. Nigel Cameron confirms the persistence of late medieval images: "The Western world remained obstinately faithful to the China of Marco Polo and of that inspired literary robber and romancer Sir John Mandeville" (qtd. in Gerhard Strasser,
"The Impact on the European Humanities of Early Reports from Catholic Missionaries from China, Tibet, and Japan between 1600 and 1700," in *From Early Modern to
Modern Disciplines*, vol. 2 of *The Making of the Humanities*, ed. Rens Bod, Jaap
Mat, and Thijs Weststeijn (Amsterdam: Amsterdam University Press, 2012), 192.

69. Johann Wolfgang Goethe, *Werke*, ed. Erich Trunz (Munich: C. H. Beck,
1982), 2:226. Henceforth cited as HA.

Goethe cast himself in this role, in order to encourage the nineteenth-century German reading public, unschooled in Asian cultures, to more quickly accept his late poem collection *West-östlicher Divan* (*West-Eastern Divan*), inspired by the Persian poet Hafez.[70]

Well into our own present, scholars debate how much Marco Polo invented or saw for himself, thereby reinforcing China's long reputation among Europeans as a half-fictional place.[71] The question of credibility was not resolved by celebrating China as an exotic place where familiar ratios were inflated. The scale and sublime excess of Chinese society appealed to baroque courtiers who expected their own monarchs to overwhelm and subdue their subjects with visible signs of power and wealth. Since grandeur was required for all rulers, it seemed appropriate, and reassuring, that the far-away emperor of China ruled in a manner so familiar to the European elite. If travel accounts indulged in hyperbole, this was appreciated as a rhetorical flourish completely in keeping with the narrator's privilege.

Within these broad terms, the seventeenth century is when China became an ideal within utopian discourse, where it hovered between anthropological reporting and theological projection. Its ambiguous representations suggested both a wonderful synthesis of political and social possibilities, while at the same time making clear that it was strikingly different from all other societies, and thus difficult to replicate.[72] The Jesuits' image of China suggested that it was possible for an earthly ruler to reconcile the historical contradictions that plagued post-Reformation Europe. Early modern literature about China exposes and masks European ideological conflicts between Christian sects, between monarchs and subjects, between competing imperial contenders. China is the focal point that seems to bring all these European forces together into a single resolution,

---

70. "Damit aber alles was der Reisende zurückbringt den Seinigen schneller behage, übernimmt er die Rolle eines Handelsmanns, der seine Waaren gefällig auslegt und sie auf mancherley Weise angenehm zu machen sucht" (Goethe, *West-östlicher Divan*, ed. Hendrik Birus [Berlin: Deutscher Klassiker Verlag, 2010], 1:139.

71. For an overview of the issues, see the first chapter of Vogel, *Marco Polo Was in China*.

72. Louis Marin, *Utopics: The Semiological Play of Textual Spaces*, trans. Robert A. Vollrath (Amherst, NY: Humanity Books, 1984), 8.

yet the largest empire in East Asia could hardly have been reduced to a mere projection from one side of the globe onto the other. The many critiques that claim to expose the falsity of chinoiserie and orientalism approach the problem only from one side, as if the system that produced and fulfilled European consumers' desires were the only apparatus engaged in the utopian construction of China. To argue that the utopia of China is just a fiction does not explain the ambiguous realities that sustain it to this day. Indeed, so many of the earliest worries that China was only a fable reflect a critical skepticism that masks its own desire to believe in its truth. The fable, as a genre, is repeatedly cited as presenting the radical opposite of theological, empirical, and philosophical truth. Any thoroughgoing critique of the utopian image of China needs to examine its own aggression against that image. What was it about the pleasure provided by fables that made them so threatening? Were fables the source of temptation? Did fables about China, unlike their Enlightenment cousins, lack a moral conclusion? Why were later readers so angry at John Mandeville and other medieval adventurers for spreading invented stories about the East?

How European interests in reading about the Orient shifted in the early modern period can be detected in the alternating reputations of Marco Polo and John Mandeville. As Jesuit descriptions of China and adventurers' accounts of Central Asia circulated in the seventeenth and eighteenth centuries, Polo's book was increasingly recognized as based on the lived experiences of an intelligent observer, while Mandeville's was increasingly regarded as proof of medieval folly—a collection of tales garnered from English and French libraries. The Jesuits recognized that the geography and imperial politics they saw in China had already been sketched out by Polo. As Mandeville's reputation declined, Polo's narrative garnered confirmation from later travelers. In his capacity as the ducal librarian in Wolfenbuettel, Gotthold Lessing would introduce his bibliographic comments on Polo with the epithet: "Polo, whose work has been confirmed by more recent travelers."[73]

---

73. Gotthold Lessing, "Marco Polo, aus einer Handschrift ergänzt, und au seiner andern sehr zu verbessern," in *Zur Geschichte und Litteratur, aus den Schätzen der*

Polo was thus the writer with whom later Europeans began their study of the Orient. His work set the standard by for trustworthiness by being contrasted with Mandeville. Scholars devoted considerable effort to finding the most accurate version of Polo's manuscript—which edition, which translation offered the true account? Reading Polo became a philological adventure in its own right. Later texts were understood as supplements, additions to Polo's information, rather than as contradictions or refutations.[74] Enlightenment scholars were eager to follow up on the many proper names mentioned in medieval narratives: Did they refer to places, people, specific rulers? In comparing manuscript versions of Polo's travels, Lessing points out many of the problems connected with names, such as the question of how many brothers did Kublai Khan have and over which peoples they ruled. Lessing mentions that the Polo manuscripts he has examined in Berlin and Wolfenbüttel refer to kingdoms that have found no mention in other sources except Joseph de Guignes's recent history of the Mongol peoples. Attentive eighteenth-century readers were thus astounded that almost half a millennium could pass in Europe before important details of Polo's description of China found any secondary confirmation. Wieland could write an ironic novel that featured the political history of an imaginary Asian kingdom, knowing full well that this vague and imprecise reference only bolstered his fable. When it came to evaluating Marco Polo, the Enlightenment pulled in two opposing directions, with Lessing seeking to clarify ambiguities and Wieland seeking to spin them out into longer tales. Polo's route from Venice to Beijing serves as the implicit model for any number of later fables about the Orient. For example, in Friedrich Schiller's *Turandot* the protagonist, Kalef, flees from Ashkedan, a city at the base of the Ural mountains, to China. Kalef's account of how he made his way from the Caspian Sea to Beijing follows Polo's orientation—the same

herzoglichen Bibliothek zu Wolfenbüttel, ed. Gotthold Lessing (Zweyter Beytrag Braunschweig: Waysenhaus, 1773), 261.

74. In another example of a wandering, imperfect manuscript, Engelbert Kaempfer evaluated Polo in his review of earlier literature about Europeans visiting Japan; see Engelbert Kaempfer, *Geschichte und Beschreibung von Japan*, ed. Christian Wilhelm von Dohm (Lemgo: Meyer, 1977), 1:227.

path Goethe will want to pursue when Napoleon's armies crash across the Holy Roman Empire.

As the epitome of the Orient, China represented a neutral third position outside the polarities that were tearing Europe apart after the Reformation; it claimed an unoccupied place of civilization beyond the already familiar divisions. In this sense, China represented an escape from conflict, military and otherwise. The European culture wherein truth was determined by a public confrontation of disputants was unable to incorporate Chinese thought into its own dialectics, though it tried to do so repeatedly. Different sides would claim to be speaking for China but these arguments never had much impact so long as China remained unfamiliar to most participants. Debaters might invoke China as an ideal representation of their particular position, but more often than not the image of China receded back into a position hovering on the horizon but not yet attainable by any party in Europe. Eventually, in the nineteenth century, Hegel and British imperialists reversed the terms of intellectual desire so that instead of remaining the utopia that European philosophy could not quite explain, Chinese thought became the remnant that could be ignored.

For the early modern period, the Jesuits set the standard for accurate reporting about China, because they had traveled there and learned the languages, and because they held a priestly office that established them in the republic of letters as credible eyewitnesses. Moreover, inasmuch as Jesuit reports from China helped remove the impression that Marco Polo had written a fable, they became the new standard for judging the plausibility of fictional writing about China. Just how respected their status was even among northern Protestants can be gleaned from their authenticating function in the first German novel about China, *Aeyquan, oder der Große Mogol* (Aeyquan, or the great Mogul), written by Christian Hagdorn and published by Jacob de Meurs in Amsterdam, purveyor of many illustrated travelogues through Asia. By the time the novel appeared in 1670, German readers were well aware that the Jesuit missionaries had established themselves as the most knowledgeable Europeans about China. Thus Hagdorn invokes their reputation to ground the verisimilitude of his novel. Anticipating his audience's questions, Hagdorn addresses the problem of his reliability as a reporter of Asian affairs on the first pages. How can an author, in no way a Jesuit, claim to know anything special about China? As behooves a baroque novelist, Hagdorn provides a multilayered response. First, he lays out the important genre distinction—namely, that he is offering a novel, not a personal travel memoir. Hagdorn is also aware that this argument is not sufficient given that the contours of the novel, particularly the epistemological status of its internal truth claims, were hardly codified in 1670. Thus, he augments his formalist defense by providing a potentially fictional tale about how he came to write the novel in the first place. This second-order personal account stands somewhere between the fictionality of the novel and the reader's reality. The plausibility of the main narrative remains in question despite the author announcing its fictional status, because the reader expects that the author of a novel about India and China has gone there himself; otherwise how could he describe the vast battle scenes with any accuracy?[75]

In the answer to the question "Did you travel through Asia?" Hagdorn answers, "No, but I met a Jesuit who had." The preface relates how the author set off on a sea voyage, during which he met a Jesuit, who was just returning from twelve years in both realms. Over the course of their ten-week voyage, the venerable father recounted his experiences and provided the author with additional written works. Unfortunately, the manuscripts were then all lost in a shipwreck in the English Channel, yet the author explains, he remembers most of what he had been told by the Jesuit. Through this elaborate side tale, Hagdorn legitimates the main narrative. Ultimately, the missionary serves as the source of the author's knowledge and the novel's integrity. Logistics, in the form of a failed ocean voyage, again figure in the author's transformation into a valid raconteur. Should this para-narrative seem implausible as well, Hagdorn promises the reader, finally, that most everything to be found

---

75. Christian Hagdorn, *Aeyquan, oder der Große Mogol. Das ist Chinesische und Indische Stahts-Kriegs- und Liebes-geschichte* (Amsterdam: Jacob von Mörs, 1670), preface: "Unterdessen möchte vielleicht der nicht al zu günstige Leser fragen: Ob ich in China oder Indien gewesen daß ich Darvon die Eigenschaften sonderlich deren Kriege zu beschreiben mich unterfinge?"

in his novel, can also be read in other books about China—intertextuality supplementing as the last line of credibility. Here, too, the Jesuits are invoked, though only indirectly, for they authored most of the important books on the subject.

Even after reports from China had increased dramatically and had begun to circulate in Europe, the wonder readers felt toward China manifested itself in diverse reactions: admiration for its moral order, suspicion that the tale was concocted, a desire to emulate Chinese manners by consuming its wares, a greed to find one's own share of such a wealthy kingdom. These responses could all be mixed in one: fascination for travel reports coupled with doubt that they were entirely true, respect for Confucian principles with the suspicion that dark practices must also involved. The slow historical shift that has so often been diagnosed as a turn from Sinophilia to Sinophobia emerges alongside the increasingly suspicious attitude European readers took toward Jesuit's media strategies. Eighteenth-century editors such as Du Halde felt obliged to argue that readers should trust the Jesuit reports sent back from Asia, not because China seemed too wonderful a place to be believed, but because the honesty of their authors of these texts was increasingly challenged. This had not been a problem in the seventeenth century when Jesuit accounts were accepted as authoritative. In the eighteenth century any serious study of China also required a critique of the Jesuit sources. The first point of concern was its utopian character; the second was the amazing, yet suspicious, consistency of the Jesuit publications.

The Uncanny Persistence of Oriental Fables

The eighteenth-century distinction between accurate ethnographic information and imaginary literary creation continues to structure contemporary scholarship. The opposition between fiction and reality plays itself out in political terms, with the presumption that imaginative projections are always ideological distortions. As the debate about Marco Polo's *Travels* became a full-fledged intellectual project in the eighteenth century, Enlightenment thinkers were

extremely proud of their ability to unveil the superstition and deception ascribed to tradition, folklore, church, and state. Yet try as one
might, it seems impossible to fully dispel the fable of the Orient.
Marco Polo's *Travels* continue to hover between fiction and fact. If its
claims seemed exaggerated, then the narrative became all the more
suitable as literature. For centuries after its publication, well into the
Enlightenment, Europeans had no simple method for dispelling the
work's influence. To discredit its veracity does not dispel its historical
significance. To deny its informational accuracy only reinforces its
literary quality. To call Polo's text fiction cannot undo its importance.
On the question of depicting China in the Enlightenment, the difference between fable and fact was never easily elucidated.

Srinivas Aravamudan makes clear that imaginative fiction, and
fables in particular, continue to define European perception of India,
Persia, China, and the Levant even as the novel became the dominant
fictional genre during the Enlightenment. Behind these genre distinctions was a rationalist epistemology that preferred scientifically veri-
fied information against imaginative narratives. Aravamudan sets the
two modes in a dialectical relation: "Two seemingly unconnected
genres—scientific dialogue and beast fable—complement each other
to form the stereoscopic perspective of Enlightenment Orientalism."[76]
Rather than accepting the simple Enlightenment charges that fables
are distortions of reality that readers naively swallow, we might consider how they unveil truths that scientific information cannot represent. Fables are often sharply critical of European society, harboring
religious, political, and sexual aspirations that could not be articulated directly.

Such an appreciation of fables has little place in Jürgen Osterhammel's *Unfabling the East: The Enlightenment's Encounter with
Asia*. Osterhammel insists that the Enlightenment did away with the
marvelous fictions about China. He claims that Europe's engagement
with Asia was carried out by "roving *philosophes*, itinerant scholars
who combined high competence with great intellectual authority."

---

76. Srinivas Aravamudan, *Enlightenment Orientalism: Resisting the Rise of
the Novel* (Chicago: University of Chicago Press, 2012), 129.

Osterhammel reiterates the Enlightenment's own heroic tale of its travelers by praising their valiant self-composure: they reflected on what they had experienced and witnessed, while refraining from "telling tall stories in the manner of many an earlier fabulist."[77]

Osterhammel's epistemological juxtapositions reflect his view of fables as moments of imaginary indulgence, rather than as the bearers of utopian aspirations. As the two modes become more distinct during the eighteenth century, he elevates information and knowledge production over artistic representation, which he faults as a form of distortion or noise. Russell Berman warns: "It is the denigration of the 'marvelous' . . . that represents both the Enlightenment's victory over superstition and its perhaps excessive confidence in its own ability to separate between the marvelous and the accurate."[78] Rather than setting reason off against the fable, we would be better served to recognize their interdependence. Siegfried Kracauer applied this dialectic directly to the Enlightenment's fascination for oriental tales: "There is profound historical significance in the fact that the *Thousand and One Nights* turned up precisely in the France of the Enlightenment and that eighteenth-century reason recognized the reason of the fairy tales as its equal."[79] For Kracauer, both modes of thought, critical reason and fables, articulate open suppressed ideals of justice.

In order to support his claim that the Enlightenment produced a steady increase in accurate, rational knowledge about Asia, Osterhammel is required to ignore the many eighteenth-century novels, poems, operas, paintings, and dramas that depict the East. Demand for Chinese porcelain, furniture, and interior design among absolutist princes was already high at the start of the eighteenth century, but most public ballets, operas, festivals, masquerades, and theater performances that included a Chinese diversion appeared in the second

77. Jürgen Osterhammel, *Unfabling the East: The Enlightenment's Encounter with Asia* (Princeton, NJ: Princeton University Press, 2018), 27.

78. Russell Berman, *Enlightenment or Empire: Colonial Discourse in German Culture* (Lincoln: Nebraska University Press, 1998), 44.

79. Siegfried Kracauer, *The Mass Ornament: Weimar Essays*, trans. Thomas Y. Levin (Cambridge, MA: Harvard University Press, 1995), 80.

half of the eighteenth century.[80] It is relatively easy for Osterhammel to claim that the eighteenth century "unfabled the East," because he specifically overlooks all the fables written during the period. Ultimately, Osterhammel is less concerned with literary culture and more interested in travel writing as data collection. His book does not consider the nuanced connections between these modes of writing—for example, the manner in which fiction and ethnography reinforce each other. It is one thing for a German historian not to appreciate contemporary theory; much more surprising is one who dismisses Goethe and Romanticism. He dispatches the *West-Eastern Divan* with a muddled quotation from Friedrich Rückert, failing to appreciate how important Persian poetry was to both poets. If one makes a point of ignoring literary culture, then it is relatively easy to claim that one particular literary form no longer matters. The formulation of world literature as a privileged genre was motivated in part by the realization that reading foreign fiction offered access to social relations otherwise hidden to travelers. The nineteenth-century value granted to philological study of Asian novels demonstrates that the earlier interest in fables was also particularly important for Europeans seeking to understand Asian cultures. Osterhammel focuses exclusively on the production and transfer of information as an abstract form of knowledge, thereby ignoring the modes of discourse grounded in more immediate experience and in traditional communication. Romanticism and world literature with their two distinctly different attitudes toward the Orient both rely on the fable in order to find compatibility with Asian societies. As translators discovered, too much information layered as footnotes in the narrative smothers most aesthetic effects, reducing the novel to a clumsy encyclopedia.

Even if we were to juxtapose ethnographic reports with fictional literature, we should not presume that only the travelogues produced knowledge. For the upper classes who did not read scholarly treatises, operas would have been a serious source of information about any number of Asian societies. As Chinese novels and poetry

---

80. *China und Europa*, 121.

were being translated into European languages, the claim was increasingly heard that fiction more accurately depicted the private life of Asians than the reports of travelers, who were never allowed anywhere near the interior of a house. For all their language skills and political connections, Jesuit priests were also not considered adequate judges of Chinese intimacy and romance. How did the Chinese express and regulate desire? Surely a novel written for a domestic audience was far more likely to reveal such secrets than any European observer. Thus, literature in translation was an important new source for understanding the Orient, although the process of translation did of course allow myriad biases and presumptions to shape the final text. Wieland's novel, like so many others, emerged only after *A Thousand and One Nights* had appeared in French; similarly Goethe's *West-Eastern Divan* responded directly to Joseph von Hammer-Purgstall's translation of Hafez.

Given these translations, eighteenth-century writers generated a succession of texts that appealed to European sensibilities about Asia. The fable, the genre that Osterhammel seeks to banish, plays a central role in the Enlightenment's conception of the Orient. Lessing's "Nathan the Wise" offers perhaps the most important example of a fable, or parable, receiving a new life within the German Enlightenment. Far from removing fables from the Enlightenment's conception of the Orient, Lessing sets a forgotten fable at the center of his drama and the Enlightenment debates about religious tolerance. For better or worse, regardless of the many critical interpretations it has received, the "three-rings parable" at the heart of Lessing's drama has become the illustrative supplement that defines rationalist arguments in favor of religious tolerance. When Saladin expects a logical disputation, Lessing has Nathan offer the parable instead, suggesting that he well understood that its open-ended undecidability gave the fable an advantage over theoretical discourse and ethnographic realism. In Lessing's presentation, the three-rings parable is clearly marked as an oriental tale. The narrator, Nathan, is a representative of the Orient, a wealthy businessman known also for his practical ethics—the mode of philosophy for which Leibniz had already praised the Chinese. His journeys take him all across the Orient. Nathan enters the play having just returned in Jerusalem after a long journey, his caravan bearing goods from across the Orient:

> He comes from Babylon.
> With twenty well-loaded camels,
> And everything, noble spices,
> Stones and Clothe, that India
> Persia, Syria, even China
> Offer up as Valuables.[81]

The image of Marco Polo returning from Asia with riches and stories from a great distant empire once again provides the precedent for Lessing. As already noted, Goethe adopted the same posture, in Islamic guise, for the opening to his *West-Eastern Divan,* a cycle of poems intent on reviving even more myths of the Orient. Even the most philological literary scholars have understood that bibliophilic writers such as Lessing studied the scholarship on Islam before composing a "Nathan the Wise." Lessing's attention to detail, down to having Saladin play chess with stone markers rather than anthropomorphic figures, demonstrates the interpenetration of theatrical performance and orientalist scholarship of the late eighteenth century.[82] Goethe's extensive notes to the *Divan* were ostensibly an attempt to aid the German reader unfamiliar with Islam, yet as a summary of the author's research, this addendum to the poems only heightened their learned strangeness. The reinvention of China as a land of fable was compatible with Weimar Classicism's view of Asia. When Schiller takes up the task of revising Carlo Gozzi's "Marchen" *Turandot,* he struggles to provide motivations for the princess's cruelty; in fairy tales actions do not require psychological justifications, yet by Schiller's understanding of the melodrama, or tragicomedy, they do. Nevertheless, even in providing a hidden reason for the princess to execute her unsuccessful suitors, Schiller does not abandon the sto-

81. Gotthold Ephraim Lessing, *Werke,* ed. Herbert Georg Göpfert and Karl Eibl (Munich: C. Hanser, 1970), 2:232 (act 1, scene 6).

82. Zahim Mohammed Muslim, "Lessing under Islam: Eine Studie zu Lessings Auseinandersetzung mit dem Islam," PhD diss., Humboldt University, 2010, 110–12.

ry's fantastical qualities. At the top of his list of *Personen* we see "Altoum—fabled emperor of China."[83]

If travel writers struggled to balance the degree to which their writing seemed fabulous, as they sought to attract audiences to their adventure tale while convincing them of its reality, the situation was quite different for writers around 1800 who were working within genres understood as fictional—Lessing, Wieland, Goethe, Novalis, Hoffmann. Even outside the question of a text's fictionality, any classically trained writer would have maneuvered between the ancient rhetorical distinction between Attic and Asiatic styles of speaking. The challenge for a learned European was to write about Asia in an Attic manner, while preserving the wonder and awe that readers clearly desired. In E. T. A. Hoffmann's romantic story "Der goldne Topf" ("The Golden Pot"), Archivarious Lindhorst offers a fable about salamanders as his own family genealogy. An audience member, sitting in the café where he is holding forth, dismisses the tale as "Orientaler Schwulst" (oriental bombast), an ironic echo of an ancient rhetorical distinction.[84] Hoffmann's story juxtaposes bourgeois rationalism with Romantic orientalism, deliberately playing Cicero's succinct Attic style against the metaphorical abundance of "Asiatic" writing. Hoffmann was completely aware of how important Cicero was for proper training of Prussian officials. In "The Golden Pot" he goes so far as to include a virtuous bourgeois administrator who reads Cicero in the evenings at home as a lucidly dull counterweight to the hallucinatory revelations the protagonist Anselmus experiences while copying an Asian manuscript written in a strange, non-European script. Cicero is after all our primary

---

83. The thematic proximity of the two plays shows itself in that Schiller staged the Weimar premiere of *Turandot* on January 30, 1802, two months after he had finished a run of Lessing's *Nathan der Weise*. The Orientalist theme continued with Goethe's *Iphigenie auf Taurus* as the next drama to be staged. Marion Müller, *Zwischen Intertextualität und Interpretation: Friedrich Schillers dramaturgische Arbeiten 1796–1805* (Karlsruhe: KIT Publishing, 2004), 105.

84. E. T. A. Hoffmann, "Der goldne Topf," *Fantasie- und Nachtstücke* (Darmstadt: Wissenschaftliche Buchgesellschaft, 1985),192–93; Eduard Norden, *Die antike Kunstprosa, vom VI. Jahrhundert v. Chr. bis in die Zeit der Renaissance* (Leipzig: B. G. Teubner, 1923), 2:783. The term "Schwulst" was used by classicists to describe an excessively ornamental Asian style of writing.

source for the ancient distinction between sober, concise Attic speech and bombastic, flowery Asiatic diction. The absolutist Enlightenment along the Spree certainly favored crisp Attic forms; thus in response to Frederick II's insistence that Christian Garve provide a modern German translation of *De Officia* as a model for all Prussian civil servants, Hoffmann offers as much oriental bombast as he can muster.

Joseph Görres turned the Enlightenment's concern for accurate travel reporting on its head when in 1807 he elevated John Mandeville's crazy medieval fables about travel through Asia into a central influence on Romantic poetry.[85] Görres fully appreciated that Mandeville cobbled together existing fables into a fully implausible first-person narration, including many about Alexander the Great's exploits on the way to India,.[86] As a philologist, Görres celebrated Mandeville for having brought together the many fables circulated in antiquity into one book, thereby preserving the ancient wonder at the distant paradise for later poets to emulate. "The fables, which were retold many times already in antiquity as Alexander's army marched to India, provide us with the basis for our poetry."[87] Far from wanting to remove the Orient's fables, Görres strove, like the Grimm brothers and so many other Romantics, to capture and archive the supernatural tales circulating without authority or credibility. Thus he lauded Mandeville's much maligned travelogue as the first truly Romantic work: "The poet collected ancient sagas that were formed in the Orient and Occident and that he strung together into a whole. Thus emerged this strange work, perhaps the first real Romantic composition."[88]

The Romantic revival of fairy tales inevitably created a rift between popular writing on the Orient and German sinology as well. When Richard Wilhelm offered a translated collection of Chinese *Märchen* (fairy tales) in 1913, he inevitably organized the volume

85. Joseph Görres, *Die teutschen Volksbüchern* (Heidelberg: Mohr und Zimmer, 1807), 55.

86. Willy Richard Berger, *China-Bild und China-Mode im Europa der Aufklärung* (Cologne: Böhlau, 1990), 34.

87. Görres, *Volksbüchern*, 57.

88. Görres, *Volksbüchern*, 59.

according to standards enunciated by the Grimms, drawing a distinction between *Kunst-und Volksmärchen* (literary and folk tales), preferring oral over literary sources, giving precedence to nursery rhymes and children's tales, even while acknowledging that this category had little place in Chinese literature. So broadly did Wilhelm define the Chinese *Märchen* that he affirmed the old notion that Chinese literature was pervaded with the marvelous. "In China, the fairy tale does not constitute a strictly separate genre. From nursery tales to fables up to myths about gods, to sagas and novellas, the borderlines are flexible. For China, the marvelous belongs to the natural course of the world, and thus it is impossible to draw sharp distinctions."[89]

By asserting the demystification of the Orient, Osterhammel touches on only one side of the persistent tension between fiction and veracity in writing about Asia. He posits an Enlightenment narrative of increasingly accurate knowledge, as if the fictional representation of Asia were merely inaccurate and distracting, when in fact nineteenth-century culture, including the German traditions, generated a rich vein of poetic fantasies about Asia, which always drew heavily from academic publications on the Orient.

89. Richard Wilhelm, *Chinesische Volksmärchen, Die Märchen der Weltliteratur, Märchen des Orients*, ed. Friedrich von der Leyen (Jena: Eugen Diedrich, 1914), 1.

Jesuit Channels between Europe and Asia

Marco Polo's travels appeared as a single narrative summarizing the most important journey in one person's lifetime. His information came in the form of personal experience: what I saw with my own eyes. Many later travelers to China wrote tomes summarizing the journey of their lifetimes, but these books were too sporadic to provide a continuous flow of news from Asia. Even after the administrative apparatus required to convey continuous information updates about China was established in the last decades of the sixteenth century with the arrival of Jesuit missionaries on Portuguese vessels, news from China reached Europe only in waves.

Founded by Ignatius Loyola and a circle of friends in 1534, the Society of Jesus grew rapidly to become a global institution. Although not explicitly created as a vehicle for the Catholic Renewal, the society soon came to define its mission in terms of education and spreading the faith after receiving papal approval in 1540. As part of its missionary work, the Jesuits established schools that taught the methods of Renaissance humanism and medieval Scholasticism along with advanced mathematics and science. Francis Xavier, an early companion of Ignatius Loyola and founder of the Asia mission, established St. Paul's College in 1542 in Goa, India. The Jesuit mission in Asia moved through Portuguese lines of communication and transport, though eventually they would find occasional passage with the Dutch East India Company (VOC), fierce competitors of the Portuguese. Securing long-distance travel and communication was fundamental to the Jesuits' intertwined goals of education and missionary work. Not only did they work with existing institutions, but they formed their own to become "a vast network of enterprising individuals who, while keeping in close communication with those in authority and receiving guidance and 'consolation' from them, adapted to local needs and tried to seize opportunities as they presented themselves."[1] Because they were not monks, the Jesuits did not retreat from worldly interactions, but instead often adopted the dress, manners, and language of the local population they were trying to convert.[2] Florence Hsia describes the strategy in popular terms: "The ideal Jesuit was thus a shapeshifter, putting on different clothes and different roles, speaking in as many tongues and modulating his message in as many forms of diction as his audiences required."[3] The Jesuits' transformation into strange cultures also provided them with a rhetorical advantage—the ability to understand the other side of a debate. Understanding others is not always motivated by sympathetic agreement; sometimes it is driven, for better or worse, by sophistry or by the need to comprehend your opposite's perspective. These rhetorical lessons were useful for both actors and debaters.

---

1. John W. O'Malley, *The First Jesuits* (Cambridge, MA: Harvard University Press, 1993), 11.

2. For a comprehensive overview of the languages Jesuits studies, see Henrike Foertsch, "Missionare als Sprachensammler, Zum Umfang der philologischen Arbeit der Jesuiten in Asien, Afrika und Lateinamerika. Auswertung einer Datenbank," in *Wege durch Babylon: Missionare, Sprachstudien und interkulturelle Kommunikation,* ed. Reinhard Wendt (Tübingen: Gunter Narr, 1998), 43–73.

3. Florence Hsia, *Sojourners in a Strange Land: Jesuits and Their Scientific Missions in Late Imperial China* (Chicago: University of Chicago Press, 2009), 1.

For most of the twentieth century, intellectual historians have traced a well-established narrative of early modern European interest in China as an arc that runs from fascination and admiration for the grandeur of Chinese civilization to racism, contempt, and the colonial urge to take over the place. Although by no means the first, Arthur O. Lovejoy neatly sketched out the rise of early modern "Sinomania," and this pattern has continued in German and French scholarship down into the present day.[4] These accounts of Europe's philosophical engagement with Chinese culture begin with the memoirs published by the Jesuits about their mission to bring Christianity to the Middle Kingdom.[5] Behind these claims of "Sinophilia" and "Sinophobia" stands the history of Jesuit writing about China. The two epochs could just as readily be divided into the period when the Jesuits set the discourse on China and the decades after the society's suppression in 1773.

To this day, intellectual histories and biographies follow the contours traced out in Matteo Ricci's and Nicolas Trigault's history of the Jesuit mission in China, published in 1617.[6] Matteo Ricci, the second leader of the China mission, is generally credited with having developed the accommodation strategy in China, which entailed missionaries learning Chinese and assimilating into the society of the Mandarin elite.[7] His predecessor, Michele Ruggieri, founded

---

4. His article "The Chinese Origin of a Romanticism" first appeared in the *Journal of English and Germanic Philology* January 1933 and was republished several times in a revised and expanded version; see Arthur O. Lovejoy, *Essays in the History of Ideas* (Westport, CT: Greenwood Press, 1978), 99–135.

5. For an excellent overview of scholarship on the Jesuit mission in China, see Ronnie Po-chia Hsia, "Imperial China and the Christian Mission," in *A Companion to the Early Modern Catholic Global Missions*, ed. Ronnie Po-chia (Leiden: Brill, 2018): 344–64.

6. The first two editions published in Germany were: Nicolao Trigault, *De Christiana Expeditione apud Sinas Suscepta ab Societate Iesu ex. P. Mattaei Riccii* (Cologne: Bernardi Gualteri, 1617) and *Historia von Einführung der Christlichen Religion in das grosse Königreich China* (Augsburg: Antony Hierat, 1617).

7. The scholarship on Matteo Ricci is vast. For starters, see Jonathan D. Spence, *The Memory Palace of Matteo Ricci* (New York: Penguin, 1985); David Mungello, *Curious Land: Jesuit Accommodation and the Origins of Sinology* (Honolulu: University of Hawaii Press, 1989); Ronnie Po-chia Hsia, *A Jesuit in the Forbidden City: Matteo Ricci 1552–1610* (Oxford: Oxford University Press, 2010).

the China mission but remained true to his identity in China as a foreign monk, a position that aligned him implicitly with Buddhists who had also brought a new religious teaching from the outside. Ruggieri wrote religious works and poetry in Chinese while courting the scholarly company of the mandarins, a strategy that Ricci would expand upon while dropping any references to Buddhism. In 1582, when the Jesuits first arrived in China, Westerners were confined to Macau. Ricci gained permission to travel away from the coast, where he initially moved through Guangdong province. He settled for a time in Nanjing, visited Suzhou, and after several attempts, was received at the imperial court, thereby becoming the first Westerner to enter the Forbidden City. Ricci and his followers were able to ingratiate themselves with the Chinese elite in large part because they adopted Chinese manners and spoke and wrote Mandarin while studying early Confucian texts, which Ricci argued were compatible with Christian teaching. He sought to demonstrate that Confucian teaching served as a natural theology that shared in the divine revelation of a single God as creator of the universe. Even further, early Confucian texts enunciated ethical teachings remarkably similar to Christianity. From 1583, when the China mission was first established, until its high-water mark in 1700, the Jesuits published around 450 works in Chinese.[8] The Jesuits' alignment with Confucianism seemed to also require a very deliberate disavowal of Buddhism, to the extent that missionaries followed the long-standing practice of arguing against (in this case, Buddhist) heresies through oral disputations, while building an alliance with Confucian scholars through written works, in both printed and manuscript forms, which sought to translate the two traditions into each other.

The early Enlightenment perception of China is generally said to have developed from the Jesuit position. Gottfried Leibniz elaborates upon the Jesuit respect for Confucian thought when he describes China in almost utopian terms, partially in order to praise

---

8. Patricia Sieber, "The Imprint of the Imprints: Sojourners, *Xiaoshuo* Translations, and the Transcultural Canon of Early Chinese Fiction in Europe, 1697–1826," *East Asian Publishing and Society* 3 (2013): 33.

China as a nation administered by responsible philosophers and partially in order to critique European politics.[9] Leibniz's correspondence with Jesuits traveling to China and his visions of China as an ideal society ruled by an emperor trained in Confucian ethics reiterated the larger European initial amazement at Chinese civilization that the first Jesuit texts had produced. His admiration was so great that without irony he reversed the whole purpose of the Jesuit mission by arguing that the Chinese ought to send missionaries to Europe to teach political philosophy and the administration of the peace.[10]

The Jesuits are generally regarded as having established a successful international communication network that operated over long distances for at least 150 years. Letter writing was integral to the general operation of the society. The obligation to report one's observations to other members was conveyed to each missionary setting out, so that over time the network of correspondences became both a historical as well as a spatial interconnection. Ignatius Loyola set the standard for later cosmopolitan societies when he counseled that "frequent interchange of letters back and forth between inferiors and superiors greatly aids the unity of spirits in the Society."[11] These communications were composed in standardized forms that followed the precedents established by the society's founding members. The first "rules that must be observed concerning writing" were issued in 1547.[12] These guidelines were eventually incorporated into the *Constitutions*, where it was explained that

---

9. "Just as Ricci praises the highly sophisticated ethical code of Confucianism as a theistic system minus the Christian revelation, so does Leibniz perceive the efficient government of the hierarchically structured Chinese society by meritocracy . . . as the real-life realization of the Platonic utopia-republic" (Yu Liu, "The Jesuits and the Anti-Jesuits: The Two Different Connections of Leibniz with China," *Eighteenth Century* 43.2 [2002]:167).

10. Gottfried Wilhelm Leibniz, *The Preface to Leibniz' Novissima Sinica*, trans. Donald Lach (Honolulu: University of Hawaii Press, 1957).

11. Grant Boswell, "Letter Writing among the Jesuits: Antonio Possevino's Advice in the *Bibliotheca Selecta* (1593)," *Huntington Library Quarterly* 66 (2003): 257.

12. Paul Nelles, "*Cosas y cartes*: Scribal Production and Material Pathways in Jesuit Global Communication (1547–1573)," *Journal of Jesuit Studies* 2.3 (2015): 425.

letters "facilitated the union of souls" and provided "mutual consolation and edification."[13]

Letters from India also became an opportunity for European Catholics to pray for the missionaries and their converts, thus completing the spiritual media cycle. Members of the laity who were excluded from traveling to the Indies, women among them, joined the mission vicariously by reading letters and sending prayers. J. Michelle Molina provides the case of Isabel Roser, a pious Catholic who corresponded with Loyola. From her position in a Franciscan convent, she participated in the expansion of Christianity: "We often see letters telling us what the Lord is working in the Indies through the fathers of the Society, the Abbess has these letters read in the refectory and bids all pray God for our Lord for the whole Society."[14] Francis Xavier was certain of the prayers' effectiveness; he stated that pagans in the Indies were more likely to convert because of European prayers than missionary preaching.[15] In due time, Xavier, as founder of the Asia mission, became himself a venerated figure, particularly within Bavaria.[16]

The Jesuit instruction for missionaries to write letters recreated the postal structure already present in the New Testament and the early Christian Church. The epistles of Paul served as a point of reference for missionary letters both in terms of allusions to specific passages and as models for how to evangelize. The preservation of letters and their translation and distribution among the laity likewise recreated an image of the early church.

For all the attention given to following precedent, the process of letter writing was not simply formulaic, but rather a highly self-conscious form in which correspondents would often call attention to their own place within the growing tradition of sending missives from Asia to Europe. Many opened their epistles with a statement

---

13. Nelles, "*Casas y cartas,*" 423.

14. J. Michelle Molina, *To Overcome Oneself: The Jesuit Self and Spirit of Global Expansion* (Berkeley: University of California Press, 2013), 56.

15. Alfons Väth, SJ, "Nicht in den Missionen, und doch Missionär," *Die Katholischen Missionen* 45.7 (April 1917): 146.

16. Luke Clossey, *Salvation and Globalization in the Early Jesuit Missions* (Cambridge: Cambridge University Press, 2008), 80.

about the importance of writing and an accounting of the letters they had recently received and sent. The most famous letters, read by other priests and the public, were themselves an affirmation of the obligation to write and a testimony to the Jesuits' successful maintenance of their networks.

We cannot simply equate the purpose and value inherent in missionaries' communications with modern models of information, even though a considerable amount of scientific data were passed along. Missionary letters produced knowledge of China through the personal relationships implied between sender and receiver, the willingness of the Christian reader to accept the authority of the missionary, the ease with which pious recipients could admire the senders. The epistolary production of knowledge, in short personalized forms, was distinctly different from other forms of scientific information gathering. All observation was embedded within the mission's religious framework. On an individual level, each letter constituted a spiritual statement distinctly different from scientific methods of communication. The value in confession lies more with the person sending information than with its recipient. What does the sender gain by conveying information? Who benefits from confession, the speaker or the audience, or perhaps both? Missionary letters show the operation and interdependence of administrative, spiritual, rhetorical, and scientific techniques as European subjects encounter previously unfamiliar cultural practices. If the Jesuits are famous for their discipline, they are equally known for their flexible adaptation to completely new circumstances. Their correspondence elucidates how the often radical personal transformations brought about by assimilating into foreign cultures depended upon, adapted, and reaffirmed the missionaries' commitment to theological truth.

As has often been noted quietly in passing, practices familiar to twenty-first-century media anthropology can already be found in the Jesuits' organizational repertoire. The international, multilingual reach of the society was not a secondary effect of its success, but rather a defining feature, both in its rise and suppression. When the language of contemporary globalization is applied to the Jesuits, the fit is not nearly as anachronistic as one might expect. Even though the early modern concept of distributing a message around the globe was not as rapid or pervasive as in our own capitalist present, Markus Friedrich can comfortably describe the Jesuits as a global organization with a hierarchical bureaucratic structure that understood itself as spatially distributed.[17] In 1975, Elida Maria Szarota suggested that modern media theory fits neatly onto the communication strategies of Jesuit school dramas.[18] From the start, Ignatius Loyola stressed the importance of reliable communication between administrative offices. Whatever religious value writing letters had for the author and the readers, correspondences between members was also important to the society's successful administration. A 1620 manual on letter writing sent by the Roman secretary Francesco Sacchini to the provincial of Germany superior spells out the point most clearly: "In every task, profit and success depends on compliance with certain routines and protocols. Persons with many obligations are particularly dependent on diligent support. In the Society of Jesus this holds particularly true for the Father General and his Provincials. Since the epistolary communication between the General and the Provincials is the backbone of our order's administration, and since this communication relies on letters, it is important that the writing of these letters is done with the utmost care and accuracy."[19] Communication was so important because in a globally distributed organization such as that of the Jesuits, local colleges and missions operated with a considerable degree of individual responsibility in adapting to local conditions. On an abstract bureaucratic level, the purpose of writing letters is to keep the letter writing system in operation. The story becomes interesting when this system runs less smoothly than the ideal would want. The enormous delays in travel and communication between Rome, Madrid, or Lisbon and the distant missions

17. Markus Friedrich, "Communication and Bureaucracy in the Early Modern Society of Jesus," *Zeitschrift für Schweizerische Religions- und Kirchengeschichte* 101 (2007) 49–75.

18. Elida Maria Szarota, "Die Jesuitendrama als Vorläufer der modernen Massenmedien," *Daphnis* 4 (1975): 129–43.

19. Cited in Friedrich, "Communication and Bureaucracy," 50.

made it all the more important that Jesuits maintain a routine correspondence, even if it meant that letters were sent only annually.

In 1553, the society's secretary in Rome sent instructions to the provincial in Brazil and the vice-provincial in India explaining that reports should provide information about the number of settlers, their clothing, food, and drink, the bedding provided society members, how high their expenses were, further information about the land, its size, neighbors, clothing and food of the inhabitants, their morals, the number of Christians, pagans, Muslims—really anything that would excite the curious and would aid Ignatius Loyola in directing the society.[20] As he departs Portugal for India, Francis Xavier reiterates the expectation that missionaries send letters back. The instruction holds true regardless of the letter writer's location. Histories of Jesuit missionaries in Canada often stress that letters sent back to France had been written in a hut deep in the wilderness. Fittingly the instruction to write letters appears in a letter, which for centuries has been circulated among those eager to commune with Xavier, who begins a typical letter with the instruction to write: "As I think it is only through the medium of letters that we shall see one another again in this life—in the next it will be face to face with many embraces—it remains for us during the little time left here below to secure these mutual glimpses by frequent writing. This is what you tell me to do and I shall see to it, as well as to your instructions about the *hijuelas*."[21] Though letter writing does not produce a shared sense of the other person's presence that compares with being physically in the same place or the expectation of a heavenly reunion, the effort to write holds out the promise of a visible encounter. The visualization of a person, place, or object was central to Jesuit devotional exercises.[22] We shall see each other again through writing, which produces an experience that is generated by

---

20. Alessandro Valignano, S J, *Historia del principle y progresso de la Campaña de Jesus en las Indias Orientates (1542–1564)*, ed. Josef Wicki (Rome: Institutum Historicum S. I., 1944), 23–24.

21. John Correia-Afonso, SJ, *Jesuit Letters and Indian History, 1542–1773* (Oxford: Oxford University Press, 1969), 11.

22. Paul Nelles, "Seeing and Writing: The Art of Observation in the Early Jesuit Missions," *Intellectual History Review* 20.3 (2010): 322.

the writing but is not itself dependent solely on the meaning of the words. The letter itself seems to convey a presence aside from its contents. Whether we understand this effect in terms of Romanticism or Latour's actants remains undecided.

The success of the Jesuit network depended on each member carrying out Xavier's instructions. Correia-Afonso thus provides us with a continuation of the command in a different location. This time Xavier is in India. As he is leaving for Japan, Xavier, instructs Flemish Jesuit Gaspar Berze: "You will relate to the College [at Goa] in great detail all the work which you there do [at Ormuz] for God our Lord, and the fruit which God produces through you, since the letters which you write to the College will be of use for transmission to the kingdom [Portugal]; and in them you will write things of edification and such as to move those who see them to serve God."[23] These are standard instructions: Xavier repeats them verbatim to Father Gonçalo Rodriguez in Hormuz as well.[24] Gaspar Berze understands Xavier's intentions so well that he repeats them December 1, 1549, to the missionaries with whom he corresponds. Again the command to write arrives in a letter: "My dear Brothers and Fathers write at length each individually, as Father Master Xavier commanded each one of us who are scattered in these pagan regions."[25] While he was in Japan, Xavier expected to stay informed about events in India and the rest of the Asia mission. Letters were to be collected in Goa, where they could be copied to be sent on to Rome and Portugal, as well as to Malacca, from whence they could be forwarded to Xavier in Japan.[26] Such logistical routing would lead to confusion even today; it is remarkable that Xavier was convinced that it would succeed in 1550. These letters found an eager

---

23. Correia-Afonso, *Jesuit Letters and Indian History*, 12.

24. Francis Xavier, *Letters and Instructions of Francis Xavier*, trans M. Joseph Costelloe, SJ (St. Louis: Institute of Jesuit Source, 1992), 364: "When you write to the college, write also with great brevity, obedience, and reverence to the lord bishop, giving him an account of what you are doing there for he is our ecclesiastical superior and has such a great affection for us and helps us in all that he can."

25. Correia-Afonso, *Jesuit Letters and Indian History*, 12.

26. Georg Schurhammer, SJ, *Japan and China 1549–1552*, vol. 4 of *Francis Xavier: His Life, His Times* (Rome: Jesuit Historical Institute, 1982), 276.

audience in Europe. Xavier's November 5, 1549, letter from Japan, a country whose conversion held great promise for him, was already circulating in translation two years later and was included in the 1552 edition of Giovanni Battista Ramusio's *Navigationi et Viaggi* (Voyages and travels), the compilation that introduced many Europeans to Marco Polo, as well.[27]

Writing letters belonged to the exercises that defined the Jesuit order. The principle instructing members to write, as it was reiterated in the letters that fulfilled that command, introduced a layer of self-examination into the correspondences. Am I fulfilling my responsibilities as I write this letter? The Jesuit reports are at least in part self-conscious reflections on the act of reporting, as are so many letters that begin by pondering: What does it mean that I am writing this letter? These brief moments of reflection about letter writing comprise a rhetorical and media self-consciousness that calls attention to the exercises that reinforced the cohesion of both the individual missionary's faith and the Society across the globe. That the instructions that produce this unity of souls is commented upon in the act of writing a letter is significant. The command to the letter writer and the recipient makes clear that the letter writers are the themselves the theorists of their own communication network. As Bernhard Siegert asserts, without having the Jesuits in mind, "a theory of the postal system always is a theory in the postal system, as well."[28]

The letters sent by missionaries in Asia provided information that editors in Europe would arrange into encyclopedic collections of strange and uplifting stories from abroad. The most important Jesuit compilations, such as Athanasius Kircher's *China Illustrata* (1667), and the collection so vital to the Enlightenment's understanding of China, *Lettres édifiantes et curieuses, écrites des Mission Étrangères par quelque Missionaires de la Compaigne de Jésus* (Edifying and curious letters, written from the foreign missions by some missionaries of the Society of Jesus, 1702–1776), clearly ac-

---

27. Donald F. Lach, *Asia in the Making of Europe* (Chicago: University of Chicago Press, 1965–1993), 1:664.

28. Bernhard Siegert, *Relays: Literature as an Epoch of the Postal System*, trans. Kevin Repp (Stanford, CA: Sanford University Press, 1999), 4.

knowledge missionary letters as their sources. That knowledge is drawn from a missionary's letter becomes a sign of authenticity within the Catholic world. While more synthetic works that combine information from diverse letters into a single document organized by chapters may have hidden or suppressed the names of correspondents in Asia, they would still insist that their information was based on letters sent from the source country. For example, Jean-Baptiste du Halde, who never left Europe, was able to gather together information for his *Description géographique, historique, chronologique, politique et physique de l'empire de La Chine (General History of China, Containing a Geographical, Historical, Chronological, Political and Physical Description of the Empire of China,* 1735) because he also edited the *Lettres édifiante et curieuses.* The editorial decisions regarding how to collect, organize, and present information were similar whether an author was writing an administrative report, an inspiring story for the faithful, or an assortment of strange customs and facts. Because the Jesuits were able to sustain lines of communication with China for long stretches at a time, missionary letters were eventually treated as ordinary and thus could easily be made anonymous. It sufficed to state that a particular statement had been written in China by a Jesuit for its credibility to be established. For much of the early modern period, the missionary network had an enunciative authority that granted a truthfulness to its reports far above those of other correspondents.[29] Of course this sense of legitimacy operated best when it did not call attention to itself. The clearest sign that the Enlightenment had started to challenge the Jesuit account of China emerges when Du Halde argues that his history of China is superior to the reports of merchants and sailors, because it is after all based on information gathered by priests. The problems that arose as letters flowed from the periphery of the Jesuit network to the administrative hub in Rome manifest themselves in the published compilations about China. Often the materials sent

---

29. Michel Foucault, *The Archeology of Knowledge and the Discourse on Language,* trans. A. M. Sheridan Smith (New York: Pantheon, 1972), 50.

to Rome received an unexpected interpretation that the missionaries in the distant countries would hardly have affirmed.

Histories of networks tend to replicate the operation of the system they are describing. They reiterate the rules that are known to each participant. Thus, scholarly histories of Jesuit letter writing tend to repeat the instructions given to each correspondent, without necessarily analyzing the contents. The presumption that the formal rules for letter writing were consistently obeyed appears in the work of John Correia-Afonso, SJ, who duplicates the correspondent's devotion while writing his 1955 dissertation, *Jesuit Letters and Indian History, 1542–1773*.[30] As C. R. Boxer pointed out in an early review, Correia-Afonso's study, now considered a classic, does not go beyond what earlier scholars had written. Indeed, one could argue that histories of Jesuit letter writing tend to replicate the instructions and motivations with which each missionary was instilled, so that these scholarly works themselves become part of the legacy that was carried forward for centuries.[31] If the point of writing letters is to fulfill the obligation to write letters, then histories of Jesuit letter writing are confirmations of that message. Jesuit historians are keenly attentive to what their predecessors have written, with the result that new works often repeat the same points made earlier with some minor additions and elaborations. In this sense, Jesuit historiography participates in the success of the network it describes. If the network depends on each member confirming the instructions that guide its operation, Jesuit histories constitute a parallel network to the one they describe.

The presumption that formal regulations about how to write are consistently obeyed is another blind spot in histories of communication. Because of the sheer volume of material, scholars tend to focus on the guidelines for letter writing rather than treating each letter as an individual text. It is often taken as a given that correspondents followed the rules. Yet there are many instances of personal digressions, resentments, and political intentions in the letters that gently

---

30. Correia-Afonso, *Jesuit Letters and Indian History*.
31. C. R. Boxer, "Review of *Jesuit Letters and Indian History* by John Correia-Afonso," *Bulletin of the School of Oriental and African Studies* 19 (1957):189–90.

contradict the image of information flowing smoothly. Correspondents were quite capable of anticipating how their letters might be read and thus would try to argue against certain positions even before they had been articulated. Matteo Ricci was surely not the only missionary to defend his methods against imagined criticisms. He undoubtedly foresaw some of the objections raised against his accommodation policy. For all their adherence to the requirements put on correspondents, missionaries were quite capable of staking out very specific policy positions. Edifying letters could for instance be met with concern and disapproval. We cannot presume that the contents of a letter always satisfied the formal instructions.

Historians of the Jesuit network are more inclined to focus on the remarkable success of its operation, while overlooking those instances when distant missionaries ignored instructions from Rome because they disagreed with them. Earlier scholars were prone to admire Jesuit letter writers for the ability to preserve organizational unity over great distances, while more recent scholars dig into the administrative challenges that faced even this most disciplined of societies. Theorists today set a very high standard for the movement of information through far-flung networks. In describing the Portuguese imperial system, upon which the Jesuits depended for their travel and correspondence, John Law depicts a sequence that was almost impossible to uphold: "Mobility, durability, capacity to exert force, ability to return—these seem to be indispensable if remote control is to be attempted. Indeed, they may be seen as specifications of a yet more general requirement: that there be no degeneration in communication between centre and periphery." Law makes clear that he is thinking about twentieth-century electronic communication when he adds: "No noise must be introduced into the circuit. Periphery must respond, as it were mechanically, to the behest of centre. Envoys must not be distorted by their passage, and interaction must be arranged such that they are able to exert influence without in turn being influence."[32] Steven J. Harris argues

32. John Law, "On Methods of Long Distance Control: Vessels, Navigation, and the Portuguese Route to India," in *Power, Action and Belief: A New Sociology of Knowledge?*, ed. John Law (Routledge: Henley, 1986), 9.

that the features Law isolated for the Portuguese network also applied to the Jesuits in Asia.[33] Although there is of course much to be gained from applying actor-network theory to understanding the correspondences among Jesuit missionaries, we should also consider how disruptions and delays in these networks could also be productive. Noise is after all the inevitable effect of an object's mobility. Indeed, the Jesuit policy of accommodation with Confucianism emerges precisely because of the long time span between messages in the correspondences between Rome and China. The farther away a missionary was stationed from Rome, the more opportunity he would have to formulate his own policies toward the local population. Since China was a civilization that inspired awe among Europeans, the need to adapt evangelical messages would have been apparent even in Rome. However, Ricci and his successors in China enjoyed a latitude made possible by the delays and breakdowns in communication. For all the merits of accommodation, it also helped that for a long time the Jesuits in China could claim that they had not received instructions to the contrary of what they were doing. This added twist requires us to read letters differently, to keep an eye out for their tactics of delay and defensiveness even while they express all the virtues required for well-drilled members of a long-distance network.

Annual Letters

As we have seen, annual letters were compiled within each province with individual chapters sending in their own local report. Markus Friedrich isolates three editorial methods of compilation. The first method entailed rewriting local letters into a single document that was organized according to geographical locations, first the province as a whole and then the individual chapters within it. The second method gathered the chapter letters within each province with minimal editorial revision, so that the annual letter became something of

---

33. Steven J. Harris, "Confession-Building, Long-Distance Networks, and the Organization of Jesuit Science," *Early Science and Medicine* 1.3 (1996): 287–318.

an anthology. The third method, which became more predominant after 1650, organized information according to themes rather than locations. These editorial decisions about how to organize information were not limited to administrators, for they were common concerns to all manner of published scientific and ethnographic compilations. Discrete local letters were rewritten into a single smooth document, or they were merely connected to one another in a sequence, or cut up into topics. The more editorial work involved in reshuffling the information gathered from local priests, the more the final document approached a published compilation. The internal administrative work of composing an annual letter entailed much of the same editorial work that organized larger compilations about curiosities collected from the world. The annual letters were collective works, in which information was drawn from different sources, and then the compiled document was circulated again within the province. The organization of annual letters into thematic chapters after 1650 reflected the need to make the documents more interesting and persuasive to readers. "For European readers these letters represented an exponential increase, both in quantity as well as in quality, compared to medieval travelogues, in which only fragmented and half-mythical descriptions had been presented. Contextually, these letters are of very high value in terms of transfer of information."[34]

Friedrich points out that the Jesuits were organized quite differently from earlier orders. While older monastic orders followed the manner of medieval kings in having an itinerate leadership that moved between churches and abbeys, the Jesuit leadership remained fixed in Rome. Furthermore, the upper administrative offices were held for life, rather than rotating between priests. Given these new structures, the Jesuits must have felt confident in their ability communicate. Their organization explicitly established a center-periphery distinction, which no medieval organization could ever have mustered.[35] Charlemagne, and most every subsequent king,

---

34. Kerstin-Katja Sindemann, "Japanese Buddhism in the 16th Century: Letters of the Jesuit Missionaries," *Bulletin of Portuguese Japanese Studies* 2 (2001): 125–26.

35. Markus Friedrich, "Organisation und Kommunikationsstrukturen der Gesellschaft Jesu in der Frühen Neuzeit/Organization and Communication in the Society of Jesus (1540–1773)," in *Etappen der Globalisierung in christumsgeschichtlicher*

was constantly moving through his territories in order to assert his authority and privileges directly in person. Moreover, in further contrast to earlier orders, the Jesuits were thoroughly hierarchical, with decisions made from the top down. Of course, the importance of an officer who visited all Jesuit institutions, spoke with every priest, reviewed the books, addressed local authorities, and provided a final report was still maintained. The provincial visitors often traveled great distances throughout the entire year, especially in the Habsburg Empire.

Despite the center-periphery organization of Jesuit communications, we should not presume that all letters sent from Rome were filled with commands and instructions.[36] The letters often provided suggestions, advice, and requests. Local autonomy was not under constant pressure from the center. Very often the Roman letters delegated authority so as to leave decisions in the hands of the priests who were on site. In all cases, these communications were grounded in Jesuit spiritual teachings. The limits of this administrative arrangement became quickly apparent in Asia, where administrators such as Alessandro Valignano worried that the distances made it impossible to govern by letter. George de Carvalhal wrote in 1581 from Goa: "From experience we know that this province cannot be administered through letters and requests sent from India to Rome, for they take too long and by the time an answer has arrived here, the many circumstance and incidents have completely altered the situation."[37] Friedrich reminds us that when looking at the operation of the international society, we need to consider the failures as much as the successes.

The tendency for analyses of Jesuit missions to replicate the terms of the society becomes most clear when actor-network theory is applied to the operation. In many ways, one would have a difficult time deciding which came first: the Jesuits or actor-network theory. In his application of the theory to the reception of missionary let-

---

Perspektive/ Phases of Globalization in the History of Christianity, ed. Klaus Koschorke (Wiesbaden: Harrassowitz, 2012), 83–104.

36. Friedrich, "Organisation und Kommunikationsstrukturen," 97.

37. Quoted in Markus Friedrich, "Organisation und Kommunikationsstrukturen," 100.

ters from Asia, Steven Harris adopts the Scholastic tendency to organize letters into types (described below).[38] One could add to this list the laity who watched Jesuit dramas, parades, and listened to sermons. Harris quotes the first line of Law's abstract for his influential 1986 article: "Long-distance control depends upon the creation of a network of passive agents (both human and non-human) which makes it possible for emissaries (also both human and non-human) to circulate from the center to the periphery in a way that maintains their durability, forcefulness and fidelity." Law himself lists three types of emissaries "devices, drilled people, and documents."[39]

Harris includes Jesuits in the cycle of information moving from center to periphery as stable forms of knowledge slowly accumulated throughout the entire system. Missionaries wrote consistently to their superiors. Very aware of previous writing in their field, they were under an obligation to continue the work done by previous scholars, whether this meant confirming Marco Polo's observations or completing assignments earlier Jesuits could not finish. Bruno Latour augments Law's model to claim that in time, after several cycles of information, European explorers could feel that they possessed more accurate knowledge than local natives. Jesuit missionaries certainly used this relative advantage to impress the Chinese court with accurate cartographic and astronomical information. Nevertheless, sympathetic observers such as Leibniz could question whether they were actually strengthening their position. Latour's model works less well when considering the relations between the Jesuit network and China's own extensive network of administrators. One question is how the two networks—missionaries and Chinese literati—interacted, given that they had such a clear affinity for each other. As much as the Jesuits paraded their mathematical sophistication, they also quickly adapted to the Chinese literati. Harris refers to Rome as the "center of concentration" rather than calculation. The Jesuits gathered and condensed information, allowing the

---

38. Steven J. Harris, "Long-Distance Corporations, Big Sciences, and the Geography of Knowledge," *Configurations* 6.2 (1998): 292.

39. Law, "On the Methods of Long Distance Control."

center to use the accumulated knowledge to recruit more missionaries to the society.

How was the information within the Jesuit network adapted once it moved beyond the control mechanisms of the society? Harris offers a history of the Jesuit letter-writing network that does not consider the flaws within its operations; nor does he consider how documents and immutables were altered once they left the immediate editorial control of the Jesuits. Unsympathetic reinterpretations of missionary letters would come from Enlightenment radicals and Protestant theologians eager to argue that the Jesuits were themselves idolaters. English and Dutch publishers were equally unfriendly as they sifted out Catholic theology in order to distill commercial information. The many popular adaptations of Jesuit primary texts appeared as translations and compilations. These many different modes of reading and republishing Jesuit information show how mutable their reports were once they left the pious Catholic circle of readers. If the Jesuit letter-writing network was part of confession building, so too were the adaptations of Jesuit texts by Protestants. One of the most inflammatory reinterpretations of missionary letters came from Christian Francken, a lapsed Jesuit from Magdeburg, who compared the idol worship attributed to Buddhist temples with the saints' prayers of Spanish and Italian priests.[40] His writings were well received in England.

As Latour, Law, and Harris would acknowledge, the missionary network was not a fixed arrangement, but rather needed to be reestablished each time that it was traversed; in other words, it had little of the stability presumed with modern communications technology. As the missionaries moved into China, they sought out contact with preexisting networks. Ricci's strategy was to seek acceptance and sponsorship from established literati so that he might find a place in Beijing. Each newly arrived missionary had to demonstrate anew his relevance to the Chinese administration. The term "network" is ap-

---

40. Christian Francken, *Ein Gesprech von Jesuiten: allen frommen Christen, die Jesuiter und ihre Religion recht zu erkennen, vast nützlich zu lessen* (Basel, 1581), 11–22. An English translation appeared later: Paulus Florenius and Christianus Francken, *The Doctrines and Practises of the Societies of Jesuites* (London: George Gibbs 1630).

propriate to missionary communications because it confirms how the individual is secondary to the larger movement and operation of the administration. The prominence of rules and procedures over personal will is a shared feature in long-distance communication systems and priestly orders. Nevertheless, the missionary network cannot be explained as just a set of fixed relations because communication requires the movement of actors. No journey between East and West was ever a simple succession of stops on a highway, even if Marco Polo's narrative along the Mongol postal network made it seem so.

The religious background of modern communication theory is sometimes acknowledged with a vague reference to Marshall McLuhan's Catholic leanings or Bruno Latour's Jesuit schooling. Given the importance of letter writing in early Christianity and the treatment of religious statements as "news," it should come as no surprise that modern communication terminology still bears the remnants of theology. For instance, Jesuit communication through missionary letters can be understood as a *Mitteilung*, an act of sharing that brings the receiver into the group of people who possess knowledge.[41] By distributing information about Asia, Jesuits were forming a community of those who agreed with the news they were receiving. The German word *mitteilen* operates with an accusative and a dative object, so that the verb means not just splitting something into parts but also involves sharing a portion of an abstract or specified quantity with someone; in this case, the "thing" is knowledge of the Catholic mission in China. *Mitteilen* implies an asymmetrical relationship between an authoritative sender and a grateful receiver—the canonical Christian example being Jesus who shares news of God's salvation with sinful mortals. "The Grimm Dictionary also mentions 'grace' and 'forgiveness' as attributes that older languages include in the act of 'Mitteilung.'"[42] In more ordinary, secular situations, a person who has information shares it with

---

41. Lea Pao's excellent dissertation first called attention to the religious etymology of *Mitteilung*: "Informational Practices in German Poetry: Ernst Meister, Oswald Egger, Friedrich Gottlieb Klopstock," Pennsylvania State University, 2017.

42. "Mittheilen" is the spelling used by Jacob and Wilhelm Grimm in their *Deutsches Wörterbuch* (Leipzig: Hirzel, 1854), http://woerterbuchnetz.de/cgi-bin

someone who lacks it. Communication in this sense involves an act of generosity that includes the recipient within the community of those who are in the know. To the extent that information is not a material object, its portioning into units does not break up the corpus of the original that is being imparted.[43] By using *mitteilen*, the speaker is not implying that a quantifiable part of some original unit is being given up. Hierarchies are, of course, involved in the distribution process, but the term *mitteilen* suggests their momentary suspension by the inclusion of an outsider who would otherwise not have been given this exclusive information. The question of whom to include or exclude when sharing information was all the more pressing after the Reformation, when Protestant seafarers were aggressively competing with Catholic nations. To the extent that information about China might aid Protestant merchants gain access to the Chinese market, Jesuits were no doubt loath to impart practical knowledge. However, if, as missionaries, they might impress Protestants with the Catholic mission's success in Asia and thereby win converts in Germany, then sharing reports would serve their purpose. This balancing act explains why Jesuits were willing to publish translations of Confucian classics that reinforced their accommodation strategy but never seemed to provide textbooks on how to read and speak any Chinese language. The Jesuit success in maintaining the authoritative position in their communications as *Mitteilungen* meant that Protestants such as Leibniz or the elector of Brandenburg were constantly eager to correspond with Jesuits who had experience in China.

As much as Friedrich Kittler sought to expel the spirit from the *Geisteswissenschaften* (humanities), any study of the Catholic communication network would have to include prayer within a complete media history. Arguing against McLuhan's Catholic aspirations for universal language, Kittler insists that "all previous development

/WBNetz/call_wbgui_py_from_form?sigle=DWB&mode=Volltextsuche&lemid=GM06319#XGM06319.

43. Samuel Weber mentions "sharing" as one connotation, but he bases his etymological reading of *Mitteilung* on the claim that the term involves a separation of a thing into parts, in the sense of a material object divided; see Samuel Weber, *Benjamin's -abilities* (Cambridge, MA: Harvard University Press, 2008), 40–44.

of technical media, in the realm of computers as well as optical technology, were the exact opposite of cosmological harmony, namely technologies of war."[44] The two realms overlap, however, when we consider the intentions of missionaries conveyed through Asia on Portuguese warships. Kittler acknowledges the convergence between Jesuit appeals to early modern curiosity and the Church's global aspirations later in his 1999 lecture series when he addresses early modern Jesuit theater. "No history of optical media should suppress the fact that entertainment media are also propaganda machines."[45] Most early modern historians focus on texts that convey what they define as information, while leaving works of edification aside. Donald Lach, perhaps the most well-read American scholar on the subject, maintains this distinction in deciding which works to include in his vast *Asia in the Making of Europe.* Thus he writes: "Between 1570 and 1588 very little information about India appeared in Europe in published form. . . . Not only was there a blackout of India during these years; those [Jesuit] letters which actually saw light contributed almost nothing to the European image and are little more than letters of edification."[46] Of course, the missionaries presumably did not consider their missives to be empty placeholders. The tendency to sift through missionary letters for information, while tossing aside spiritual discourse, began among Protestants eager to cull secrets they might use against their mercantile rivals and was then continued by Enlightenment scholars looking for encyclopedic knowledge of the world. (From a Catholic perspective, the difference between these two groups might be difficult to discern.)

As explained earlier, maintaining communication between Catholic Europe and Asian missions was originally intended to spur the laity to include Asia within its spiritual horizons by encouraging them to pray for the faithful overseas. Letters sent from Asia were intended to establish a religious circuit of communication. Menahem

---

44. Friedrich Kittler, *Optische Medien, Berliner Vorlesung 1999* (Berlin: Merve, 2002), 23.
45. Kittler, *Optische Medien,* 92.
46. Lach, *Asia in the Making of Europe,* 1:446.

Blondheim provides a succinct justification for expanding the definition of media to include spiritual speech:

> Prayer is a communicative practice intended to bridge the insurmountable gap between the human and the divine, by trying to convey purposeful messages from people to an entity they deem is everything they are not. Indeed, the gulf separating the parties is a key to a series of communicative dimensions on which prayer stands out: It is a most highly conscious and highly venerated act of communication, conveying the most important and most urgent messages people have, and it therefore commonly holds a privileged position among people's speech acts.[47]

Particularly if one wants to understand the edification that missionary letters were supposed to elicit in European Catholics, then it becomes clear that missives shipped from Goa represent only the postal portion of a larger spiritual economy in which the laity respond by praying for the conversion of Asian heathens and the success of the same missionaries who wrote in the first place. The global Catholic Church conceived itself within this global circulation of letters and prayers. If we understand prayer as a form of media communication with the divine—an assumption most early modern Christians would have considered self-evident—then we can better understand how the Asia missions were perceived as reinforcing the religion on both continents. After all, the missionaries did not dispatch information for its own sake but rather hoped that their exhaustive descriptions and reflections would to arouse spiritual petitions in return.[48] As an immaterial response to missionary letters, prayers completed the devotional feedback loop between Europe and East Asia, thereby conditioning Catholics to form an ardent attachment to missionaries and converts on the other side of

---

47. Menahem Blondheim, "Prayer 1.0: The Biblical Tabernacle and the Problem of Communicating with a Deity," paper presented at the Sixty-Second Annual Meeting of the International Communication Association, Phoenix, AZ, May 28, 2012, https://www.academia.edu/5915336/Prayer_1.0_The_Biblical_Tabernacle _and_the_Problem_of_Communicating_with_a_Deity.

48. Luke Clossey also argues that the missionaries' frequent request for prayers point to a global economy of spiritual expression; Clossey, *Salvation and Globalization*, 217–20.

the world. In addition to serving as a form of communion, prayer became a means of feeling the suffering of others. Even as he lists common superstitions in his history of the China mission, Matteo Ricci insists that the Christian reader should sympathize with the Chinese: "I would request of the reader that he recognize . . . a reason for sympathizing [*condolendi*] with this people and for praying God for their salvation, rather than becoming impatient with them and losing all hope of remedy for their misfortune."[49]

Missionary letters attracted enthusiastic readers to the church. Max Weber ignored the importance of recruitment when he claimed that Catholics do not have a sense of calling (*Beruf*), for the appeal of working as a missionary to the point of martyrdom was widespread.[50] Peter Canisius's frequently uttered the wish to serve in India even as he accepted his prominent role in the Holy Roman Empire. His aspirations underscored the long-standing parallels made within the church between Germany and Asia—two areas equally in need to Catholic ministry. Canisius and Jeronimo Nadal both understood the importance of publishing missionary letters from India because they motivated the laity in Central Europe to prayer.[51] In the church's global accounting, conversions in Asia provided consolation for Catholics lost in Europe.[52] Across Europe, interest in India was so strong that the Jesuits published over fifty editions of India letters in the first thirty years.[53] For many devout young men, the ideal response to a missionary letter was for them to join the mission as well.[54] If the opportunity to sail to

49. Matteo Ricci, *China in the Sixteenth Century: The Journals of Matthew Ricci (1583–1610)*, trans. Louis J. Gallagher (New York: Random House, 1953), book 1, chap. 9, 82.

50. Max Weber, *The Protestant Ethic and the "Spirit" of Capitalism*, trans. Peter Baehr and Gordon Wells (New York: Penguin, 2002), 28.

51. Väth, "Nicht in den Missionen, und doch Missionär," 178.

52. "In der Einleitung zu den *Avvisi farticolari delle Indie di Portugallo*, die 1552 zu Rom gedruckt wurden, wird ausdrücklich darauf hingewiesen, dass die Kirche durch die Bekehrung zahlreicher Heiden in den Missionsländern für den Abfall vieler Katholiken in Europa entschádigt werde" (Valignano, *Historia del principle y progresso de la Campañia de Jesus*, 20).

53. Harris, "Confession-Building," 304.

54. On missionary recruitment in early modern Germany, see Clossey, *Salvation and Globalization*, 136–142.

India never appeared, then the next best answer was prayer. One such young Jesuit recruit was Eusebio Kino, who, inspired by the example of Japanese martyrs, hoped to join the Asia mission to follow in Xavier's footsteps. Kino wrote: "Most fortunate are these missionaries en route to the Church's vineyard in the Orient! If we do not follow and accompany them in body, we can do so in mind and unceasing prayer poured out to God."[55] In the end, Kino was assigned to Mexico, where he also played a decisive role. To modern thinking it seems paradoxical that the prospect of being killed served as a recruitment incentive: "Martyrdom promised both a rich harvest of new Christians and new missionaries. As the most heroic form of death, it engendered moral exemplars whose redemptive suffering in faraway lands drew other men into the missions, thus extending the reach of the order's corporate body in space and time. Given its dual effects, martyrdom may have been the most potent means of successful clerical reproduction."[56] If missionaries complained that their letters from Asia went unanswered for long stretches, they nevertheless understood that they generated spiritual responses.

Theodor Schneider was another priest inspired by letters from Asia, though as a German he was not kept in Central Europe to convert Protestants. Instead, he was deployed where other Germans had emigrated outside Europe. His assignment suggests the complexity of Jesuit priorities around the globe. Born 1703 in Geinsheim, Schneider became the rector of Heidelberg University at an early age. A large, strong, learned man, he applied repeatedly to be sent to India; eventually in 1740 he received a letter from the Jesuit general calling him to Pennsylvania instead. After a few days Schneider left for Lüttich to begin English lessons. In March 1741, he sailed from London to Maryland, then continued on to the mission in Conestoga, near Lancaster, twenty hours travel west of Philadelphia. His work required him to search through the woods for Germans

55. Ernest J. Burrus, SJ, ed., *Kino Writes to the Duchess: Letters of Eusebio Francisco Kino, S.J., to the Duchess of Aveiro* (Rome: Jesuit Historical Institute, 1965), 80, November 16, 1680.

56. Ulrike Strasser, "Copies with Souls: The Late Seventeenth-century Marianas Martyrs, Francis Xavier, and the Question of Clerical Reproduction," *Journal of Jesuit Studies* 2.4 (2015): 560.

scattered about. He founded schools, taught children to read and write, erected a church, preached in Philadelphia—mornings in German, afternoons in English. For twenty years, he remained healthy until in 1763 he collapsed suddenly and died four weeks later.[57]

Clearly the intentions behind missionary letters were complicated. In addition to the obligation to write, specific instructions were sent to priests on what to report. In 1547 missionaries were ordered to include edifying material and to compile them into a separate mailing every four months. From the 1560s onward a series of norms was established for communication, so that eventually in 1620 a detailed manual was composed on letter writing.[58] While the first letters were administrative, with the inclusion of edifying stories added on later, there came to be three types of letters from Asia: those intended to inform superiors, those intended to inspire members and close supporters of the society, and those meant to be circulated in the general public by being read aloud in churches and schools. Harris provides neat terms for the three types of intended audiences: the *studiosi*—external students at Jesuit colleges; the *virtuosi*—aristocratic supporters and collectors who delighted in their missions and provided funds; the *cognoscenti*—intellectuals and skilled readers in the republic of letters interested in scientific knowledge from Asia.[59]

When modern scholars classify Jesuit letters into types, they are merely following the advice offered by the society's earliest school administrators, who were themselves relying on Aristotle's distinctions between different forms of public speaking. Missionary letters would be distinct from medieval business correspondences, which had their own conventional forms.[60] In defining how Cicero's letters

---

57. Bernhard Duhr, SJ, *Deutsche Auslandsehnsucht im achtzehnten Jahrhundert, Aus der überseeischen Missionsarbeit deutscher Jesuiten* (Stuttgart: Ausland und Heimat Verlag, 1928), 16–17.

58. Markus Friedrich, "Circulating and Compiling the *Littrerae Annuae*. Towards a History of the Jesuit System of Communication," *Archivum Historicum Societatis Iesu* 77 (2008): 7–9.

59. Harris, "Confession-Building," 292.

60. See for example the letters of Indian Ocean traders in S. D. Goitein and Mordechai Akiva Friedman, *Indian Traders of the Middle Ages, Documents from the Cairo Geniza* (Leiden: Brill, 2008), 10.

should serve as guides for sixteenth-century students, Antonio Possevino differentiated among epistles that were persuasive, judicial, and demonstrative, with further Scholastic distinctions in each category.[61] Thus, the first lesson any young Jesuit learned about writing a letter was to identify its rhetorical purpose. Having isolated specific types of letters, the student and scholar of Cicero would of course quickly come to understand that many letters mixed their styles and that the lessons from Cicero's example had to be adapted for Christian purposes. When Ignatius Loyola instructed missionaries to write with care, keeping these three genres in mind would have been an important step in deciding how and what to write. In other words, correspondents were supposed to understand that their communications were in no way private, in the modern sense of confidential and intimate. This tripartite division of letters has itself been passed down in the instructions given to missionaries, which means that it has been repeated in many histories of the Jesuits as well, so that scholarship on the Jesuit mission serves to reiterate its goals.[62] The official tripartite organization of letters called for distinct rhetorical strategies, with each type of letter requiring circumspection and a particular mode of address. A. Lynn Martin makes this point explicitly: "Different genres of communication—prayer, eulogy, sermon, disputation, instruction—required different rhetorical forms, and even within the single genre of letter writing the Jesuits used a variety of styles."[63] As the leadership well understood, not all correspondents were adept in adjusting to their rhetorical situation.

---

61.   Boswell, "Letter Writing among the Jesuits," 250.

62.   Correia-Afonso cites as his source on the three categories the following contemporary work: Andre Rétif, "Breve histoire des Lettres édifiantes et curieuses," *Neue Zeitschrift für Missionswissenschaft = Nouvelle revue de science missionaire* 7 (1951): 37–50. Rétif in turn cites a nineteenth-century history of the Jesuits in Canada reinforcing the principle that the instructions on letter writing apply regardless of location: Camille de Rochemonteix, SJ, *Les Jésuites de la Nouvelle France au XVIIe siècle* (Paris: Letouzey et Ané, 1895), 1:10, "Les lettres des missionnaires étaient de trois sortes." Two pages earlier, Rochemonteix quotes Xavier's instructions to Barzee.

63.   A. Lynn Martin, *The Jesuit Mind: The Mentality of an Elite in Early Modern France* (Ithaca, NY: Cornell University Press, 1988), 4.

Despite all this training, the Jesuits were far from thinking as a single monolithic mind. We can see how closely intermingled the different types of writing were in a letter Xavier wrote to Ignatius Loyola and Pietro Codacio on March 31, 1540, wherein he affirms their friendship by stating that their letters will recreate the presence of being in each other's company. He also distinguishes between writing that lends the impression of seeing each other and Loyola's instruction to send sensitive political analysis on a separate sheet (*hijuelas*). "As I think it is only through the medium of letters that we shall see one another again in this life—in the next it will be face to face with many embraces—it remains for us during the little time left here below to secure thee mutual glimpses by frequent writing. This is what you tell me to do and I shall see to it, as well as to your instructions about the *hijuelas*."[64] The friendship shared through writing was compatible with separate notes on political, administrative issues. Alluding to 1 Corinthians 13:12, Xavier posits a parallel between the visual encounter provided by corresponding and an embrace between friends in the afterlife.[65] Writing offers one kind of substitution that will itself be compensated for again in heaven. Advice was repeatedly given that letters should reviewed and edited before they were sent, for correspondents could not assume that later officials would perform this task as the letters circulated among the laity. As the society and its paperwork grew, the task of editing letters before they were passed along or published became daunting. Juan Alfonso de Polanco, the society's secretary in Rome, warned the provincial of Castile about the need to carefully edit correspondences: "And for the love of God, be careful that what has been written has been carefully reviewed. Do not imagine that they will be corrected here as they have been until now"[66]—advice every professional email writer would readily appreciate.

In addition to administrative and religiously uplifting news, missionaries outside Europe were urged to include observations to satisfy the curiosity of readers. No casual observers, missionaries took

---

64. Quoted in Correia-Afonso, *Jesuit Letters and Indian History*, 11.
65. Xavier, *Letters and Instructions*, 11.
66. Nelles, "*Cosas y cartas*," 430.

notes to record their impressions in order to respond to the high demand for more information about the wider world. From the start, Loyola distinguished between different forms of curiosity. Thus, in a letter written February 24, 1554 to Gaspar Breze, he confirmed the need to indulge European readers

> Some leading figures who in this city [Rome] read with much edification for themselves the letters from India, are wont to desire, and they request me repeatedly, that something should be written regarding the cosmography of those regions where ours [Jesuits] live. They want to know, for instance, how long are the days of summer and of winter; when summer begins; whether the shadows move towards the left or towards the right. Finally, if there are other things that may seem extraordinary; let them be noted, for instance, details about animals and plants that are either not known at all, or not of such a size, etc. And this news—sauce for the taste of a certain curiosity that is not evil and is wont to be found among men—may come in the same letters or other letters separately.[67]

What religious purposes lie within the injunction to write regularly? To what extent does data collection overlap with confession and the spiritual life of the priest writing? These letters from Asia, starting with Xavier's reports, became the basis for the Enlightenment's much larger project of publishing missionary letters by Du Halde in *Lettres edifiant et curieus* and the German *Neue Welt-Bott* (New world messenger).

Built into any correspondences from Asia to Europe was the possibility of failure, including that the letter would never arrive but be lost along the way. Missionaries would often send the same letter with different carriers: the Portuguese from Goa, the Dutch from New Batavia, and the Spanish from Manila via Mexico to Spain.[68] Still, it was well understood that even if several copies were sent along different routes, a document might never reach its intended recipient. Indeed, the delay in letters arriving was itself a topic of letter writing. Jesuits in India requested that copies of letters be sent from Lisbon on four or five different ships because even when sent in trip-

---

67.   Quoted in Correia-Afonso, *Jesuit Letters and Indian History*, 14.
68.   Burrus, *Kino Writes to the Duchess*, 34n69.

licate, they sometimes did not arrive.[69] Xavier opens a letter to his friends in Rome written on January 15, 1544, with a reflection on the paucity and uncertainty about letters reaching their destination: "Two years and nine months ago I sailed from Portugal, and, including this letter, I have written to you three times since then. During the time that I have been in India, I have received only one letter from you, written on January 13, 1542, and God our Lord knows how much consolation I received from it. The letter was given to me around two months ago. It was so late in arriving in India because the ship which brought it wintered in Mozambique."[70] Letter writers of course frequently began their correspondence by commenting on how much time has passed since the last time they had written, so Xavier's remarks are quite expected. Still, they call attention to how far stretched and tenuous the connections between Rome and its missionaries were, as well as how intensively one letter could be read—repeatedly and exhaustively for every bit of meaning.

The posthumous publication of Matteo Ricci's memoirs was justified in terms of the need to inform future generations of missionaries about the first efforts in China but exactly who those future readers were differed. From individual letters to massive treatises, the circulation of Jesuit reports was intended to inspire and inform readers about the society's mission. Yet, how these reports were recirculated depended on the audience. The German translation of Ricci's memoirs stressed the need for readers to understand the missionaries' penetration into the closed kingdom of China, whereas the Latin does not explicitly refer to China at all, but instead underscores the mission's function of spreading Christian teaching through its many allusions to the metaphorical language about seeds falling on hard ground or fallow.[71] The German translation (published 1617 in

---

69.   Paul Nelles, "*Cosas y cartas*," 437.

70.   John Patrick Donnelly, SJ, ed., *Jesuit Writings of the Early Modern Period, 1540–1640* (Indianapolis: Hackett, 2006), 67.

71.   "Das die Nachkömling wissen/wie/und durch das mittel/dise Societet in das so lang und scharpff verschloßne Königreich China/den süssen Namen JESU eingeführt/ auch was sie gethan und gelitten" (Nicholas Trigault, *Historia von der Einführung der christlichen Religion in das große Königreich China durch die Societet Jesu* [Augsburg: Antony Hierat, 1617], 2; Nicholas Trigault, *De Christiana*

Augsburg) gives a slightly adventurous tone to the spreading of seeds, whereas the Latin original (published 1617 in Cologne) may well have been more concerned with providing a sophisticated invocation of Matthew 13.

Becoming Chinese in German

For leading Jesuits, Germany was as important a place to make converts as India. Both Peter Canisius and Hieronymus Nadal were eager to have letters from missionaries in the Indies translated into Latin for the benefit of the shaky believers in Germany. In 1555, Nadal instructed Canisius to begin translating letters from the Indies into Latin for learned Germans. All the centers of Catholic scholarship in Germany would eventually translate and print missionary letters—Cologne, Augsburg, Ingolstadt, Munich and Dillingen.[72] While these two founding figures of the society were too busy to undertake the task themselves, Canisius arranged in 1563 to have missionaries' letters published in Dillingen, located in northern Bavaria. In the first decades, Latin was the language intended for German readers. Humanists in Rome were employed to translate missionary letters from Spanish, Portuguese, and Italian into Latin so that they could be printed in Dillingen.[73] Copies were then distributed to bishops and cardinals, church diplomats in Trient, Duke Albrecht V of Bavaria, and the emperor Maximillian II. Of considerable importance was the translation of Francis Xavier's letters from the Indies. Canisius and Nadal both believed that the spread of information from the Asian missions had an important propaganda effect in the European regions shaken by the Reformation.[74] Just how

---

Expeditione apud Sinas Suscepta ab Societate Iesu ex. P. Mattaei Riccii [Cologne: Bernardi Gualteri, 1617], 2).

72. Clossey, *Salvation and Globalization*, 197–202.

73. Valignano, *Historia del principle y progresso de la Campañia de Jesus en las Indias Orientates*, 34.

74. Christoph Nebgen, *Missionarsberufungen nach Übersee in drei Deutschen Provinzen der Gesellschaft Jesu im 17. und 18. Jahrhundert* (Regensburg: Schnell and Steiner, 2007), 36–37.

important the China mission was in the effort to reinforce German Catholicism is demonstrated by the speed with which Jesuit treatises and letters were translated from Latin into German. By contrast, the church made little effort to provide English versions.

Individual printers were obviously important transmitters as well as readers of such literature. To better understand what pious German readers would have learned about China, we can examine a German compilation printed in Dillingen in 1589. This collection includes both administrative reports and passionate personal reflections, offering German Catholics a glimpse into the Jesuit hierarchy and its missionary soul.

In his preface, the printer, Johannes Mayer, reports that he had been reading letters and reports sent by Jesuits from East Asia to Rome for the last six years.[75] Encouraged by the well-intended advice of highly placed persons, he began to print these writings. His decision was hardly surprising given his location. The printer's city, Dillingen, also housed a university that, starting in 1564, was administered by Jesuits who also opened a collegium at that time. The town also served as a residence for the university's founder, Otto Truchseß von Waldburg, cardinal bishop of Augsburg, a leading figure in the Catholic revival. In addition to receiving Jesuit administration and instruction, the university also obtained additional papal funding for the education of twenty-five priests dedicated to serving in Germany. The city was on the list of locations approved by the Duke of Bavaria for printing ecclesiastical books such as hymnals. Peter Canisius's catechism was printed there in the 1580s.[76] Mayer's print shop eventually produced a version of the catechism with 103 illustrations, intended for distribution in China—each picture was accompanied by a blank page that a missionary was supposed to later complete with an accompanying Chinese text.[77]

---

75. *Sendtschreiben auß den weit berhümpten Landschafften China, Japon un India . . . Sampe Angehenecker erzehlung eines mercklichen Schiffbruchs wie in andern schreiben des P. Petri Martonez an den Ehrwürdigen P. General der Soceitet Jesu* (Dilingen: Johannem Meyer, 1589).

76. Wilhelm Weiß, *Chronik von Dilligen im Regierungsbezirke Schwaben und Neuburg des Königreichs Bayern* (Dilligen: Kränzle, 1861), 20–28.

77. Väth, "Nicht in den Missionen, und doch Missionär," 178.

From the moment the university was reorganized under the Jesuits, book printing took on a vital function. Bishop Truchseß recruited Sebald Mayer to serve as the university book printer, an office he held from 1555 to 1575. After his death, his widow, Anna, and son, Johannes, continued printing. Johannes in turn was succeeded by his widow, Barbara. The family persevered in the business until 1620.[78] Because both father and son were constantly in debt, the Jesuits were particularly important clients for Mayers.[79] The Dillinger press was well known as "a stronghold of Catholic printing in southern Germany"[80]—a commitment Mayer displays openly in his dedication to Wolfgang von Hausen, the prince provost of Ellwangen and future bishop of Regensburg, where he stresses the need to combat heretical errors in the name of the Catholic Church.

Mayer states that as he started translating and printing missionary letters, he learned that they provided not only pleasurable entertainment, but that good Christians found them to be fruitful and encouraging of their faith. As much as he explains his motivations as personal, his republication of Jesuit letters belongs to a European-wide network of Jesuit institutions passing along correspondences. In practical terms, we can assume that Mayer received local academic assistance in translating the letters "from a strange foreign language into our German." The subjective first-person voice of missionary letters made them more affectively appealing than commands. Rather than delivering their message from above, the letter's intimate tone allowed readers to share in another believer's Christian adventure. The letters conveyed both spiritual commitment and exotic action.

Mayer organizes the sequence of letters hierarchically, so that the first letter is written by Alexander Valignagni, the provincial for India, the highest Jesuit office in Asia. His letter introduces

78. Lorenz Stempfle, *Bericht über die königlichen Studien-Anstalten zu Dilingen am Ober-Donau Kreise* (Dilingen: Roßnagel, 1832), 21.

79. Otto Bucher, "Der Dillinger Buchdrucker Johann Mayer (1576–1614)," *Gutenberg Jahrbuch* (1955): 162–69.

80. Christian Thomas Leitmeir and Bernard Klingenstein, "Catholic Music in the Diocese of Augsburg c. 1600: A Reconstructed Tricinium Anthology and Its Confessional Implications," *Early Music History* 21 (2002): 121.

the reader to the mission in China, in particular the most prominent priests stationed there. Matteo Ricci is praised for already
being quite advanced in learning Chinese.[81] Within the first two
installments—Mayer's preface and Valignagni's letter—translation
is presented as a necessary function in spiritual edification and
conversion. This requires as much attention to the target language
as to the original. Mayer, or whichever Jesuit apprentice provided
the translation, needed to portray the mission in a religious and
literary discourse that was not only familiar, but also inspiring to
pious Germans. Hence, we must examine the language of the
receiving end of the translation sequence as well as that of the
sender.

Valignagni's letter rounds to a conclusion by stressing two strategic concerns. He notes that the mandarins have, so far, shown a
friendly attitude toward the Jesuits by allowing them to move beyond the entrepot of Canton and Macao. Then he warns that this
tolerance could be undermined with the arrival in Macao of so many
other orders who do not understand Chinese manners and mores. If
too many missionaries arrive from the Philippines, Valignagni warns,
the Chinese governors will ban all Christians from the land. In a few
pages the average pious reader in southern Germany has been introduced to the primary cast, the institutional framework, the foreign
places, and the central threat to the mission's success. As behooves
his office, Valignagni writes in the optimistic, watchful, yet cautious
tone of an administrator addressing his superior. His style differs
greatly from the naïve enthusiasm of the novice missionary.

The second letter provides the spiritual inspiration pious readers
sought and offers a clear invitation for them to identify with the
missionary as he adapts to China. Far from seeking to convey information about China, this letter describes a missionary's travel in
terms of self-discovery. If anyone is to be converted, it is the self-
reflective missionary who comes to a deeper awareness of his own
soul. The letter offers emotional insight into the education of a martyr.

---

81. "Er habe ein gute un starcke hoffnung eines grossen frucht und nutz, dann
Er ergreifft un lernt die Chinisch Sprach durch hilff und beystand P. Ricci, so diser
Sprach schon zimlich wol erfahren" (*Sendtschreiben auß China*, 3).

His travel account was far more in line with later notions of *Bildung* and the metamorphosis of migration than with geographic discovery. Antonio Almeida, newly arrived in China, writes to his superior, Eduardo de Sande, about his first voyage into the Chinese countryside with the more experienced Father Michele Ruggieri. His letter provides a sensitive psychological reflection on a person's self-transformation as he enters into a foreign culture. Like many correspondents, he begins with a preface reflecting upon the moment and particularly the place from which and in which he is writing. In Almeida's letter the administrative voice drops away, as the young man marvels both at what he is about to encounter and the transformation that it has already wrought in himself. His letter is both travelogue and self-discovery. As Markus Friedrich notes, systematic self-observation often augmented the study of foreign lands.[82] Francis Xavier wrote to Loyola following his travel in Japan that he had come to understand himself there, "for, being outside of myself, I did not know how many evils existed within me, until I saw myself amidst the labors and dangers of Japan."[83]

Almeida's naïve, enthusiastic tone in his letter invites readers to identify with his position as a newcomer to China. Almeida announces his amazement in the first sentence—that he is becoming Chinese: "Nunmehr bin ich ein Chineser worden." Like many foreigners immersed in an utterly different culture, Almeida is responding with the mimetic obligation to conform to his surroundings. However, he is hardly a passive recipient, for he has yearned for this day and has gone to great lengths to reach it; and yet, he is still not in command of his own transformation. The opportunity to write a letter allows him to reflect on the alterations he is undergoing. The language in which he is writing the letter belongs to his European identity, yet he is eager to learn Chinese, both as a language and a manner of

---

82. Markus Friedrich, *Der lange Arm Roms: Globale Verwaltung und Kommunikation im Jesuitenorden 1540–1773* (Frankfurt: Campus Verlag, 2011), 14.

83. Xavier to Ignatius, Cochin, January 29, 1552 quoted in Ananya Chakravarti, *The Empire of Apostles: Religion, Accommodatio, and the Imagination of Empire in Early Modern Brazil and India* (Oxford: Oxford University Press, 2018), 118.

existence. He knows well enough not to present himself as the agent who controls the process of becoming Chinese; rather, he understands it as something that he is allowing to happen to him, an anticipated transformation that is now finally happening. As he moves into his metamorphosis, Almeida opens up to the possibility that he, and his readers, will form an affective bond with "being Chinese." This emotional connection has clear theological precedent for Almeida. For in the next sentences, he summarizes the Jesuit approach to becoming Chinese in the name of Jesus, for the sake of converting. His own transformation emulates Jesus's, who became human even though he is the eternal God ("meinetwegen Mensch worden / da er ewiger Gott"). Because of Christ's transformation and sacrifice, Almeida believes he has nothing more to do on earth than improve his life by converting the Chinese, even it means losing his own life.

To what extent does his transfiguration into Chinese follow the medieval mystical injunction to imitate Christ? Almeida writes with inspiration about his inspiration; he apologizes that he cannot contain himself in this letter. Like a good writer, he reflects on his position writing this letter. As he starts writing about his river cruise, he states that he imagined that he was in China writing—an odd position because he was actually there at that moment. He wondered whether his imagination (the word appears twice) led him to live in a dream as if he were asleep, so that he hoped his superior would write back to him so as to wake him up to the reality that he really was in China, the kingdom Francis Xavier tried for so long to enter. In this reverie, Almeida shows his imagination to be completely enveloped by Jesuit teaching, so that he has assumed the desire and place of the mission's founder. His own yearnings are so completely aligned with the society's history, that even in fantasy he dreams like a good Jesuit. As a confession, the letter reveals much about the psyche of a young missionary in Asia; as a document published in southern Germany, it offers a model of desire: it shows missionary work to be the culmination of profound yearning. Xavier is also characterized as a desiring agent ("so groß verlangen gehabt"). If he should lose his life—martyrdom is always an option—Almeida would still have joined his desire with Xavier's. The German phrase here is "meins hertzlichen begerens."[84] As things would go, Almeida died in 1591 in Shaozhen of malaria.[85]

Xavier's biography, in particular his sojourn in Japan and his dying aspiration to reach China, provide the mold for Almeida's own yearning.[86] He models himself on Christ generally, but in China on Xavier in detail. For the next two centuries, Jesuit missionaries would reiterate Almeida's identifications; they, too, would cite their school lessons about Xavier's life as reasons for applying to an overseas post.[87] Reading the letters and biographies of early missionaries could be spiritually transformative. Unlike eighteenth-century explorers in the Pacific, Almeida is not trying to disprove or even surpass his predecessor, so much as fulfill his earlier intentions. Enlightenment explorers took a competitive stance with each other, each striving to collect more information and travel farther than his predecessor: Goethe wanted to explore Italy more thoroughly than his father, Cook to survey more of the southern arctic zone than any previous expedition, and members of the Macartney expedition sought to disprove the entirety of the Jesuit presentation of China, while outmaneuvering the Dutch in trade negotiations. Jesuits in China, however, defined themselves as building upon their predecessors, completing and confirming what they had begun, rather than overturning their goals.

The main body and ostensible purpose of Almeida's letter describes the journey he undertook with the more senior Michele Ruggieri from Canton to Shaoqing. The trip runs along one of the established channels through China. The priests are being taken along on the boats belonging to a merchant closely related to the mandarin administering Shaoqing. Almeida perceives it as divine

---

84.   *Sendtschreiben auß China*, 8.

85.   Ana Caroline Hosne, *The Jesuit Missions to China and Peru, 1570–1610: Expectations and Appraisals of Expansionism* (London: Routledge, 2013), 31.

86.   Ulrike Strasser provides a lively, gender-conscious account of how young men strove to emulate Xavier in "Copies with Souls," 558–85.

87.   Nebgen, *Missionarsberufungen nach Übersee*, 130–32. For an earlier, somewhat nationalist review of applications for overseas missions, see Duhr, *Deutsche Auslandsehnsucht*.

guidance that they have such a powerful patron for their journey, for they are allowed to pass any number of tolls, bridges, and city gates undisturbed. Almeida once more compares his journey with Francis Xavier, who was also dependent on a Chinese boatman in his final attempt to land on the coast.

Almeida aligns his own transformation with the boat's movement into the Chinese countryside, away from the harbor: "Just as our ship has begun to advance, so have I begun to become Chinese."[88] Like so many language learners, Almeida feels that he has been reduced to a helpless child because he cannot speak the language around him. A second defining quality of adulthood—the ability to eat food competently—also eludes him in China.[89] Like many visiting Europeans after him, Almeida sees China from the vantage point of a river. If trains, highways, and airplanes have conditioned modern perceptions of territory, it is the river that provides Almeida any number of lessons about China. When one of the boats catches fire and the crew blame the presence of the Jesuits, Almeida perceives the work of the devil. Along the shore he sees many great and beautiful buildings dedicated to worshipping the devil and idols. With an implicit contrast to his ocean voyage, he describes the river as beautiful, great, and wonderfully sweet, filled with many types of fowl. Almeida's geographical descriptions are typical for an entire genre of travel literature in China that would be repeated with any number of official visits and embassies. Most officially sanctioned visits by European missionaries and merchants followed the same canal and river system as they moved from south to north, the same axis merchants and administrators took.

The greatest amazement is provided of course by the cities, and here Almeida's narrative becomes important in scholarship, because later commentators will state that he provides one of the first European descriptions of Chinese urban life. The trip commences in Canton on November 20, 1585. When, almost a month later, they

---

88. "Wie nun unser Schiff angefangen fortzurucken/hab ich auch angefangen ein Chineser zuwerden" (*Sendtschreiben auß China*, 10).

89. "Gleichwohl noch ein unmündig Kind [zuwerden]/ dann ich weder reden nich essen/ mich auch nicht anzulegen gewißt/ nach Chinischem brauch" (*Sendtschreiben auß China*, 10).

arrive at Nanchang, the capital of Ciansi (Jiangxi) Province, he writes that this city is much larger than Canton, making it obvious that the interior of China offers far more than the narrow coastal harbors. The other contrast: people within China are much less suspicious of foreigners, much more modest in their negotiations compared with those in Canton and Macao. So enamored of Nanchang is Almeida that he would like to establish a collegium there. The priests linger to celebrate Christmas. Almeida defines some of the cities through epithets, so the next major stop, Chindeshen, is defined by its porcelain production. The German translator or printer must have been unfamiliar with China and porcelain, given that he refers to Chindeshen as the place where they manufacture "Pozzotanische dishes . . . which are sold throughout India and Europe"—a simple error involving one letter, as the Italian text from Antwerp refers to Pozzolane.[90] Later commentators on the German epistle cannot help but smile at the error.[91] When they finally arrive at their last city, Shaoqing, Almeida quotes his superior Ruggieri that the city looks like Venice.[92] Almeida's letter is filled with optimistic prospects for the mission even though only one person is actually baptized on the journey. The prospects for future conversions remain hopeful, for he reports that the *Bonzen* from local temples gather to listen politely to the priests, and that even if one cannot tell what thoughts lie in their hearts, they are respectful in their manner.[93] The young priest concludes by saying that he wishes he had a thousand lives to dedicate to converting this kingdom[94]—a line that clearly invites readers to become missionaries themselves, so that they too may supplement the one life Almeida has to offer the church.

Almeida's letter clearly left a strong impression on lay readers, for it is reprinted in several compilations in different European vernaculars. The Jesuits in Dillingen must have been encouraged to

90. *Avvisi della Cina et Giapone del fine dell'anno 1586* (Antwerp: Plantin, 1588), 12.

91. Adolf Reichwein, *China und Europa: Geistige und Künstlerische Beziehungen im 18. Jahrhundert* (Berlin: Oesterheld, 1923), 24.

92. *Sendtschreiben auß China*, 24.

93. *Sendtschreiben auß China*, 26.

94. *Sendtschreiben auß China*, 27.

turn to their local printer after an Italian edition of Chinese correspondence was published 1586 in Antwerp by the Spanish monarch's official typographer, Christophe Plantin.[95] This family of printers served as a conduit between Dutch and Spanish networks, so that on occasion VOC vessels would deliver Jesuit packets to the Plantin/Moretus printers, where they would be copied before being passed along to their Catholic recipients.[96] Although the two editions contain different correspondence, they are all of course from the same handful of missionaries in China, and both editions feature a translation of Almeida's letter about his river voyage at the very beginning of their collection.[97] In the Italian version, Almeida's opening reads as "Fatto io hormai Cinese." Clearly, readers in all European languages were fascinated by his becoming Chinese.

---

95.   *Avvisi della Cina et Giapone del fine dell'anno 1586.*

96.   Noël Golvers, *Building Humanistic Libraries in Late Imperial China* (Rome: Edizioni Nuova Cultura, 2011), 117–18. On the printer's complex political maneuvers, see Dirk Imhof, "Between Philip II and William of Orange: The Correspondence of Christopher Plantin (ca. 1520–1589), in *Between Scylla and Charybdis: Learned Letter Writers Navigating the Reefs of Religious and Political Controversy in Early Modern Europe*, ed. Jeanine De Landtsheer and Henk Nellen (Leiden: Brill, 2011), 218–32.

97.   The Almeida letter of February 10 is also in *Avvisi della Cina*, 5.

A Genealogy of
Cosmopolitan Reading

A genealogy of secret cosmopolitanism runs from the Jesuit policy of accommodation in Asia to Goethe's notion of world literature. Without giving primacy to one level over all others, my argument concerns information networks and their interpretive techniques, as they mediate the history of concepts and discourses. In the end my goal is to move past the early modern masquerade to show how the long history of cosmopolitanism informs our debates today about refugees and migrants. This chapter focuses on the question of how Europeans developed textually mediated compassion for unfamiliar peoples. If Europeans were going to recognize their affinity with others, they would need to develop information channels and reading techniques to overcome distance and lack of interest.

In order to understand how people have come to feel sympathy with the suffering of distant strangers, we need to examine specifically the avenues through which affective bonds formed across distances during the seventeenth and eighteenth centuries. Modern cosmopolitanism entails an emotional response to strangers—in contrast to the ancient Stoic disavow of sympathy, even for family members. Feeling sympathy for victims was not a feature of Roman ethics, nor was it particularly common to Confucianism. Indeed, the proper Stoic individual was supposed to act as if the fate of others had no impact on him. The question of how to care about the suffering of others, both far and near, emerges in Western ethics through Christianity and takes on global dimensions with the spread of missionaries in the Counter-Reformation. Reading techniques developed in late medieval monasteries and refined through Jesuit pedagogy were important first steps. By the eighteenth-century the ability to imagine scenes denoted in texts became a vital secular means for Enlightenment and Romantic readers to identify with foreigners. By the end of this chapter, it will be clear that James Chandler's definition of identificatory reading common to the sentimental novel shares more than a few similarities with Jesuit practices: both are meant "to enable readers to imagine the perceptual and affective field of characters understood to be embodied in time and space, an exercise that depends on giving the sensorium of a fictional character a local habitation, embedding the sensibility in a world."[1]

Early modern studies of European-Chinese relations tend to be divided between a concentration on the Jesuit mission from the 1690s through to the Rites Conflict and then on Enlightenment treatments of the "second wave of exploration" ending in the early nineteenth century with the memoirs published after the failed Macartney embassy. Although this division has its obvious sense in that it separates the religious mission from the Enlightenment's secular anthropology, such periodization also overlooks the long influence of Jesuits. Most histories of the Jesuits in China are understandably weighted toward Matteo Ricci and the founding generation. The abundance of serialized information published in the eighteenth century is always acknowledged as it appeared first in Du Haldes's *Lettres edifiante et curieux* and then in Joseph Stöcklein's *Der Neue Weltbott* (The new world messenger), followed by the *Mémoires*

---

1. James Chandler, *An Archeology of Sympathy: The Sentimental Mode in Literature and Cinema* (Chicago: University of Chicago Press, 2013), 168.

concernant l'histoire, les sciences, les arts, les moeurs, les usages des Chinois (Memoirs concerning the history, the sciences, the arts, the customs, the customs of the Chinese) after the Society's suppression; however, these sources are rarely analyzed with any of the intensity applied to Ricci and company. We should not presume that the decision against the Jesuits in the Rites Controversy resulted in a decline in their publications about China. Enlightenment reports on China continued to be shaped by the 140 years of Jesuit writing on the place. For all its methodological ambitions to free itself from a religious understanding of humans, the Enlightenment anthropological approach to China continued to deploy Jesuit accommodation techniques for thinking with, rather than against, the foreign.

By focusing on the images and tropes that were carried over from missionary reports into the Enlightenment, we can see how modern cosmopolitanism with its sympathetic appreciation of foreign otherness is indebted to missionary accommodation to diverse languages and religious rites as part of the larger drive to establish a world church. Specifically, the Jesuit efforts to foster European compassion for Chinese and Japanese martyrs led indirectly to the modern cosmopolitan belief that affluent Europeans and Americans should feel sympathy for the suffering of distant foreigners. The Enlightenment adapted the Catholic fascination for martyrs by insisting that suffering had to have a general purpose rather than a particular sectarian one, yet the psychology and visuality of both are related.

Europeans identified most readily with distant foreigners if they were perceived as suffering victims deserving compassion. The first East Asian figures for whom early modern Catholics could feel sympathy were Japanese and Chinese Christian converts who were martyred for their faith. In his *Theory of Moral Sentiments*, Adam Smith described the historical transformation that the term "sympathy" underwent as a movement from crisis to intellectual identification. He explained that shared emotions began as a reaction to suffering and sadness, but that eventually the ability to place oneself in the position of another person became the basis for a cosmopolitan feeling. Smith implies that the feeling has its own history, perhaps a genealogy, as it acquires new meanings quite separate from earlier ones. "Pity and compassion are words appropriated to signify our fellow-feeling with the sorrow of others. Sympathy, though its meaning was, perhaps, originally the same, may now, however, without much impropriety, be made use of to denote our fellow-feeling with any passion whatever."[2] For the purposes of my study, I would describe the shift from pity to sympathy as following a path from Christian compassion for the suffering of martyrs or the audience's horrified bond with a tragic character to a more general ability to feel identity with other humans. In his *Laokoon* essay, Lessing elaborates the aesthetic forms that most effectively draw sympathy from the onlooker, while at the same time establishing a new mode of emotional masculinity. Greek drama replaces the Gospel and saints' lives, yet the quest remains to demonstrate a higher principle through restrained suffering. "Laokoon suffers, however he suffers like Sophocles' Philoktet: his misery reaches down into our soul; still, we wish to endure the misery like this great man."[3] Over time the insistence on Stoical forbearance is loosened to allow a greater, increasingly wider expression of sentiment. In the history of early modern European literature, this path can be traced as a shift from the aesthetics of the martyr drama and the *Trauerspiel* to a cosmopolitan openness that allowed readers feel the nuances of an another person's everyday life and to expand the range of figures worthy of such identification from kings and saints to unknown foreigners. Here, I trace feelings of pity, compassion, or sympathy as they are evoked by increasingly secular literature over the course of the seventeenth and eighteenth centuries.

Martyrs and Sympathy

In his very first review of his *Hamburgische Dramaturgie* (*Hamburg Dramaturgy*), Gotthold Lessing elaborates on the difference between

---

2. Adam Smith, *The Theory of Moral Sentiments* (Indianapolis: Liberty, 1976), 49.

3. "Laokoon oder über die Grenzen der Malerei und Poesie," in *Lessings Werke*, ed. Paul Stapf (Berlin: Deutsche Buch Gemeinschaft), 1957; Gotthold Lessing, "Laokoon oder über die Grenzen der Malerei und Poesie," in Stapf, *Lessings Werke*, 2:276 (part 1, sect.1).

Christian martyr plays and tragedies.[4] In discussing the play
Olint und Sophronia, Lessing points out that the author, Johann
Friedrich von Cronegk, portrays Islam as a polytheistic religion in
which diverse idols are worshipped in mosques. Aside from insisting that dramatists correctly represent oriental religions, Lessing
also dismisses Christian martyr dramas generally. We live in a time
of healthy reason, he argues, and so we do not accept that every religious fanatic who races off to his death is a martyr. Lessing does
not rule out the possibility that someone might die for his or her
beliefs, but he insists that audiences distinguish between false and
true martyr, and thereby leaves room for his tragic drama, *Emilia
Galotti*. Empathy for a martyr is limited to a sense of melancholy at
the blindness and idiocy that drives people to such sacrifice. Lessing
distinguishes tragedies from martyr dramas, wherein the protagonist
readily marches off to death rather than valiantly defying it. If the
victim dies too willingly, then the play calls into question the religion
it was trying to validate. Christian tenets, he argues in the next review, such as quiet acceptance or unwavering meekness, the expectation of a reward in the afterlife, or complete unselfishness do not
lead to the kinds of conflicts that nurture tragedy.

Carl Niekerk notes that in discussing plays set in the Orient, Lessing judges characters based on their motivations: even if a play
shows a spectacular exotic palace, the characters must present plausible reasons for their behavior. Behind Lessing's argument is the
simple assumption that foreigners on the European stage must share
the psychology of their audiences. Friedrich Schiller struggles with
the same problem as he adapts Gozzi's *Turandot*—namely, how to
explain the princess's cruel dismissal of all her suitors. Once the audience has accepted the frame within which a character acts, the
playwright must carefully balance out his or her motivations. They
must ring truthfully within the accepted understanding. Lessing is
not suggesting that all humans share the same psychological makeup,
but he does insist that theatrical characters act out of "natural" as
opposed to supernatural motivations. Miracles may happen in the
world, but not in the moral universe of the theater, where all opin-

4. Stapf, *Lessings Werke*.

ions and desires are judged according to whether they really do fit the character. While Lessing recognizes that this expectation has the effect of transforming foreigners into Europeans, he nevertheless admires the ancient Greek convention—from Homer onward—wherein Greek attributes are ascribed to foreigners, so that Trojan warriors, for example, follow the same code of honor as their attackers. The goal is not to strip away the particularities of foreign cultures, but more importantly to avoid projecting stereotypes on to them.[5] In the absence of more accurate knowledge, presume that Asians act for the same reasons Europeans do. The ultimate goal of this strategy is to take foreigners as seriously as domestic rulers. Thus, the question of who deserves the audience's sympathy depends on how recognizable the character's motivations are. Since foreigners who seem "opaque" to Europeans are less likely to receive sympathy, dramatists often feel obliged to attribute familiar thoughts to their behavior, thereby making them less strange.

The path from Asian martyrs to world literature starts with the basic Christian lesson of identifying with the suffering condition of others—for pious Catholics, foremost with the image of Christ on the cross and then the instructive examples of martyrs. Later secular models of sympathy and emulation drew lessons from the affective piety that the Catholic Church nurtured in the late Middle Ages and then intensified following the Council of Trent. With the formulation of each new mode of sympathy, different qualities of the medieval believer's union with Christ's suffering were either adapted or suppressed.

For early modern Catholics the promise of salvation was conjoined with the practice of contemplating and incorporating the representation of Christ's suffering into one's own life. By drawing Christ's suffering into their own physical and emotional experience, Catholics were acknowledging their own sinful nature and their belief that Christ's suffering could rescue them. Very often this maneuver was made while meditating on a text or image. Out of the shared sense of misery, a more transcendent happiness was supposed

---

5. Carl Niekerk, "Der Orient-Diskurs in Lessings *Hamburgische Dramaturgie*," *Lessing Yearbook/Jahrbuch* 41 (2014): 186.

to emerge. The theological contemplation of Christ sought a spiritual union with God, allowing the possibility of feeling love for the other as the other suffers. Christian art tends to construct the image of the suffering Christ in terms that are familiar to the contemporary viewer, thus easing the act of identification. Inevitably emulation and identification began locally, only to move out across space as the church could show the extended reach of its own teachings. Martyrs participate in a geographical ring of emulation for they both demonstrate their own successful emulation of Christ on the cross across the world while serving as models for later, often distant believers. The post-Tridentine missionaries were very much inspired by earlier images of martyrdom. The globalization of the Catholic mission also revived the veneration of martyrs. For inspired young men, to spread the gospel abroad offered the exciting possibility of attaining martyrdom.[6] Japanese Christians whose stories and images appeared in European churches were admired by European Christians for their faith-driven sacrifice, proof that the church lived on around the world. Jesuit school dramas reenacted the sacrifices made by Japanese Christians who refused to recant their new faith.

The primary source for such performances was Nicholas Trigault's *De Christianis apud Iaponios Triumphis* (On Christian triumphs in Japan), published in 1623. Trigault's book provided news of martyrs in its account of how the Japanese church was founded and then suppressed in a manner reminiscent of the early church. Even Protestants were fascinated. Later Dutch publishers catered to the reading public's desire for further graphic portrayals of Japanese martyrs, less out of a sense of piety than to satisfy a fascination in seeing what punishment the Japanese inflicted. The pious interest in Japanese martyrs centered on the suffering of fellow Christians. While Jesuit histories of China provided an increasing array of social and historical information, the first dramas about Japan con-

---

6. Kristina Müller-Bongard, "Konzepte zur Konsolidierung einer jesuitischen Identität. Die Märtyrerzyklem der jesuitischen Kollegien in Rom," in *Le monde est une peinture. Jesuitische Identität und die Rolle der Bilder*, ed. Elisabeth Oy-Marra and Volker Remmert (Berlin: Akademie, 2011), 153–75.

centrated exclusively on the protagonists as Christian martyrs without any digressions into society at large.[7]

A morality based on sympathy uses the image of another person's suffering to compel an emotional response, in speech or action, from the observer. It operates most effectively in close proximity, yet can be extended beyond localities as information channels deliver news of foreign events. The Scottish Enlightenment understood that the ethical person cannot completely share the suffering of another; there is no possibility of a complete union—or rather, Scottish philosophers maintained a skeptical attitude about such mystical claims. For this reason, moral philosophers sought to distinguish their own psychology from Catholic spiritualism. Nevertheless, the image was fundamental to both systems. The sight of the victim compelled the observer to imagine the suffering of the other. Adam Smith describes the victim as "our brother," thereby changing the love felt for the other from a religious union to a fraternal caring. Within moral philosophy, the process of imagining an other's pain replaces the spiritual connection the Christian seeks while contemplating the crucifixion. Enlightenment moralists tended to view martyrdom as an excessive and misguided passion. The Earl of Shaftesbury would have understood it as a primitive enthusiasm, for which a love of humanity had replaced the more cultish dedication of the martyr. "'Tis well we have the authority of a sacred author in our religion to assure us that the spirit of love and humanity is above that of martyrs."[8] Instead of the concentrated focus on a single figure of piety, Shaftesbury advocated a more cosmopolitan sympathy: "To love the public, to study universal good, and to promote the interest of the whole world, as far as it lies in our power, is surely the height of goodness and makes that temper which we call divine."[9] In the moral scenario, sympathy extends to a wider range of situations than the Christian focus on the crucifixion and its emulation through martyrdom. By moving away from the singular moment of crucifixion,

---

7. Goran Proot and Johan Verbercknoes, "Japonica in the Jesuit Drama of the Southern Netherlands," *Bulletin of Portuguese-Japanese Studies* (2002): 27–47.

8. Anthony, Earl of Shaftesbury, "A Letter Concerning Enthusiasm," in *Characteristics of Men, Manners, Opinions, Times* (Indianapolis: Bobbs-Merril, 1964), 19.

9. Shaftesbury, "A Letter Concerning Enthusiasm," 27.

moral sympathy still has a fixation on visual contemplation, but it allows a variety of such images, thereby shifting its own analogy with Christianity to the broader principle of showing compassion for others.

In researching the scholarship on Catholic missionaries in China, I was waiting for the point when some expert on Church history would link the Jesuit's accommodation of the Confucian canon with later forms of cosmopolitanism. Furthermore, it seems clear that accommodation in China was grounded in a search for analogies rather than a drive to refute errors. The underlying assumption of a shared human experience of divine revelation allowed for the possibility that Confucian teachings, at some fundamental origin, were not different from Christian. As the last chapters will show, Goethe's approach to world literature shares with Jesuit accommodation the inclination to find analogies between Chinese and European traditions that allow for identification with the foreign despite the obvious differences. His secular approach allows a much broader range of analogies, without requiring a far-reaching reinterpretation of Confucian texts, yet it clearly emerged from the track already dug out by the Jesuits. Unfortunately, such a connection has always remained unspoken and implicit. Thus this book offers an initial historical path connecting missionary accommodation with world literature.

I argue that eighteenth-century sentimentalism with its preference for epistolary expression incorporated reading practices developed in the Catholic Church's missionary networks—a coupling that most Enlightenment thinkers in Germany and Scotland would have rejected. The Enlightenment and sentimentalism are rarely associated with this older Catholic lineage, yet any eighteenth-century person curious about Asia would have inevitably consulted the vast seventeenth-century literature produced by missionaries. Indeed, these texts would have been the primary source of information about East and South Asia available to even the most sophisticated reader. German media scholars have concentrated on sentimental epistolary forms as a principle moment in the formation of emotional inwardness, while overlooking the earlier Catholic culture of missionary letter writing. Bernhard Siegert in his groundbreaking study of postal systems and literature, treats the history of eighteenth-

century letter writing as a transition from feudal rhetoric to intimate confession, thereby overlooking the long Catholic tradition,
which long preceded Pietist first-person narratives.[10] In his later
work, however, Siegert makes clear that the history of postal delivery is much older than the eighteenth century.[11] There is no doubt
that Germans were reading letters sent from the other side of the
world already at the end of the sixteenth century. My study tries to
draw the sentimental and early modern histories together to show
that postal systems stretched from the global missionary church to
world literature.

Most analysis of world literature and Enlightenment cosmopolitanism focuses on the most progressive qualities in these ideas, or
it critiques their absence. Why not read these terms backward to
look for what is oldest in them? How do they emerge from far more
aged versions of global relations? How have they adapted Christian teaching while removing its theology? What religious principles does cosmopolitanism preserve even as it positions itself
critically against the church? How were the reading strategies of
world literature an expansion of monastic meditation, despite
Goethe's thorough aversion to the medieval church? Accommodation and world literature share a wonderful open-mindedness as
well as an archaic belief in the fundamental sameness of human existence. Cosmopolitanism owes more to religious and mythic thinking than it perhaps wants to admit.

Critics of cosmopolitanism still argue that spatial "closeness" between people is crucial to their feeling compassion and that humans
have a far more difficult time sympathizing with someone on the
other side of the globe than with their neighbor. How could information about China seem relevant to European readers? What reading
techniques bring the reader to form a strong affinity for events and
people in China? While the flow of information from Asia to Europe
was a remarkable development, it alone did not suffice to make that

---

10. Bernhard Siegert, *Relays: Literature as an Epoch of the Postal System*,
trans. Kevin Repp (Stanford, CA: Stanford University Press, 1999), 14.
11. Bernhard Siegert, *Passage des Digitalen: Zeichenpraktiken der neuzeitlichen Wissenschaften, 1500–1900* (Berlin: Brinkmann and Bose, 2003).

news important to the laity when it arrived. Scholars were immediately drawn to the new reports, but less curious readers had to be trained to incorporate information into their daily environment. As with so many literary questions, the problem of how to process the unfamiliar text was addressed by adapting methods first formulated to make the Bible more familiar.

Early modern global networks quickly developed modes of emotional identification that allowed Europeans to form a sympathetic bond with foreigners and foreign places despite the alienation created by distance and difference. Without the Jesuit practices, Europeans would not have possessed the intellectual techniques to perceive and identify with foreigners. Long after readers stopped attending Mass and reading missionary letters, the intellectual maneuvers developed by seventeenth-century Catholics as a means of providing spiritual support for global missions were applied to scientific travel reports.

Roland Barthes was clearly confining himself to his own nation when he wrote: "The Jesuits, as we know, have contributed much to forming our notion of literature. The heirs and propagators of Latin rhetoric, through teaching, over which they had in the past, to all intents and purposes, a monopoly in Europe, they left bourgeois France with the concept of 'fine writing.'"[12] When tracing discursive channels across early modern Europe, it would take little exaggeration to extend his argument to encompass Spain, Italy, and Germany. Few would deny that Jesuit pedagogy and theatrics shaped baroque literature. And while the various strands of the Enlightenment sought to seal themselves off against the Jesuits, their general influence persisted, at least in a negative form, as the atheist insistence on always reversing Jesuit theology (Goethe) and in mainstream thinkers' combined critique and acquiescence (Voltaire). On any questions related to China, their authority declined slowly at first, then suddenly, only to find a quiet revival once the polemics had died down.

---

12. Roland Barthes, *Sade-Fourier-Loyola*, trans. Richard Miller (New York: Hill & Wang, 1976), 39.

The techniques for visualizing and identifying with distant events were outlined in the foundational text of Jesuit spirituality, Ignatius Loyola's *Spiritual Exercises*, and in the medieval devotions that preceded it. The theological intent in using these techniques was to lend biblical narratives, which after all were set far from European localities, an immediate relevance first to monks, then to a wider laity. The yearning pious reader was supposed to visualize how Mary and Joseph sat around the manger, how crowds gathered as Christ was crucified, the terrors of the Last Judgement. "The immediate force of this desire is to be read in the very materiality of the objects whose representation Ignatius calls for: places in their precise, complete dimensions, characters in their costumes, their attitudes, their actions, their actual words."[13] Spiritual narratives were organized by detailed scenes that the reader contemplated almost as if they were illustrations.[14] These readerly views provided the setting for later theatrical adaptations of missionary writings in Jesuit schools. The theatricality was already present in the *Spiritual Exercises*: "The 'mysteries' excerpted by Ignatius from the Christian narrative take on a theatrical quality which relates them to the medieval mysteries: they are 'scenes' the exercitant is called upon to live out, as in a psychodrama."[15] The techniques were initially applied to the life of Christ but extended to other spiritual narratives, such as saints' lives, missionary reports, and martyrs' deaths.

Eventually the ability to imagine distant scenes, both spatially and temporally, as if they were happening "right before our eyes" could be applied to secular fiction with much the same intensity as a monk in his chamber contemplating the crucifixion. Kant, for example, in the *Critique of Pure Reason*, defines imagination as "the faculty of representing in intuition an object that is *not itself present*."[16] In order to prevent outright inventions, Kant cautions that the representation of what is not itself present be based on established analogies with nature as it is already known. To avoid excessive speculation,

---

13. Barthes, *Sade-Fourier-Loyola*, 62.
14. Barthes, *Sade-Fourier-Loyola*, 55.
15. Barthes, *Sade-Fourier-Loyola*, 61.
16. Immanuel Kant, *Critique of Pure Reason*, trans. Norman Kemp Smith (New York: St. Martin's Press, 1965), 165 (B 151), (emphasis in original).

Kant requires that the imagination to be accompanied by reason—
"Einbildungskraft in Begleitung der Vernunft"[17]—much as the Jesuits expect the reading of sacred texts to be accompanied by the
explanations of a priest. Barthes traces this coupling, typified by
Loyola's *Exercises*, back to Roman rhetoric and the mysticism of the
High Middle Ages.[18] Manuals on oratory stressed the importance of
speech making a scene visible to an audience. Aristotle refers to
phantasia and *energeia* to describe speech's visual productivity.[19] In
the *Poetics* he advises: "In constructing the plot and working it out
with the proper diction, the poet should place the scene, as far as
possible, before his eyes. In this way, seeing everything with the utmost vividness, as if were a spectator of the action, he will discover
what is in keeping with it."[20] Within eighteenth-century fiction, German critics refer to such readerly spectatorship as arising from a
text's *Anschaulichkeit* (vividness).[21] The graphic effect emerges from
both the manner in which the text is composed and the reader's attentiveness to details. Loyola incorporates these tropes into his meditation. He instructs pious readers to imagine a biblical scene by
filling in the physical properties of the space within which events
occur. The moral aim of such visualization was for the reader not
only to perceive the meaning of religious texts, but to imitate them,
particularly the life of Christ.

The emotional concentration on the scenes from Christ's life was
first developed in the monasteries of the eleventh century, but over

17. Immanuel Kant, "Mutmasslicher Anfang der Menschengeschichte," in
Schriften zur Anthropologie, Geschichtsphilosophie, Politik und Pädagogik 1, in
vol. 11 of *Wekausgabe*, ed. Wilhelm Weischedel (Frankfurt: Suhrkamp, 1981), 85.
18. Barthes, *Sade-Fourier-Loyola*, 55.
19. Debra Hawhee, "Looking into Aristotle's Eyes: Toward a Theory of Rhetorical Vision," *Advances in the History of Rhetoric* 14.2 (2011): 139–65.
20. Aristotle, *Aristotle's Theory of Poetry and Fine Art*, trans. S. H. Butcher
(New York: Dover, 1951), 61 (sect. 17).
21. For an excellent account of *Anschaulichkeit* in Loyola's spiritual exercises, see Paul Rabbow, *Seelenführung, Methodie der Exerzitien in der Antike* (Munich: Kösel, 1954), 70–90. Dorothea von Mücke explains the difficulty in translating
the term into English, while defining *Anschaulichkeit* for Enlightenment semiotics,
in *Virtue and the Veil of Illusion: Generic Innovation and the Pedagogical Project in
Eighteenth-Century Literature* (Stanford, CA: Stanford University Press, 1991),
18–44.

time became widespread among the laity, first by Franciscans, and then after Trent even more widely by Jesuits and other Catholic orders.[22] The compassionate mode of reading about Christ included an attention to detail, to the physical and emotional state that Christ must have undergone, to the look and tone of his immediate environment. This mode of reading drew the believer to imagine additional details, to fill in gaps in the text to provide a more vivid understanding of the biblical scene, to pull the space, sound, emotions, pains from their own life into their contemplation of the text. Medieval Christians who practiced this form of meditation on the figures of Christ and Mary were drawn to imagine how Jerusalem looked and sounded. In a broad sense, reading the Bible obliged Christians to perceive the Orient.

With the spread of missionaries around the world, the compassionate gaze of the believer with its inventive construction of sacred scenes was redirected toward other locations. Catholics in Europe were thus drawn to imagine the sites where Xavier preached in Asia, a practice encouraged by missionary letters and reports. While this intense mode of identifying with Christ's Passion started off as secluded monastic practice that would lead devotees to cloister themselves from the world, Jesuits took an entirely different approach, for they refused seclusion in order to place themselves deliberately in the arenas from which older orders retreated.[23] Although medieval monastic practices such as praying the rosary did spread into the laity, the Jesuits took a more active stance towards the world as

---

22. R. W. Southern notes that new medieval meditative practices had long-term effects on the history of emotions in his *The Making of the Middle Ages* (New Haven, CT: Yale University Press, 1953): "The theme of tenderness and compassion for the sufferings and helplessness of the Saviour of the world was one which had a new birth in the monasteries of the eleventh century, and every century since has paid tribute to the monastic inspiration of this century by some new development of the theme" (232); "It was the Franciscans who first brought the fruits of the monastic experiences of the eleventh and twelfth centuries to ordinary people" (255).

23. J. Michelle Molina, *To Overcome Oneself: The Jesuit Self and Spirit of Global Expansion* (Berkeley: University of California Press, 2013), 36–38. Molina strikes a Foucauldian tone when she writes: "Early modern Christians were monasticized when Christian technologies of the self that had hitherto remained the realm of the spiritual elite began to percolate more rapidly than ever before into lay society" (45).

they propagated Loyola's version of medieval spiritual exercises. Jesuit instructions were often cautious about a spiritual posture that
might require withdrawal into mystical inwardness or social detachment. Rather than remain in monastic isolation, they introduced
such practices to the pious urban elite by teaching students across
Catholic Europe to use this imaginative mode of reading. "Affective imagination was the key means by which individuals were sum-
moned to be active in worldly service to God."[24] What started off
as an esoteric practice of spiritual retreat became a pedagogical
principle for Jesuit versions of worldliness.

Pierre Hadot has argued that Loyola inherited certain concerns
from the spiritual exercises of Greek antiquity.[25] Hadot claims
that ancient practitioners read philosophy not so that they could
formulate systematic knowledge of the world but in order to reinforce their exercises. Both Stoic and Jesuit exercises thus sought to
instill *prosoche* (attention and vigilance over oneself) and its goal,
apatheia (tranquility and equilibrium of mind, an indifference to
worldly matters). The position of the monk, Hadot explains, was
one of attention in the form of a constant vigilance over the mind,
a self-consciousness that never rests and holds the spirit in constant tension, allowing the philosopher to always be aware and to
regulate his actions. The ultimate purpose of attentiveness was to
free the self from the passions that overwhelm it. Hadot's own attentiveness to the many continuities between ancient philosophy
and the *Spiritual Exercises* allows us to recognize new formulations as they emerge. Missing from Hadot's list of shared goals is
the distinctly Christian interest in expressing compassion for the
suffering of others. In his moral philosophy, Adam Smith similarly
updates Stoicism by rejecting its coldness, its apathy toward others,
while at the same time dispensing with an overtly Christian spirituality. Sympathy for others constitutes a major difference between
his moral philosophy and ancient practices. By sympathizing with
the suffering of others, one often loses the detachment and com-

24. Molina, *To Overcome Oneself*, 52, 131–33.
25. Pierre Hadot, *Philosophy as a Way of Life*, trans. Michael Chase (Oxford:
Blackwell, 1995), 82.

posure intended by the ancient exercises. Instead practitioners are thrown into an excited state in which they want to act quickly to alleviate the other's misery.

While Samuel Taylor Coleridge called on readers in 1817 to "suspend disbelief" while reading about the supernatural because he presumed that skepticism was always at play, Ignatius Loyola, the Society of Jesus's founder, wrote with an entirely different orientation to the divine: well before the critiques of the Enlightenment, he calls on the reader to activate belief, to bring all the powers of the imagination into play in order to give shape and color to a reality that is unquestioned in a religious text. Learning how to project oneself into the thoughts of an Old Testament patriarch eventually made it possible for Europeans to imagine that they could think and feel like a Persian prince or a Chinese emperor. The remaining chapters of this book will trace the shifting forms of emotional identification, starting with early Jesuit representation of Asian martyrs and ending with Goethe's reading of a Chinese novel.

The Jesuit's appeals to visualizing a scene became a means of understanding a narrative. To read one's way into a text was to see it unfold around oneself. The capacity to imagine a spatial reality allowed the act of reading to become transformed into a visual experience. German Romanticism adopted an extreme form of this identification, wherein metaphors were perceived as actually existing realities. This notion, however, has a long history preceding the eighteenth century, for the ability to think about ideas as vivid images situated in a familiar space had been codified in Roman rhetorical treatises as the correct way for a public speaker to store and then retrieve information: the anonymous *Rhetorica ad Herennium*, which had long been credited to Cicero, then Cicero's own *De Oratore*, and Quintilian's *Instituio oratoria*.[26] The practice of mnemonics required the speaker to picture a familiar place (*locus*) wherein they could store information by associating it with striking

---

26. The scholarship on the Christian adoption of Roman mnemonics is vast. Caroline Behrmann, "'Le monde est une peinture': Zu Louis Richeômes Bildtheorie im Kontext globaler Mission," in *Le monde est une peinture: Jesuitische Identität und die Rolle der Bilder*, ed. Elisabeth Oy-Marra and Volker R. Remmert (Berlin: Akademie Verlag, 2011): 15–44.

visual cues (*imagines*). Imagining foreign locations was an added challenge, for the Romans had used buildings in the forum as their memory sites. Still this mental maneuver was fundamental to Christian meditation, for most Europeans had never visited the Holy Land. If they were going to construct visual images of biblical scenes, they needed to conjure them up with the assistance of sacred art and the transference of scenes from their own environment. Ignatius Loyola's *Spiritual Exercises*, which were intended to help guide the individual's development, often begin with a prelude that calls on the meditator to compose an image of a physical place in order to concentrate his or her thoughts on it.[27] The first prelude to the first exercise states generally the manner of imagining a sacred space that precedes most meditations.

> First Prelude. This the composition of the place. It should be noted at this point that when the contemplation or meditation is about something visible, such as when we contemplate Christ our Lord, the composition will consist in seeing with the imagination the physical location of the object contemplated. I said the physical place such as the temple or mountain where Jesus was, according to the subject matter of the contemplation.[28]

At least initially, the practice of imagining a place is dependent on reading from the Bible. Imagination is coupled with a very well-known text. Over time, the exercises are more freely based on sources other than scripture, as when the exercitant is asked to imagine the tortures of hell or the Babylonian battlefield of Satan, both scenes that have been represented many times. The exercises go beyond the familiar, to encompass a global survey of diverse cultures. "First Point. This will be to see the different persons. First, those on the face of the earth, with such diversity of dress and custom. Some are white, others are black; some at peace, others at

---

27. Philip Endean, "The Spiritual Exercises," in *The Cambridge Companion to the Jesuits*, ed. Thomas Worcester (Cambridge: Cambridge University Press, 2008), 52–68.

28. Ignatius Loyola, *The Spiritual Exercises of St. Ignatius Loyola*, trans. Elisabeth Meier Tetlow (Lanham, MD: University Press of America, 1987), 23.

war."[29] Paul Rabbow points out that the meditative reader's ability to visualize spaces belongs to a long rhetorical tradition intended to activate the passions. "It is the fully self-conscious, methodical and well-versed application of the profound force that the visual image possesses for exciting the affects, as rhetoric teaches and practices in its lessons on comparisons [*de similititudinibus*]."[30] Loyola writes that the meditative reader does not view the image as image, but rather as fantastical animation immediately present as his or her own experience.[31] This insistence on a rhetoric that excites the passions to the point of hallucinating the presence of a scene described in words clearly distinguishes the Jesuit exercises from those practiced by the ancient Stoics, who sought precisely to tamp down all such excitement.

Not every spiritual image or text automatically produced such responses.[32] Only if they are embedded in spiritual practices, within the church service, meditation, or structured prayer do they rise up to the level of immediate visualization of distant places. In the case of missionaries in China, Jesuit correspondences and the spiritual practices they fostered were placed within a larger liturgical context, so that when Europeans learned to care about Asians—first about their souls, eventually about their daily lives—they did so within the church's rituals.

Jesuits were always clear that the source for Loyola's exercises reaches back into late medieval monastic practices.[33] The society's founding legend recounts that in 1521 as Ignatius Loyola lay wounded from a cannonball during the French army's siege of Pamplona, he

---

29. Loyola, *Spiritual Exercises*, 42.

30. Rabbow, *Seelenführung*, 74.

31. Rabbow, *Seelenführung*, 75.

32. Evonne Levy warns that it is crucial to consider the specific context within which the exercises are pursued rather than allowing them serve as the blanket explanation for all Jesuit images in "Early Modern Jesuit Arts and Jesuit Visual Culture: A View from the Twenty-First Century," *Journal of Jesuit Studies* 1 (2014): 81.

33. David Freedberg provides the definitive art historical analysis of medieval meditation before a sacred image. He also shows how these practices were revived after the Reformation by the Jesuit *Exercises* in *The Power of Images: Studies in the History and Theory of Response* (Chicago: University of Chicago Press, 1989), 161–88.

had only three books available to read. *Vita Christi*, composed by Ludolph of Saxony (1295–1378), was one. It had long circulated as a written manuscript; eventually a Spanish translation was printed in 1503. A Carthusian monk, Ludolph compiled the meditative techniques for reading the Gospels.[34] The Carthusian tendency was to offer works of practical mysticism.[35] *Vita Christi* pulls together an array of medieval approaches focused on the life of Christ as a model for religious life. This technique of reading sacred texts inspired a wide array of religious movements. Another devotional work in the same tradition, Thomas á Kempis's (1380–1471) *Imitation of Christ*, became the most widely read and translated Christian book of devotion. As Karl Phillip Moritz mentions in his autobiographical novel, *Anton Reiser*, Kempis's *Imitation of Christ* was included in children's Latin lessons well into the eighteenth century.[36]

In contemplating the events depicted in the Gospel, Ludolph urges the faithful to read what once happened as if it were happening here and now.[37] The act of reading becomes a compassionate meditation in which readers place themselves visually within the scenes: "Be present at his Nativity and Circumcision like a good foster-parent with Joseph. Go with the Magi to Bethlehem, and worship with them the infant king. Assist with his parents to take him and present him at the Temple. Be in escort with the apostles as the Good Shepherd performs his glorious miracles. Be present at his death with his blessed Mother and John to suffer with them and to console them: and with a certain devout curiosity, feeling your way, touch each of the wounds of your Saviour, who has thus died for

---

34. John O'Malley, *The First Jesuits* (Cambridge, MA: Harvard University Press, 1993), 26.

35. Ignatius Loyola, *The Spiritual Exercises and Selected Works*, ed. George E. Ganss, SJ (New York: Paulist Press, 1991), 21.

36. Karl Philipp Moritz, *Anton Reiser, Ein psychologischer Roman* (Frankfurt: Insel, 1979), 40. Anton Reiser generally read sacred biographies with the intention of imitating the saints: "As tasteless and strange as their stories often were, the old fathers were still the most venerable model for Anton to emulate" (20).

37. Milton Walsh, "'To Always Be Thinking Somehow about Jesus': The Prologue of Ludolph's *Vita Christi*," *Studies in the Spirituality of Jesuits* 43.1 (Spring 2011): 1–39.

you."[38] Placing hands in Christ's wounds becomes the paradigmatic metaphor for the reader's hermeneutic *Einfühlung* (empathy). The preface makes clear that Ludolph has specific procedures in mind that will encourage the reader to imagine sensually the events signified by the text. Ludolph's meditation is unconcerned with historicizing even as it does try to simulate a physical environment for speeches and actions. The biblical scene is supposed to appear as if it were part of the viewer's familiar environment. This explains in part why biblical paintings are never "historically accurate" in the modern sense. They were never intended as costume dramas. Ludolph continues: "As you read the narrative, imagine you are seeing each event with your own eyes and hearing it with your own ears, because the sweetest thoughts are born of desire—and these are much more pleasing to the taste. Although these accounts describe events that occurred in the past, you must meditate upon them as if they were taking place now: there is no question but that you will savor them with greater pleasure. Read what once happened as if it were happening here and now."[39]

Ludolph's example of how to meditate on the book of Christ's life was eventually transported all the way to China via into the widely admired *Evangelicae historiae imagines* (Pictures of the Gospel history), composed by one of the founders of the Jesuit Society, Jerónimo Nadal (1507–1580). Published in Antwerp by the Plantin press in 1593 and 1594, Nadal's book provided 153 illustrated meditations on the Gospel.[40] It became the standard for illustrating the narrative of Christ's life. Nicolai Longobardo and other missionaries in China requested that Nadal's book be sent to them, so that they might show the pictures as objects of meditation to potential converts. If Ludolph urged readers to imagine the scene in

38. Charles Abbot Conway Jr., *The Vita Christi of Ludolph of Saxony and Late Medieval Devotion Centred on the Incarnation: A Descriptive Analysis* (Salzburg: Analecta Cartusiana, 1976), 126–27.

39. Ludolph of Saxony, Carthusian, *The Life of Jesus Christ*, trans. Milton T. Walsh (Collegeville, MN: Liturgical Press, 2018), part 1, 1:17.

40. Paul Begheyn, "The Jesuits in the Low Countries 1540–1773: Apostles of the Printing Press," *The Jesuits of the Low Countries: Identity and Impact (1540–1773)* (Leuven: Peeters, 2012), 135.

which Christ's life takes place, Nadal's work provided illustrations on the page for readers to contemplate, meditate, and remember. The title page resembles an altar piece. Similarly, the frontispiece to Nadal's *Adnotationes et meditations* (Annotations and meditations) portrays saints as sculptures standing in niches within a church's façade, thereby establishing a triangular reiteration of sacred architecture, reading the book, and contemplating the image. So successful was the book-church-saint sequence that it was reiterated in countless publications, including Guilo Aleni's translation with images into Chinese.[41] The illustrations allowed Nadal's work to address readers who did not understand Latin by providing a visual framework around which translations of text could be organized. If the visualization of biblical scenes was the secondary effect of Ludolph's reading strategy, the new techniques of Antwerp printers allowed images to become the equal to the written word, thereby allowing meditations on the Gospel to drift away from a singular focus on the text and into the more diffuse impressions of the visual.

The purpose of visualization in this context was not merely to perceive more intensely with more senses, but also to feel compassion for the figures. Ludolph and the early Jesuits understood visualization as a means of strengthening the reader's emotional affinity for Christ. The point of identification was for the reader to be absorbed into the image that arises from reading, to pass over into it, and thereby to be so transformed that he or she adopts a new form of living. By placing themselves within the text's scene, it became easier for readers and their pious listeners, for reading aloud was certainly the most common method, to feel compassion for other religious figures, such as the missionaries and their converts. Herein begins the psychological process whereby European Christians could develop sympathy for distant people.

Antoine Sucquet advises that a faithful reader preparing to contemplate a religious book should imagine the space in which the book transpired—under a heading "imagining the place is almost

---

41. Nicholas Standaert, "Jesuits in China," *The Cambridge Companion to the Jesuits*, ed. Thomas Worcester (Cambridge: Cambridge University Press, 2015), 182.

always useful."[42] Ralph Dekonick suggests that these instructions
are replicated in Jesuit frontispieces generally. The architecture
shown in a book's opening page implicitly encourages the reader to
imagine this space while moving through the text. "This metonymic
dimension inaugurates the act of reading by an act of imagining,
which constructs a virtual and prospective image of the text to be
discovered."[43] For example, the widely read and influential 1687
introduction to Confucius's life and philosophy, *Confucius Sinarum philosophus* ("Confucius, the philosopher of the Chinese"),
opened with a page showing the Chinese thinker dressed in robes,
which could also have been worn by a European scholar or Church
father, while standing in a building that had the checkerboard floor
tiles along with a high vaulted ceiling that culminated in the same
rounded arch found in many classically designed European churches
(see figure 3).[44] Only his facial features, the script on the books,
and the hats worn by small figures in the background identify the
representation as Chinese; otherwise, the Confucian temple could
easily have been taken as a European library. Similar to drawings
and paintings from Raphael to David of Greek philosophers debating in Athens, the title page at the start of Confucius's biography
offers readers an image of the space within which to situate the
short dialogues between teacher and student that organize classical
Chinese philosophy.

The inclusion of illustrations in devotional books did not super-
sede the link between text and imagination. As we have seen, classical rhetoric well understood that poetry could employ language
so vivid that readers would have the impression that they could see

---

42. Antoine Sucquet, *Wege zum ewigen Leben*, trans. Carl Stengel (Augsburg: Langenwalder, 1627), 7.

43. Ralph Dekoninck, "On the Threshold of a Spiritual Journey: The Appeal-ing Function of a Jesuit Frontispiece (Antwerp, 1593–1640)," in *Le monde est une peinture: Jesuitische Identität und die Rolle der Bilder*, ed. Elisabeth Oy-Marra and Volker R. Remmert (Berlin: Akademie Verlag, 2011), 80.

44. *Confucius Sinarum philosophus*, trans. Prosperi Intorcetta, Christian Herdtrich, Francisci Rougemont, Philipp Cpuplet. (Paris: Daniel Horthemel, 1687), 122.

Figure 3. Depiction of Confucius in a European styled library.
Source: *Confucius Sinarum philosophus*, trans. Prosperi Intorcetta,
Christian Herdtrich, Francisci Rougemont, and Philipp Couplet
(Paris: Daniel Horthemel,1687), 122.

the scene for themselves.[45] Without abandoning this ideal, medieval
Christianity also reversed the formula when it approached texts
meditatively.[46] Faithful readers took it upon themselves to conjure

---

45. G. Zanker, "Enargeia in the Ancient Criticism of Poetry," *Rheinische Museum für Philologie* N.F. 124 (1981): 297–311.

46. Mary Carruthers's insistence that monastic practice deployed the memory arts, in particular their reliance on mental visualization, for the sake of inventive composition rather than passive information storage reflects this shift toward the reader rather than the orator. See her *The Craft of Thought: Meditation, Rhetoric, and the Making of Images, 400–1200* (Cambridge: Cambridge University Press, 1998).

up the image through their own effort, even if the text was not brimming with visual detail, thereby conjoining rhetoric with contemplative hermeneutics.

The European inclination to identify with foreign figures, to feel an emotional bond with them based on a written description, to sympathize and even share in their suffering and happiness has a long genealogy. We will begin with the martyr. Three types of dramatic scenes—the emperor's court, the martyr's death, and the idyllic retreat—were introduced by the first missionaries into the European discourse on China in order to foster identification from West to East. The first two place the Asian within a nexus of power and violence, the third removes him entirely from it. All three scenes appealed to humanist Christians as familiar from history, literature, and philosophy of the Mediterranean antiquity. Contemporary cosmopolitan appeals to aid and support suffering people outside the West descend from the staging of martyr dramas in the early modern period. Modern cosmopolitanism still uses the images of suffering that were at the core of the Catholic Church's claim to be represent the universal Christian church. Without the stagecraft of early martyr dramas, we would not have the modern media spectacle of cosmopolitan appeals to rescue the Third World. The cruel deaths of Christian converts in East Asia established the possibility that Europeans could sympathize with complete strangers on the basis of a shared religion. The stories of how Japanese Christians were tortured and killed circulated widely in seventeenth-century Europe: they were the basis for school plays performed in public markets; they were shown on church walls, eulogized in sermons; and their stories circulated widely in church literature. While Europeans might have no other basis for seeking affinity with Japanese peasants, a shared religious faith was enough to open an imaginary emotional connection. From theatrical depictions of Asian Christians dying for their faith, it was a small but crucial step for plays to depict non-Christian Asians, often Chinese, who shared certain virtues in common with Christian Europeans—indeed who might even have had an inclination to convert. Martyr dramas contributed strongly to the image of the Asiatic despot who mercilessly and with absolute power subjugated all subjects, foreigner as well as native. Europeans sympathized with the suffering of Asian converts specifically because they had abandoned their traditional religion in favor of Christianity. That they had fallen away from their own culture made them objects of long-distance identification—an alignment quite different from Enlightenment curiosity, which fixated on difference.

Harsh autocrats were a staple of baroque tragic dramas, as in Andreas Gryphius's *Catharina von Georgien*. The longevity of this stereotype was reinforced by its frequent adaptation, so that the despotism of the Asian ruler was portrayed as operating against different types of victims. In the nineteenth century, it was not Christian converts so much as English merchants with free-market principles who were at least figuratively tyrannized by Chinese and Japanese rulers uninterested in opening their markets. However, Asian monarchs were not all type cast as harsh tyrants; some were reflective rulers cautiously interested in Western teachings. Already in the seventeenth century, urban theater splits away from Jesuit school dramas, so that tyrannical power is often shown to be operating against the monarch rather than at his behest. These almost-Christians could also be the objects of sympathy for naïve Europeans. For humanist Europeans, such as the Jesuits, Confucian moral philosophy could also become an object of admiration worthy of emulation. The Jesuit efforts to establish a connection between the ethical and cosmological principles in a humanist Christianity and Confucian texts broadened the terms of an abstract emotional bond between cultures. If Scholastic Christians could incorporate Greek and Roman philosophy, then the Jesuits postulated that they ought try the same with the classical works transcribed by the students of Confucius. In this manner there emerged a very real possibility for the Catholic seventeenth century to find an affinity with a small, refined sector of Chinese culture.

As these affinities became more abstract, they were often turned against each other. The spectacle of martyrdom could be turned against Europeans if one contemplated the possibility that Christian campaigns to convert others were themselves tyrannical, especially if these critiques reinforced divisions within Christianity. Thus, Protestants could present resistance to Catholic conquest as a form of martyrdom based on abstract principles such as autonomy and sovereignty. In *The Indian Emperour*, John Dryden could portray Montezuma as a martyr suffering for his civilization at the hands of obsessed conquistadores. As the monarch he is, of course, representative of the fate of his civilization, which is driven by *fortuna*, the sheer chance that Spanish strangers have landed on his shores. In either case, whether the violence was administered by or to the head of state, the victims were portrayed in Stoic terms, as calmly accepting horrific bodily punishment without blinking. The calm of the medieval martyr was revived in representations of Asia. If certain Japanese and Chinese converts seemed capable of quietly undergoing torturous misery, it was because missionaries ascribed to them the virtues they perceived in early Christian martyrs. By the end of the eighteenth century, English philosophers took for granted that Londoners could feel sympathy for the suffering of distant Asians; the question for Edmund Burke and Adam Smith was no longer whether it was possible to feel for the misery people in China or India, but how strong were these feelings? Were they as strong as the emotional affections Englishmen had for each other? If they were not as strong, was this then a sign of moral failure?

One problem with the figure of the martyr is he or she is understood to represent an entire nation, yet we can easily say that the suffering Japanese Christian convert is by no means typical of Edo Japanese society. By the tragic conventions of baroque martyr dramas, the suffering monarch was the embodiment of his or her nation. Montezuma tortured by conquistadores is understood by the conventions of tragedy to embody the fate of all native peoples in the Americas. As compelling as these images are, we must ask to what extent do they summarize the history of two societies' interaction? Does the refugee who has landed on an island represent his homeland just because Europeans and Americans have formed an emotional bond with him on account of his suffering? What pressure does the theatrics of martyrdom place on the refugee to be the perfect Syrian or to speak for all Sudan? Furthermore, to what extent is the West aware of a place when it is not in crisis? If sympathy is the first bond between cultures, how do those connections develop when there is no longer a desperate situation? How can sympathy lead to a more complete cultural exchange rather than relying on the breakdown of culture as the basis for building an emotional bond? The reliance on spectacles of suffering to find a shared humanity may reinforce the cycle of forgetting that typifies the early modern European connection with China—foreign societies matter only in moments of crisis or, in that clear contrast to cosmopolitan unity, when they threaten the West militarily. Outside of such emotional peaks, they run the risk of being forgotten. Sympathy for martyrs always entails an emotional appeal for a person and often a culture on the brink of destruction, whereas accommodation entails a respectful integration of the self into the other. Only when the conditions of fatalistic *Trauerspiele* are preceded by dialogue in advance of disaster, only when sympathy is expanded to become identification so that observers come to believe that they share a complex identity with the other, does a sophisticated cultural exchange such as in accommodation or world literature commence.

A second line of identification fostered by missionary discourse was predicated on the perceived similarity between European intellectuals and their counterparts in Asia. Its emotional success depended on a sense of equality between the two cultures. Eighteenth-century continental thinkers, bureaucrats, and courtiers themselves, could find a strong affinity for the Chinese ruling class, mandarins, or literati, who not only engaged in learned study, but also exercised real political power under the guidance of a wise and just monarch. While the Jesuits saw the literati as scholars with a similar cosmological and ethical philosophy, Enlightenment thinkers followed a similar track of identification, though without a particularly strong faith in an omnipotent deity. As the Enlightenment turned to reexamine the first translations of Confucian texts, rationalist philosophers continued to accept the Jesuit claim that the European and Chinese intellectual elite shared similar ethical principles, but they did so precisely for the opposite reason than the missionaries. Chinese intellectuals were appealing to the Enlightenment precisely because they showed little sign of believing in God the creator. Each one of these encounters with China came almost anew. If European depictions of China follow a continuous line, it depends on the remarkable consistency and discipline of the Jesuit missionaries' discourse. How could such a far-flung association of intellectuals maintain such a consistent position for almost two centuries?

Jesuit Techniques Shared

The similarities between Catholic missionary communities and eighteenth-century sentimentalism deserve greater attention.[47] Eighteenth-century German media scholarship has treated emotional subjectivity as a circuit that begins with Pietism in the late seventeenth century and emerges as a literary form with sentimentalism in the late eighteenth. Recent work has made explicit how important communication systems were in providing the conditions for long-distance expressions of feeling. The privacy and direct address made possible by postal delivery allowed writers to heighten the intensity of their subjective utterances to recipients living far away, so much so that without mail delivery, one might suspect that the moral psychology of sentimentalism would not have been possible. Christian Gellert's discourse on letter writing, *Praktische Abhandlung von dem guten Geschmack in Briefen* (Practical treatise on good taste in letters), is regularly cited as the turning point from letters composed according to a rhetoric intent on demonstrating feudal, courtly status to a personalized inner voice of emotional vulnerability.[48] Most every German literary historian overlooks the Catholic history of reading practices that precedes Gellert's advice on how to narrate a story: "Tell a story not so that one simply understands the matter, but rather so that one believes to see it before oneself and to thus be a witness thereof. This is what it means to narrate in a lively manner. This comes about through the small portraits that one composes in a story about the circumstances, or people."[49] Gellert's practical recommendation recapitulates the medieval reader's relationship to sacred and edifying scripture. Gellert's

---

47. Astrida Tantillo offers a singular analysis in "The Catholicism of Werther," *German Quarterly* 81.4 (2008): 408–23.

48. Siegert, *Relays*, 33.

49. Christian Fürchtegott Gellert, "Praktische Abhandlung von dem guten Geschmack in Briefen," *Sämtiche Schriften* (Berlin: Weidmann, 1867), 4:68.

radical innovation in lies in switching a mode of reading into a style of narrating. The medieval mode of reading sacred stories by envisioning them becomes a method of writing secular stories so that they may be visualized. No medieval believer would have assumed the authorial position of sacred literature, and Gellert extends his advice only to personal narratives, yet the reversal opens up the possibility that the successful modern author could claim the position of a "second Creator," an aesthetic that Goethe and the Sturm-und Drang actualized decades after Gellert's rather sensible advice.

A second blind spot in eighteenth-century German media studies is the manner in which they sometimes reinforce the periodization of traditional literary history. Although media history has often claimed that its chronology is driven by technologies and practices, all too often the history of postal systems reinscribes canonical German literary historiographies by presenting Pietist literature as a precursor to the young Goethe, who inevitably becomes the decisive starting point for German literature's tradition of intensely subjective writing. Werther's presumption that court life is filled with cold wooden puppets who cannot express an inner genius finds its media equivalent in the claim that rhetorically organized letters written by aristocrats were formulaic and without feeling. Most scholars follow Goethe's recollections in book 8 of *Dichtung und Wahrheit* (*Poetry and Truth*) that Pietist circles offered the natural link between sentimentalist reading and religious practices.[50] All too often Pietism is treated as the origin of German soulfulness. Nevertheless, a glance at letters circulating within the early modern Catholic world reveals that a passionate epistolary culture flourished in the church, not as a rebellion but as an actively

---

50. Johann Wolfgang Goethe, *Dichtung und Wahrheit*, in *Werke*, ed. Erich Trunz (Munich: C. H. Beck, 1982), 9:308–53; *Werke* is hereafter referred to as HA. The title will be translated henceforth as *Poetry and Truth* in order to preserve poetry's primacy. As a general note on translations in eighteenth-century German scholarship: For philosophers writing in English, there exist standard translations of Immanuel Kant's three *Critiques* and many other works in the German tradition, from which quotations are commonly taken. English scholars of German literature, on the other hand, do not rely on standard translations. Even though translations from German abound, scholars are obliged, in the case of Goethe's work as well as most every author since, to provide their own as part of their analysis.

encouraged communication that was understood to motivate the faithful. In his history of German letter writing, Albrecht Koschorke notes that Gellert reactivates the Roman view that a written correspondence substitutes for a personal conversation, implying that this was an entirely new rediscovery, as opposed to having been a staple of humanist friendship.[51] The long history of Catholic epistles with their manifold proclamations of faith and yearning is thereby discounted. Missionary correspondents constituted one of the communities where intimacy and the desire to be reunited with distant friends were expressed frequently and with complex tropes. Missionaries often stressed that their great separation from old friends meant that they would never again be able to speak with one another in person and that letters would thus have to stand in substitution. Gellert's distinction between the formality of baroque administrative style and the oral simulation of private letters appears in Jesuit letter-writing advice over a century before.

In tracing out these comparisons between letter writing and conversation as an ideal, we must bear in mind that interpersonal conversations have their own history. Cicero and Gellert may have held the private conversation as the model for letter writing, but we can hardly imagine that their speech was much the same. How a patrician Roman spoke with a favorite friend would have differed considerably from a dialogue between two sensitive German poets, just as it would surely have varied from any conversation between two Jesuit priests. Thus, even if a sentimental conversation sounded different from the pious talk between Ignatius Loyola and Francis Xavier, we can still recognize that they shared a similar model of written communication—to simulate spoken intimacy. Despite their historical differences, we can imagine similar problems arising for anyone taking advantage of a postal system. In writing their personal letters, Jesuits, Pietists, and sentimentalists would all have had to negotiate the curious paradox of writing about personal feelings for a friend with the understanding that the more successfully their text reveals the nuances of spiritual or emotional intimacy, the more

---

51. Albrecht Koschorke, *Körperströme und Schriftverkehr: Mediologies des 18. Jahrhunderts* (Munich: Wilhlem Fink, 1999), 191–92.

likely it was that it would be shared publicly. Church readings of
missionary letters and their republication in vernacular translatio
inspired many young men to apply for missionary positions in the
East and West Indies, just as Sturm-und-Drang epistolary novels encouraged swarms of emulators. Young missionaries' greatest aspirations had more than a little in common with Werther's ultimate
end: to demonstrate their everlasting faith by dying a martyr's death.
Rather than seeing sentimentalism as a wholly new mode of expression, we should consider it a secularized, sensualized revision of
earlier postal communications. Hans Robert Jauß argued already
in the 1970s that *Werther* drew from and indeed exhausted the older
religious tradition of edifying literature that urges readers to identify compassionately with Christ's suffering.[52]

The aesthetic practice of sympathizing with fictional characters
still places great importance on the suffering of others and the observer's ability to imagine him- or herself in the same situation, however the range of scenes expanded over time. If late medieval
readers shared Christ's suffering as they read, eighteenth-century
readers applied similar techniques to very different characters. By
all accounts Pietism served as conduit between medieval mysticism
and eighteenth-century sentimentalism.[53] Karl Phillip Moritz was
not the only such child raised on Thomas a Kempis's *Imitation of
Christ*. Johann Caspar Lavater read the book daily while a student.
The model of emulating Christ led Lavater to see the divine in every
person, to find the highest ideals in humanity. Lavater adapted the
Christian medieval model of reading as involving compassionate
identification to an Enlightenment faith in progress.[54] While his enthusiastic reiterations of Kempis's *Imitation of Christ* may have

---

52. Hans Robert Jauß, *Ästhetische Erfahrung und literarische Hermeneutik*
(Frankfurt: Suhrkamp, 1982), 173.

53. "[Der Pietismus] überliefert vor allem starkes mystisches Gut dem 17. und
18. Jahrhundert, in ihm wurzelt, wie erwähnt, der Subjectivismus des 18 Jahrhunderts, der in der Romantik einen Höhenpunkt erreicht" (August Langen, *Der
Wortschatz des deutschen Pietismus* [Tübingen: Max Niemey er, 1954], 3).

54. Kurt Guggisberg, "Johann Caspar Lavater und die Idee der 'Imitatio
Christi,'" *Zwingliana* 7.5 (1941): 337–66; Gerhard Kaiser, *Pietismus und Patriotismus im literarischen Deutschland: Ein Beitrag zum Problem der Säkularistion*,
2nd ed. (Frankfurt: Athenäum, 1973), 21.

been seen by contemporaries such as Goethe as excessive, unrelenting, and a model of uncritical readerly reception, the basic notion of identifying through the text with a revered figure resonated broadly among German readers.

The medieval model persisted within sentimentalism, though in a secularized form. Martyrdom was one obvious trope that carried over into a poetic and unreligious use in the eighteenth century. The structure of Richardson's most famous novels mirror a basic conflict in baroque tragic drama, an absolute male tyrant demanding the sexual submission of a virtuous virgin or mother through rape, marriage, or both. These configurations hearken back to medieval martyr plays, such as Hroswitha von Gandersheim's Latin *Dulcitus*, also known as *Die Leiden der heiligen Jungfrauen Agaoe, Chionia und Irene* (The sufferings of the holy virgins Agaoe, Chionia and Irene). In noting the affinities, Margaret Ann Doody is also quite clear that the martyrdom was disregarded in the eighteenth century. An avowed aversion to martyrdom does not prevent its recuperation as sentimentalism. Doody elucidates the ways in which Richardson's Lovelace recreates the rape and desire of Dryden's tyrannical lovers, thereby drawing a lineage from baroque tragedy to the emerging novel.[55]

German religious authorities sensed that sentimental fiction was encroaching on their own terrain. The conservative Hamburg pastor Johann Melchior Goeze, for example, was outraged by how many readers of *The Sorrows of Young Werther* tended to treat the protagonist's suicide as a martyrdom.[56] The novel is saturated with allusions to the Gospel's account of Christ's passion even as it elaborates a pantheist worldview.[57] In Jakob Michael Reinhold Lenz's *Briefe über die Moralität der Leiden des jungen Werthers*

---

55. See Margaret Ann Doody's chapter on "Tyrannic Love and the Virgin Martyr" in her *A Natural Passion: A Study of the Novels of Samuel Richardson* (Oxford: Clarendon Press, 1974).

56. Johann Melchior Goeze, *Kurze aber nothwendige Erinnerungen über die Leiden des jungen Werthers* (Hamburg: Schröders Wittwer, 1775), 9.

57. For a close reading of the biblical references as they mix with Ossian and pantheism, see Herbert Schöffler, *Deutscher Geist im 18. Jahrhundert: Essays zur Geistes- und Religionsgeschichte*, 2nd ed. (Göttingen: Vandenhoeck & Ruprecht, 1967) 155–81.

(Letters on the morality of the sorrows of young Werther), itself one of the most intense glorifications of identificatory reading, Werther is characterized as a martyr with whom the reader strives to share every emotion.[58] The eighth letter states: "Werther is the image . . . of a crucified Prometheus whose example offers you a mirror with which to contemplate yourselves."[59] Rather than suffering for the sake of transcendence in the afterlife, Werther is seen as martyr for sensual love in the here and now. Goethe revived the image of the martyr on the last page of *Elective Affinities*, when Eduard is found dead and, despite his wife Charlotte's fears that he might have killed himself, is then buried in a chapel alongside his beloved Ottilie. His last lines in the novel made the comparison explicit: "I feel indeed . . . that there is a genius to everything, even to martyrdom."[60]

Reception theory in the 1970s sought to integrate pious edification and secular fiction by considering how the novel's discourse guided its reception. As book historians point out, sentimental novels increasingly took the place of edifying religious books in the late eighteenth century. While this shift did not require that the older modes of reading for religious edification be abandoned, in the secularized mode of the Enlightenment, identificatory reading was treated as a natural practice, rather than as an explicitly Christian one. Lenz's fifth letter on *Werther* points out that readers gladly mimic what they find in texts: "The human heart is inclined to imitate that which has moved it extraordinarily, as Cicero already recognized."[61] Lenz suggests further that Werther's virtues have much more in common with martyrdom than with Roman Stoics: "Sacrifice, self-denial, renunciation of the purest pleasures for the sake of a higher purpose."[62]

Another trait that sentimentalism acquired from earlier devotional works was the expectation that readers would visualize narrative scenes. Scholarship on *Werther* used to characterize identificatory

58. Klaus R. Scherpe, *Werther und Wertherwirkung, Zum Syndrom bürgerlicher Gesellschaftsordnung im 18. Jahrhundert* (Bad Homburg: Gehlein, 1970), 77.

59. Jakob Michael Reinhold Lenz, *Werke und Schriften*. Band 1 (Stuttgart: Gouverts 1966),1:396.

60. Goethe, *Die Wahlverwandschaften*, HA, 6:490.

61. Lenz, *Werke*, 1:388.

62. Lenz, *Werke*, 1:399.

readings of the novel as naïvely mistaken, though since at least the 1960s, such enthusiastic modes of literary apprehension have gained greater academic respect, as more than just the antithesis of autonomy aesthetics.[63] Despite his later efforts to distance himself from the *Werther* emulators, Goethe often wrote about author's need to provide an image through the text. In his notebook while traveling through Switzerland in 1797 he reflects that human nature has a fierce desire to give words to everything we see and that the desire to see with our own eyes what we have heard described is even greater. As universal as this statement sounds, he immediately situates these urges within his own era. The English and the Germans have in recent times been drawn particularly to this experience, he claims. They embrace any artist who sets a landscape before their eyes, who can make the protagonist of a novel or poem appear visibly in action. Just as welcome is the speaker or poet who can transport an audience through his description into a place, either by reviving memories or stirring up fantasies. Reverting again to the model of reading presented in *Werther*, Goethe concludes that readers are happy to wander through the landscape with book in hand.[64] Decades later he attributes this poetic ability to produce visions to Shakespeare, whom he characterizes as a poet to whom one listens, and who could transport readers into another world by giving words to what he saw within himself. Goethe isolated "inneres Anschauen," inner observation, as Shakespeare's particular genius. "The eye may be called the clearest of the senses, with which we can convey most readily. Yet the inner sense is even more clear and it succeeds in conveying meaning better and more quickly through the word. . . . Shakespeare speaks through this inner sense through which the imagination's world of pictures springs to life."[65] Goethe is again drawing from the ancient

---

63. For further analysis, see chapter 2 in my *The Tyranny of Elegance: Consumer Cosmopolitanism in the Era of Goethe* (Baltimore: Johns Hopkins University Press, 1997).

64. *Goethes Werke* (Weimar: Hermann Böhlaus Nachfolger, 1887–1919), 1.34:1, 354–55; henceforth referred to as WA. See also Karl S. Guthke, *Goethes Weimar und "Die große Öffnung in die weite Welt"* (Wiesbaden: Harrassowitz, 2001), 29–30.

65. Goethe, "Shakespeare und kein Ende," HA 12:288.

tradition of the memory arts by presuming that the artist possesses
a treasure chamber of images that evoke dramatic stories. Recollection and speaking both originate from the author's theatrical imagination, and if performed well, they produce the same internal
vision within the listener. Both author and audience indulge in
their own ability to produce inner visions.

As familiar as this characterization is to readers of sentimental
and Romantic literature, it shares many qualities with Ignatius
Loyola's sixteenth-century instructions. Kurt Weinberg suggests a
correlation between the two traditions: "Goethe's quite secular idea
of theatricality seems to owe . . . much to his childhood experiences
with Protestant Pietism. . . . [His] notion of theatricality emerges
from his remote Christian past as an *inneres Anschauen* . . . —the
urbane crystallization of religious meditation in the sense of Loyola's
Exercises, with the addition of the Illuminists' 'inner light.'"[66] The
eighteenth-century literature reader was more likely to waver ironically in and out of a text's diegesis, but for the sentimental being
absorbed by a narrative description remained an ideal.[67] Falling
into the illusion of being transported by travel literature was a desired effect, even for the most analytical. Carl Linnaeus, surely the
Enlightenment's most seasoned reader of travel reports, praised Peter Osbeck's *Voyage to China and the East Indies* for its ability to
conjure of the illusion of a foreign landscape's presence: "I seem
myself to have travelled with you, and to have examined every object you saw with my own eyes. If voyages were thus written, science might truly reap advantage from them."[68] Science writing, as
Linnaeus enjoyed it best, should adopt the narrative techniques of
devotional and adventure literature. The addition of illustrations
enhanced the illusion already provided by imagistic reading of the
text, as the philosopher John Locke suggests in his summary of Jan
Nieuhoff's account of his travels with the Dutch East India Com-

66. Kurt Weinberg, *The Figure of Faust in Valery and Goethe* (Princeton, NJ:
Princeton University Press, 1976), 223–24.
67. Michael Bell, *Sentimentalism, Ethics and the Culture of Feeling* (Basingstoke, Hampshire: Palgrave, 2000): 57–65.
68. Peter Osbeck, *A Voyage to China and the East Indies*, trans. John Reinhold Forster (London: Benjamin White, 1771), 2:128.

pany: "He leaves nothing worth relating untouched . . . from China all along the coast of India and Persia; so plainly representing all things observable or strange there, that with the help of his [wood] cuts we seem to be conversing with the people of those parts, to see all their towns and living creatures, and to be thoroughly acquainted with their habits, customs, and superstitions.[69] Both Locke and Linnaeus praised authors not only for their abilities to observe and take notes about Asia, but also for actualizing their impressions in the reader, thus combining scientific practice with literary effect by encouraging readers to construct their own images of distant places—a move enhanced by the Nieuhoff's tendency to draw Chinese cities from a vantage point along a body of water, in a manner very similar to Dutch cityscapes of the seventeenth century. Like many philosophers, Locke treated metaphors with suspicion, denouncing the beautiful deceit of figural language;[70] however, the readerly inclination to visualize a narrative scene seems to fall outside such hostility to the extent that it recreates an observation originally professed by the travel writer.

In positing similar reading practices from Loyola to Pietists to sentimentalism and the Enlightenment, we should not presume that these sects shunned each other. Max Weber already noted that Catholic and Calvinist exercises share similar aims and techniques in self-examination: "This absolute self-control, like the aim of the *êxercitia* of Saint Ignatius and the highest forms of all rational monastic virtues, was also the decisive practical ideal of Puritanism."[71] Such overlapping traits emerged out of the competition between confessions, with each studying the other as part of their long disputation. For the larger argument that Catholic strategies for fostering and managing a long-distance missionary operation while inspiring support from European congregations, it is important to point out that all sides kept track of each other: "Just as the Calvinists

---

69. John Locke, "A Catalogue and Character of most Books of Voyages and Travels," in *The Works of John Locke* (London: Thomas Davison, 1823), 10:557.

70. David Porter, *Ideographia: The Chinese Cipher in Early Modern Europe* (Stanford, CA: Stanford University Press, 2001), 25–26.

71. Max Weber, *The Protestant Ethic and the "Spirit" of Capitalism*, trans. Peter Baehr and Gordon Wells (New York: Penguin, 2002), 81.

are wont to quote the Catholic moral theologians, and not only Thomas Aquinas, Bernard of Clairvaux, or Bonaventura, but also contemporaries, so did the Catholic casuists regularly take note of the heretical ethic."[72] Maximilian Sandaeus was perhaps the most important Jesuit mediating between the medieval tradition and Pietism. Writing in Cologne, he identified and interpreted some 800 mystical terms in his *Pro theologia mystica Clavis* (The key to mystical theology, 1640), providing Pietists a frequently cited point of access to medieval mystical sources.[73] While Weber does not worry himself with readers' imagination or emotional expressions as they arose from the Catholic devotions, for eighteenth-century sentimentalism, medieval and Jesuit exercises were important not only because they taught practitioners to be attentive to their own internal states, but also because they intensified readers' emotional relationship to the text, inspired them to fill in details with their own reservoir of images, and provided a general model of devotional reading.

Halle Pietists were also well aware of the Jesuit's efforts in Asia, for they aspired to compete directly with them. They often framed their own missionary efforts in terms of the Jesuits who preceded them.[74] The first Pietist missionaries in Asia learned many of the same logistical and theological lessons that the Jesuits learned in China: that the long distance from Europe allowed missionaries to accommodate themselves and their teachings to their audience's culture. Eighteenth-century Pietists did not reach China, but they did found a very small mission in India. They lacked the logistical network that Catholic seafaring nations could provide, ye they were able to develop a working relationship with the Dutch East India Company. The first important Pietist mission in Asia was established 1706 in the small Tamil village of Tranquebar by Bartholomaeus

---

72. Weber, *Protestant Ethic*, 186.

73. Langen, *Der Wortschatz des deutschen Pietismus*, 402.

74. Hans-Jörg Hintze, "Christian Missionaries and their Perceptions of Hinduism: Intercultural Exchange," in *Halle and the Beginning of Protestant Christianity in India*, ed. Andreas Gross, Y. Vincent Kumaradoss, and Heike Liebau, (Halle: Verlag der Franckeschen Stiftungen, 2006), 2:885–902. See also the complaints of the fallen Jesuit, Maturin Veyssiere La Croze, *Abbildung des Indianischen Christenstaates*, trans. G. Chr. Bohnstedt (Leipzig: Samuel Benjamin Walther, 1739), 715.

Ziegenbalg (1682–1719) and Henry Plütschau (1677–1746) under the political authority of the Danish king Frederick IV (1671–1730), but with the spiritual and financial support of Halle.[75] The Tranquebar mission also received indirect influence from the British Society for Promoting Christian Knowledge and the Society for the Propagation of the Gospel in Foreign Parts. The mission remained small yet enthusiastic, with its members learning Tamil in order to approach the local population in their own idiom. Ziegenbalg commenced the task of translating the New Testament into Tamil. The preachers sent reports from India back to Halle, which after 1710 were published at regular intervals. These *Hallesche Berichte* (*Halle reports*) provided German readers a media avenue into India and an opportunity for intellectuals to comment upon and critique the India mission.[76] August Francke, the founder of the Pietist foundation in Halle, had been wary of Ziegenbalg's sympathetic portrayal of Hindu culture, allowing "only a select few of his most trusted allies full access" before prohibiting the publication of his two major works.[77]

Ziegenbalg is credited as having opened an ethnological dialogue on the sources for Hindu traditions that led him to set aside European stereotypes about so-called "heathens."[78] Gita Dharampal-Frick considers his writings to be an extraordinarily rich source for

75. Daniel Jeyaraj, "Mission Reports from South India and Their Impact on the Western Mind: The Tranquebar Mission of the Eighteenth Century," in *Converting Colonialism: Visions and Realities in Mission History, 1706–1914*, ed. Dana L. Robert (Grand Rapids, MI: William B. Eerdmans, 2008), 21–42. Hanco Jürgens, "On the Crossroads: Pietist, Orthodox and Enlightened Views on Mission in the Eighteenth Century," in *Halle and the Beginnings of Protestant Christianity in India*, ed. Andreas Gross, Y. Vincent Kumaradoss, and Heike Liebau (Halle: Verlag des Franckeschen Stiftungen, 2006), 1:7–36.

76. These reports were published intermittently from 1735 to 1772. The first volume: *Der Königlich Dänischen Missionarien aus Ost-Indien eingesandter Ausführlichen Berichten*, ed. Gotthilf August Francken (Halle: Waysen Hauses, 1735). A digitalization of the entire run is available at https://digital.francke-halle.de/fsdhm.

77. Anthony Gregg Roeber, *Hopes for Better Spouses: Protestant Marriage and Church Renewal in Early Modern Europe, India, and North America* (Grand Rapids, MI: William B. Eerdsmann, 2013), 199.

78. Monica Juneja, "'Malabarian' Dialogues: The Encounter between German Pietists and the Tamilian Populace during the Early Eighteenth Century," *Medieval History Journal* 5.2 (2002): 344.

the oral history of southern India.[79] Monica Juneja implicitly compares him with Jesuits in China by characterizing his writings as an
attempt to find "accommodation" between his beliefs and his observations.[80] Even as Ziegenbalg's writing from India was attempt-
ing to understand local beliefs, back in Germany, Francke made a
point of censoring the letters before they appeared in the *Hallesche
Berichte* because they highlighted the discrepancy between a dangerous ethnographic interest in Tamil culture and what leading Pietists thought European Christians should know about India.[81] The
ancient anxiety that all missions struggle to contain is the fear that
efforts to understand non-Christian culture will introduce heretical
ideas into the home country. In order to learn Tamil and to engage
the people he was intent on converting, Ziegenbalg opened an
interfaith dialogue by soliciting letters with Indians about their religious tenets. Traveling to Madras in early 1711, Ziegenbalg participated in religious disputations and gathered explanations from
Hindus on their faith. Between October and December 1711, he collected fifty-eight letters and later another forty-eight. These he
translated into German and then sent them with the originals on to
Halle for publication. Ziegenbalg followed a familiar Pietist form
when he engaged Hindus by asking them to write personal letters
about their faith. These were intended to be the kind of first-person
narratives that came to define eighteenth-century subjectivity in the
epistolary novel. Rather like Goethe's "Bekenntnisse einer schönen
Seele" (Confessions of a beautiful soul), Ziegenbalg solicited confessions of a Hindu soul. In writing about Brahmin learnedness, he
strikes a pose similar to Werther: "Oh, you Brahmans! you who instruct in many disciplines and carry on with so many books. When

---

79. Gita Dharampal-Frick, *Indien im Spiegel deutscher Quellen der Frühen
Neuzeit (1500–1750): Studien zu einer interkulturellen Konstellation* (Tübingen:
Niemeyer, 1994), 105–6.

80. Juneja, "'Malabarian' Dialogues, 345: "The missionary's deepening ethnological engagement with the sources of Hindu traditions led him to question
more openly European stereotypes by setting aside the language of Christian universalism in favour of alternative frameworks of 'civility' within which he sought
to accommodate his observations of the Tamilian socio-religious order."

81. Dharampal-Frick, *Indien im Spiegel*, 100.

you die, what use will these books be to you. If you would only know God and live according to this knowledge, then you would have life."[82]

Francke was decidedly unimpressed and did not wish to publish any personal Hindu confessions, but was obliged to respond to pressure from the Danish crown prince. In the end, for the work published under the title of *Malabarische Correspondenz* (Malabarian correspondences), he removed some letters and expunged the sections he felt were too critical of Christians in India. An English translation based on the original German translations also appeared shortly thereafter. It provides a more complete version of Ziegenbalg's views than the Halle publication. Sensing the danger that curious German readers might be attracted to Asian beliefs, Francke also refused to publish Ziegenbalg's longer treatises on the genealogy of the South Indian gods, stating: "The missionaries were sent out to exterminate heathenism in India, not spread the heathen nonsense all over Europe."[83] Although Ziegenbalg had originally been inspired by Lange to take up the call to India,[84] his written accounts of the place met with such disfavor that they were not published in their completed version until the nineteenth and twentieth centuries. He composed his *Genealogie der malabarischen Götter* (*Genealogy of the Malabarian Gods*) in 1713, but it did not appear in full until 1791.[85]

---

82. Quoted in Dharampal-Frick, *Indien im Spiegel*, 363.

83. Brijraj Singh, *The First Protestant Missionary to India: Bartholomaeus Ziegenbalg (1683–1719)* (Oxford: Oxford University Press, 1999), 78. Singh quotes Arno Lehmann, *Es began in Tranquebar: die Geschichte der ersten evangelischen Kirche in Indien* (Berlin: Evangelische Verlagsanstalt, 1956), 56. Lehmann in turn quotes a paraphrase of August Francke from the forward to the nineteenth-century publication of Ziegenbalg's treatise: *Genealogy of the Malabar Gods*, ed. Wilhelm Germann (Madras: Christian Knowledge Society Press, 1867), vii.

84. Ziegenbalg was a student at the gymnasium in Berlin Lange directed. See J. F. Fenger, *History of the Tranquebar Mission* (Tranquebar: Evangelical Lutheran Press, 1863), 19; Daniel Jeyaraj, *Genealogy of the South Indian Deities: An English Translation of Bartholomäus Ziegenbalg's Original German Manuscript with a Textual Analysis and Glossary* (London: RoutledgeCurzon, 2005), 10.

85. Modern scholars uniformly overstate the time lag to publication because they rely on Wilhelm Germann's incorrect claim in 1867 that Zeigenbalg's manuscript had lain in the archives for 150 years until he provided for its publication

His interest in Hindu beliefs as a form of natural theology would have drawn the attention of Goethe and the Romantics.[86] As a regular reader of the *Hallesche Berichte* from 1770 to 1830, Goethe kept up with Pietist missionary reports.[87] Zeigenbalg's opening line shows the sympathy he carried for the Indians he was sent to convert: "The Indians recognize God from the light of nature. This truth was not brought to them first by Christians, but rather witnessed in their souls through their conscience."[88] His acceptance of natural theology as an alternative to Christian preaching leads Ziegenbalg to recognize Hindus as bearers of a shared religious truth. The similarities between their respective teachings created for him an obvious emotional bond. As Francke correctly understood, Ziegenbalg's turn to natural theology was a threat to dogma, for he seemed willing to include thoughtful Hindus in his "invisible church of saints."

Pietist missionaries were yet another link between late eighteenth-century sentimentalism and Jesuit adaptations of medieval reading practices, thereby reinforcing the eighteenth-century ideas about a global union of sympathetic spirits. Without providing the many reports and translations the Jesuits produced in China, the first Pietists missionaries did replicate the lessons of accommodation in a smaller, less imperial Indian context.

(*Genealogy of the Malabar Gods*, x). Germann seems to be unaware of the 1791 edition, which is largely identical, and most scholars have continued to accept his claim to have rescued Zeigenbalg's work from the archive.

86. Ziegenbalg, *Beschreibung der Religion und heiligen Gebräuche der Malabarischen Hindous* (Berlin: Königl Preußischen akademischen Kunst und Buchhandlung, 1791).

87. Lehmann, *Es began in Tranquebar*, 47.

88. Both the 1791 and the 1867 edition include this opening.

NEWS OF THE MING
DYNASTY'S COLLAPSE

For Europeans far removed from the battlefields, the 1644 collapse and defeat of the Chinese empire was a major media event, and the sensation of reporting history as it unfolded "before our eyes" drew early modern audiences just as it does today. Wars generate demand for information. The 1527 sack of Rome by Spanish troops and Lutheran mercenaries became an immediate sensation attracting the attention of everyone who connected to the postal system. A century later, the Thirty Years' War pulled together an audience of focused news readers. Precisely because their ultimate outcomes were uncertain, battles in which cities were besieged and destroyed quickly turned into European events. One notorious example was the "blood marriage" of Magdeburg, in which the Protestant city, famous for its publishing industry, was surrounded and destroyed during a Catholic army's siege. The catastrophe produced a two-sided media storm: Catholic and Protestant images and explanations circulated within a week of the city's ruin.[1] The military destruction of civilizations beyond Europe also provided spectacular images for the printing press and the baroque stage. The Black Legend of Spanish cruelty in the devastation of the New World's great kingdoms attracted as much interest from the Protestant media as Jesuit reports about the Manchu invasion of imperial China.

After decades of extreme religious warfare, sixteenth-century news reports were well prepared to ascribe familiar labels—barbaric deed, divine punishment, or horrifying tragedy—to the military defeat of foreign nations and the violent destruction of great cities. With the first images of Asian martyrs, Europeans depicted recent converts who died torturously because they refused to bend to the pagan will of a tyrannical ruler demanding they recant. Reports from Japan included such stories along with the more familiar figures of missionaries killed gruesomely. When the Manchu invasion of imperial China was reported in Europe, the clear demarcations that defined a Christian martyr were expanded, as historians and travelers described the drawn-out sieges in southern China during which the last Ming resistance was overwhelmed. Jan Nieuhof wrote his travel account having read earlier Jesuit histories, but he included his own personal conversations with Chinese victims of the wars to present an image of the Manchus as invading barbarians, capable of any cruelty against the genteel, civilized Chinese in the south.[2]

There is of course a great difference between propaganda against a neighboring enemy and graphic descriptions of distant warfare between unfamiliar combatants. News of Spanish atrocities in the Americas was immediately important to Protestants in northern Europe, but what of Asian wars in which all the combatants were unfamiliar? How can an unknown, yet powerful foreign ruler along with his people become figures of empathy? At least since Tacitus,

1. Hans Medick and Pamela Selwyn, "Historical Event and Contemporary Experience: The Capture and Destruction of Magdeburg in 1631," *History Workshop Journal* 52 (Autumn 2001): 23–48.

2. Johan Neuhof, *Die Gesantschaft der Ost-Indischen Gesellschaft in den Vereinigten Niederländern and den Taryarischen Cham/und nunmehr auch Sinischen-Keyser/ Verrichtet durchdie Herren Peter de Gojern und Jacob Keisern* (Amsterdam: Jacob Mörs, 1669).

Western writing has always had a minor tradition that sought to elevate people living outside its boundaries as noble, praising the foreigner for possessing virtues that one's own civilization has lost. This chiasmic argument operates most effectively when a powerful civilization is confronted with people over whom they still feel superior. The gesture of a self-ascribed civilized writer identifying with barbarians implies a temporality of growth, wherein the foreigner's present corresponds to the writer's past. How could Europeans care about the fate of foreigners from whom they had no immediate military threat, either because they were far removed or because, as in the case of colonial conquest, they were so clearly overpowered that they did not pose a threat. How did admiration for the enemy mingle with pity? These questions appear of course in Homer, where similarities between the Achaeans and the Trojans imply an admiration for one's enemies—a parity that extends from the battlefield to the moment when Priam appears as a supplicant before Achilles in order to beg for Hector's corpse. While classical examples figured prominently within Christian Europe as its missionaries and merchants encountered nations far removed from its borders, the outpouring of sentiments for foreigners during the early modern period was much more complex that the ancient admiration between warriors.

The Homeric tradition of conquest both acknowledges and denies respect to the foreigner has had a long life, reaching well into modernism, so that in *To the Lighthouse* when Virginia Woolf describes Mr. Carmichael who lies awake, keeping his candle lit longer than the others, while reading Virgil, she could be confident that her readers would readily perceive how classical literature reinforced British colonialism. Still, for all its persistence, the model of the Trojan War and its aftereffects cannot explain all instances of confrontation and empathy for the foreign. How did Europeans learn to identify with nations that were already extremely sophisticated? The emotional investment in distant peoples often ran through an identification with its leading citizens, so that in the case of China, Confucius and the emperor were treated as representative of a coherent civilization. Jesuits and early Enlightenment thinkers could assert analogies by setting the image of Confucius in relation to Socrates,

Mohammad, or Christ. If more contemporary and less abstract comparisons were required, then the reigning Chinese emperor functioned as a handy representative, at least until the eighteenth century.

In the two and a half centuries under discussion in this book, we can see a transition in rhetorical and theatrical modes of sympathy as the humble citizen slowly begins to share the tragic stage with the monarch. European attitudes toward China follow the wider changes in how tragic drama was received by its audience. Walter Benjamin was not alone in pointing out that for seventeenth-century drama, the monarch was "the principle exponent of history," almost serving as its incarnation,[3] yet in the eighteenth century this concentration on one representative person was augmented by stories about more humble figures. When Peter Szondi argues that bourgeois tragedy emerges in the eighteenth century, he cites George Lillo's dedication of *The London Merchant*, wherein it is argued that there is no loss of dignity in accounting for the generality of mankind rather than just the misfortunes of princes.[4] Compassion and pity need no longer be attached only to the representative sufferings of monarchs or martyrs. Lillo proposes to "enlarge the province of the graver kind of poetry" so as to include "moral tales in private life."[5] It would take another century before this geographical imagination expanded so far that the private life of Chinese families would seem comparable with those known in Europe.

How could relations be established between societies without relying solely on the conventions of diplomacy between monarchs? How did information networks facilitate emotional connections to distant cultures? Long-distance trade with its not so veiled threat of military violence had of course always provided an avenue of exchange, but in the eyes of intellectuals it was only a first, albeit necessary, stage toward establishing a moral, religious, philosophical intimacy. Liberalism, from Adam Smith to Ferdinand Braudel,

---

3. Walter Benjamin, *The Origin of German Tragic Drama*, trans. John Osborne (London: Verso, 1985), 62.

4. Peter Szondi, *Die Theorie des bürgerlichen Trauerspiels im 18. Jahrhundert* (Frankfurt: Suhrkamp, 1973), 1:24.

5. George Lillo, "The London Merchant," *Eighteenth-Century Plays*, ed. Ricardo Quintana (New York: Modern Library, 1952), 288.

celebrated the peace-bringing influence of mercantile trade. Even Immanuel Kant's cosmopolitanism was predicated upon nations recognizing the economic benefits of cooperation over conquest.

In this chapter, I consider how the ancient links that trade and war established between foreigners were supplemented by compassion, pity, and identification. My broad thesis is that secular twenty-first-century appeals for affluent readers and viewers to extend humanitarian relief and aid to distant sufferers have an origin in the religious theater of early modern Europe, specifically in dramas depicting the suffering and triumph of non-European converts to Christianity at the hands of cruel pagans.[6] These early depictions of merciless rulers slaughtering innocents became a source for later nineteenth-century images of the Asiatic despotism. While we will discuss seventeenth-century Christian plays as the wellspring for this pervasive colonial stereotype, the tyrant's victim is the more influential figure in this genealogy: the suffering stranger deserving of the audience's admiration and investment, emotional and financial, continues to pervade appeals for solidarity across cultural divides, while the figure of the merciless dictator has been cast in monochrome. Starting at this obscure religious source—a genre that cosmopolitans would almost certainly dismiss as far removed from our postcolonial present—I consider how distant rulers and peoples, in Asia and elsewhere, became the object of European sympathy during the seventeenth and eighteenth centuries. My analysis focuses on how the staging of performances in religious and secular theater directed the emotional connection of European spectators to foreigners. This required a shift of feelings from their own to the other, from the sailors and priests who traveled out from Europe to the people they encountered.

I begin my argument with the raw spectacle of seventeenth-century martyr dramas, which provide a graphic, turbulent, and unstable supplement to the ancient rules of trade and war. In the process, I trace a shift from the first martyr dramas about Asia, which depicted

---

6. For a genre-specific analysis of the complexities inherent to secularization, see Elida Maria Szarota, *Künstler, Grübler und Rebellen, Studien zum europäischen Märtyrdrma des 17. Jahrhunderts* (Bern: Francke, 1967).

Christians suffering at the hands of pagan rulers, to portrayals that presented these rulers as martyrs themselves, suffering stoically at the hands of cruel invaders, often Europeans themselves. If, as Eric Hayot has argued, the Chinese are depicted in the twentieth century as enduring misery almost without feeling, this stereotype can be traced back to the stoicism performed in martyr plays.[7] For as theater conventions changed in the first half of the eighteenth century so as to allow ordinary individuals to become the objects of tragic drama, so too did the cosmopolitan structure of feeling shift so as to empathize with foreign peoples generally, and not just their rulers. By the time Christoph Wieland, Adam Smith, and Goethe cast their thoughts towards Asia, this ability to feel the condition of foreign peoples had, for better or worse, become a prerequisite for Enlightenment cosmopolitanism.

Within the context of Jesuit strategies, martyrdom and accommodation would seem to stand in opposition to one another, for the respectful adoption of Chinese culture by missionaries is readily seen today as an ideal of intercultural relations, whereas martyr dramas staged in public squares made little attempt to understand the foreign. Japan was depicted as the devil's kingdom, filled with hostile idol worshippers, who tortured Christian converts mercilessly. While one might argue that the Jesuit priest's disciplined striving to integrate into Chinese learned society was itself a form of renunciation and martyrdom, this would too easily reduce all Christianity to a single ascetic model. There is more nuance in not pursuing genealogy down to its most common denominator, but stopping instead at the level of media representations to acknowledge the contradiction between the Jesuit effort to interpret Chinese philosophy so that it sounded compatible with Christian cosmology and the more popular appeals to support the mission in Asia by depicting priests as combating idolatry. Peter Burschel distinguishes between different modes of martyrdom by insisting that the Jesuits staged martyrs as heroic figures rather than as passive recipients of

---

7. Eric Hayot, *The Hypothetical Mandarin: Sympathy, Modernity, and Chinese Pain* (Oxford: Oxford University Press, 2009), 14–16.

pain. The suffering of Asian martyrs stood in defiance of the pressure to renounce their Christianity according to this basic formula: the higher the pain, the greater the faith. If one studies the existing scripts of Jesuit school dramas, it becomes clear that they were not so concerned with maintaining Stoic indifference to suffering, as in showing Asian Catholic martyrs to be suffering actively as heroic figures opposing idolatrous attempts to suppress their faith.[8] James Parente also differentiates between Catholic and Protestant conceptions of martyrdom, with Catholics being interested in mobilizing of classical virtues for ecclesiastical ends. All martyr dramas are not alike. For example, Gryphius's *Catharina von Georgien* was written to counter the Catholic celebration of valiant action for the sake of the church. The Protestant martyr was not an extraordinary person of limitless courage, but rather a fallen sinner constrained by circumstance to die for faith.[9]

Historians who follow Jesuit representations of Confucian culture from Matteo Ricci up to Du Halde, find a remarkably consistent lineage, one that was thrown off its trajectory only at the end of the seventeenth century as it tried to adapt to the Rites Controversy with a new allegorical interpretation of Confucianism known as Figuralism. These intellectual histories of the Jesuit mission focus on annual reports and treatises published in Latin, along with letters, notebooks, and other material secured in Roman archives. When we take a broader view to consider first how the Catholic laity and then how the republic of letters, curious merchants, or worldly courtiers received news from China, a much more complex and at times sporadic distribution of news appears. Jesuit reports from China were carefully divided between those that advocated accommodation and those that presented the missionaries as combating heresy. In its most intense form, the struggle against heresy resulted in the martyrdom of missionaries and Christian converts. Jesuit reports sent two sets of messages—accommodation and martyrdom—two positions not

8. Peter Burschel, *Sterben und Unsterblichkeit. Zur Kultur des Martyiums in der frühen Neuzeit* (Munich: Oldenbourg, 2004), 281.

9. James Parente, *Religious Drama and the Humanist Tradition: Christian Theater in Germany and in the Netherlands, 1500–1680* (Leiden: Brill, 1987), 188.

easily reconciled with each other. Scholars today separate them by distinguishing between the Jesuit positions on Confucianism (accommodation) versus Buddhism (heresy). To the seventeenth-century European, however, these nuances were not at all obvious.

In addition to their two distinct agendas for the China mission—accommodation for princes, clerics, and scholars, conversion and martyrdom for the wider laity—Jesuits tried to control the type of information distributed in Europe and the audiences who were allowed access. While Catholic churchgoers were drawn into the China mission through sermons and prayers, the Protestant North often scrounged for new information about China. Scholars such as Leibniz or Jacobus Golius were willing to undertake the most unusual social maneuvers to gain just a little more access to Jesuit sources on China. For readers who were eager to learn more about China but who stood outside Jesuit circles, news from China came and went without consistency nor with any of the systematic organization that the Enlightenment would demand of any discipline that called itself a science.

Once information about China did begin circulating within European discourses, these bits were incorporated, or folded, into all other forms of knowledge, so that "China" did not constitute its own field of study. Instead information about East Asia was woven into larger collections of interesting facts about the world. Baroque compilations arranged stories and events according to the author's grand and arbitrary intentions. Chinese figures thus could appear in sermons, operas, histories, paintings, festivals, dinner plates, theological treatises, and sailor's tales without any sense that they were being misappropriated from an authentic origin.

Martyrdom was not just a Christian value. During the late Ming dynasty, the Christian martyr tradition could be seen to intersect with Chinese veneration for virtuous literati who had maintained Confucian principles in the face of unjust, cruel executions. The history of the 1402 Yongle usurpation in the early stages of the Ming dynasty, when an uncle overthrew his legitimate nephew to assume the imperial mantle while executing many who opposed him, provided many examples of cruelly murdered and heroic individuals, who eventually received rehabilitation and respect two centuries later.[10] Perhaps the most famous of these was Fang Xiaoru, a court official who refused to proclaim the ascent of the Yongle emperor and was therefore publicly sliced in half at the waist before a Nanjing gate, with 870 of his followers and clan members also being put to death. Western scholars readily use the term "martyr" to describe such historical figures, suggesting an easy coordination between the Chinese and Christian traditions that might require closer examination.[11] The term is used broadly today, but in the seventeenth century there might have been considerable disagreement about who deserved the appellation. Jesuits would probably have applied the term to persons whom local mandarins would have considered undeserving of the honorific. Nevertheless, both sides would have understood the sentiment of the Hanlin academician Huang Zuo, when he commemorated the victims of the Yongle usurpations as "righteous deaths of our predecessors. . . . Their great virtue radiates just as the sun and moon shine"[12] Baroque readers would likewise have understood the late Ming fascination with the gory deaths of their virtuous predecessors.[13]

Reflecting the bifurcated message of the Jesuit mission in China, scholars working on Catholic accommodation with Confucianism do not pay sufficient attention to the importance martyr stories held in the mission's own self-representation within Europe. The split between the mission's methods in China as opposed to within Europe means that it even today it is difficult to define accommodation solely as a respectful engagement with Confucianism. Early modern Catholics believed that martyrdom at the hands of violent pagans exemplified a missionary's highest achievement.[14] To die as a

---

10. Maria Franca Sibau, *Reading for the Moral: Exemplarity and the Confucian Moral Imagination in Seventeenth-Century Chinese Short Fiction* (Albany: State University of New York Press, 2018), 85–95.

11. Nicolas Standaert, *Yang Tingyuan, Confucian and Christian in late Ming China* (Leiden: Brill, 1988) 15.

12. Peter Ditmanson "Venerating the Martyrs of the 1402 Usurpation: History and Memory in the Mid and Late Ming Dynasty," *T'oung Pao* 93.1 /3(2007): 142.

13. Ditmanson, "Venerating the Martyrs," 146.

14. A recent, superb exception is Adrian Hsia and Ruprecht Wimmer, eds., *Mission und Theater, Japan und China auf den Bühnen der Gesellschaft Jesu* (Regensburg: Schnell and Steiner, 2005).

sign of your faith was literally the ultimate test for a believer, and Jesuit histories insisted that in dying at the hands of cruel pagans, Catholic martyrs were assuring the ultimate victory of their faith. Peter Burschel argues that frescos of martyrs—often prominently displayed in seminaries—offered an image-oriented meditation in which the faithful took up Christ's crucifixion and the martyrdom of his followers in order to immerse themselves in the representation of the passion and to prepare themselves for a comparable fate.[15] In an implicit comparison with eighteenth-century critiques of excessive reading practices, Burschel writes about the seventeenth-century "euphoria" if not "hysteria" for martyrdom.[16] Even without adopting later psychological terms, we can recognize the intense desire that missionary reports about Asian martyrs stirred up.[17]

As part of its Trentine reforms, the church fostered the veneration of saints. Large compilations of their lives were published. Pope Gregory XIII (1572–1585) commissioned a catalogue of all the martyrs since the earliest records of the church, entitled *Martyrologium Romanum*, editions of which were published in 1597 and 1613 in Antwerp.[18] From 1570 onwards poems recounting the stories of martyrs appeared in large numbers. Japanese killings of Christians were particularly important in the 1620s.[19] Modern scholarship on accommodation has avoided the literature celebrat-

---

15. Peter Burschel, *Sterben und Unsterblichkeit. Zur Kultur des Martyiums in der frühen Neuzeit* (Munich: Oldenbourg, 2004), 256.

16. Burschel, *Sterben und Unsterblichkeit*, 252.

17. "Undoubtedly, the biggest influence on the decision to apply for missions in the Far East were the reports of the Jesuits in the region. In the first half of the seventeenth century, books and brochures describing foreign peoples and their customs, emphasizing the important, difficult, and even martyr-making work of the missionaries in Asia and the New World were published by the Society of Jesus every year" (Monika Miazek-Mecynska, "Polish Jesuits and Their Dreams about Missions in China, According to the *Litterae indipetae*," *Journal of Jesuit Studies* 5.3 [2018]: 408–9). Miazek-Mecynska suggests that most applications to serve in the East Asian missions that directly mentioned the readiness to become a martyr were not accepted (413).

18. Willibald Sauerländer, *The Catholic Rubens, Saints and Martyrs*, trans. David Dollenmayer (Los Angeles: Getty Research Institute, 2014), 78.

19. Henry Ettinghausen, *How the Press Began: The Pre-Periodical Printed News in Early Modern Europe* (Coruña: Janus, 2015), 129–30.

ing martyrdom probably because it does not correspond to a cosmopolitan view of Ricci's accommodation strategy. From within the martyr drama's framework of the loyal Christian's steadfastly refusing to abandon his or her own faith by bowing down before pagan idols, it would be difficult to explain the accommodationist willingness to acquiesce to make offerings to images of ancestors and Confucius. How could Catholics admire martyrs for resisting pagan gods while accepting ancestor rituals within the church liturgy? Chinese and Japanese martyrs stood halfway between European piety and Asian culture. As the dramas developed in the seventeenth century these oppositions softened so that eventually even the foreign monarch became a martyr rather than an oppressor, a figure of sympathy rather than dread, a victim rather than a tyrant—a shift that made it more plausible for the Enlightenment to represent non-Christian foreigners as objects of empathy without having to rely on dogmatic theological distinctions.

How did the Chinese emperor become a martyr? The 1644 Manchu conquest of the Ming dynasty was recognized immediately as a cataclysmic shift that sharply altered the European attitude toward Chinese emperors. Nicola Cosma points out that Jesuit missionaries instantly perceived it as an "epochal transformative 'revolution,'" that it was the most important event not just in Chinese, but in world history.[20] With that cataclysm, the last Ming emperor took on, in the eyes of some European observers, the qualities of a baroque tragic figure. The European perception of the Manchu invasion opened the possibility that China was undergoing convulsive wars similar to the sectarian conflicts of Europe. News from the wars was provided first by Martino Martini's *De Bello Tartarico Historia* (History of the Tartar war, 1655) and then reiterated in dramas such as Joost van den Vondel's *Zungchin* (1667) and Elkanah Settle's *The Conquest of China by the Tartars* (1676).

Martini and his pious readers interpreted the end of the Ming dynasty in terms of its consequences for the spread Christianity. In this light, the figure of the Chinese emperor killing his daughter and

---

20. Nicola di Cosmo, "The Manchu Conquest in World Historical Perspective: A Note on Trade and Silver," *Journal of Central Eurasian Studies* 1 (2009): 58.

then himself was transformed into a stoic patriarch worthy of empathy and admiration. Far away Europeans could recognize the tragic resonance of the Ming defeat and the devastation that would ensue. This echo on the European stage suggests an interconnectedness that was mediated by the Jesuits but whose wider implications were recognized by missionaries as well as by worldly Europeans. Even if writers made vague references to a chain of military invasions that could lead from the Manchu victory in China to Europe, the actual mediation ran along different lines: through the sea vessel carrying Martino Martini and then the rapid European dispersion of his book. The reverberations running from north of the Great Wall to Amsterdam were transported by ships and printing presses. Martino Martini's history of the Tartar war, which replaced the oral stories of the returned seafarer with a text written while sailing from China, found an eager audience. These technologies—sailing and printing—moved more rapidly and reached more people than Marco Polo's manuscript. From their first encounters, Portuguese captains confirmed Polo's image of China as a massive and powerful kingdom, far too large for Europeans to conquer. Before the destruction of the fleet sent against England, Spanish officials in the Philippines had briefly considered sending an armada to conquer China, an idea that never materialized presumably because it seemed implausible. Thus, when the Chinese empire was suddenly overwhelmed by invaders this seemed to portend divine intervention and punishment—the kingdom too grand for Spain or Portugal to conquer was now overrun by barbarians.

Martino Martini was born in Trent within the province of Tirol, the city famous as a mediating point between German and Roman princes and cardinals. His family were merchants living in the German side of the city. The Jesuits opened a school in Trent when Martini was eleven, and he soon began to receive the classical education in humanism and scholasticism for which the Jesuits were known. At eighteen, he began studying in Rome in order to prepare himself for his calling as a missionary. Like others before him, he studied first rhetoric under the mantle of Cicero and then philosophy in the form of a Thomist scholastic understanding of Aristotle. Athanasius Kircher, the German polymath who published *China Illustrata* among other works, was an important professor for Martini at the Collegio Romano, and the two corresponded after Martini had left for the Indies. In 1638, Martini traveled to Lisbon, where he prepared himself further for his mission by studying Portuguese and theology. His movements have long fascinated historians because they display the European rivalries between maritime nations as well as the affinities between scholars.[21] He was just twenty-six when he sailed from Lisbon in 1640, eventually arriving in Macao in 1642, where he studied Chinese for another year before walking to Nanjing just as the Manchu invasion broke in from the north during the winter 1643–1644. Judging from his biography, Martini studied the history of the Jesuit mission, yet he never became one of the important figures at the court. Instead he preached initially in Hangzhou, where his grave lies. In 1650, he was called to Beijing, where he met Adam Schall along with the other Jesuits at the new dynastic court. Martini was sent in 1651 to answer to the Rites Controversy back to Europe. On the journey, he was taken captive by the Dutch as he passed the Philippines, from whence he was taken to Batavia. While languishing there, Martini provided the governor-general and the council of the Dutch East India Company with information about the commercial and political conditions in China.[22] On February 1, 1653, he sailed to Europe, where his ship avoided the channel, presumably because of the war between the Dutch and the English, passed north of England, and landed at Bergen in Norway on August 31, 1653. From there Martini traveled via Hamburg to Amsterdam, where his *Atlas* was published by the famous printer Joan Blaeu.[23] In June 1654, Martini left for Antwerp and Brussels, meeting Jacobus Golius of Leiden (1596–1667),

---

21.   David Mungello, *Curious Land: Jesuit Accommodation and the Origins of Sinology* (Honolulu: University of Hawaii Press, 1989), 106–10.

22.   Karel Davids, "Dutch and Spanish Global Networks of Knowledge in the Early Modern Period: Structures, Changes and Limitations," paper presented at the International Workshop on Iberian-Netherlandish Knowledge Exchanges, Barcelona, Institut d'Estudis Catalans, November 27–28, 2009, 10.

23.   Willem Janszoon Blaeu, Joan Blaeu, Martino Martini, and Jacobus Golius, eds., *Novus Atlas, Das ist, Weltbeschreibung: Mit schönen newen außführlichen Land-Taffeln in Kupffer gestochen, vnd an den Tag gegeben*, vol. 6, *Novus Atlas Sinensis Das ist ausfuhrliche Beschreibung des grossen Reichs Sina* (Amsterdam, 1655), http://digi.ub.uni-heidelberg.de/diglit/blaeu1655bd6.

who had just been appointed professor of Arabic, along the way. Pressed for time, the two scholars met on Martini's barge as it passed Leiden and later continued their conversation at the Burgermeister's estate in Antwerp. The exchange was quite important for Golius, given that Martini was one of the very few people in Europe who knew the Chinese language. In the manner typical for early modern scholars, Martini is presumed to have presented Golius with his first Chinese volumes.[24] The example of these two scholars going to great lengths to meet for a short time is often cited as an example of how the republic of letters was not constrained by religious or political differences.[25] Furthermore, it reiterates that scholars interact on many levels, not only in the form of publications or even correspondence, and that certain activities—such as answering questions about a foreign language or interpreting a text—can be carried out more swiftly in person.

Martini arrived in Rome 1655 on his primary mission to convince the Vatican to reverse its 1645 decision forbidding Christians from bowing and lying prostrate before images of ancestors and Confucius.[26] During his journey through Europe meeting church officials, scholars, and Catholic princes, Martini sought to build public support for the Jesuit mission and its approach to elite Chinese society. Martini must have been a persuasive conversationalist and narrator, and his books, both the popular history and his more specialized reports, extended the range of his influence. His skill in speaking about the divine purpose of the Jesuit mission was elaborated in his writing. Knowledge of China was never removed from his religious preaching, and Martini's writing carries on where his voice or the memory of his listeners falters.[27] His justification for writing a history of China reflects the larger question missionaries

24. J. J. L. Duyvendak, "Early Chinese Studies in Holland," *T'oung Pao* 32.1 (1936): 293–344.

25. Davids, "Dutch and Spanish Global Networks," 10.

26. Franco Demarchi, "Martino Martini und die Chinamission der Jesuiten im 17. Jahrhundert," in *Martini Martini (1614–1661) und die Chinamission im 17. Jahrhundert*, ed. Roman Malek and Arnold Zingerle (Sankt Augustin: Institut Monumenta Sinica, 2000), 25–49.

27. Ulrich Johannes Schneider, "Der Aufbau der Wissenswelt. Eine phäno-typische Beschreibung enzyklopädischer Literatur," in *Kulturen des Wissens im 18. Jahrhunderts*, ed. Ulrich Johannes Schneider (Berlin: De Gruyter, 2008), 94.

faced in replacing preaching—the preferred mode of addressing the laity—through written, that is, printed, works. China had long possessed a print culture used by its administrative elite, and Europe was developing one quickly. Jesuits such as Matteo Ricci and Martini were consciously augmenting their spoken performances with printed works that distributed an ideal representation of the original rhetorical event to a wider readership.

The scene of writing was important in establishing the author's legitimate voice. Judging by the preface to *Bello Tartarico*, the ocean voyage from China back to Europe weighed on Martini as he composed the book, giving readers the impression that they were receiving a traveler's tale just as he had landed. The immediacy of an adventurer's return to Europe lends credibility to Martini's narrative.[28] He describes his voyage in detail, not only where he went and under whose control, but also the hazards of sea travel—such as being becalmed for twenty days and the the sailors being in an uproar. The more he focuses on logistics, the more he establishes his own authority to deliver the latest information from China. Indeed, he cements the image of the homeward-bound missionary as the embodiment of Asian knowledge—a trope Christian Hagdorn would use soon in *Aeyquan, oder der Große Mogol* (Aeyquan, or the great Mogul, 1670). Even the experience of arriving in Europe serves to justify his book. Martini explains that he is writing his history because people of all ranks surrounded him on his journey through European cities asking about China. While acknowledging the need to distribute information widely and calmly, he underscores the textual sources for his own representation of history, thereby reiterating the standard of scholarly legitimacy that the Jesuits long used to distinguish their treatises from less learned travelers'

---

28. The Jesuits also called attention to the great distance they had traveled across the ocean in their Chinese works, as Matteo Ricci does in his *Treatise on Friendship*: "I, [Ma]dou [Matteo], navigated to the Middle Kingdom by sea from the Far West because of my reverence for the good government of the Son of Heaven of the Great Ming Dynasty and the teaching of ancient Chinese rulers" (quoted and translated in Dongfeng Xu, "The Concept of Friendship and the Culture of Hospitality: The Encounter Between the Jesuits and Late Ming China," PhD diss., University of Chicago, 2011, 108).

accounts. In justifying the need to write, he cites the unreliability of oral tales: it is not always possible to relate events in a calm, detached tone; future generations will hardly benefit from these spoken accounts; and he recognizes that has not been able to reach all the people curious to know about China. Martini explains that he began researching the events recounted in the book once he had been ordered to return to Rome in 1651. Here Martini emphasizes the importance of written sources: on the one hand, annual publications (*Jahrschriften* in the German), maps of the empire and its provinces, and ancient books (*uhr-alte Bücher*), which he read with great care in order to learn Chinese history from the time of Noah's flood onwards.[29] Martini presents his ability to read these texts as being based on having lived in country for ten years and having long collected books. The historian may not been an eyewitness to all that he related, but he was capable of reading the official bulletins and gazettes that circulated among the imperial magistrates. Because he was tapped into this official network, rather than because he was close to the scene, Martini could claim a certainty of knowledge that was far less mediated than most Western reports. Without question, Martini's hierarchy of research and its codification were fully convincing to early modern scholars, and it continues to appeal to academics. In addition to the fact that Martini's text is based both on first-hand experience in the country and bookish investigations, it also remains consistent with earlier Jesuit scholars writing on China. In the German and Latin editions, Martini sees himself as fulfilling a promise made by Trigault in 1615 to inform Europeans about the chronology given in Chinese annuals.[30] The English edition calls attention on its title page to Martini having been in China as the events unfolded, but, aside from the promise of more maps to be published in his *Atlas*, it leaves out any complex narration establishing Martini's sources.[31]

---

29. Martino Martini, "Vorrede An den günstigen Leser," in *Historische Beschreibung deß Tartarischen Kriegs in Sina* (Munich: Lucas Straub, 1654), n.p.

30. Martini, "An den Leser," n.p.

31. Martin Martinius, *Bellum Tartaricum, or the Conquest of the Great and Most Renowned Empire of China, by the Invasion of the Tartars* (London: John Crook, 1654).

Martini's rich narrative of political change in China could be understood as an early attempt at global history, and its reception in Europe indicates that this idea was understood at least implicitly, at first through biblical chronology, but then as an effort to interpret history as it was recounted by others, most notably in terms of Chinese chronology and its incompatibility with biblical dating. Martini was very concerned to present both the ancient Chinese chronology and the immediate history of the invasion. One concern of global history for the early modern period was measuring the age of the earth and human civilization; the two were still interconnected so that dating one would explain the other. A second priority of global historiography for Martini was establishing points of connection between distant events. Martini's narrative interprets Chinese events in Christian terms, but it also lays out political analogies and generalizations that operate independent of religious affiliation. The comparison between the Manchu conquest and Europe's sectarian wars required a strict theological distinction between divine and earthly power. Trained in a humanist approach to historical narration that leans more toward Thucydides than the Old Testament, Martini provided a mostly political assessment of Chinese wars.

Only at certain key moments does he briefly and self-consciously interrupt his history to ponder the role of divine will in shaping historical events. He suggests that the Ming dynasty fell because God was punishing it for having persecuted Christians. This interlude in the otherwise secular history shows that Martini was still very much the missionary priest. These references to divine will seem to the modern reader as mere minor moments in the overall history, yet they are a telling nod to the audience. In this instance, Martini's discourse takes up the eschatology of a martyr play. In preparing Martini's history for the stage, the Dutch dramatist Joost van den Vondel would later expand this pious perspective by inserting an entire chorus of Jesuits commenting on the imperial drama. Similar gestures appear in the work of Nicolas Trigault, Martini's predecessor. While relaying a history of the early Christian mission in Japan, Trigault also steps out of his role as humanist historian at key moments. After having related the story of Titus, an early convert, Trigault states that the Japanese Christian deserved more praise than he was allowed to give as an historian; indeed he compared Titus to Abraham and Job. To strengthen the point, Trigault describes the fate of Titus expressly as a "tragicomedy" which he does not have space to narrate in full.[32] These nods were well understood in Europe. Not long after Trigault's book was published, Jesuit schools started putting on plays depicting the suffering and eventual triumph of Titus and his family. Some of the brochures for these plays also allude to Titus's similarity with Abraham and Job.[33] In Germany, versions of Trigault's initial report were performed as early as 1629 in Augsburg and as late as 1768 in Ingolstadt.[34] Stories of Titus and other East Asian martyrs circulated through many church publications in the seventeenth century, allowing them to be adapted and augmented with new scenes and characters. Masahiro Takenaka compares English, Irish, and German sources to show how the play became more complex with an increasing number of allegorical figures over time, even as the core plot remained constant.[35]

Martini's history found an audience in Europe because he had written a compelling recital of a dynastic upheaval, independent of his theological views. His success was such that he received challenges from the Jesuit mission's most persistent Dominican critic, Domingo Navarrette, who wrote a series of critical notes on Martini's history.[36] In Martini's history and later more so in Vondel's play, the last Ming emperor becomes a figure of sympathy, partially because

32. Nicolao Trigault, *De Christianis apud Iaponios Triumphis* (Munich: Sadeler, 1623), 228.

33. Ruprecht Wimmer, "Japan und China auf den Jesuitenbühnen des deutschen Sprachgebietes," in *Mission und Theater: Japan und China auf den Bühnen der Gesellschaft Jesu*, ed. Adrian Hsia and Ruprecht Wimmer (Regensburg: Schnell and Steiner, 2005), 22.

34. For an English translation of Latin manuscript for performances in Freising between 1736 and 1743, see Charles Burnett, "The Freising Titus Play," in *Mission und Theater: Japan und China auf den Bühnen der Gesellschaft Jesu*, ed. Adrian Hsia and Ruprecht Wimmer (Regensburg: Schnell and Steiner, 2005), 413–67.

35. Masahiro Takenaka, "Jesuit Plays on Japan in the Baroque Era," in *Mission und Theater: Japan und China auf den Bühnen der Gesellschaft Jesu*, ed. Adrian Hsia and Ruprecht Wimmer (Regensburg: Schnell and Steiner, 2005): 379–410.

36. Dominick Fernandez Navarete, "Notes upon F. Martin Martinez His Treatise de Bello Tartarico," in *An Account of the Empire of China, Historical, Political, Moral and Religious* (London: Lintot, 1732), book 6, chap. 33, 366–71.

he is the accepted authority representing all of China, but also because he is presented as a patriarch betrayed by members of his household, an identification much more accessible to seventeenth-century readers. The illustrations for the many printings of Martini's work show at what point in the story seventeenth-century readers stopped to contemplate the dramatic conflicts in emotional terms. The emperor's murder/suicide is depicted in a number of different illustrations, often with the iconography of a Christian martyr, as David Mungello has suggested.[37] This extension of empathy for the emperor moves the emotional investment of readers past a simple pro or contra for Christian faith to see the emperor's demise in comparatively figurative terms. Martini, and certainly Vondel after him, understood Chinese history in relation to Mediterranean antiquity, creating a triangle of references that affirmed a stoical moral view. The parallels between Europe and China were not have been confined to classical allusions, but would also have taken on an immediate importance for Europeans who had just barely survived the terrible religious wars of the Reformation. Furthermore, Martini and Vondel interpret Chinese history within a Stoic framework that had been one of the strands in the accommodationist approach. Chinese history confirmed the instability of all power just as much as European wars.

The similarities between European and Asian rulers figure prominently in tragic dramas of the seventeenth century. Walter Benjamin reminds us that the history of the Orient, embodied in the figure of the absolute ruler, was a favorite topic in baroque tragic drama.[38] Not only was this genre an international construct that stretches across northern Europe, but it often directly responded to reports describing political conflicts in Asia. Missionary letters provided material for these tragic dramas while Jesuit school performances shaped the popular theological and aesthetic understanding of these events.[39] Contemporary events in China, particularly the

37. David Mungello, *Curious Land: Jesuit Accommodation and the Origins of Sinology* (Honolulu: University of Hawaii Press, 1989), 111.

38. Benjamin, *Tragic Drama*, 68.

39. Irene Wegner, "'China' in der Fest- und Theaterkulturs Bayerns," in *Die Wittelsbacher und das Reich der Mitte, 400 Jahre China und Bayern*, ed. Renate Eikelmann (Munich: Hirmer, 2009), 344.

Manchu conquest, reinforced the seventeenth century's distinct notion of the tragic; they provided the genre with new historical material while confirming its ancient stoic worldview.

The network of Jesuit schools shaped the popular Catholic image of Asia by including Japanese and Chinese topics alongside biblical and antique stories in their public theater.[40] Johannes Müller, a Jesuit who taught in Tokyo, lists sixty-seven Japanese martyr dramas performed in Germany between 1607 and 1767, while Takenaka offers the figure of more than 600 plays performed across Europe.[41] Plays involving Japanese martyr stories were often preformed in celebration of St. Francis Xavier's feast on December 3. Young Jesuit students would be assigned to perform as Japanese converts punished for their new faith, thereby preparing these novices for the idealized possibility of becoming an actual martyr.[42] Staged often in town squares and performed in Latin, with a program guiding viewers in the vernacular, school plays were another Jesuit foray into public entertainment. Asian events were a minor but attractive theme for staging spectacles. Mime, slapstick, and backstage machinery augmented the multilingual entertainments offered by English and Dutch actors in the north and commedia d'elle arte troupes everywhere. Shadow plays, called *ombre des chinois* in the eighteenth century, could depict supernatural events—demons flying through the air, pacts with the devil, talking animals, bodily dismemberment. These different genres competed as well as augmented each other. Shadow theaters, for example, often quickly adapted stories told in other formats, so that a few days after a troupe of human actors had dismantled their stage, a nearby puppet theater could revive their performance with a few new twists

40. For a thorough examination of martyr dramas with Chinese figures, see Adrian Hsia, "The Jesuit Plays on China and Their Relation to the Profane Literature," in *Mission und Theater, Japan und China auf den Bühnen der Gesellschaft Jesu*, ed. Adrian Hsia and Ruprecht Wimmer (Regensburg: Schnell and Steiner, 2005).

41. Johannes Müller, SJ, *Das Jesuitendrama in den Ländern deutscher Zunge vom Anfang (1555) bis zum Hochbarock (1665)* (Augsburg: Benno Filser, 1930) 2:111–12; Masahiro Takenaka, "Jesuit Plays on Japan in the Baroque Era," 379.

42. Miazek-Mecynska, "Polish Jesuits and Their Dreams about Missions in China," 410.

provided. Commedia d'elle arte presented Asian rulers as comical figures, to be feared at first and mocked at the end. Marketplace commedia became a vital source for later large-scale operas about Asia. Adrian Hsia traces a link between a cluster of Jesuit plays about the martyr Chaocungus and eighteenth-century comic opera by Metastasio *Le Cinesi* (The Chinese women, 1735), and its further adaptations by Gluck in *L'eroe Cinese* (The Chinese hero, 1753) and *Le Orfano della Cina* (The orphan of China, 1766).[43] A Chinese spectacle presented in the royal gardens might have had its first formulations in an Italian troupe's improvisations. Jesuit drama operated at the high end of these low entertainments. Its influence stretched into the literary canon of northern Baroque *Trauerspiele*. These pedagogical plays also interpreted the curious Asian reality for a local European audience, but they did so with a theological point. The school drama marks the intersection of advanced Jesuit scholarship and the popular demands placed on early modern theater companies to entertain, attract, inspire, and shock audiences. While the two realms were clearly connected discursively, given that the priests composing school plays read the bulletins and treatises from their brothers in Asia, the plays performed in the marketplaces and schools of small European towns had little of the cosmopolitan, philosophical qualities attributed to Matteo Ricci's "accommodation."

We can trace the popular reception of Martini's history by concentrating on a pivotal scene in its adaptation in Joost von der Vondel's 1667 tragic drama, *Zungchin*. Vondel's play is significant because, without representing the Jesuit accommodation with the imperial elite in China, it makes a first attempt at presenting the emperor as a figure of empathy, akin to martyrs embodying Stoic dignity. Vondel presents the emperor as a personification of martyrdom in the face of immoral violence. In this regard, Vondel's portrayal of the Zungchin competes with John Dryden's 1664 presentation in *The Indian Queen* of the Aztec ruler, Montezuma, as the torture

---

43. Adrian Hsia, "Jesuit Plays," 216–21, argues specifically that these operas and ballets were derived from Jesuit dramas as opposed to Du Halde's compilation of Jesuit reports, which served as the source for Voltaire's "The Orphan of Zhou."

victim of the conquistadores. Vondel fosters European empathy with Zungchin, establishing a lineage of identifications, distinct from but building off martyr plays, in which non-European rulers, who represent their peoples as they collapse, are portrayed as deserving moral support. From Vondel to Dryden we can move on to Adam Smith's broader late Enlightenment account of an imaginary European's sympathies for the Chinese population at large and Burke's assertion that members of Parliament ought empathize with ordinary Indian victims of the East India Company's policies. The Aztec ruler became an operatic figure first in Vivaldi's *Motezuma*, which premiered November 14, 1733, in Venice's Teatro Sant'Angelo.[44] Michael Talbot writes that the libretto "evinces a rare degree of sympathy for the Mexican emperor and his queen Mirena," yet this gesture was by no means unusual.[45] Even Frederick II's 1755 opera libretto presents an almost rococo Montezuma, who appears as a martyr warning against relying on the sympathy of Europeans to stop their own cruelty. The Prussian version suggests that it is better to stand opposed to the arrival of European enemies than to become an object of their pity later.

The extension of sympathy, as if it were a diplomatic courtesy, is possible precisely because of the distances involved. German baroque tragedy did not present Muslim rulers in empathetic terms because they were too close by to become figures of poetic imagination. To Silesian playwrights, Muslim empires seemed too a plausible military threat to serve as screens for utopian projections. The distinctions between distant and approximate rulers on European stages suggest that from early on China's remoteness allowed it become the object of daydreams.

44. Steffan Voss, "Die Partitur von Vivaldis Oper 'Motezuma' (1733)," *Studi Vivaldiani* 4 (2004): 52–72.

45. Michael Talbot, *The Vivaldi Compendium* (Woodbridge, UK: Boydell Press, 2011), 125.

5

VONDEL'S TRAGIC CHINESE EMPEROR

For Joost van den Vondel, the poet of the Dutch Golden Age, and for many other European observers in the mid-sixteenth century, the Manchu conquest demonstrated that China was not the eternally stable empire. The proverb that political power never lasts had been relearned many times during the sectarian wars. The Manchu conquest was interpreted in similar terms and quickly assimilated into the rhetoric and theology of instability and violence that defined the European discourse from the Reformation to the baroque *Trauerspiel*. The admiration for China as an ancient and stable kingdom that David Porter identifies as a characteristic of the early eighteenth century emerged most strongly after European absolutism had become the norm following the religious wars. To celebrate the venerable age of Chinese civilization, requires one to perceive a continuity that extended across dynastic shifts—a perspective seventeenth-century Europeans did not share with the Enlightenment. For Christians witnessing the Thirty Years' War or the Dutch rebellion, the Manchu conquest showed that China was subject to a familiar catastrophe. The invasion by northern barbarians and the infiltration of rebels into the Forbidden City constituted precisely the "state of emergency" that, according to seventeenth-century political theory, legitimated the monarch's absolute power. The tragic aspect of Vondel's 1667 drama, *Zungchin* (Chongzhen), centers on the Chinese emperor's failure to use his authority to prevent the calamity.[1]

Vondel's *Trauerspiel* about the last Ming emperor, who executes his daughter and hangs himself just as the Forbidden City is about to be overrun by rebels, calls attention to the genre's connections with Jesuit drama. The link between missionary's letters and European theater becomes most intense in school plays, which often drew on biblical themes and Roman history but when they staged an Asian performance always relied on Jesuit reports and treatises for their plot. Jesuit school performances represent the mediating moment between princely Latin treatises and the laity. In tracing the reception of Jesuit writing on China and Japan, school dramas and independent plays such as Vondel's *Zungchin* as well as Voltaire's *Orphan* were important venues for distributing images and news of Asia to a less learned audience. As an important component in the Jesuit's pedagogy, school plays allowed students to practice their rhetorical skills while spectators witnessed the character's self-sacrifice. To be sure, Vondel's *Zungchin*, set inside the imperial court, provides a more complex image of ruling elite than the polarized image of school dramas, in which absolute rulers in Asia viciously torture and execute foreigners, yet Vondel was clearly writing in conjunction with that tradition, which had a strong presence in Flanders.[2] While Matteo Ricci in China and Francis Xavier in Japan were admired for their diplomacy, the adaptation of Jesuit reports in school plays makes clear that the society operated at very different registers in representing its mission in Asia.

---

1. Walter Benjamin, *The Origin of German Tragic Drama*, trans. John Osborne (London: Verso, 1985), 65.

2. Goran Proot and Johan Verberckmoes, "Japonica in the Jesuit Drama of the Southern Netherlands," *Bulletin of Portuguese-Japanese Studies* 5 (2002): 27–47.

Jesuit reports from Japan in the 1600s strongly emphasized martyr histories. Annual and individual letters recounted the hundreds of Japanese who were baptized only to include follow-up stories about their persecution.[3] One of the popular martyr dramas in the school repertoire involved the story of a Japanese convert named Titus, who was forced to chose between his faith and his love for his family. The script is derived from Nicolas Trigault's *De Christianis apud Iaponios Triumphis* (The triumph of Christians in Japan, 1623).[4] When this story was performed in 1724 at a school in Mindelheim, the program underscored the exemplary faith of Japanese martyrs in contrast to more distracted European youths. Addressing German rather than Japanese school children, the play made Asia out to be the scene of extraordinary faith, worthy of emulation. Distance here served as a strategy of conversion.[5] The play shows Titus, a Japanese Christian convert, refusing to abandon his faith even in the face of a warlord's threat to kill his son. Faced with the plots of idol worshippers to wipe out Christianity in Japan, Titus hands over his son to death rather than deny his faith. After his two other sons have been handed over to be sacrificed, Titus himself stands ready to be executed, at which point the warlord is so impressed with his fortitude that he restores Titus and his three sons, who now appear alive and well. The tyrant then has the idol-worshipers thrown into a chasm where they remain buried. Having children on stage demonstrating their constancy was clearly part of the lesson, as it was in Flanders where similar performances were staged.[6] Their steadfast willingness to die for their faith stood in sharp contrast to the powerful but unstable tyrant, who

---

3. A catalogue of European publications is available, often with summaries, in Robert Streit, *Bibliotheca Missionum*, vol. 5, *Asiatische Missionsliteratur 1600–1699* (Aachen: Franziskus Xaverius Missionsverein, 1929), 362–598.

4. Nicolas Trigault, *De Christianis apud Iaponios Triumphis* (Monachii: Sadeler, 1623), book 3, caput 11.

5. Harold Jantz, ed., *Fortitudo christiana in Tito Japone exhibita—Obsigende Glauben-Lieb Titi Eines Edlen Japonesers, Vorgestellt auf der Schau-Bühne von der Studierenden Jugend des Chur-Fürstlichen Gymnasii Societatis JESU zu Mindelheim, den 4. Und 6. Tag Herbstmonats 1724* (Middelheim: Adolph Joseph Ebel, 1724).

6. Proot and Verberckmoes "Japonica in Jesuit Drama," 35.

shifts from one position to the other in the face of the martyr's example.

Such spectacles attracted European audiences and drove young men to volunteer for mission work so that they too might find glory. The more graphic the violence against Christians, the more compelling the play. Thus, for example, a drama performed in September 1664 at the Academy in Ingolstadt, which in English would have been "The Glorious Martyrdom and Blessed Life of Jacobi Macaximi," opened by characterizing Japan as "the Empire of martyrs swimming not in water but blood, to which the Holy Father Francis Xavier brought the first light of faith and which has often shown the strength of martyrs."[7] East Asia appears as a theater of violence. While the less devout may have been fascinated with the cruelty practiced upon victims, the pious were moved to follow the mission, so that they too could demonstrate the strength of their belief in the face of horrible torture. These performances stood at the tail end of a long sequence of communication. In her commentary on the Ingolstadt play, Elida Maria Szarota traces the drama's beginnings to the annual letters from Japan, *Literae Annuae Japonenses* (1630), even as she underscores how carefully the dramaturge arranged the scenes, distributing displays of exquisite cruelty and unimaginable suffering evenly across the play's three acts.[8]

Martyr plays are clearly an important phase in the genealogy of the Asiatic despot trope. When members of the English Macartney embassy to the imperial court in 1794 recycled the image of the cruel tyrant who oppresses his free-thinking subjects, they were working with a figure that stretched back to the earliest heroes of the Christian Church. In describing *Fortitudo Japonica, Das ist Christliche Standhaftigkeit, Dreyer starckmütigen Blut-Zeugen Chrsiti in Japonien* (The strength of the Japanese, this is Christian fortitude, three strong-willed blood witnesses to Christ in Japan), a play derived from Trigault's *De Christianis apud Japonios Triumphis* and performed in 1665 in Constance with the local bishop's approval,

---

7. Elida Maria Szarota, *Das Jesuitendrama im deutschen Sprachgebiet: Texte und Kommentare* (Munich: Wilhelm Fink, 1983), 3.1:190.

8. Szarota, *Jesuitendrama*, 3.2:2069.

Szarota points out that the figure of the steadfast martyr and the vicious tyrant are as old as Christianity itself. "We have here before us a martyr drama of the classical type: the Christian defies the tyranny of the ruler, does not follow his commands, refuses to sacrifice to pagan gods, and joyfully accepts martyrdom as a knight of Christ. The entire family in *Fortitudo Japonica* maintains this attitude."[9] Given the critical Enlightenment reception of the Jesuit mission, there would seem to be discrepancy between the school drama's focus on martyrdom and the missionaries' efforts to interweave Christian and Confucian thought, or at the very least a lack of coordination between different aspects of the society's mission, as it adapts itself for different audiences. After all, the question of what happens when one sector overhears a message intended for another part of the world became an enormous problem during the Rites Controversy. While Chinese literati probably never had the opportunity to attend a South German martyr play, Vatican and Sorbonne officials were clearly unnerved and outraged by the mission's accommodationist statements in Beijing.

If China and Europe share parallel fates of political instability in the mid-seventeenth century, just two generations later that same instability was remobilized to justify the absolute monarch's authority over his subjects. China continued to be seen as the equivalent of Europe, so that by the end of the seventeenth century European courts celebrated the perceived similarities in asymmetrical monarchical power by adopting chinoiserie as the court fashion. Dramas about colonial conquests became lessons affirming royal concentrations of power. The Spanish conquest of the New World became a political warning for European nations wanting to avoid the fate of the Aztecs and Mayans. The Dutch playwright Joannes Antonides van der Goes compared the Jesuits in China with the Spanish in Mexico, reinforcing the suggestion that Montezuma shares the same role as the last Ming emperor—a kingly sacrifice. By the start of the eighteenth century, the conquests of China and Mexico were readily interpreted as demonstrating the need for a strong centralized monarchy that can fend off rebellion and invasion. Frederick II

---

9. Szarota, *Jesuitendrama*, 3.2:2070.

staged the opera *Montezuma*, wherein the Aztec emperor's suffering serves as an admonishment against weakening monarchical power. Already in *Bello Tartarico*, Martini cautioned against monarchical decay. The Manchus appeared in his telling as vigorous, if somewhat barbaric warriors replacing an indolent southern order.

The last Ming emperor was a transitional figure not just between dynasties, but also religions. In baroque accounts, he has all the features of a powerful but indecisive tyrant—a king who is quite capable of executing anyone but who is so unsure that he drifts from one position to the other.[10] In this sense, the emperor appears as a potential convert. Just as the warlord who is so impressed by the self-sacrifice of Japanese Christians that he turns against his own idols, the Chinese emperor holds a two-sided position. He can persecute the Christians at his court, but he might also be drawn over to them. In the Jesuit narratives, Chongzhen plays much more the role of the potential proselyte, the Asian Constantine.

Walter Benjamin argues that the tyrant and the martyr are two faces of the baroque sovereign—as extreme opposites, they both embody excess.[11] In Vondel's play, the two merge. The marginal figure of the martyred Asian convert moves from the periphery, where he would have stood as a figure defying traditional religions, to the (decaying) ontological center of the emperor. As the great ruler is shown to have become increasingly powerless, he becomes a figure of sympathy, yet the most important step, as far as European drama is concerned, lies in the emperor's conversion to Christianity. Because tragic dramaturgy presumes from the start that the ruler stands in as the embodiment of his people, the chance that he might have converted, but died beforehand as bandits and Manchus approached, suggests within theatrical conventions that all of China might have done the same.

The legend of Chongzhen's near conversion runs through Jesuit treatises and becomes explicit in personal letters. What Martin Martini does not include in his history, but what he and Adam Schall mention in other writings, is their belief that the last Ming emperor

10. Benjamin, *Tragic Drama*, 71.
11. Benjamin, *Tragic Drama*, 69.

was inclined toward Christians and in the eyes of Jesuits at court willing to be baptized.[12] In dramatizing the demise of the Ming dynasty, Vondel is following closely Adam Schall's own account of why Chongzhen was a flawed figure, worthy of sorrow:

> So this monarch, almost the greatest in the world and second to none in the goodness of his character, with no companion and abandoned by all, through his imprudence perished by an unworthy death at the age of thirty-six. And the name of the empire Ta Ming (that is, Great Clarity) after it lasted 276 years with the royal clan which numbered almost 80,000 persons, was extinct. Although the emperor, to my sorrow, did not follow me when I showed him the way to salvation, yet he merits a deep lamentation because he not only sustained Christianity, which had been maintained in China and in the court by his grandfather, but he also praised and fostered it, to the maximum advantage of his subjects. He would have done even more had he not died such a violent and untimely death.[13]

In the dedication to his play, Vondel marshals examples from antiquity and his era, from Asia and Europe, to argue that no empire is secure in its dominion. He opens with Jupiter's promise to Aeneus—"Imperium sine fine dedi"—that the Roman Empire will rule eternally without limits.[14] Vondel underscores the failure of such grand claims by emphasizing the corresponding theological claim that only divine rule lasts forever. Human politics will always lead to ruin; whereas the deaths of martyrs confirms the divine truth.

---

12. Adrian Hsia, "The Jesuit Plays on China and Their Relation to the Profane Literature," in *Mission und Theater, Japan und China auf den Bühnen der Gesellschaft Jesu*, ed. Adrian Hsia and Ruprecht Wimmer (Regensburg: Schnell and Steiner, 2005), 223.

13. Adam Schall, quoted in John W. Witek, SJ, "Johann Adam Schall von Bell and the Transition from Ming to Ch'ing," in *Western Learning and Christianity in China: The Contribution and Impact of Johann Adam Schall von Bell, S.J. (1592–1666)*, ed. Roman Malek, SVD (Sankt Augustin: China-Zentrum & Monumenta Serica Institute, 1998), 112.

14. "*Imperium sine fine dedi*: from the days of Quintilian down almost to the present, any schoolboy who was forced to read Book I of the *Aeneid* would, coming upon those words for the first time, know precisely (if unconsciously) what they meant" (W. R. Johnson, review of *Virgil's Aeneid: Cosmos and Imperium*, by Philip Hardie, *Classical Journal* 83 [1988]: 269).

Further drawing on Virgil, Vondel suggests a parallel between Troy and China, Priam and Chongzhen, as he concentrates on Virgil's account of the Trojans' destruction in order to emphasize the monumentality of the play he is about to present.[15] A quotation from book 2 of *The Aeneid* raises the motif of the decapitated ruler:

> That was the end
> Of Priam's age, the doom that took him off,
> With Troy in flames before his eyes, his towers
> Headlong fallen—he that in other days
> Had ruled in pride so many lands and peoples
> The power of Asia.
>   On the distant shore
> The vast trunk headless lies without a name.[16]

From the butchered corpse of Priam, Vondel passes to Chongzhen, whose body fell before his triumphant enemy and was cut to pieces. Having cited Virgil, Vondel then draws a distinction between antiquity and the seventeenth-century understanding of the globe. Priam ruled over a small territory that could be considered the eastern edge of Europe, whereas the borders of the Chinese empire stretched much farther. The key distinction between the recent fall of the Ming dynasty and Troy was the presence of Christian missionaries in Beijing. The tropes Vondel uses are a first attempt at global history, comparing vast territories and subsuming them under rhetorical terms. He emphasizes the interconnectedness of Asia and Europe repeatedly, often in terms of an allegorical interpretation that isolates difference and connectedness as two extremes of the one continent. Shifting attention away from the Hellespont, a symbolically laden stretch of water, he shows Europe and Asia to be less clearly distinguished from one another. Separated by a succession

15.   Nieuhof also describes the devastation he observed while on the Dutch embassy to the Manchu court as "a second Troy"; see Donald F. Lach and Edwin J. Van Kley, *Asia in the Making of Europe* (Chicago: University of Chicago Press, 1993), 3:1669.

16.   Virgil, *The Aeneid*, trans. Robert Fitzgerald (New York: Vintage, 1981), 52.

of distances over the same land mass, they stand in a range of extended relations, rather than oppositions.

Vondel not only relies on Martini's political history of the Manchu conquest of China, but also includes Adam Schall (1592–1666), court astronomer and mathematician at the imperial court in Beijing, alongside the ghost of Saint Francis Xavier, as figures on the stage.[17] Schall was well known in Europe. Leibniz refers to him as a "famous Mandarin" in a 1672 letter about the history of the Jesuit mission.[18] Alexander Baumgartner ascribes the play to Vondel's deep admiration for the Jesuits and his "glowing enthusiasm for the spread of Christian faith."[19] Alfons Väth, the twentieth-century biographer of Schall, explains further that the Jesuits were decisive in Vondel's conversion to Catholicism. In Amsterdam he belonged to a circle of friends around the printer Joan Blaeu, who shared an interest in the Jesuit mission. Given that the play is based on a scene depicted in Martino Martini's *De Bello Tartarico Historia*, it would be reasonable to expect that Vondel spoke directly with Martini in 1654 while he was visiting with Blaeu as his *Novus Atlas Sinensis* was being prepared. Martini would have imparted direct information about Schall's role at the imperial court.[20] Indeed, Martini states in the preface to his history that he wrote the work in part to answer the many curious persons who wanted to know about events in China. Even before Martini's arrival in Amsterdam, Vondel seems to have corresponded with Father Philipp Couplet who was in in China and who later published a Latin translation

---

17. It was not usual for Jesuit school plays to include in the cast the missionary who wrote the treatise upon which the play is based. A 1732 performance in Amberg, Bavaria, about a Chinese martyr baptized as Joseph, also includes the Father Parrenin, who first described the case in a letter, as a member of the cast. Adrian Hsia, "The Jesuit Plays on China," 214.

18. Letter to Gottlieb Spitzel Augsburg February 7/March 8, 1672, Gottfried Wilhelm Leibniz, *Sämtliche Schriften und Briefe*, Deutsche Akademie der Wissenschaften zu Berlin (Darmstadt: O. Reichl, 1923), first series, 1:193.

19. Alexander Baumgartner, *Joost von den Vondel, sein leben und seine Werke* (Freiburg: Herder'sche Verlagshandlung, 1882), 261.

20. Alfons Väth, SJ, *Johann Adam Schall von Bell S.J. Missionar in China, kaiserlicher Astronom und Ratgeber am Hofe von Peking 1592–1666 Ein Lebens- und Zeitbild*, new ed., China-Zentrum und Instituts Monumenta Serica (Sankt Augustin: Steyer, 1991), 349.

of Confucian works, *Confucius Sinarum Philosophus* (1687).[21]
Vondel's play, in turn, is dedicated to Cornelius von Nobelaer, whose
two sons were both Jesuit priests.[22]

In Vondel's telling, the Christian mission becomes a factor in the
fate of the Chinese rulers. Unlike Virgil, the Chinese were offered
"the Apostolic light of truth"; hence, they do not have they do not
have the same standing as Dante's pagan philosophers. Vondel cites
Xavier's mission to Japan and the martyrdom of Karel Spinola, who
also inspired many young men to join the Jesuits.[23] Alongside the
image of the dismembered emperor stands the martyr suffering willingly for divine truth. In Vondel's play, the convergence of emperor
and martyr is implied cautiously, because ultimately the Zungchen
did not convert to Christianity.

Walter Benjamin's thesis that the emperor and the martyr are two
sides of the same political order comes clearly to the fore in John
Dryden's 1665 play, *The Indian Emperour*, in which Montezuma
is tortured on stage by Spaniards seeking gold. Performed two years
prior to Vondel's drama, Dryden's states directly that the tortured
ruler suffering represents his martyred civilization. In act 5, scene
2, Montezuma along with his high priest lie stretched out as they
are interrogated for information about their hidden gold. Dryden
inaccurately places Pizarro in the scene in Mexico so that he can
perform as the cruelest conquistador. While critics have noted that
Dryden does not devote many lines to the debate over Christian
injustice in conquering natives, Montezuma's defiance quickly
touches on the main topics of eighteenth-century discussions: natural reason versus divine revelation, the immorality of European ex-

---

    21.   Väth, *Schall*, 235n62.
    22.   Baumgartner, *Joost van den Vondel*, 261.
    23.   The German Jesuit Kino wrote on November 16, 1680: "As far as I am
concerned, I admit that from my earliest years (but especially after reading the life
and martyrdom of Reverend Father Charles Spinola) I longed to go to the missions
of the Orient. Hence I often worked hard at mathematics" (Ernest J. Burrus, SJ, ed.,
*Kino Writes to the Duchess, Letters of Eusebio Francisco Kino, S.J., to the Duchess
of Aveiro* [Rome: Jesuit Historical Institute, 1965], 79). Kino was also inspired by
Beatus Amrhyn and Adam Aigenier, who accompanied the Sicilian Prospero Intorcetta and died on the voyage out caring for plague victims onboard. Kino never
had his desire to serve in China fulfilled, but he was quite important in Mexico.

pansionism, justice as a standard transcending religious conflict, the heroic ideal of restrained expression under torture. The point of Montezuma's defiance, "The gods will Punish you, if they be Just; / The gods will Plague your Sacrilegious Lust," his moral argument against the Spanish, is ignored by the Christian priest who takes it to be based on heathen worship.[24] The Spanish insistence that Montezuma convert to Christianity on the spot, without the slightest theological explanation, and their military conquest of Mexico stand as the obvious alternative to the Jesuit accommodation in China. The Mexican priest's despair, "Can Heaven be Author of such Cruelty?" was a common Buddhist and Confucian challenge to the Christian claim that God created evil as well as good, yet on Dryden's stage it draws the audience's attention even more closely to the graphic suffering of the two Aztecs. Pizarro heightens the torture: "Fasten the Engines; stretch 'um at their length, / And pull the streightned Cords with all your strength." Montezuma demonstrates his nobility by refusing to reveal where his gold is hidden, thereby setting up the principle that Lessing and Smith will debate: Does the noble man suffering express his anguish and do cries of pain weaken the spectator's empathy for the victim? To heighten his defiance, Montezuma pledges his eventual revenge, a long-running motif, one that Heine revisits in "Vitzliputzli." When the high priest weakens, Montezuma demonstrates his superior resolve: "Shame on thy Priest-hood, that such pray'rs can bring! / Is it not brave to suffer with thy King?" The conversation between victims, as with the crucifixion, guides the audience on how to judge their suffering. Montezuma sets the Stoic standard: "I charge thee dare not groan, nor shew one sign, / Thou at the Torments does the least repine"

Having asserted his ancient defiance and willingness to die suffering, the Christian priest urges Montezuma to convert. By raising the question of the soul and its afterlife, the priest shifts the discussion away from the classical depiction of the heroic death. The subsequent

---

24. Dryden, John. *The Indian Emperour* (London: 1667), act 5, scene 2, http:// ezaccess.libraries.psu.edu/login?url=https://www-proquest-com.ezaccess.libraries.psu .edu/books/indian-emperour-1667/docview/2138574641/se-2?accountid=13158. All following quotations in the text appear in act 5, scene 2.

debate covers topics familiar to all Christian missionaries and the point from which Enlightenment critiques commenced: the sufficiency of natural reason. The Christian priest argues the Thomistic point that revelation supplements reason as nonbelievers practice it. "Though Nature teaches whom we should Adore, / By Heaven's Beams we still discover more." Unable to convince Montezuma in what is the play's only extended attempt at proselytizing, the Christian priest heightens the pressure on the rack, killing the Aztec priest who was about to reveal the gold's location. To the last, even as Cortez arrives to release him, Montezuma asserts his defiance under torture, refusing the sympathy the Spaniard extends:

> Am I so low, that you should pity bring,
> And give an Infant's Comfort to a King?
> Ask these if I have once unmanly groan'd;
> Or ought have done deserving to be moan'd.

When Cortez (unhistorically) falls before Montezuma weeping at the sight of his tortured body, Montezuma refuses all sympathy, insisting on his own standard of masculinity: "Your grief is cruel, for it shews my shame." Ultimately Aztec honor shames the Spanish, so that Cortez, having conquered Mexico, declares "It makes me blush to owne a Victors name."

Zungchin's suicide similarly enacts the Ming dynasty's self-inflicted collapse. The emperor's death confirms the impermanence of political power. In Jesuit and baroque tragic dramas the death of the martyr makes the instability of human institutions spectacularly explicit: "Der 'Fall' des Martyrs ist Exempel der irdischen Unbeständigkeit" (The martyr's fall [in German meaning both the "case" and the "fall" of the martyr] is the exemplar of earthly inconstancy).[25] As Vondel states in his preface, certainty lies only in Christian faith, not in political power.

The connections between Dutch and German tragic drama were once well understood. Unfortunately, the national boundaries de-

---

25. Joachim Harst, *Heilstheater: Figur des barocken Trauerspiels zwischen Gryphius und Kleist* (Munich: Wilhelm Fink, 2012), 60.

fining literary studies today are much less permeable than in the early modern period, when Andreas Gryphius attended the university in Leiden for six years, met Descartes there, and learned the tragic arts from Vondel. Even transnational studies are too often centered on one territory so that they focus more on just one foreign culture in one European country, while traditional comparative literature sifts through linguistic variations rather than political juxtapositions.[26] Although Benjamin regularly refers to the "niederländische Literatur" in his *Trauerspiel* book, German scholarship on baroque drama rarely considers Joost Vondel directly, and when it does engage his work, it does so either to dispel an anxiety about Gryphius's debt to him or to insist upon it.[27] The question of influence raises the much broader question of how, during the seventeenth century, Germans of all strata and professions were attracted to the Low Countries.[28] Edward Verhofstadt noted in 1969 that when scholars compare Vondel and Gryphius, they hope to use these authors to explain the enormous influence Dutch culture had on the rest of the Holy Roman Empire.[29] As an indication of the ease with which (low) German readers approached Dutch literature, one could point to the fact that through the nineteenth century, German libraries acquired Vondel editions in the original language, a sure sign that the differences between the languages were not enough to inhibit a reader already interested in the complexities of baroque writing.[30] One quality German and Dutch *Trauerspiele*

---

26. Adrian Hsia is the exceptional scholar who draws connections between Jesuit martyr plays about China and German-Dutch tragic dramas in *Chinesia: The European Construction of China in the Literature of the 17th and 18th Centuries* (Berlin: De Gruyter, 1998), 25–33, 55–73.

27. A recent exception is James Parente, *Religious Drama and the Humanist Tradition: Christian Theater in Germany and in the Netherlands, 1500–1680* (Brill: Leiden, 1987).

28. Joseph Eugene Gillet, "De Nederlandsche letterkunde in Duitschland in de Zeventiende eeuw," *Tidjschrift voor Nederlandsche Taal- en Letterkunde* 33 (1914): 1–31.

29. Edward Verhofstadt, "Vondel und Gryphius: Versuch einer literarischen Topographie," *Neophilologus* 53 (1969): 290.

30. English translations have been made of many plays that show Milton's affinity with Vondel, and a complete French translation was published in the nineteenth century. What was once self-evident in Germany has now become blocked.

share is their engagement with Jesuit theater. Scholars have long noted the international importance of school dramas in the development of the baroque *Trauerspiel*.[31]

In having Schall speak as the leader of the chorus, Vondel allows the Jesuit priest to guide the spectator's identification toward the doomed emperor. The chorus, led by Schall, interprets the political drama in theological terms, searching for two modes of historical causation in a way that tries to find the divine triumph in political catastrophe. However, the priests are never certain of how the two dimensions interact. They speculate while drawing analogies between China and other kingdoms where Christianity emerged out of political disaster: Japan, Rome, Europe in general.

Vondel's fondness for Schall is obvious immediately. The dramatis personae identifies Schall as an "Agripyner," which is to say, a native of Cologne (Colonia Claudia Ara Agrippinensium under the Romans), the city where Vondel was born as his Mennonite parents had fled there from Antwerp. As is appropriate for the court astronomer, Schall calls attention to the heavens as he stands in the imperial courtyards addressing the chorus of priests. He looks to "hemels ring," an old-fashioned reference to the stars, one invoking the star over Bethlehem.[32] As he describes the stars, Schall explains that the city has been surrounded by the rebel Li Zicheng's army, thereby suggesting a connection between the constellation's appearance and the arrival of war, but only cautiously, for later in the play Schall dismisses all manner of Chinese soothsaying. At what point do the heavens reveal the Christian God's will and when are they misunderstood by idol worshippers constitutes a serious question. The central conflict, and the title of play, concerns the col-

---

The linguistic convergence of Dutch and German no longer seems negotiable for readers, so that they now require a translation into modern German.

31. John O'Malley, *The First Jesuits* (Cambridge, MA: Harvard University Press, 1993), 223, nevertheless argues that much research needs to be done on the importance of theater along with music and ballet in Jesuit schools.

32. A hymn celebrating Christ's birth uses the phrase. See Jodocus van Lodenstein, "Jesus Geboren," *Uyt-spanningen, behelsende eenige stigtelyke liederen* (Utrecht: Willem Clerck, 1676), http://www.dbnl.org/tekst/lode002uyt_01_01/lode002uyt_01_01_0077.php.

lapse of the Chinese empire and the missionaries who stand in the middle. The end of civilization promises martyrdom. Schall declares that the priests are prepared to die if the catastrophe would further the spread of Christianity. Vondel shares Martini's claim that the fate of dynasties in China depends on how much they foster Christian teaching. Will the invading Manchus prove more lenient toward the missionaries? Is the current emperor in jeopardy for having failed to support the priests? Schall, like all good missionaries, speaks in metaphors of sowing seeds and gathering harvest. Matteo Ricci and Nicholas Trigault's *Ad Christiana* opens with the same references to the parable of the sower and the seed.[33] The scene unfolds as the imperial chancellor arrives and asks the priests to pray for the emperor. Schall's query into the political situation produces a brief history of China's conflicts with the Tartars to the north, which hints to the reader that more could be learned elsewhere—namely, in Martini's book. Schall points out that the Portuguese in Macao provided cannons for the emperor's war, which then leads the chancellor to give a typical baroque statement on the inconstancy of fortune:

> Time does not permit us to speak in detail
> About how fickle fortune follows neither rule nor direction.
> But tumbles round and round, like a turning wheel.
> Anyone who hangs on, and holds on to what he can grasp,
> Sits in the middle, or ends up above, then below.[34]

Added to the difficult wars in the north, the empire suffers from the administrative elite's massive corruption and oppression of the populace, which ultimately strengthens the appeal of rebels such as Li Zicheng. The dialogue concludes with Schall promising to keep watch over the city's gates with prayers—an inconclusive or perhaps double-sided message of practical and spiritual support.

---

33. Nicolas Trigault, *Historia von Einführung der christilichen Religion in das große Königreich China durch die Societet Jesu* (Augsburg: Antony Hierat, 1617), 1.

34. The Department of Dutch Language and Literatures at Leiden University offers a very helpful English translation online, last accessed November 17, 2019: http://www.let.leidenuniv.nl/Dutch/Ceneton/VondelZungchin1667English.html. All subsequent quotations from Vondel's play refer to this translation; line numbers are given in the text.

As the chorus of priests prays for protection, they hold the hope that Asia might be born again like Europe. The Jesuits are fascinated with the analogy between the Roman emperor Constantine's conversion before the Battle of Milvian Bridge and the possibility that the Chinese emperor might similarly dedicate himself in order to win a battle. The chorus of priests sings:

> And if the Emperor respected Christ's laws,
> As did the Great Constantine;
> Then you would see the enemy flee (174–76)

Like chaff blown away in the wind, China finds itself in a state of emergency, which grows worse in the second act as the emperor is informed that the rebel army threatens to take the city by stealth and deception. The ministers debate how the situation could have deteriorated so completely, leaving the court with nothing to do but stand watch lest the rebels sneak past the walls. The chorus of priests accompanies these political stratagems with a history of the Jesuit mission in China. Matteo Ricci and Trigault are named as the first to have unlocked China so as to combat idolatry. Vondel shows no particular sense for an accommodationist approach. Rather than consider a synthesis of Christian and Confucian teaching he instead portrays the Chinese as heretics by equating the idol Fo with Beelzebub, the Christian devil. Francis Xavier is praised in turn for having won converts in Japan. Vondel follows Martini's tendency to equate setbacks in the mission as matters of divine will, while victories for nonbelievers are characterized as fortune. Thus, the mission's reversal in Japan and the thousands of Christians killed there are described as a triumph for martyrs who demonstrate their faith in death. The sacrificial logic of Japan's Christians points to a similar figuration in China: the ultimately success of Christianity in death. Vondel's distinction between spiritual and earthly kingdoms resolves the contradiction by having dying martyrs ascend to heaven, the only stable order in contrast to the upheavals of worldly politics. The threat of disaster opens the opportunity for conversion. Only in desperation may the Chinese chose Christianity. However, the chorus of priests is hardly infallible, for they worry that a change in regime from Ming to Qing would weaken the mission. The Japanese reaction against Christianity could happen in China as well, and thus the priests resolve to keep watch and pray more intensely.

The third act brings together Schall and the empress in a dialogue comparing Christianity and superstition. The empress, Jasmine, sees the signs of a new authority coming:

> The dogs howl at night. There are ghosts along the backroads.
> The ravens caw ominously. The ground of the earth trembles.
> Fog occludes the sun. All that breathes and live,
> With soul o without, monsters on the beaches
> Indicate that a change of regime is at hand. (574–88)

Vondel's presentation of Chinese beliefs does not put much emphasis on Ricci's synthetic interpretation of Confucian teaching. Only once briefly does Schall praise the Chinese teacher. Instead, the empress and court are shown to be thoroughly superstitious. Europe is presented as enlightened, as having risen above superstitious habits, as the source of Christian teaching. Confucius is praised for having "planted golden morals," yet he is cited more as the local authority who confirms European disdain for soothsayers (592–94).

Some balance must be asserted between the two continents; otherwise it makes little sense for the Jesuits to so assiduously pursue their mission, or for the audience to be carried along by the empire's demise. The troubling images equating Asia with Troy from the preface are countered when, at the end of act 3, the chorus praises Asia and China unreservedly as the site of divine creation, affirming the ancient presumption that humans came into existence there:

> Happy Asia, trodden by God
> The gardener of Eden,
> And angels, and God the son,
> You are the greatest of three regions
> Of the earth, and among majestic lands
> You, with reason, wear the best crown. (901–6)

China is thus physically closer to the creation than Europe, and it enjoys a paradisiacal abundance. China, in a sense, is the Edenic garden, the geographical origin of humanity and its original bond with the divine:

> All that the first man was given
> In paradise, so richly blessed
> Flows to you out of heaven's lap. (913–15)

This ideal is immediately dashed by historical events, as the last two acts lead to the turning point in the Martini's narrative and the culmination of Vondel's play: the emperor's suicide and murder of his daughter. Both versions hint that this sacrifice might produce a more just political order—that it fosters Christian teaching as well. Neither telling includes an overt reference to Livy's account of Verginius's murder of his enslaved daughter, yet the prominence given to this scene both within Martini's text and its many illustrations suggests that the analogy was familiar enough to seventeenth-century readers. Vondel also revives the comparison to Priam given in the preface, when the imperial chancellor describes a city and court without a monarch as headless torso (1199). When, in act 5, the rebels swarm the city, the analogy is reiterated:

> The whole of China is in meltdown.
> Beijing has been abandoned and looks like headless torso,
> A body without the head. (1345–47)

The catastrophe has become unstoppable; the chancellor announces his intention to die just before the emperor presents a letter written in his own blood, denouncing his own betrayal to his apparent successor, the rebel Li Zicheng. The emperor then turns to his daughter, explaining that he must kill her to prevent her being raped by the conquerors. Even as he acts to avert his daughter's fate he describes how she would be stripped naked, raped in front of her family with her chest torn open and her heart pulled out with hot pinchers and fed to dogs, her body's mutilation demonstrating ostentatiously the collapse of her family's power. Not quite as extreme as Emilia Galotti later, yet still stoical enough, the crown princess affirms her father's resolve, upon which they walk off stage. The chancellor immediately lauds her in a manner that suggests the intermixing of the Chinese imperial and Christian sense of having heaven's mandate: "O glorious, agreeable one chosen by heaven [*hemelsche*] . . . You, most beautiful phoenix-flower in the holy valley of crowns" (1383–85).

In the end, tragic drama relies on potentiality: events that might have happened but never came to pass. The emperor and his court die, while the Christian message, and the Jesuits who deliver it, survive. Before a European audience, the play fosters continued evangelizing, continued prayers for the salvation of the Chinese. Zungchin becomes an object of sympathy because the ambidextrous dramaturgy of baroque tragic drama presents him in the double Christian role of ruler and subject, a more nuanced figure than the Asian despot character of earlier plays. The emperor receives sympathy because he has been incorporated into a fully theological account of Chinese history. The brief moments of religious reflection in Martini's history became the metaphysical basis for Vondel's fully Catholic incorporation of the emperor into the emotional economy of baroque tragic drama. Vondel's play compensates for the missionaries' inability to convert Zungchin by placing Chinese history within a Catholic eschatology.

6

Wieland's Secret History of Cosmopolitanism

Literary and theological cosmopolitanism requires a psychological bond between humans that reaches beyond the rational adherence to universal principles. How did the eighteenth century imagine the emotional relations between distant people? The sentimental side of the Enlightenment offered a secular alternative to Christian compassion for distant members of the global church. Rather than relying on a shared faith as the basis for intercultural compassion, the new eighteenth-century network of feelings stretched across cultural differences to encourage like-minded Europeans to develop identifications with foreigners based on aesthetic and moral terms. This new secular form of emotional cosmopolitanism invoked the conventions of friendship rather than faith. In the trajectory traced by this book, sentimental internationalism served as an intermediary stage and precursor to world literature. This chapter considers Christoph Wieland's assertion that cosmopolitanism had a long secret history. Looking back on Jesuits in China, we know that they would never have described themselves in such terms, yet, as with colonialism, they inadvertently contributed to its emergence.

In order to pick up the diffuse strands of these secular sympathies, it might be helpful to concentrate on one author. Wieland was vital to the Enlightenment even if he is overlooked now. One of his few remaining claims to fame is that he was probably the first German intellectual to scribble down the word "Weltliteratur." In the many texts written around his Oriental tale, *Der goldne Spiegel, oder Die Könige von Schechian* (The golden mirror, or the king of Scheschian, 1772) from his youthful first fragments through his mature essays as the eldest Weimar author, Wieland outlined the contours of a sentimental cosmopolitanism that encouraged Europeans to identify with temporally, spatially, theologically, and linguistically distant figures. His description of the mystical union that holds sentimental cosmopolitanism together is not particularly focused on China or any other location, but it does lay out an emotional network that allows readers to form imaginary bonds with strangers far off in Asia.[1] Wieland's writings outline the discursive and psychological preconditions for cosmopolitan feelings. Without his model, cosmopolitanism might have continued to follow the rational principles Leibniz and Wolff had formulated, rather than the ethical and aesthetic identification it became for Adam Smith and Goethe. Emerging from Pietism, Wieland's model provides a secular alternative to the global church(es) postulated by missionaries, by reconceptualizing their contemplative practices to justify a new ethics.[2]

---

1. Recent scholars analyzing the worldly linkages that make up sentimental communities have relied on the term "imaginary" to characterize the bonds of these readerly communities. However I want to trace the genealogy back to before the Enlightenment in order show the long continuities between sentimentalism and the earlier, global Christianity. On "imaginary," see, for example, April Alliston, "Transnational Sympathies, Imaginary Communities," in *The Literary Channel*, ed. Margaret Cohen and Carolyn Dever (Princeton, NJ: Princeton University Press, 2009), 133–48.

2. "A new system of axioms on thought and action moves initially into a third position, between the adversary churches of Catholic and Protestant denomination. It progressively defines the very ground which is uncovered beneath the fragmentation of beliefs. An autonomous ethics is thus established, one whose frame of reference is either the social order or conscience" (Michel de Certeau, "The Formality of Practices, from Religious Systems to the Ethics of the Enlightenment [the

Wieland's sentimental network stands between Catholic prayers connecting laity to the missionaries and nineteenth-century sentimentalism's obsession with mourning the beloved dead. Wieland's model allows for a relation between someone alive in the present and another long-dead soul in a far-off distant place, but he does not fall into the hyperbole of later sentimentalism. Instead Wieland offers a connectedness that will reappear as the aged Goethe's identification with Hafez and mandarins—that is to say, as world literature.

Moral cosmopolitanism in Germany, particularly the notion that all people around the world deserve equal respect, is often characterized as a continuation of ancient Stoic worldliness. Pauline Kleingeld presents Christopher Wieland as a representative of this cosmopolitan strand.[3] As much as Wieland and other Enlightenment thinkers agreed with the ancient Stoic rejection of local patriotism, they also added important ideas that have no place in Stoicism. Enlightenment cosmopolitanism augments Stoicism to the point that the two positions are distinctly different, if not in disagreement. Wieland, like other Germans influenced by Shaftesbury, insisted that cosmopolitans belong to a global network of like-minded spiritual beings who share intellectual and emotional enlightenment that set them apart from their surroundings. They communicate with each other by participating through often invisible lines. His position tacitly assumes reaching across cultural boundaries, whether in the form of letters or translated books. He presumes the work of global postal networks, and he anticipates the notion (in Gosch, Goethe, Nietzsche) that writers can address each other across time, finding companion spirits in far removed places. As a preindustrial social formation, Wieland's cosmopolitanism did not depend on living within a large city, such as Paris or Rome. In fact, his model presumes that all cosmopolitans live in isolation within societies opposed to their own beliefs. Reading, more than urban socializing, is the medium for composing such

---

Seventeenth and Eighteenth Centuries]," in *The Writing of History*, trans. Tom Conley [New York: Columbia University Press, 1988], 149).

3. Pauline Kleingeld, "Six Varieties of Cosmopolitanism in Late Eighteenth-Century Germany," *Journal of the History of Ideas* 60.3 (1999): 505–24.

communities. Cosmopolitanism's dependence on long-distance media led to a critical reflection about the aesthetic quality of the texts circulating between senders and receivers. World literature unsurprisingly begins as texts that move within these circuits, first letters and small-form writing, but eventually larger works. The movement of these texts through international media inevitably required them to undergo translation, often more than once.

While the term became famous after Johann Peter Eckermann published his *Gespräche mit Goethe* (*Conversations with Goethe*), Hans-Jürgen Weitz has shown that the first recorded enunciation of "world literature" was made by Christoph Wieland as a marginal correction to his translation of Horace's epistles.[4] This first putting pen to paper to write the word *Weltliteratur* happened sometime between 1790, when Wieland's translation first appeared, and 1813, when he died, well before Goethe started discussing the idea in 1827. Taking the imagined position of American students and teachers, John Pizer asks provocatively: "What difference does it make if Wieland preceded Goethe in using the German term for 'world literature'?"[5] Of course it does. The point of this archival discovery is not who said it first, so much as the context in which it was written. First, it is telling that the term "world literature" pops up initially while Wieland is correcting the dedication of a translation. World literature is always coming from some other place, some other language. Second, the term is applied to letters, rather than to any established genre of literature. Epistolary novels became an enormously popular form of sentimental literature in the eighteenth century, and Wieland had of course written his own. The genre was itself a manifestation of expanded European postal systems. Wieland's text with its corrections shows that mail delivery not only created new forms of subjective writing, but also helped bring translated texts into movement within Europe. Horace's letters were not written as fiction; they evolved into literature as they passed beyond

---

4. Hans-Juergen Weitz, "'Weltliteratur' zuerst bei Wieland," *Arcadia* 22.2 (1987): 206–8.

5. John Pizer, *The Idea of World Literature: History and Pedagogical Practice* (Baton Rouge: Louisiana State University Press, 2006), 2.

their initial communication circuit, which allowed them to acquire addition significance within a larger audience, meanings that went beyond the message they first conveyed between sender and receiver. As with Jesuit reports sent from abroad, the secondary circulation of letters turned them into objects of contemplation above and beyond their original articulation.

Wieland begins the preface to his edition, as many translators do, by modestly acknowledging how much of the grace and urbanity in Horace's writing was lost in his German rendition. No matter how sensitive, hard-working, and learned he was, Wieland could not overcome all the difficulties of turning Horace's Latin into German, yet at the same time, he is pleased with what he had accomplished. To understand the singular qualities of Horace's epistles, it was necessary to appreciate that they were actual letters sent to historical people about real events. Such letters now required commentary in order to explain their original intentions, which might be unfamiliar to modern readers, and to reveal the stylistic nuances—their "true meaning and secret beauty." Wieland describes these almost indescribable qualities as revealing Roman "urbanity"—a term that we might now associate with sophisticated, metropolitan cosmopolitanism, but in eighteenth-century Germany was more a literary style than a downtown attitude. After all, Weimar was quite a small place. Now here comes the important moment. In his published preface, Wieland struggles to fill out a definition of urbanity, so he offers a list of its characteristics: erudition, knowledge of the world, and civility (*Gelehrsamkeit, Weltkenntniß,* and *Politesse*). Reading over this passage, years later, after the translation has already been published, Wieland starts scribbling corrections onto the printed page, crossing out words, adding new ones. This is the point where the word *Weltliteratur* appears, as a long unnoticed interlinear correction. Wieland was generally inclined to create compound words—an easy feature in German—that begin with "world." The characteristics that he now attributes to urbanity in his scribbled revision are "knowledge of the world and world literature, as well as mature character formation and well-manneredness." The list has grown as Wieland has invented new words: *Weltkenntniß, Weltliteratur, reifer Charakterbildung,* and *Wohlbetragen.* All these qualities, he concludes, come from reading the best writers and from socializing with the most cultivated and excellent people in a very refined era.

In the course of making his corrections, Wieland keeps urbanity as the defining feature of Horace's style, but he reassesses the subtleties that define this term. Knowledge of the world he supplements with world literature, and classical learnedness he drops altogether. In his list of urbane qualities, the scholarliness demanded in the republic of letters has been replaced with worldliness, suggesting that literary salons have supplanted universities as the preferred intellectual venue. In Wieland and then in Goethe's telling, world literature is not conceived as an academic pursuit, nor as a field of knowledge. Instead it brings together an ineffable community of readers, dispersed across time and space. Wieland hopes that his translation of Horace's letters will draw together sophisticated readers by offering them a model for their own urbane sociability. While Wieland's *Weltliteratur* is still focused on Mediterranean antiquity and echoes of this orientation appear in Goethe's later comments, as we will see later when Goethe discusses Chinese literature, the early modern distinction between ancient and modern maps of the globe lies implicit within *Weltliteratur*. Countless explorers, from the first Portuguese to round the Cape to Captain Cook in the South Pacific, called attention to the fact that they were venturing into territory unknown to the Greeks and Romans. Much the same applies to reading habits. For Europeans, reading world literature entailed moving beyond the horizon known to antiquity, literally surpassing their classical models.

This literary worldliness feels remarkably delicate when compared to later formulations. In the first section of the *Communist Manifesto*, Marx and Engels correlate world literature with the global expansion of markets, a far cry from the invisible community of sympathetic souls Wieland imagines.[6] Nevertheless, the two systems were interdependent. The market relations expressed in nineteenth-century notions of competing *Weltkulturen* were

---

6. Robert C. Tucker, ed., *The Marx-Engels Reader*, 2nd ed. (New York: Norton, 1972), 477.

built upon the trading systems established by the Portuguese, Spanish, and Dutch Empires. From the earliest, sensitive cosmopolitanism and its literary affiliations followed along the circuits of European mercantile trade routes. This interdependence between global economies and literary culture was already quite visible to ordinary readers in eighteenth-century Germany. We need not wait for industrialization and direct colonialism to find texts and audiences reacting against the mercantile underpinnings of their own literary institutions. Already in the Enlightenment, sentimental cosmopolitanism was defining its own international consciousness as standing apart from the sanctioned exploitation of East India Trade Companies, slave traders, and colonial plantations.

Through her close readings of smaller genres, Birgit Tautz shows that northern German salons nurtured spaces and dialogues at odds with louder, more aggressive discourses intent on defining national influence and identity.[7] Tautz claims that German salons and literary correspondences enacted several of the six varieties of cosmopolitanism defined by Pauline Kleingeld.[8] Far from creating literary works that staked out positions within the polemics of the public sphere, these salons enacted their culture more tenuously through conversation and correspondence. Their networks were based on friendship and intimacy, rather than the ethical and aesthetics polemics that defined the Enlightenment. There was an important difference between the fine strands connecting like-minded friends and the public free-for-alls thrown up by controversies, such as Christian Wolff's praise for Confucianism, Lessing's supposed Spinozian leanings, or Kant's racial theories. Salons avoided the *Streitkultur* that has often been equated with *Aufklärung*. Jürgen Habermas's model of the public sphere includes constellations from family reading circles to coffee house conversations to philosophical debates printed in established journals. The networks Wieland describes tend toward the quiet side, where intellectuals are free to ponder

---

7. Birgit Tautz, *Translating the World: Toward a New History of German Literature around 1800* (University Park: Pennsylvania State University Press, 2018), 130.

8. Tautz, *Translating the World*, 152.

without fear of public disclosure. From the outside, these configurations might seem opaque and exclusive. Weimar gatherings were certainly described in exactly those terms by outsiders. Goethe and Schiller's communications through letters and conversations constitute one such closed circle where confrontations were politely avoided. Tautz shows convincingly that cosmopolitan ideals were often expressed first in these small bubbles of intimate thought.

Bookish Friends

Friendships are always intertwined with media not only because letter-writing and its later descendants have fostered relationships over long distances that might otherwise have faded away, but also because the act of reading, mailing, writing, and operating media generally forms friendships in the first place. Sharing the excitement of having read the same book together was central to sentimental friendship, but it was hardly invented there. The European networks of humanist scholars both before and after the Roman Empire's collapse created, as well as depended upon, friendships stretched across space and eventually time. The eighteenth century was noteworthy for bringing women into the wider media circuits of bookish affection. Nuns and aristocratic women had always found partners in reading, but the literary republic of scholars was largely a masculine operation, in Europe as well as in China, a parallel that we will analyze in the last chapter on the Chinese novels Goethe read.

Friendship has been a trope and a psychological model for transcultural relations between same-sex individuals since antiquity. Because they are usually less hierarchical and more malleable than sovereign politics, such intimacies could serve as the pattern for public concepts such as cosmopolitanism and world literature. In their early stages within the eighteenth century, these international networks were often described in terms of the bonds held between friends. The pleasure in sharing letters and literature across time and space depended so much upon the movement of texts through communication channels that the two seemed interchangeable. Reading and exchanging missives could be portrayed as an act of friendship rather than treated as the functional transmission of money, instructions, or news.

With the adaptation of Catholicism to China, male friendship was used in the sixteenth century as a means of fostering agreement, rather than confrontation, between Confucian mandarins and Jesuit priests. As he ingratiated himself into the administrative class of Ming China, Matteo Ricci recognized that homosocial affections reinforced the subtle relations between mandarin scholars. In keeping with his mediating role, Ricci surmised that the sentiments shared by Confucian literati were comparable to the bookish friendships between humanists. The first line of the *Analects*, a work Ricci would have consulted, reinforced this impression: "Confucius said: 'Is it not a pleasure to learn and to repeat or practice from time to time what has been learned? Is it not delightful to have friends coming from afar? Is one not a superior man if he does not feel hurt even though he is not recognized?'"[9] As an opening gesture in the Jesuit campaign to accommodate themselves to Confucius society, Matteo Ricci's translated a Latin compilation of aphorisms on friendship into Chinese.

The shared interest in the philosophy of friendship would have allowed Jesuits to develop social connections with the literati. Jesuit humanist education emphasized Stoic teachings on ethics, which include maxims on obligations between friends, and the early modern network of scholars well understood itself in these terms, as friends sharing their writings on classical texts that first laid out these principles. Peter Sloterdijk defines "the quintessential nature and function of humanism: It is the telecommunication in the medium of print to underwrite friendship. That which has been known since the days of Cicero as *humanism* is in the narrowest and widest sense a consequence of literacy. Ever since philosophy began as a literary genre, it has recruited adherents by writing in an infectious way about love and friendship. Not only is it about love of

---

9. Wing-Tsit Chan, ed. and trans., *A Source Book in Chinese Philosophy* (Princeton, NJ: Princeton University Press, 1963), 18.

wisdom: it is also an attempt to move others to this love."[10] Of the five important Confucian relationships, friendship was the only one available to foreigners and one that had a long humanist tradition.[11] Missionaries composed compilations of ethical maxims translated into Chinese on topics such as friendship in order to demonstrate the compatibility of Western ethics with Confucianism. Relying on compilations already published in Europe that drew primarily on classical, especially Stoical, sources, both Matteo Ricci and Martino Martini after him collected and translated aphorisms on friendship.[12] The practice of collecting statements from Cicero, Plutarch, Aristotle, and Plato about a specific theme—in this case one that resonated strongly with Chinese literati—reflected similarities between the educational methods of the two intellectual classes. Ricci's Chinese book on friendship was entitled *The Book of 25 Paragraphs* and was published in 1605, though he seems to have composed it some five years earlier. Both the book's subject and its means of distribution allowed Ricci to develop and deepen important friendships. In this work Ricci sought to demonstrate that the two classes of scholars shared a similar ethical interest; at the same time he fostered his circle of friends by sending the manuscript around among his acquaintances. The exchange of books, so important in establishing contacts with the republic of letters, was also a means of entering into literary circles in China. The book's contents were carefully composed to appeal specifically to the administrative elite: "Because we needed this book to spread our message in a short time through that whole kingdom . . . several curious things were tossed in, like spices to entice the reader. . . .

---

    10.   Peter Sloterdijk, "*Rules for the Human Zoo*: A Response to the *Letter on Humanism*," trans. Mary Varney Rorty, *Environment and Planning D: Society and Space* 27.1 (2009): 12.
    11.   Norman Kutcher, "The Fifth Relationship: Dangerous Friendships in the Confucian Context," *American Historical Review* 105.5 (2000): 1615–29.
    12.   Lucia Longo, "Martino Martinis *Traktat über die Freundschaft (1661)*," in *Martini Martini (1614–1661) und die Chinamission im 17. Jahrhundert*, ed. Roman Malek & Arnold Zingerle (Sankt Augustin: Institut Monumenta Sinica, 2000), 184–199.

Given their deep-seated propensity for reading, such magistrates always made more time for reading than for conversation"[13] Ricci explains that he circumvented restrictions on foreigners publishing in China by offering the manuscript of his maxims on friendship to a mandarin he knew, who then in turned published it in book form. The book's broadest implication was to express the Europeans' intentions to approach China without hostility. Thus, friendship operates both as an internal motivation holding together the long-distance connections between European scholars and as a cross-cultural avenue of identification. Social rituals are built into the networks of scholarly exchange; friendship has rules and codes within the republic of letters and among Chinese literati. The Jesuits' initial appeal to friendship focused on the elite Confucian enclaves; they did not use it as an emotional appeal to mediate between China and Europe en masse. Intimacy was a means of finding acceptance within small ruling circles in China and within the society itself; the friendships preserved through letter-writing were instruments of the Jesuits' own administrative culture, but they were not the theological lesson to be delivered to the laity. Seventeenth-century European Catholics were not urged to see the Chinese as their friends. Only in the second half of the eighteenth century was friendship invoked within Europe as a supplement to the sympathetic appeal of the Asian martyr. Only after the first adaptations of Chinese literature appeared, did it become plausible for European readers to form affinities with Chinese characters. Friendship became a basis for literary identification as the intense feelings inspired by sentimental reading became more dispersed, less exclusive. Once translators insisted that Chinese romance included features found in European novels, it become plausible to adapt familiar modes of sociability to foreign literary figures.

The idea of world literature stretching out between readers separated by political and linguistic boundaries was one unexpected

---

13. Nicholas Trigault, *The Christian Expedition Undertaken among the Chinese by the Society of Jesus, from the Commentaries of Father Matteo Ricci*, in *Jesuit Writings of the Early Modern Period, 1540–1640*, ed. John Patrick Donnelly, SJ (Indianapolis: Hackett Publishing, 2006), 93.

consequence of these intimate circles. For in its early stages, around Weimar, world literary reading practices were modeled on literary friendships. The social setting of Goethe's comments about Chinese literature is just as important as his performative rhetoric. Eckermann's conversations recreate the language of intimacy, albeit in a rather asymmetrical fashion. The key point is that world literature makes its cosmopolitan appearance during a salon conversation. Only later does it take on the language of manifestos. Goethe's conversations with Eckermann are really a stiff repetition of his earlier, more even-handed exchanges with Friedrich Schiller. This friendship between poets provides the emotional and intellectual openness that allows world literature to become an aesthetic project. As we will examine in chapters 8 and 9, Schiller's recommending a Chinese novel to Goethe could set off a series of discussions seeking to understand, translate, and appropriate the foreign within terms familiar to the two friends. Such literary ensembles, Tautz argues, allowed for greater diversity and complexity than larger, more public forums.[14] The friendships fostered within these circles—Wieland and Goethe both experienced Pietist communities in their youth—were extended to include artists and authors from Europe's expanding library of translated texts. Before long, Goethe approached Hafez and the characters in Chinese novels with the same sympathetic tone that he cultivated with his best friends.

At least two factors in this model of cosmopolitanism suggest that the historical sources for perceiving distant figures as spiritual mates lie in the missionary channels of the post-Reformation Catholic Church: the incorporation of long-range communication networks into local church services and the spiritualization of information channels. Like the early modern church, Enlightenment cosmopolitanism sought to teach its practitioners compassion, sympathy, and identification with strangers, as opposed to Stoic detachment from the polis and family. Adapting the arguments of Shaftesbury and Hume, Adam Smith supplements ancient Stoicism, to the point of thoroughly revising it, by insisting that worldly morality requires feeling sympathy for the suffering of strangers. Smith's

---

14. Tautz, *Translating the World*, 131.

morality takes full advantage of the global circulation of news as it reduces the muting effect of physical distance by offering cosmopolitans access to enough information about distant cultures that they are compelled to care about foreigners as if they were nearby. Already in the sixteenth century, with the expansion of Catholic missionary networks, the European laity were taught similar lesson in prayer, meditation, and compassion for new converts on the other side of the world. To the extent that modern liberal cosmopolitanism insists on empathy and identification with foreign cultures, it professes a secularized version of the global church's teachings. The urge to be informed about distant peoples so that one can empathize with their conditions would seem foolish and unsettling to most any ancient sage. While Stoics looked for the interconnectedness of humans and events, they understood them as driven by cosmological forces. An ancient cosmopolitan, such as Democritus, had to be well traveled in order to learn about foreigners; in the seventeenth century, by contrast, a clear distinction emerged between Europeans who moved about in the world and those who remained home reading reports. This readerly form of cosmopolitanism was unfamiliar to Greek philosophy. Modern cosmopolitanism encourages an individualized and imaginative, sometimes, mystical, connection between people. The new moral obligations— to follow the news and to sympathize—emerged during the sixteenth century as supplements to Stoicism in large part because Jesuit missionaries compiled a global circuit of information and care about their activities. Sympathetic moral cosmopolitanism emerges within global information circuits, thereby altering its obligations fundamentally. News and morality become intertwined more intensely and on a much larger scale than ever.

Once the notion of a global network is posited, the character of its intellectual content is open to variation. From the earliest, the notion of a global church was accompanied with its own negation, a global atheism, shared by the intellectual elite in China and Europe. Not only was the radical Enlightenment quick to reverse pious assertions about shared intercultural revelations, but the mission in China included a minor voice that suspected the mandarins of really being just atheists, with no clear sense of a ruler in heaven and no particular affinity for Christianity. For every assertion of a theological globalism, there followed the possibility that the comparative study of religion would demonstrate the universality of atheism—defined in broad terms.

In its fully developed form, Enlightenment cosmopolitanism represented the explicit rejection of the Jesuit mission to Christianize the world. If Jesuit accommodation acknowledged the self-sufficiency and legitimacy of Asian cultures, the Rites Controversy made clear that the Catholic hierarchy was willing to cast aside other traditions to assert its own dogma. From this anticlerical vantage, even accommodation appeared as a sly maneuver to subjugate Confucianism. Radical Enlightenment thinkers often portrayed the Jesuit mission as a subtle power move. In *Rameau's Nephew*, Denis Diderot provides a double-reading of Jesuit accommodation as a secret maneuver. Diderot argues that their modest introduction of Christ into the syncretic environment of Chinese and Indian religions had the intention of conquering both without violence or armies:

> The True, which is the Father and engenders the Good, which is the Son who creates the Beautiful, which is the Holy Spirit. The foreign god humbly goes to sit down next to the local idol on the altar; bit by bit, he grows stronger; and one fine day, he gives his companion a little shove, and boom boom, down the idol falls. That's how they say the Jesuits planted Christianity in China and the Indies. And the Jansenists can say what they like, but this way of doing politics, which achieves its goal without making a stir, without any bloodletting, without creating martyrs, without so much as a tuft of hair being pulled out, seems the best to me.[15]

German intellectuals were quite familiar with such ideas. In a curious historical turn, Diderot's original French manuscript of *Rameau's Nephew* was lost for decades presumably to avoid censure, so that the only copy available to the eighteenth-century reading public was Goethe's German translation.[16] Wieland's more rationalist

15. Denis Diderot, *Rameau's Nephew—Le Neveau de Rameau: A Multi-Media Bilingual Edition*, ed. Marian Hobson, Kate E. Tunstall, and Caroline Warman (Open Books Classics, 2016), 75–76.

16. Johann Wolfgang Goethe, *Goethes Werke* (Weimar: Hermann Böhlaus Nachfolger, 1887–1919), vol. 45; hereafter cited as WA.

cosmopolitanism had an anticolonial vein to the extent that it refrained from the Catholic insistence that its truth would ultimately replace others. Enlightenment critics well understood that the missionary network offered a model of global spiritual union at the price of Catholicism's long view approach to conversion.

The political stakes were apparent to later Romantics as well. Joseph von Eichendorff's Catholic interpretation of the eighteenth century lays bare the genealogical relation between missionary networks and the Enlightenment worldliness, while also making clear that the rejection of church dogma, martyrdom, and drive to convert were crucial principles for cosmopolitans. For Eichendorff, the secularization of Catholic institutions was never a quiet, peaceful process; it always involved the expulsion of priests and the erasure of theology. Rather than surrender to secularism, Eichendorff hoped to revive the Catholic worldliness of the Jesuits.[17] Writing against what he perceived as the fragmentations created by political parties generally, from Enlightenment liberals to ultramontane monarchists, he reinterprets eighteenth-century cosmopolitanism as a secularization of an even older Catholic tradition.[18] Striking a melancholy chronological tone, Eichendorff summarizes: "Thus, there emerged in stages and parallel to each other, cosmopolitanism, along with philanthropism, humanity, tolerance, natural religion, the religions of sentimentalism, art, reason, etc. In part, praiseworthy virtues were presented independently as something previously unheard of and new, thereby forgetting entirely that they were once subordinate to a higher principle and that each one, when put its proper place, was already included within Christianity."[19] If Wieland felt a pre-Revolutionary optimism that cosmopolitanism could finally emerge from its secret social network, the situation was quite reversed in

---

17. Andrea Albrecht, *Kosmopolitismus: Weltbürgerdiskurse in Literatur, Philosophie und Publizistik um 1800* (Berlin: De Gruyter, 2005), 354.

18. Jutta Osinski, "Eichendorffs Kulturkritik," *Aurora: Jahrbuch der Eichendorff-Gesellschaft* 61 (2001): 89.

19. Joseph von Eichendorff, *Der deutsche Roman des achtzehnten Jahrhunderts in seinem Verhältnis zum Christentum*, in *Eichendorff Werke: Geschichte der Poesie, Schriften zur Literaturgeschichte*, ed. Hartwig Schultz (Frankfurt: Deutscher Klassiker Verlag, 1990), 456. See also Albrecht, *Kosmopolitsimus*, 353.

1850 when Joseph von Eichendorff was composing a literary history of the eighteenth century. Writing right after the failed revolution in 1848, Eichendorff sought to revive what he considered to be a Catholic cosmopolitanism as a response to rising Protestant hostility and liberal-leftist assertions of the Enlightenment.[20] Positioned within a Eurocentric perspective that accepted the rapid expansion of its colonial territories, he sought to demonstrate that cosmopolitanism was not confined to a single political party, but had a much wider and longer history within Christianity as a whole. Wieland, in turn, had also claimed that cosmopolitans had maintained a secret history for thousands of years, though he did so without ascribing it to one religion. The survival of cosmopolitans depended in part on their ability to communicate with local authorities as they sought each other out. Wieland claims that cosmopolitans make excellent citizens: they adapt to the laws under which they live, they never ferment revolution, even as they carry on discretely with their international allegiances.

While the belief in a global Christian church continues to motivate missionaries to this day, in the middle of the eighteenth century the European Enlightenment formulated an emotional cosmopolitanism that distinguished itself from the older, colder Stoic formulations and from the Catholic missionary model.[21] Some of the earliest secular articulations of how emotions could constitute moral intercultural relationships appeared in England. "To love the public, to study universal good, and to promote the interest of the whole world, so far as lies within our power, is surely the height of goodness, and makes that temper which we call divine."[22] Shaftesbury's position may sound quite pious from a twenty-first-century point of view, yet it constitutes an important moment in the slow transformation of Christian teaching based on scripture to a secular morality intent on applying specific rational claims universally. Christoph Martin Wieland's literary career

---

20. Eichendorff, *Der deutsche Roman*, 354.

21. Luke Clossey's account of the Jesuit's global missions, *Salvation and Globalization in the Early Jesuit Missions* (Cambridge: Cambridge University Press, 2008), is particularly sensitive to its discursive forms and thus quite useful for literary scholars.

22. Anthony, Earl of Shaftesbury, "A Letter Concerning Enthusiasm," in *Characteristics of Men, Manners, Opinions, Times* (Indianapolis: Bobbs-Merril, 1964), 27.

spans this transition. He was one of Shaftesbury's most enthusiastic German readers.

Secret Sentiments

Wieland's effort to define cosmopolitanism runs self-consciously through a succession of works, with the later ones alluding the earlier statements. His first formulation is fragmentary and sentimental, written at a time when he still moved within Pietist circles. In a collection of intimate letters, entitled "Sympathies," the young Wieland imagined a global community of emotionally connected readers dispersed over time and place.[23] Out of Pietism's "invisible church of saints," Wieland draws a similar community of cosmopolitans, who, like Calvinists, were predestined from birth to assume a worldly affinity.[24] Wieland saw, in 1754, the possibility for an imaginary communion of sympathetic souls with fewer social obligations and conventions than the scholarly networks already dispersed throughout Europe. While Pietist circles were usually composed of a small, local coterie, Wieland has little trouble dispersing his aspirations across the globe. The young thinker offers a convergence of Pietistic missionary aspirations with an enthusiastic language of the heart comparable to Europe's republic of letters or the Jesuits' global mission. He celebrates the joy kindred spirits feel when they meet each other, as if they were once together in an earlier existence but then had been separated. Wieland explains that time and geography often prevent sympathetic unions: "How fortunate when sympathetic souls find each other. . . . Fate may have separated them as they departed from those blessed shores to take

---

23. Christoph Martin Wieland, *Sämmtliche Werke* (Leipzig: Göschen, 1857) 29:1–63. For a contextualization, see Bernhard Seuffert, "Der junge Wieland," *Zeitschrift für deutsches Altertum und deutsche Literatur* 26 (1882): 252–87; Roderick R. Milne, "Line of Desire: The Body and the Spirit in the Pre-Erotic Texts of Christoph Martin Wieland," PhD diss., University of Toronto, 1998.

24. Here I am applying Max Weber's terminology from *The Protestant Ethic and the "Spirit" of Capitalism*, trans. Peter Baehr and Gordon Wells (New York: Penguin, 2002), 88, 89.

up their challenges in this foreign land. Still, their friendly angel brings them closer together, even when the years, mountains, and rivers lie between them."[25] Like Leibniz, Wieland attributes the physical separation of such souls to forces beyond anyone's control. Not unlike the Jesuit ideal of the worldwide church in its spiritual organization, Wieland's global network is composed of those who share a bond of sympathy.[26] "And can it be any different than that all those who have been blessed with this manner of thinking are connected in a secret spiritual union and thus stand close to each other, even if their glances have never encountered one another and their lips have never parted for each other?"[27] He clearly borrows the Church's spiritual language, though only with the broadest, least concrete notion of God: "Their inclinations meet one another, their purest wishes rise up together toward God, their spirit strives in parallel lines toward perfection, their hope flows toward the same center together."[28] Intellectual desire, what Wieland calls "wit," serves as the driving force that brings this spiritual network together despite geographical distances: "And if place and time separate them, then their wits and the desires of their heart come to their aid, to find a means of bringing the inhabitants from remote regions together in an instant."[29] Farther along in the text, a correspondent belonging to this union insists that "no dislocation of place shall hinder the spirit, whose thoughts do not allow themselves to be confined within any boundaries."[30]

Similar to Kafka's recipient of the imperial message, Wieland sinks into a daydream as he contemplates the temporal and geographical enactment of these global connections. He imagines sympathetic souls as existing in a spiritual relationship even as they are dispersed around the earth, so that they could at any given moment be thinking about each other: "How often does my soul flee from

---

25. Wieland, *Sämmtliche Werke*, 29:3.

26. Sigrid Thielking, *Weltbürgertum: Kosmopolitische Ideen in Literatur und politischer Publizistik seit dem achtzehnten Jahrhundert* (Munich: Fink, 2000), 32.

27. Wieland, *Sämmtliche Werke*, 29:5.

28. Wieland, *Sämmtliche Werke*, 29:5.

29. Wieland, *Sämmtliche Werke*, 29:5.

30. Wieland, *Sämmtliche Werke*, 29:40.

the distractions of the day into the quiet lonely shadow, into its favorite thoughts in order to entertain itself with invisible objects;
how often do I delight myself there with the sweet idea that the spirits are related to each other and that many of my sibling spirits
scattered across the earth's surface have also in this very moment
fled into their lonely shadows in order to entertain themselves with
the same thoughts and objects!"[31] As part of the Pietist aspiration
to escape feudal confines, Wieland's prose avoids specific references
to class and identity; coupled with a missionary sensibility of the
global reach that his sympathetic community, Wieland allows his
thoughts to fly around the world in order to find similarly sensitive
souls. Perhaps they too are looking for a friend who would share
their perceptions, to whom they could open their heart. Further,
Wieland reveals that writing is indeed the means to bring about this
cosmopolitan union, and thus he addresses the reader directly as
just such a sympathetic soul, thereby making explicit that his sympathetic union can be actualized as a literary exchange. Because the
parties to the union may never see or speak with each other, writing and reading are the only avenues for exchange. "You alone understand these pages; you alone will know and feel this language,
and only in your hearts will my sympathetic feelings find their
answer."[32] Wieland sets no physical or temporal limits on the possibility of exchange between sympathizers.

While his language may be typical for German sentimentalism,
his emotional aspirations extend far beyond Central Europe, so that
it would be quite plausible for Novalis to have shared Wieland's Pietist cosmopolitanism as he wrote "Die Lehrlinge von Sais" (The
apprentices to Sais) and for Goethe to remembered him as he read
Hafez.[33] Wieland's conceptualization of a sympathetic community

31. Wieland, *Sämmtliche Werke*, 29:6.
32. Wieland, *Sämmtliche Werke*, 29:7.
33. Fritz Martini, "Nachwort," in Christoph Martin Wieland, *Werke*, vol. 3,
ed. Fritz Martini and Reinhard Döhl (Munich: Carl Hanser, 1967), 960: "Die
'Sympathien' sind nicht nur in Form und Wortschatz ein signifikantes Dokument
der Empfindsamkeit, sie sind auch eine wirkungskräftige Etappe innerhalb der Geschichte der deutschen poetischen Prosa und haben noch in der Frühromantik, wie
bei Novalis, ein Echo ausgelöst."

extended far beyond the small reading and prayer groups for which German Pietism was known. In another early essay, "Gesicht von einer Welt unschuldiger Menschen" (The face of a world of innocents), Wieland conceptualizes his ideal emotional community on a planetary scale. This essay offers a mixture of Christian harmony and intergalactic wandering, inspired by Milton but written as a utopia, wherein angels travel across the galaxy to visit a planet where people lived in spiritual harmony.[34] Wieland's Pietist science fiction phase was short lived, but his conceptualization of an international community persisted into his later, much more circumspect discussions of Enlightenment cosmopolitanism.

In his most famous formulation, Wieland defines cosmopolitans in terms of a secret network of friends, who recognize one another immediately even though they have never met before. Cosmopolitanism is constituted by interpersonal bonds: it operates as an emotional network between singular people, rather than as a morality that detaches itself from family and city. The frequently quoted definition appeared in *Geschichte der Abderiten* (*The History of the Abderites*), first published in installments from 1773 to 1779 in his journal, *Der teutsche Merkur* (*The German Mercury*), and then a year later as a volume. The novel is set in the ancient Greek city of the title, though its intent is a satire of German provincial town. The occasion for defining cosmopolitans arises in a chapter in which the two great Greek thinkers, Democritus and Hippocrates, meet each other for the first time: "There exists a type of mortal, known since the ancients and referred to under the name of cosmopolitans, who without prior agreement, without special insignias, without lodge meetings, and without being bound by oaths, have constituted a kind of brotherhood, that holds together more tightly than any other order in the world."[35] This union spans across distant soulmates: "Two cosmopolitans come together, one from the East, the other from the West, see each other for the first time and are friends." Already in

34. Wieland, *Sämmtliche Werke*, 29:77–102.

35. C. M. Wieland, *Geschichte der Abderiten*, in *Sämmtliche Werke* (Leipzig: Göschen, 1796), 19:216. The first printed version includes a clause contrasting the bond between cosmopolitans with those of Free Masons or Jesuits. For the very first version of the novel, see *Teutscher Merkur* 6 (1774): 149.

this passage, Wieland holds out the possibility of spiritual and intellectual connections between Asians and Europeans. When, decades later, Goethe finds a warm affinity with the Persian poet Hafez and with Chinese mandarins, he could be easily understood as an exemplar of such cosmopolitans. Wieland's earlier invocation of sympathies finds an ironic recuperation in *The History of the Abderites*, where he states that the cosmopolitan connection does not arise from any secret sympathy, for those can only be found in novels. Moving away from the hyperbole of his youthful *Sympathien*, he now refers to cosmopolitans as brothers and intimate friends.[36] Consistently, though, Wieland holds to the proposition that cosmopolitanism is defined, first and foremost, through the emotional rapport between members.[37]

Wieland returned to the proposition that cosmopolitans constitute a worldwide society of sympathetic intellectuals in 1788, during the earliest stages of the French Revolution, when he published "Das Geheimniß des Kosmopoliten-Ordens" (The secret of the cosmopolitan order) in the *Teutsche Merkur*. Sensing that a major political transformation was on the horizon, Wieland declared that cosmopolitanism need not be considered the exclusive concern of secret organizations. His cautious phrasing suggests that he is describing a clandestine philosophy. Wieland's reticence demonstrates that cosmopolitanism has long been treated with suspicion. While scholars today may look back to the late Kant's defense of a cosmopolitan world order and Goethe's world literature as founding statements, it is vital to recognize the domestic hostility such pronouncements faced. Goethe's pronouncements on world literature were criticized throughout the nineteenth century and often turned on their head by imperialists as a hierarchical ranking of civilizations.

Many of the Enlightenment concerns about secret societies (the ostensible topic of Wieland's cosmopolitan essay) were reiterations of long-standing conspiracy theories leveled against the Jesuits. They

---

36. Wieland, *Abderiten*, in *Sämmtliche Werke* (1796), 19:217.
37. Klaus Manger, "Wielands Kosmopoliten," in *Europäische Sozietätsbewegung und demokratische Tradition: Die europäischen Akademien der Frühen Neuzeit zwischen Frührenaissance und Spätaufklärung*, ed. Klaus Garber, Heinz Wismann, and Winfried Siebers (Tübingen: Niemeyer, 1996), 2:1659.

also demonstrate both the limitations and curious affinities in Reinhold Koselleck's and Jonathan Israel's (radical Enlightenment)
claim that secrecy was a central strategy of the Enlightenment. By
arguing for cosmopolitanism as an open citizenship in the world,
Wieland is decisively redefining the terms of the Enlightenment as no
longer confined to a chosen circle. But in acknowledging the end of
secrecy, Wieland is also revealing that there had been any number of
subterranean connections in previous epochs. Now, he states, in an
age of Enlightenment, on the eve of the French Revolution, such
speculations are no longer required. Wieland seems to be announcing the end of clandestine philosophy, as if it were no longer necessary to hide radical thought at odds with church and monarchy.[38]

By making this declaration, Christoph Wieland exposed the previously unspoken assumption that cosmopolitanism had indeed been
practiced in secret, as it would not be tolerated by monarchs, popes,
and princes. In a sense, the Enlightenment could now abandon the
closet that features in so many eighteenth-century dramas. Much as
Goethe would later try to do for world literature, Wieland announced
a new era in which intellectuals could openly espouse cosmopolitan
principles. Indeed from now on they were obliged to do so, in order to
avoid the compromises to rational critique that secrecy entails. "Cosmopolitans will benefit in the eyes of the public only by explaining the
revelation of their secret."[39] While Wieland's understanding of cosmopolitanism is closely akin to definitions of Enlightenment, his focus on
crossing the boundary from secrecy to publicity shows that cosmopolitans have always existed; thus, the public appearance of cosmopolitanism does not entail a dramatic rupture with the past so much
as the revelation of something that has always been there, just hidden.
There is nothing in their constitution, in their purposes, or in their
means that has to hide itself behind allegorical veils and hieroglyphic
obscurity. They are allowed to show the world who they are and for

---

38. Antony McKenna, "Klandestine Philosophie," trans. Astrid Finke and Gloria
Buschor-Kotzor, in *Radikalaufklärung*, ed. Jonathan I. Israel and Martin Mulsow
(Berlin: Suhrkamp, 2014), 149–86.

39. C. M. Wieland, "Das Geheimniß des Kosmopoliten-Ordens (1788)," in
Sämmtliche Werke (1857), 30:401.

what they stand."[40] By unbinding cosmopolitanism from the logic of the closet, Wieland also opens up the possibility that any number of historical positions could now be interpreted as having shared cosmopolitan principles.

Wieland's essay was motivated as a response to the kind of sweeping denunciations made by another Weimar figure, the conservative courtier Ernst August Anton Göchhausen, who railed against "world citizens, Enlighteners, Jesuits and Free Masons."[41] Göchhausen proposed the theory that the Illuminati Order was conspiracy run by the Jesuits. Without bowing to reactionary hysteria, Wieland directly affirms the established reputation: "Cosmopolitans bear the name, 'citizens of the world,' in its original and most meaning, for they view all people on the earth as so many branches of one family. The universe they view as a single state, in which they are citizens along with countless other rational beings."[42] He boldly affirms the ancient notion that a cosmopolitan rejects allegiance to his clan and polis: "What the old Greek republics and the proud citizens of these cities, who believed they were born to dominate the world, called love for the fatherland is, according to cosmopolitanism's fundamental concepts, attitudes, and obligations, an unacceptable passion."[43] Added to this negative definition, Wieland insists that they are joined together "by a certain natural relation and sympathy."[44] "Despite all distances of space and time, they stand in the closest connection to each other"[45] His spiritual language climbs back into the enthusiasm of his youth—the very opposite of Stoic detachment—when he concludes that "cosmopolitans, as much as they may be scattered about in the world, are all together, in the clearest meaning of this expression, *one heart* and *one soul*."[46] These sympathetic supplements to

---

40. Wieland, "Das Geheimniß," 30:401.

41. Ernst August Anton Göchhausen, *Enthüllung des Systems der Weltbürger-Republik, In Briefen aus der Verlassenschaft eines Freymaurers* (Rome,1786); Albrecht, *Kosmopolitanismus*, 98.

42. Wieland, "Das Geheimniß," 30:406.

43. Wieland, "Das Geheimniß," 30:406.

44. Wieland, "Das Geheimniß," 30:410.

45. Wieland, "Das Geheimniß," 30:411.

46. Wieland, "Das Geheimniß," 30:411 (emphasis in original).

the restrained notion of cosmopolitanism represent a fundamental break with the Stoic definition, and they embody a humanist and secular adaptation of Christian universalism—the belief that the faithful around the globe constitutes a single spiritual union. Wieland and Eichendorff both assert that cosmopolitanism has an unrecognized, or secret, history that stretches much farther back than the Enlightenment and that includes more than ancient Greek philosophy. From the vantagepoint of Goethe's world literature, one could posit that both Hafez and Matteo Ricci belonged to this broad, loosely defined society.

7

Adam Smith and the Chinese Earthquake

To the extent that sentimentalism emerged across Europe in the eighteenth century, with parallel formulations in different languages, we may ask how self-aware such writers were about the international reach of their discourse. To what degree did sentimental writers reflect upon the cosmopolitan character of their own feelings? When did they start looking for emotional correspondences between themselves and distant foreigners? Adam Smith's *Theory of Moral Sentiments* (1759) provides a striking passage challenging readers to consider just how capable Europeans were in feeling with peoples they knew only through textual mediation. The resonance of his inquiry among Germans became a measure of how far his ideas on sympathy could extend. By incorporating the moral claims from Smith, as well as elements from Lord Shaftesbury, Francis Hutcheson, and David Hume, German Enlightenment writers were already implicitly demonstrating their own inclination to identify with foreign sentiments.

The reception of English fiction and philosophy was decisive in fostering the German Enlightenment. Moral weeklies such as the *Tatler*, *Spectator*, and *Guardian*, along with Fielding's and Richardson's novels, established an affinity between sentimental writing on both sides of the channel. Gotthold Lessing translated the work of Smith's teacher, Francis Hutcheson's *A System of Moral Philosophy* (1756) into German, an activity that helped him adapt the moral philosophy of sympathy into *Mitleid* (pity).[1] The shared German and English investigations into the psychology of spectatorship went into minute detail. In section four of *Laokoon oder Über die Grenzen der Malerei und Poesie* (*Laocoon, or the Limits of Painting and Poetry*, 1767), Lessing draws on Smith's *Theory of Moral Sentiments*, quoting a long passage on the semiotics of extreme suffering and the viewer's ability to sympathize.[2] In recounting the German reception of Adam Smith's philosophy, economic historians have long focused solely on *Wealth of Nations*. Since the 1980s, however, literary scholars have called more attention to Smith's less competitive side by highlighting the affinities between *Theory of Moral Sentiments* and Lessing's *Laokoon* essay. Ellwood Wiggins claims that Lessing and Smith complement each other, because Smith's moral psychology has a theatrical structure. Lessing, on the other hand, insists that the most moral person is the one with the most sympathy, yet he does so without formulating clear ethical principles in the manner of Smith.[3] Katherine Harloe insists that Lessing incorporated Smith's psychology into his own arguments about tragedy, even if he claimed to be debating the Englishman.[4]

---

1. Thomas Martinec, "Übersetzung und Adaption, Lessings Verhältnis zu Francis Hutcheson," in *'ihrem Originale nachzudenken': Zu Lessings Übersetzungen*, ed. Helmut Berthold (Tübingen: Niemeyer, 2008), 95–114.

2. For a clear account, see Arnold Heidsieck, "Adam Smith's Influence on Lessing's View of Man and Society," *Lessing Yearbook* 15, ed. Edward Harris (1983): 125–44.

3. Ellwood Wiggins, "Pity Play: Sympathy and Spectatorship in Lessing's *Miss Sara Sampson* and Adam Smith's *Theory of Moral Sentiments*," in *Performing Knowledge: 1750–1850*, ed. Mary Helen Dupree and Sean B. Franzel (Berlin: De Gruyter, 2015), 85–111.

4. Katherine Harloe, "Sympathy, Tragedy, and the Morality of Sentiment in Lessing's Laocoon," in *Rethinking Lessing's Laocoon: Antiquity, Enlightenment,*

Kant also appreciated Smith's moral philosophy without offering footnotes, by praising him in the 1770s for offering insights into human moral understanding beyond those offered by German writers on the subject. The Königsberg philosopher was particularly drawn to Smith's visual model of an impartial spectator who stands over the subject, holding him accountable for his moral feelings.[5] In 1777, when Johann Heinrich Georg Feder reviewed the first translation of Smith's *Wealth of Nations*, he noted that German readers were already familiar with his work: "Through his *Theory of Moral Sentiments* the name of author has long been known already as an excellent philosopher, leading us to expect nothing mediocre from him."[6]

How emotional identification with foreigners serves to establish a cosmopolitan sense of similarity can be seen in Smith's reflection in the fourth edition of *The Theory of Moral Sentiments*, wherein he asks the reader to contemplate how a civilized European might react to news that all of China had been destroyed by an earthquake: "Let us suppose that the great empire of China, with all its myriads of inhabitants, was suddenly swallowed up by an earthquake, and let us consider how a man of humanity in Europe, who had no sort of connection with that part of the world, would be affected upon receiving intelligence of this dreadful calamity."[7] From the vantage point of media history, Smith offers probably the first moral conjecture predicated specifically upon the flow of news reporting across continents. Smith sets the absence of a personal relationship with China as a condition to his query, while focusing instead on how the mere conveyance of mediated news could produce sympathy. Writing less than a decade after the devastating Lisbon

and the 'Limits' of Painting a Poem, ed. Avi Lifschitz and Michael Squire (Oxford: Oxford University Press, 2017): 158–78.

5. Samuel Fleischacker, "Philosophy in Moral Practice: Kant and Adam Smith," *Kant-Studien* 82.3 (1991): 249–68.

6. Johann Heinrich Georg Feder, [Review of *Wealth of Nations*], *Göttingischen Anzeigen von gelehrten Sachen* (March 10, 1777): 234.

7. Adam Smith, *The Theory of Moral Sentiments* (Indianapolis: Liberty, 1976), 233–34.

earthquake, Smith takes it for granted that the delivery of such long-distance information has, by the mid-eighteenth century, become commonplace. The shock lies in the content of the news—namely, the massive earthquake—and not in the fact of its delivery from the other side of the world. His assumption that Europeans regularly receive news about both China and distant earthquakes was quite reasonable. Newspapers and their forerunners, on the continent and in Great Britain, had been transmitting updates about shocking natural catastrophes long before the Lisbon earthquake of 1755.[8] His scenario is really concerned with analyzing the recipient's emotional response to the media. The first German translation refers to the subject of the thought experiment as an emotional European.[9] Are these emotions intense enough to establish a cosmopolitan sense of unity? Does distance mitigate our feelings for the suffering of others? In his provocative question, Smith suggests that once our sympathy has found expression, once we have given voice to our shock and dismay, we would be quickly distracted by the smallest of personal complaints. The sympathetic spectator would, in other words, move from the sublime to the domestic. This sequence of diminishing sympathy reverses the hierarchy of baroque tragic drama in which the audience's emotions are directed toward the monarch as representative of the people. Ever since George Lillo's *London Merchant* (1731), English drama had allowed that tragedies occur not only to the great

8.   Carlos H. Caracciolo, "Natural Disasters and the European Printed News Network," in *News Networks in Early Modern Europe*, ed. Joad Raymond and Noah Moxham (Leiden: Brill, 2016), 756–78.

9.   Adam Smith, *Adam Smiths Theorie der sittlichen Gefühle*, trans. Ludwig Theobul Kosegarten (Leipzig: Graff, 1791), 218: "Laßt uns annehmen, daß das ganze große Kaiserthum China, mit allen seinen Millionen Einwohnern, jähling von einem Erdbeben verschlungen würde, und laßt uns erwägen, wie ein gefühlvoller Europäer, der mit diesem Welttheil in gar keiner Verbindung stände, durch die Zeitung dieses fürchterlichen Unglücks affizirt werden würde." For a quick and easy overview of Smith's and the Scots' reception in the German Enlightenment, see Norbert Waszek, "The Scottish Enlightenment in Germany," in *Scotland in Europe*, ed. Tom Hubbard and R. D. S. Jack (Amsterdam: Rodopi, 2006), 55–72. For a thorough examination of sources, translations, reviews, and philosophical adaptations of Scottish thinkers in Germany, see Norbert Waszek, *The Scottish Enlightenment and Hegel's Account of 'Civil Society'* (Dordrecht: Kluwer, 1988).

and powerful. Smith's reasoning follows this turn toward the ordinary person as the bearer of tragic fate. From baroque to Enlightenment, Vondel to Smith, sympathy for China shifts from the emperor to the populace at large.

Smith is also addressing David Hume's earlier argument that the strength of our sympathy depends on how distant we are from its object. "Sympathy . . . is much fainter than our concern for ourselves, and sympathy with persons remote from us much fainter than that with persons near and contiguous."[10] Our own concerns trouble us much more than those of 100 million distant foreigners. Hume's notion of sympathy concentrates on the similarities between humans in terms of our recognition of resemblances; he seems less concerned with the expression of strong emotion than with epistemology. Hume takes an affectively neutral position, preferring to define sympathy in terms of the subject's ability to identify with another on the basis of shared traits. In this sense he preserves the ancient Stoic detachment while not giving his hypothesis over to a more intense understanding of compassion. Käte Hamburger argues in this regard that to the extent that it implies a "suffering with another," the German *Mitleid* fails as an adequate translation of Hume's meaning. Hamburger admires Hume's concept of sympathy precisely because it preserves the awareness of the other as distanced from oneself: it constructs a bond through shared humanity rather than an affective kinship.[11] Hume grounded the recognition of similarities, or sympathies, in human nature: "There is a remarkable inclination in human nature, to bestow on external objects the same emotions, which it observes in itself; and to find everywhere those ideas, which are most present to it."[12] In Smith's more complex formulation, the relationship between the sufferer and the spectator does not involve emulation or projection; instead, he posits a parallel between the two, thereby importing the language of cosmo-

---

10. David Hume, *Enquiries Concerning Human Understanding and Concerning the Principals of Morals*, ed. P. H. Nidditch (Oxford: Clarendon Press, 1975), sect. 186, 229.

11. Käte Hamburger, *Das Mitleid* (Stuttgart: Klett-Cotta, 1986), 110–16.

12. David Hume, *A Treatise of Human Nature* (New York: Barnes and Noble, 2005), 173.

logical harmony into psychology: "When the original passions of the person principally concerned are *in perfect concord* with the sympathetic emotions of the spectator, they necessarily appear to this last just and proper, and suitable to their objects."[13]

Adam Smith's choice of China for his thought experiment was not random. Much more than serving as a placeholder for "some distant place," China embodied a great civilization parallel to Europe. As Phil Dodds has shown, "China played a vital role in Scottish Enlightenment thought."[14] For both Hume and Smith, China represented the great "other" civilization that challenged the universal validity of any European hypothesis. If Smith argued that wealth was established through international commerce, China's closed market and vast wealth offered a potential counter argument. Smith's information came in part through his acquittance with Edinburgh merchants who traded in Canton.[15] While he also turned to French Jesuit treatises, most prominently Du Halde's *Description géographique, historique, chronologique, politique, et physique de l'empire de la chine et de la tartarie chinoise (General History of China, Containing a Geographical, Historical, Chronological, Political and Physical Description of the Empire of China,* 1735), he was skeptical about their reports, famously stating "The accounts of [Chinese public] works, . . . which have been transmitted to Europe, have generally been drawn up by weak and wondering travellers; frequently by stupid and lying missionaries.'[16] Smith's attitude was clearly much more influenced by the views of merchants than of the philosophically inclined Jesuits. In *The Wealth of Nations*, Smith states: "The Chinese have little respect for foreign trade. Your beggarly commerce! was the language in which the Mandarins of Pekin

---

13.   Smith, *Theory of Moral Sentiments*, 58 (emphasis added).

14.   Phil Dodds, "'One Vast Empire': China, Progress, and the Scottish Enlightenment," *Global Intellectual History* 3.1 (2018): 49.

15.   For a microhistory of Scottish private traders working in Asia outside the parameters of the East India Company, see Jessica Hanser, *Mr. Smith Goes to China: Three Scots in the Making of Britain's Global Empire* (New Haven, CT: Yale University Press, 2019).

16.   Adam Smith, *An Inquiry into the Nature and Causes of the Wealth of Nations*, ed R. H. Campbell, A. S. Skinner, and W. B. Todd (Oxford: Oxford University Press, 1976), 2:729.

used to talk to Mr. De Lange, the Russian envoy, concerning it. Except with Japan, the Chinese carry on, themselves, and in their own bottoms, little or no foreign trade."[17] As for so many Europeans, China was an object of fascination precisely because of its refusal to engage in trade. Smith was no different: "China has been long one of the richest, that is, one of the most fertile, best cultivated, most industrious, and most populous countries in the world."[18] *The Wealth of Nations* presents one of the first formulations of an argument that would be deployed sharply by British diplomats later. "[China] seems ... to have been long stationary. Marco Polo, who visited it more than five hundred years ago, describes its cultivation, industry, and populousness, almost in the same terms in which they are described by travellers in the present times."[19] While the key economic question for Smith was whether China would open its ports to foreign traders, this did not deter his positing an affinity for Chinese people in his moral philosophy. The theatrical position of his typical moral agent has often been noted, and Smith clearly has recent plays in mind when contemplates sympathy for China: "In that beautiful tragedy of Voltaire, the Orphan of China, while we admire the magnanimity of Zamti, who is willing to sacrifice the life of his own child, in order to preserve that of the only feeble remnant of his ancient sovereigns and masters; we not only pardon, but love the maternal tenderness of Idame, who, at the risque of discovering the important secret of her husband, reclaims her infant from the cruel hands of the Tartars, into which it had been delivered."[20] Smith's reflections present a cosmopolitan triangle involving a Scottish admirer of a French play about a Chinese family. His summary of Voltaire's adaptation based on a Jesuit translation of a Yuan-era drama concentrates on the intimacies of family life more than on the drama's imperial politics in a way that calls attention to the sentimental potential for cross-cultural literary identification

---

17. Smith, *Wealth of Nations*, 2:680.
18. Smith, *Wealth of Nations*, 1:89.
19. Smith, *Wealth of Nations*, 1:89.
20. Smith, *Moral Sentiments*, 371.

The question of whether it was possible for people to feel sympathy over long distances had immediate relevance to the emerging British Empire. While grounded in the suffering of others, sympathy could motivate colonial policies. Such feelings could be translated into concrete policies, particularly if they were intended to alleviate the pain of oppressed subjects. In his speech on the India Bill of 1783, aimed against corruption among the British agents on the subcontinent, Edmund Burke stressed the need for the English voter to sympathize with the ordinary inhabitants of India in order to understand what it feels like to be ruled by the arbitrary power of the East India Company.[21] Meant to inform members of Parliament, the speech includes a geographical survey of India along with a critical review of the East India Company's misalliances and broken treaties. Like Smith, Burke is well aware that distance coupled with ignorance could hamper sympathy. "But we are in general . . . so little acquainted with Indian details; the instruments of oppression under which the people suffer are so hard to be understood; and even the very names of the sufferers are so uncouth and strange to our ears, that it is very difficult for our sympathy to fix upon these objects."[22] At the start of his speech, Burke asserts his authority as an expert on India by providing a geographical review of the subcontinent. India's sublimity has immediate political implications for the British. With vast territory come monumental responsibilities. In other words, Burke is preparing his suggestion that the company now rules like an Asian despot over vast territories and that it needs to be reformed lest the abuses of power undertaken abroad be brought back to England—an anticolonial argument that stretches back as far as Euripides and Thucydides.

To build India up as an object of concern, Burke lists off the variety of traditions and populations within. He admonishes members of Parliament for focusing the debate about the India bill primarily on coalition politics within England, rather than on the Indian people,

---

21. For a broader discussion of Burke's speech and orientalism, see Frederick Wheelan, *Enlightenment Political Thought and Non-Western Societies: Sultans and Savages* (London: Routledge, 2012), 103–29.

22. James Burke, *The Speeches of the Right Honorable Edmund Burke* (Dublin: Duffy, 1854), 249.

instead it has focused. Much the same could have been said about the scandal surrounding Christian Wolff's speech on Chinese ethics at the University of Halle—the participants had nothing to say about China, but devoted vast reams of paper to church-state politics. Burke is eager to display his many years of study devoted to India. Like Wolff, Burke published his China speech with a long critical apparatus of footnotes that dwarfs the original text. Then as now, the Orient was a territory that attracted scholars eager to display their own learnedness. The overwhelming complexity of the place, which Burke alone seems to have comprehended, leads him to catalog Indian geography. So great is the space, that it threatens to confuse the audience, making it seem more fabulous than ever. As Sara Suleri notes: "In seeking to represent the physical tangibility of the subcontinent, he succeeds only in essentializing size into a numbing sequence of figures."[23] Burke's display of his knowledge about India inadvertently generates greater uncertainty.

In order to help his Parliamentary listeners come to terms with the vastness of India, he builds a comparison with Germany—imperial humor for the home audience:

> If I were to take the whole aggregate of our possessions there, I should compare it, as the nearest parallel I can find, with the empire of Germany. Our immediate possessions I should compare with the Austrians, and they would not suffer in the comparison. The nabob of Oude might stand for the king of Prussia; the nabob of Arcot I would compare, as superior in territory, and equal in revenue, to the elector of Saxony. Cheyt Sing, the rajah of Benares, might well rank with the prince of Hesse, at least; and the rajah of Tanjore (though hardly equal in extent of dominion, superior in revenue) to the elector of Bavaria.[24]

Burke's plea for sympathy sets the Holy Roman Empire as the mediating domain in order to awaken familiarity for an even more remote and cloudy object. If one can feel for the Germans with their diversified empire of different religions, classes, and principalities—the ruling British dynasty descended from Hannover—then why

---

23. Sara Sulieri, *The Rhetoric of English India* (Chicago: University of Chicago Press, 1992), 29.

24. Burke, *Speeches of Edmund Burke*, 238.

not for India as well? Europe can itself already be half oriental, at least from the perspective of a nationalist Englishman. As Russell Berman has argued, alterity was attributed not only to far-off lands, but was also found within the Enlightenment's conceptual boundaries of Europe.[25] The chaotic constitution of Central Europe served as a familiar middle term, standing somewhere between the Orient's overwhelming diversity and England's insular coherence.[26] India's patchwork of principalities might have remind the audience of Pufendorf's famous description of the Holy Roman Empire as a monstrosity: "If we want to name Germany according to the rules of political classification, then nothing remains for us but to call it a monstrosity of related political bodies, that, because of the Emperor's sluggish yielding, the princes' ambition, and the clerics' restlessness, has over time been transformed into such a clumsy political form."[27]

The India bill before Parliament, Burke stated, was intended to become the "*magna charta* of Hindostan" and if that analogy seemed far-fetched, Burke inserted a comparison with the equally arcane Treaty of Westphalia.[28] When Burke's speech appeared a year later in German translation, this passage skipped over all direct references to Brandenburg, Saxony, or Hessen. The text includes Burke's explanation as to why he drew an analogy between Germany and India, but without giving specifics.[29] German critics of the Holy Roman Empire's constitution would recognize a not-so-quiet thrust at the composite character of the Holy Roman Empire, its disparate small and larger principalities, yet the ostensible reason for Burke's comparison is his desire to instill sympathy for India. He presumes that his British audience is familiar with Germany,

---

25. Russell Berman, *Enlightenment or Empire: Colonial Discourse in German Culture* (Lincoln: Nebraska University Press, 1998), 22.

26. A little more than a century later, Adolf Loos would again apply this geographical valuation to the Habsburg Empire to show how it lagged so far behind London's modernity that it was almost Asian.

27. Samuel von Pufendorf, *Ueber die Verfassung des deutschen Reiches*, trans. Harry Breßlau (Berlin: Heimann, 1870) 107.

28. Burke, *Speeches of Edmund Burke*, 235.

29. "Edmund Burkes Schilderung der gegenwärtigen Lage der Englisch-Ostindischen Gesellschaft," *Historisches Portefeuille* 3.7 (July 1784): 82.

so if they can imagine an emotional bond that far over the channel, then they should take the next leap to identify with Indians living under arbitrary British rule. The German text does include Burke's explanation: "[India] I have compared to Germany . . . not for an exact resemblance, but as a sort of middle term, . . . in order to awaken some thing of sympathy for the unfortunate natives, of which I am afraid we are not perfectly susceptible; whilst we look at this very remote object through a false and cloudy medium."[30] Burke's call reinforces the contention that Europeans in general were familiar with the emotional configuration.

Whereas Smith imagined a Chinese earthquake, Burke describes the very real Indian suffering caused by British administrators. Given the ease with which Asian countries were interchangeably organized under the rubric "The Orient," it would not take much to draw the further analogy between India and China. While Smith asks the reader to sympathetically consider suffering Chinese, Burke wants them to do so for Indians. Smith sidesteps the colonial debate by using China in his speculation to focus solely on the problem of sympathy. Likewise, by having a European as the agent of his thought experiment, rather than an Englishman or a member of Parliament, Smith was abstracting away from the particulars of British rule in Asia. Burke's call would have been a much more political and commonly discussed challenge in late eighteenth century London. To sympathize with China allows for the possibility that one could do same for India—a point Smith would well have understood.

If sympathy serves as a cornerstone to ethics, it does so in part because the ability to share emotions depends upon communication connecting moral agents. Human beings resemble each other in the "fabric of the mind, as with that of the body," and this resemblance allows them to embrace opinions of others.[31] The emotions Smith ponders reveal a lived connection between eighteenth-century Europeans and China. First, sympathy for Chinese victims shows that the emotionally sensitive European is enmeshed in a media system

---

30. Burke, *Speeches of Edmund Burke*, 238.
31. Ute Frevert, *Emotions in History—Lost and Found* (Budapest: Central European Press, 2011), chap. 3, paras. 8, 9.

that includes China as its extreme limit. Eighteenth-century information networks gathered information from around the world, so much so that Immanuel Kant asserted the existence of world human rights because whenever European empires committed violations anywhere in the world, the public learned of these crimes and *felt* with the suffers. It is not quite enough for Kant that international crimes became known to the public; he also insisted that their misery was shared as a feeling. Kant's insistence on a moral feeling is quite striking in his late essay on "Perpetual Peace," because his categorical moral imperative is famously grounded in rational judgment, and specifically not in emotions. "The peoples of the earth have thus entered in varying degrees into a universal community, and it has developed to the point where a violation of rights in *one* part of the world is felt *everywhere*."[32] Kant, like Smith, takes for granted that media convey suffering from around the world. In moral psychological terms, these networks have taken on a function previously attributed to an omniscient deity. The role Nietzsche ascribes to the mythic gods to witness even the most remote spectacle of suffering has already in the eighteenth century been assumed by news media. "So as to abolish hidden, undetected, unwitnessed suffering from the world and honestly to deny it, one was in the past virtually compelled to invent gods and genii of all the heights and depths, in short something that roams even in secret, hidden places, sees even in the dark, and will not easily let an interesting painful spectacle pass unnoticed."[33] In addition to acknowledging the spread of information, Adam Smith's speculation also questions how far emotions can range and how long their intensity can be sustained over great distances. Indirectly, he is asking how securely the media circuits bearing news of the world are lodged in the psyche of the ordinary subject. Does information from such a distance have an impact on the domestic reader? That Smith answers in the affirmative reveals that such emotions are embedded

---

32. Immanuel Kant, "Perpetual Peace: A Philosophical Sketch," in *Kant's Political Writings*, trans. H. B. Nesbit, ed. Hans Reiss (Cambridge: Cambridge University Press, 1970), 107–8 (emphasis in original).

33. Friedrich Nietzsche, *On the Genealogy of Morals*, trans. Walter Kaufmann (New York: Random House, 1967), 68.

in the flow of information from Asia to Europe. That Smith could sensibly offer his speculation also confirms how common such a feeling could be among his readers. His insistence that the sympathizing person not turn away from China to concentrate on personal worries shows that information from abroad had enough presence to compete with immediate events.

Bernard Mandeville argued in more radical terms against the presumption that Europeans would feel real compassion for the suffering of distant foreigners. In his 1723 essay on (or rather, against) charity and charity schools, Mandeville contemplates a smaller-scale analogy to Smith's thought experiment: "When we hear that three or four thousand Men, all Strangers to us, are kill'd with the Sword, or forc'd into some River where they are drown'd, we say and perhaps believe that we pity them." Humanity and reason compel us to commiserate over an event completely removed from us, yet Mandeville argues that such thoughts are mere politeness to be forgotten in less than two minutes.[34] In dismissing any expression of compassion for distant suffering, he is forced to discount the effect that performance and reading have. Mandeville does acknowledge that "those who have a strong and lively Imagination, and can make Representations of things in their Minds" might feel "something that resembles Compassion." However, this emotion is "done by Art": it is not heartfelt, but is as faint as "what we suffer at the acting of a Tragedy."[35] With his disregard for theater, Mandeville shows that his argument does not consider the heightening effects of rhetoric or performance, indeed, mediation of any kind—a curious stance given that tragedy and Aristotle's comments on it were the locus of most eighteenth-century reflections on pity and sympathy. It was precisely the intensity of the audience's identification with the protagonist that made it a favored scenario for analyzing sympathies as the basis for moral responses.

Smith was not satisfied with skeptical assertions such as Mandeville's, for he argues that feeling sympathy for the Chinese victims is

34. Bernard Mandeville, "An Essay on Charity and Charity Schools," in *The Fable of the Bees* (London: Penguin 1970), 266.

35. Mandeville, "Charity," 266–67.

a moral obligation. Our conscience shames us into feeling. Smith concluded his thought experiment by stating: "And hence it is, that to feel much for others, and little for ourselves, that to restrain our selfish, and to indulge our benevolent, affections, constitutes the perfection of human nature."[36] This obligation to restrain greed and feel compassion was the basis for Smith's cosmopolitan conscience. The two-step maneuver—having the sociable emotions and then analyzing their moral implications—goes back to Shaftesbury's sense that the two stages can exist in sequence. Shaftesbury's concept of moral judgment attempts to synthesis two elements: first, a rational, reflective process utilizing such standards as consistency and the general welfare; and second, an intuitive process in which one responds directly to moral objects, being either attracted or repelled by them.[37] Shaftesbury takes a rhetorical approach to this moral self-examination in that he refers to the practice as "soliloquy"—a conversation, or even disputation, that one carries out with oneself rather than in a public forum. Ian Watt underscored the theatrical quality of these inner debates, seeing them as a continuity connecting Shaftesbury, Smith, and the new novels. "It would be left to Adam Smith . . . to take the notion of spectatorship implicit in the writings of Shaftesbury, Steele, and Richardson, and to develop all of this into a full-blown moral system in his *Theory of Moral Sentiments* (1759)."[38] James Chandler adds that for Smith the human capacity for functioning as a sympathetic spectator of others as well as oneself was "cultivated in the daily life of commercial civil society."[39] Smith "elaborated the innovative idea of an impartial spectator as an internal principle of general perception that is able to counteract our egoism."[40]

Smith's sequence begins with the emotional response, followed by moral reflection. In twenty-first-century terms, the gap between

---

36. Smith, *Theory of Moral Sentiments*, 71.

37. Stanley Graen, Introduction, in Anthony, Earl of Shaftesbury, *Characteristics of Men, Manners, Opinions, Times* (Indianapolis: Bobbs-Merrill, 1964), xxxii.

38. James Chandler, *An Archeology of Sympathy: The Sentimental Mode in Literature and Cinema* (Chicago: University of Chicago Press, 2013), 171.

39. Chandler, *Archeology of Sympathy*, 172.

40. Chandler, *Archeology of Sympathy*, 172.

sympathy that wears off quickly and a moral recommitment to care for the suffering foreigner constitutes the difference between a privileged ignorance about the suffering of others and a self-conscience obligation to sacrifice one's own selfish interests for others. What makes Smith's account of sympathy interesting is his explanation of how to overcome its limitations. By recognizing the failure of sympathy to sustain an emotional engagement with distant suffering, the subject becomes more self-aware and feels compelled to correct the first fading of sympathy. Sustained engagement requires more than a burst of emotion; it takes a second-order observation to hold the subject's focus on the object of pity.[41] Over time, the effect of sympathy for foreign suffering leads to greater self-observation and regulation.

In *The Passions of the Soul* (1649), Descartes had already noted that the theater was the most important institution for conveying sympathy, or "fellow-feeling" of the elevated, noble variety in which the observer feels for the victim without considering that he, too, might share the same fate.[42] Outside the theater, however, other sources of information could induce sympathy without indulging in dramatic excess. To the extent that tragic dramas were based on missionary reports and travelogues, the spectator uninterested in theater could turn to these newer forms of communication. Descartes, like many other early modern thinkers up to Kant, adopts a neo-Stoical attitude that holds compassion to be dangerous when it leads to excessively sentimental behavior. Feelings of pity elicited by dramatic suffering seemed a threat that had to be contained by reason.

For critics who see Smith as an advocate for self-interest and the free market, this thought experiment is another example of the limits of a morality based on sympathy. However, Smith's critical reflections do not come to rest here; he pursues the question beyond pointing out how selfishness counteracts empathy when he postu-

---

41. Albrecht Koschorke, "Selbststeuerung: David Hartley's Assoziationstheorie, Adam Smith's Sympathielehre und die Dampfmachine von James Watt," in *Das Laokoon-Paradigma, Zeichenregime im 18. Jahrhundert*, ed. Inge Baxmann, Michael Franz, and Wolfgang Schäffner (Berlin: Akademie Verlag, 2000), 179–90.

42. Katherine Ibbett, "Fellow-Feeling," in *Early Modern Emotions: An Introduction*, ed. Susan Broomhall (London: Routledge, 2017), 62.

lates the existence of a conscience that shames selfishness into act-ing in the interest of others. "And hence it is, that to feel much for others, and little for ourselves, that to restrain our selfish, and to indulge our benevolent, affections, constitutes the perfection of human nature."[43] The Chinese thought experiment occurs two hundred pages into a treatise in which Smith argues that sympathy for the suffering of others is the very basis of ethics. He insists that the imaginary spectator of another person's suffering fully invest himself in the effort to think like the victim.

The Chinese earthquake example is but one of many hypotheti-cal situations that Smith posits, the most famous being his example of watching our brother on the torture rack. Like Foucault, who begins *Discipline and Punish* with the famous 1757 execution of Damiens, Smith opens his argument with a graphic and extreme case, to draw our attention as readers: "By the imagination we place ourselves in his situation, we conceive ourselves enduring all the same torments, we enter as it were into his body, and become in some measure the same person with him, and thence form some idea of his sensations, and even feel something which, though weaker in degree, is not altogether unlike them."[44] While scholars debate over Adam Smith's religious views, the fact that the image that elic-its a moral feeling based on sympathy is that of a man tortured on the rack does invite comparisons with martyr dramas or the pious contemplation of altar paintings depicting Christ's crucifixion. The brother tortured on the rack is but a secular, political variation on the much older Christian coupling of compassion, vision, and mo-rality. Torture appears in baroque tragedies, both German and En-glish, as the exemplary moment in which the protagonist his or her Stoic virtue in the face of excruciating pain and dismemberment.[45] Smith rigorously eschews any such religious connotation in his lec-tures, concentrating instead on the psychological challenges in es-tablishing an emotional economy with the other. For compassion

---

43. Smith, *Theory of Moral Sentiments*, 71.
44. Smith, *Theory of Moral Sentiments*, 48.
45. Reinhart Meyer-Kalkus, *Wollust und Grausamkeit: Affektenlehre und Af-fektdarstellung in Lohensteins Dramatik* (Göttingen: Vandenhoeck & Ruprecht, 1986), 245.

to become moral philosophy, it must negate its theological origins. Smith offers a psychological process to guide the moral movement of sympathy that previously would have been undertaken with the supervision of a priest. The sequence with which his moral logic unfolds, including a sense of necessity that drives it, follows those laid out by earlier spiritual exercises: "In all such cases, that there may be some correspondence of sentiments between the spectator and the person principally concerned, the spectator must, first of all, endeavor as much as he can put to himself in the situation of the other, and to bring home to himself every little circumstance of distress which can possible occur to the sufferer. He must adopt the whole case of his companion, with all its minutest incidents; and strive to render as perfect as possible the imaginary change of situation upon which his sympathy is founded."[46] Smith's psychological rhetoric stripped of religious tones translates readily into aesthetic spectatorship. The dramaturgical purpose of the victims' torture lays not so much in their Stoicism than in the onlookers' sympathy. In both cases torture sets the extreme limit that reveals the moral order: in the baroque tragedy, the torture victim struggles against the complete loss of self-control, while in Smith's moral philosophy the sight of the torture victim establishes the paradigm requiring moral sympathy for the suffering of others. Smith's secular discussion of how best to represent the tortured body is but one of many that permeated eighteenth century criticism, most notably in Gotthold Lessing's Laokoon essay.[47]

The question of why the victim is suffering, to what end and under whose hand, does not define the victims' moral courage but it does influence the audience's ability to feel sympathy. While Chris-

---

46. Smith, *Theory of Moral Sentiments*, 66.
47. Lessing and Smith overlapped to such a great extent in their psychology of sympathy that Lessing mentions "the Englishman" only once in a quibble over whether the expressions of suffering diminish the spectator's empathy for the victim. Lessing cites Smith so little because they agree on so much. For a masterfully lucid account of their mutual sympathies, see Helmut J. Schneider, "Empathy, Imagination, and Dramaturgy—A Means of Society in Eighteenth-Century Theory," in *Empathy*, ed. Vanessa Lux and Sigrid Weigel (London: Palgrave MacMillan, 2017): 203–21.

tian martyrs suffering at the hands of pagan rulers formed the earliest version of these moral spectacles, the terms where soon reversed in the eighteenth century, so that the martyr dramas presented the Church's missionaries as the oppressors. Images of torture on the stage, particularly as they depict encounters between Europeans and indigenous people, allegorized the violent failure of intercultural relations. The martyr figure thus became an avenue for Europeans to identify with the victims of colonialism. Already in the seventeenth century, the tortured native served as a vivid image of colonial greed, so often depicted in Protestant countries as a particularly Spanish vice. Smith is quite careful to separate out the theological implications of sympathy. Unlike missionary accounts that sought to inspire Europeans to dedicate themselves to China, Smith's sympathy for the earthquake victims ignores their possible Christian salvation. The death of Chinese does not raise the question that seemed to torment so many missionaries: What will become of their heathen souls in the afterworld?

Contra his reputation as *the* spokesperson for self-interest, Smith insists that compassion for others is the very basis for masculine virtue: "Our sensibility to the feelings of others, so far from being inconsistent with the manhood of self-command, is the very principle upon which manhood is founded."[48] Smith is one of the first modern thinkers to make explicit that he is providing a gender theory along with his ethics. Thus each aspect of his moral subject defines a different masculine quality: the conscience is an imposing father figure who forces the selfish subject to act nobly, not to slink away from responsibility but stand up for virtue before the eyes of the impartial spectator. In this scheme, sympathy for others and the ability to imagine their emotional state were not confined to the foppish figures we commonly associate with eighteenth-century sentimental literature. Smith insists that his ideal man of virtue has nothing in common with fashionable clowns who flatter their way into courtly favor.[49] Rather than making an open display of his feelings for everyone else to share, Smith insists that the sympathizing

---

48. Smith, *Theory of Moral Sentiments*, 254.
49. Smith, *Theory of Moral Sentiments*, 129.

moral subject is composed, particularly under the most difficult conditions. In drawing a distinction between public demeanor and private sensations, Smith still admires Stoical self-command even as he rejects the ancient call for apathy toward oneself and others.[50] That the modern male feels the suffering of others, yet maintains his composure, suggests that Smith has the training of public servants in mind.[51]

Alongside a morality of sympathy, Smith provides a "philosophy of vision" to serve as a second-order correction. His observing spectator shares some but not all characteristics with Stoicism, another explicitly masculine moral system, whose paradigmatic example is that of a man who must grapple with the news that his wife and son have just been heartlessly killed. For Smith, the moral spectator is an allegorical figure functioning as a conscience. In many ways, he places the reader of his book in the position of the impartial spectator, who evaluates the hypothetical European's sympathy for China. His thought experiment functions as an adapted spiritual exercise. Whereas pious Catholics were asked to share the suffering of Chinese martyrs, Smith provides a secularized model for extending sympathy based on one of the oldest disaster scenarios in Western philosophy. Since antiquity, earthquakes have been a paradigmatic test of Stoical forbearance. Seneca, for example, recounted the shock Romans felt upon news of Pompeii's destruction by earthquake. An earthquake underscores the ancient and baroque lesson that nothing in this world is stable. As Seneca writes,

> Comfort needs to be found for the fearful, and their great terror needs to be eradicated. For what can anyone regard as sufficiently secure, if the world itself is shaken, and its firmest parts crumble; if the one thing in it that is immovable and fixed, so that it supports everything that converges on it, starts to waver; if the earth has lost its characteristic property of standing still? Wherever will our fears find rest? What shelter will our bodies find, where will they escape to in their anxiety, if the fear arises from the foundations and is drawn from the depths? There is general

---

50. Fonna Forman-Barzilai, "Adam Smith as Globalization Theorist," *Critical Review* 14.4 (2000): 391–419.

51. A. L. Macfie, "Adam Smith's *Theory of Moral Sentiments*," in *The Individual in Society: Papers on Adam Smith* (London: George Allen & Unwin, 1967), 44.

panic when buildings rumble and their collapse is signaled. Then everyone rushes straight outside, abandons his home, and entrusts himself to
the open air. What hiding place can we see, what help, if the earth itself
cracks, and the very thing that protects and supports us, that cities are
built on, that some have called the foundation of the world, gapes open
and trembles?[52]

When Smith mentions the inevitable philosophizing that follows an
earthquake, he surely has these lines form Seneca in mind. How to
take the news, how not to crumple in despair, how not to moan before other people, but to preserve one's own dignity and composure—
these are virtues that distinguish a Stoic from a man of unrestrained
feelings.

Pierre Hadot summarizes the ancient position: "The exercise
of meditation allows us to be ready at the moment when an
unexpected—and perhaps dramatic—circumstance occurs."[53] The
perfect Stoic attitude consisted in *apatheia*—the complete absence
of passions.[54] Included in the list of Stoic virtues is the cosmopolitan claim that he is a man of the world. The Chinese earthquake
thought experiment is Smith's means of linking ancient and modern cosmopolitanism through a chiasmic opposition. If the death
of one's nearest kin is a shock that requires the survivor to restrain
his emotions, the distant disaster calls upon him to stretch out his
feelings. If Stoicism requires us to maintain the composure of powerless Roman slave, the modern man of feeling is supposed to assume the position of the generous master who extends his
compassion outward. Smith sets the two philosophical outlooks
in juxtaposition so often in *The Theory of Moral Sentiments* that
the difference between Stoical and sentimental morality almost
constitutes a master-slave dialectic in the manner of Hegel. Stoic
cosmopolitanism insisted that the individual detach himself from his
family and community in order to treat everyone in the world

---

52. Lucius Annaeus Seneca, *Natural Questions*, trans Harry M. Hine (Chicago: University of Chicago Press, 2010), 87–88.
53. Pierre Hadot, *Philosophy as a Way of Life*, trans. Michael Chase (Oxford:
Blackwell, 1995), 85.
54. Hadot, *Philosophy*, 136.

equally. Within ancient Stoicism, being a citizen of the world meant you were *not* a citizen of your family and city. The universal affirmation required a renunciation of the more proximate bonds of affection. Much as he admired self-command, Smith considered the call for apathy toward ones nearest kin detestable.[55] Likewise, and somewhat more controversially, he considered the call to love all people in the world as equally absurd and unattainable.[56]

The alternative means for extending sympathy beyond our immediate circle are commerce and literature. In considering the modes of writing that foster the circulation in feeling Smith sets contemporary eighteenth-century literature above ancient maxims. "The poets and romance writers, who best paint the refinements and delicacies of love and friendship, and of all other private and domestic affections, Racine and Voltaire, Richardson, Marivaux, and Riccoboni, are, in such cases, much better instructors than Zeno, Chrysippus, or Epictetus."[57] Through his praise of poets, Smith shows that his thought experiment presumes the ability of representations to evoke emotions, and in his case without immediately presenting the audience any images, though Smith's moral philosophy depends on the ability of the philosophical subject to imagine the sight of the suffering person worthy of sympathy.[58] Smith presumes that the news of another person's suffering suffices to conjure up a corresponding image. While news of a Chinese earthquake today would most likely include still and moving images (unless the earthquake site were too remote), Smith presumes that the eighteenth-century recipient of news had enough visual memories

---

55. Smith, *Theory of Moral Sentiments*, 240.

56. Fonna Forman-Barzilai, *Adam Smith and the Circles of Sympathy: Cosmopolitanism and Moral Theory* (Cambridge: Cambridge University Press, 2010), 120–31.

57. Smith, *Theory of Moral Sentiments*, 241–42.

58. Ingo Berensmeyer sees Adam Smith as the central figure in Scottish and English sentimentality whose model of subjectivity fits neatly into recent German media histories. Only through his reading of later, satirical works by Lawrence Sterne and Thomas Rowlandson does Berensmeyer counter Koschorke's claim that sentimentalism represented a convergence of media, affect, and bodily sensation. See his "Empfindsamkeit als Medienkonflikt: Zur Gefühlskultur des 18. Jahrhunderts," *Poetica* 39.3/4 (2007): 397–422.

to construct a plausible image in their own minds. The importance of such images when stirring sympathy runs counter to the Protestant prohibitions on images, whether of Christ or martyrs, at the site of pious reflection.

Lynn Festa connects the inward turn of the sentimental mode with the outward expansion of empire in order to explain the eighteenth-century emergence of humanitarian feelings (a term central to cosmopolitanism and world literature). She argues that sentimental literature created the tropes that enabled readers to imaginatively grasp foreign culture, without wholly assimilating foreign figures. A key question is how this detachment is maintained and what end it serves: in breaking off sympathy is the sentimental reader acknowledging the strangeness of foreign literature or is the reader avoiding an excess of identification that might overwhelm? Rather than arguing that sentimental literature sugarcoats the nasty operations of European expansion, Festa argues that "sentimentality fashions the tropes that render relations with distant others thinkable."[59]

In his autobiography, Goethe describes a similar sympathetic response to reading newspaper reports of distant events. Not only does his characterization hearken back to Smith's moral sentiments, it also anticipates his famous description of world literature, in which new journals circulate across borders after warring nations have ended their hostilities. "During a period of peace, there is no more cheerful kind of reading than indulging in the public press, which speedily delivers the most recent world events."[60] Ordinary readers feel as if they were participating with those far removed from themselves. In a few strokes Goethe combines Smith's ethics with Lessing's dramaturgy, when he compares newspaper readers' sense of "participating" or "being there" (*Teilnahme*) with theater audiences imaginatively sharing the fortunes of a character on stage,

59. Lynn Festa, *Sentimental Figures of Empire in Eighteenth-Century England and France* (Baltimore: Johns Hopkins University, 2006), 8.

60. Johann Wolfgang Goethe, *Werke*, ed. Erich Trunz (Munich: C. H. Beck, 1982), 10:112; hereafter cited as "HA."

and while these affections often may seem arbitrary, they have a moral foundation.[61]

Smith's account of sympathy is important because he explains how moral thinkers can and should overcome mental and spatial limitations on fellow-feeling. By recognizing the failure of sympathy to sustain an emotional engagement with distant suffering, the subject becomes more self-aware and feels compelled to correct the decline. Sustained engagement requires more than a burst of emotion; it takes a second-order observation to hold the subject's focus on the object of pity.[62] Over time, the experience of sympathy for foreign suffering leads to greater self-observation and regulation, the hallmarks of modern subjectivity.

---

61. HA, 10:112–13.
62. Koschorke, "Selbststeuerung," 186.

GOETHE READS THE JESUITS

The proposition that China and Europe stand parallel to each other has a long history. In 1694, Leibniz opened his *Novissima Sinica* (The newest from China) by suggesting that fate had purposively set European and Chinese civilizations at opposite ends of the same continent. When Leibniz advocated for the intensification of this alignment through further intellectual exchange, he was clearly following the lead already put forward by Jesuit missionaries.[1] Later, when the first European translators of Chinese literature perceived clear similarities in narrative conventions, they left out any reference to a divine order. In the twentieth century, the idea reemerged when Karl Jaspers proposed the term *Achsenzeit* (Axial Age) to describe the simultaneous development of philosophical

---

1. Gottfried Wilhelm Leibniz, *The Preface to Leibniz' Novissima Sinica*, trans. Donald Lach (Honolulu: University of Hawaii Press, 1957).

thought in ancient China and Greece.[2] In the early 1980s, Joseph Fletcher elaborated on Jasper's suggestion that these parallels would make historical sense only if they could be connected through underlying horizontal influences.[3] More recently, comparative literary scholars have argued that Chinese and European novels share certain formal features because they participate in the same global economy.[4] Goethe's inclination to perceive correspondences between Chinese and European civilizations provide a variation of this established theme.

While his predilection for finding resemblances between disparate texts and cultures proliferated in many directions, the Orient was an inevitable focus. Goethe's propensity for analogies became obvious through his biological writings; however this disposition also guided his interpretation of foreign literature. Unlike Jaspers or Fletcher, Goethe's literary pairings were not concerned with organizing knowledge so much as finding creative inspiration. Rather than positing and applying an overarching concept of humanity, his readings offered a method for detecting repetition in poetic expression. His humanism was imbedded within his interpretive technique. His attentiveness to literary likeness depended upon the ability to place oneself in the position of others. Goethe's intuitions about resemblances between Chinese and European literature were motivated initially by a sentimental attitude that sought affinities between kindred souls—a modus that can be traced back beyond Pietism to late medieval devotional reading practices but that by the late eighteenth century had already manifested itself as a secular moral psychology.

The Jesuits had famously asserted the existence of a shared metaphysical foundation between Christianity and Confucianism, yet a minor countertradition stretching back to the earliest reports from China also suggested the opposite: the possible absence of any the-

2. Karl Jaspers, *Vom Ursprung und Ziel der Geschichte* (Frankfurt: Fischer, 1955).

3. Joseph Fletcher, "Integrative History: Parallels and Interconnections in the Early Modern Period, 1500–1800," *Journal of Turkish Studies* 9.1 (1985): 37–57.

4. Ning Ma, *The Age of Silver: The Rise of the Novel East and West* (New York: Oxford University Press, 2016).

istic belief among the ruling elite. This continuous, radical potential shows itself in an analogy that Goethe puts before Schiller, in which he compares a Chinese debate between a Jesuit missionary and a Buddhist monk with contemporary Weimar disputes between Kantians and Idealists. Goethe joins two divergent philosophical cultures in a parallel constellation. Both debates revolve around the question of atheism, broadly defined. In drawing these comparisons, Goethe and Schiller themselves remain the discreet third pair, commenting on the other two. These three duos stretch across two hundred years and great distances to form an intellectual continuity based on the eternal repetition of the same fundamental questions. Goethe's correspondence with Schiller shows that academic institutions and their publications (treatises, letters, encyclopedias, poems, plays) are central to preserving and recognizing these repetitions. Similar philosophical debates may spring up over time and space, but unless they are consolidated in institutional nodes, they vanish into nothingness. The similarities between the Nanjing and Weimar debates are conveyed through discourse, often obscure and archived yet readily revitalized by a curious reader. Distant, old epiphanies are stored in libraries waiting to be recalled again in a new setting capable of familiarizing the old.

Like any eighteenth-century German studying China, it was perfectly natural that Goethe followed up his reading of Marco Polo by turning to the Jesuit mission and Matteo Ricci. Jesuit treatises were the obvious, and often the only, source for further information about China. The succession of these three pairs (Jesuit-Buddhist, Kantian-Idealist, Goethe-Schiller) demonstrates the long continuum in the European reception of China, as well as its sporadic, on-off movement: China did not rise and fall in the esteem of European intellectuals, so much as come and go in an elaborate "fort-da" play of similarities and differences. The link between Weimar and Nanjing shows that connections were not drawn only between political or economic capitals. Intellectual logistics were far more flexible. To engage China, one did not have to study in Paris or Rome. Writers in small German towns could feel fully engaged with Chinese events. Leibniz once joked with a Prussian princess that his office in Hannover could become the central exchange for news from China. In the early modern period, the links between Germany and China were understood in textual terms, as more dependent upon mediation rather than personal observation. Running between the three duos are Jesuit reports and baroque compilations. As we shall see in this chapter, the arguments about atheism in Nanjing share much with those in Weimar, even as they reverse and refute each other.

Goethe's heterodox interpretation of the Jesuit position in China starts with an epiphany. On January 3, 1798, Johann Wolfgang Goethe wrote to Friedrich Schiller that he had just come across a curious story in an old tome describing a debate held in China during a banquet in 1599 involving a Jesuit missionary, Matteo Ricci, and an unnamed Buddhist scholar, who today is identified as the renowned abbot Xuelang Hong'en (1545–1607); the Jesuit texts refer to him as Sanhoi.[5] Goethe wrote, "This discovery amused me unbelievably and gave me a good idea of how sharp witted the Chinese are."[6] Typical for how humanists combined friendship, letter writing, and intellectual labor, Goethe promised to send Schiller a handwritten copy of the passage. Three days later Goethe followed through with his promise and went on to speculate about how the Buddhist might have even more wittily turned the tables on the Jesuit. Rather than agreeing with the Jesuit arguments about the creation of the earth, Goethe takes the heterodox step of siding with the Buddhist—not a complete surprise, as he had resumed working on *Faust* the previous summer. In telling Schiller about the Chinese dinner conversation, Goethe assigns eighteenth-century philosophical positions to each participant: the Buddhist he characterizes as a creative Idealist ("ein schaffender Idealist") whereas the Jesuit is given the position of a Reinholdianer, a loyal interpreter of Imman-

---

5. For modern scholarly treatments of this dinner debate, see Ronnie Po-chia Hsia, *A Jesuit in the Forbidden City: Matteo Ricci 1552–1610* (Oxford: Oxford University Press, 2010), 194–98, and Iso Kern, "Matteo Riccis Verhältnis zum Buddhismus," *Monumenta Serica* 36 (1984–1985): 88–94.

6. Sigfried Seidel, ed., *Der Briefwechsel zwischen Schiller und Goethe* (Leipzig: Insel, 1984), 2:8 (hereafter cited as *Briefwechsel*): "Dieser Fund hat mich unglaublich amüsiert und mir eine gute Idee von dem Scharfsinn der Chineser gegeben."

uel Kant.[7] The two writers had been sharing the latest work by Johann Gottlieb Fichte, as well as an anonymously written Chinese novel. For Goethe these disparate topics suddenly converged in an insight. Ever the sympathetic friend, Schiller was quick to align himself with Goethe's interest: "The father's metaphysical conversation entertained me very much." China was already an established topic between the two writers. After a few of his own sharp-witted remarks, Schiller asks, "Where did you find this morsel?"[8] and this is where the story gets complicated. Where did Goethe first read this story? Not in any source one would expect.

Goethe discovered the debate while searching for poetic plunder in a 1670 collection of stories about East Asia compiled by Erasmus Francisci. The tome had a wonderfully long-winded title, which listed off the Asian peoples with whom Europeans had come into contact. Rendered into English here, the title resounds as the "Newly-Polished Mirror of the History, Art and Morals of Foreign Peoples, Especially the Chinese, Japanese, Indostanese, Javanese, Malabarese, Peguese, Siamese, and Some Other Nations in Addition."[9] Subdivided into six volumes, this opus had been printed in Nuremberg, a center of the seventeenth-century publishing industry. Records show that Goethe had checked out the volume from the Weimar royal library for almost a year, between December 6, 1797, to November 10, 1798. Francisci was one of Germany's first professional writers, which is to say that he lived off the income his publications produced—a hard life in the seventeenth century. A cripple confined to his study after having broken both his legs in a horse-riding accident, he was unable to travel anywhere in the world he described. To make matters worse, as a scribe and compiler, he was

---

7. Iso Kern translates the debate into Western metaphysics by distinguishing between Buddhist phenomenology and Jesuit realism ("Riccis Verhältnis zum Buddhismus," 88–94).

8. *Briefwechsel*, 2:17.

9. Erasmus Francisci, *Neu-polirter Geschicht- Kunst- und Sitten-Spiegel ausländischer Völcker fürnemlich Der Sineser, Japaner, Indostaner, Javaner, Malabaren, Peguaner, Siammer, . . . und theils anderer Nationen mehr* (Nürnberg: Johann Andreae Endters and Wolfgang des Jüngern Erben, 1670). The Nanjing Disputation appears in book 1, 41–60.

also obliged to give up his family's noble title. During his long convalescence in Nuremberg, he wrote a succession of enormous compilations synthesizing travel reports from all hemispheres for the bookdealer Johannes Endter.[10] Goethe explains that he is reading Francisci's compilation precisely because it brings together so many unusual anecdotes. He was, after all, well-versed in prowling through old collections for new inspiration. The legend of the magician and trickster Faust had come down to him through a series of compilations. Francisci had himself been involved in editing Endter's influential collection. Its descriptive title sounds just as dramatic when rendered into English. "The Troubling Life and Horrible End of the Very Notorious Black Artist Dr. Johannis Fausti" was a collection that went through six editions with an appendix written on the magical practices of Lapplanders.[11] From his years of research into the Faust legend, Goethe would have well understood how popular stories in the seventeenth century would find publishers who would reissue the same material, with new editorial additions.[12] The publishing history of the many Faust editions provides a genealogical model of how curious tales grew more complex, acquiring additional characters, descriptions, locations, adventures, and connotations as they circulated within the early modern publishing industry, so that eventually later versions put forward meanings completely at odds with the original text. Baroque literature was a complex circulatory system of stories rewritten and republished, compiled, expanded, and annotated by new authors copying old ones. These tomes full of stories, shocking anecdotes, and

---

10. See Georg Andreas Will, *Nürnbergisches Gelehrten-Lexikon oder Beschreibung aller Nürnbergischen Gelehrten beyderley Geschlechtes* (Nürnberg: Lorenz Schüpfel, 1755), part 1, A–G; Gerhard Dünnhaupt, "Erasmus Francisci, ein Nürnberger Polyhistor des siebzehnten Jahrhunderts. Biographie und Bibliographie," *Philobiblon* 19.4 (1975): 272–303.

11. *Das ärgerliche Leben und schreckliche Ende des viel berüchtigten Ertz-Schwartzkünstlers D. Johannis Fausti . . . und einem Anhang von den Lapponischen Wahrsager-Paucken wieauch sonst etlichen zauberischen Geschichten* (Nürnberg: Endters, 1717).

12. Jochen Schmidt, *Goethes Faust Erster und Zweiter Teil Grundlagen-Werk-Wirkung* (Munich: Beck, 1999), 28.

foreign histories were mined for inspiration long after their publication. By way of excusing his perusal in such dusty tomes, Goethe tells Schiller that while Francisci's writing displays awful taste, it offers up many useful stories. By following Goethe's route through such a compilation, we can better understand the broader reception of Chinese culture from the later sixteenth to the early nineteenth century.[13] Along the way, we might ask how far reaching was Goethe's analogy between Weimar and Nanjing? Was it confined to this one theological disputation, or did it reveal an underlying affinity between literati in both places? Were Weimar's poets flattering themselves with their imagined affinities with China?

Nineteenth-century colonial ideology, beginning with the memoirs written after the British attempt in 1793 to open trade with China, known as the Macartney embassy, sought to dismiss baroque knowledge of Asia by arguing that its categories were defined foremost by theological concerns. While making these arguments, the later expansionists also disparaged the earlier era's sympathetic bonds with China. In order to understand the long history of European attitudes toward China, we need to trace out how knowledge of the Orient was transmitted across through Europe and down through generations of readers. This requires us to wander into the labyrinth of baroque literature that transcribed, compiled, and revised the initial Jesuit accounts of China. If we constantly refer back just to the primary missionary reports, we will never understand how readers who were removed from and often critical of the Jesuits would have understood their descriptions of China. Goethe, for example, reads Matteo Ricci's report of his debate with the Buddhist directly against author's intention. Other eighteenth-century

---

13. Among German sinologists, opinions vary on Goethe's reading of Francisci. Günther Debon considers it to be without consequence (*folgenlos*), while Wolfgang Bauer sees it as a turning point in Goethe's views on China. Günther Debon, "Goethes Berührungen mit China," *Goethe Jahrbuch* (2000): 47. Wolfgang Bauer, "Goethe und China: Verständnis und Missverständnis," in *Goethe und die Tradition*, ed. Hans Reiss (Frankfurt: Athenäum, 1972), 177–78. It seems noteworthy that in his book on Goethe and China, Debon does not once mention his Kommiliton and Munich sinology colleague Wolfgang Bauer's essay on the same topic.

readers did much the same. What the devout missionaries meant to convey by recounting Ricci's dialogues was not at all what Goethe, and presumably others, took from the tale. Even as he reads counter to the Jesuit aims, Goethe posits an affinity between Chinese and German thought without claiming a hierarchical superiority.

The first notable point of Goethe's comparison is that he sets all four positions on an equal footing, an unusual move given that both Jesuits and Buddhists would have had little credibility in German philosophical circles.[14] He aligns his own interest with the Buddhist position in part because the disputation provides an intellectual arena in which such choices are possible. A disputation provides a broadly applicable framework for ideas and arguments to be compared and transferred between debaters. Goethe seems to have had an inclination to identify with the unchristian position all his life. As he recounts in book 15 of *Poetry and Truth*, as a young man he would read aloud from Pietist missionary reports to Susanne von Klettenberg, a pious friend of his mother's. Klettenberg was the most important source for the mystical Pietist language that entered into his early sentimental writing and the model for the "schöne Seele" in *Wilhelm Meister's Apprenticeship*.[15] In reading the pietist missionary *Hallesche Berichte*, whenever the narrative came to a scene in which a missionary would try to convert the indigenous population, Goethe inevitably sided with the locals against the preacher.[16] In reading the Jesuit report, Goethe is still operating within the logic of the scholastic disputation that presumes an intellectual parity between the two cultures, when his allegiance again crosses over to the foreign and heretical position,

---

14. On the exclusion of Asian thought from the Western philosophical canon, see Peter Park, *Africa, Asia, and the History of Philosophy: Racism in the Formation of the Philosophical Canon, 1750–1830* (Albany: State University of New York Press, 2013).

15. Burkhard Dohm, "Radikalpietistin und 'schöne Seele': Susanna Katharina von Klettenber," in *Goethe und der Pietismus*, ed. Hans-Georg Kemper and Hans Schneider (Tübingen: Franckesche Stiftung and Niemeyer Verlag, 2001), 111–34.

16. *Goethes Werke* (Weimar: Hermann Böhlaus Nachfolger, 1887–1919), 1.28:301; hereafter cited as WA.

one that he domesticates by comparing it to early Weimar Idealism. Martin Mulsow describes a similar transfer of heretical beliefs from Islam into the radical Enlightenment, through a complex series of untraceable transmissions: "On the one hand there was perhaps a subliminal continuity of heretical ideas in astrological, alchemical, or medical treatises, but on the other hand we need to take a simple fact into consideration: orthodoxy of one particular religion is automatically a heresy in the eyes of another. This means that those who argue especially for the truth of the doctrines of their own religion may in fact have a subversive effect on another religion."[17] For Goethe these transfers appeared directly on the pages of Francisci's compilation. In researching for *Faust*, Goethe was clearly fascinated with the long tradition of heretical texts, but in the Nanjing Disputation he followed the more automatic heresy of adopting a foreign religion's belief. Completely absent from Goethe's affinity with China is the modernist presumption (typified by Hegel's history of philosophy) that Europe had superseded East Asian civilization.[18] Goethe's letter to Schiller succinctly encapsulates the long transformation whereby sympathy for China was understood first in theological terms as a shared participation in the divine truths revealed at the world's creation but then reversed itself into a secular history of parallel cultures. Underlying both belief systems was the technological presumption that shared experiences could be transmitted across a single global space. Both Ricci and Goethe were acutely aware of how written texts communicated over great distances, thereby conditioning the recognition of identities and differences between Europe and China. The likelihood that these insights are predicated upon a misrecognition of similitude is always present, not only because the viewing subject is apt to find confirmation of his own condition whenever looking off

---

17. Martin Mulsow, "Socinianism, Islam and the Radical Uses of Arabic Scholarship," *Al-Qantara* 31 (2010): 549–86.

18. The two most important passages appear in G. W. F. Hegel, *Vorlesungen über die Philosophie der Geschichte* (Frankfurt: Suhrkamp, 1986), 142–74, and *Vorlesungen über die Geschichte der Philosophie* (Frankfurt: Suhrkamp, 1986), 138–47.

into the distance, but also because the long relays involved in conveying the message are also likely to rearticulate the foreign so that it appeals to the end consumer.

Ricci's Arguments

The dialogue entitled "Father Ricci Debates with a Minister of the Idols" was first published for Europeans in Matteo Ricci's posthumous account of the Jesuit mission to preach Christianity in China, entitled *De Christiana Expeditione apud Sinas* (The Christian mission in China), published 1615 in Augsburg.[19] The book was based on an Italian manuscript found in Matteo Ricci's desk after his death. It was then augmented and edited into a 645-page Latin volume by the Belgian priest Nicholas Trigault. *De Christiana Expeditione* was the most influential work on China in the seventeenth century. David Mungello claims the book reached more readers than any other contemporary work on China.[20] The original Latin text was translated within a decade into French, German, Spanish, Italian, and English. The German title appeared in 1617 as *Historia von der Einführung der christlichen Religion in das große Königreich China durch die Societet Jesu* (History of the introduction of the Christian religion in the great kingdom of China by the Society of Jesus).[21] Ricci also provided a Chinese account of the debate in chapter 7 of *The True Meaning of the Lord in Heaven*, a work intended to offer a synthetic account of Christianity and Confucianism.[22]

Matteo Ricci's support for Confucian thought was coupled with a very clear antipathy against Buddhism, which most missionaries

19. Nicholas Trigault, *De Christiana Expeditione apud Sinas Suscepta ab Societate Iesu ex. P. Matthaei Riccii* (Augsburg: Christoph Mangius, 1615).

20. David Mungello, "Die Quellen für das Chinabild Leibnizens," *Studia Leibnitiana* 14.2 (1982): 234.

21. Nicholas Trigault, *Historia von der Einführung der christlichen Religion in das große Königreich China durch die Societet Jesu* (Augsburg: Antony Hierat, 1617).

22. Matteo Ricci, SJ, *The True Meaning of the Lord in Heaven*, trans. Douglas Lancashire and Peter Hu Kuo-chon, SJ (St. Louis, MO: Institute of Jesuit Sources, 1985), 347.

in East Asia perceived as idolatrous.[23] The first European reports stressed Ricci's decisive rejection of Buddhism as both pagan and pantheist. Ricci wrote: "Their great error, fatal to the idea of divinity, namely that God and all things material are one and the same substance, taken from the doctrine of the idol worshippers, has gradually crept into the schools of the literary class, who imagine that God is the soul of the material universe; the one mind, as it were, of a great body. After the debate at the banquet, some of the disciples of the host became frequent callers on Father Ricci and soon put aside their pantheistic ideas."[24] While the original debate may have been intended to impress Nanjing literary circles, the official Jesuit circulation of the dialogue in print was clearly intended to rouse European audiences. In each version, whether in Nanjing or in Europe, the Buddhist serves as the third man who is purposefully excluded from the sender-receiver communication. Whether as a rhetorical strategy or as a condition in the operation of any successful media channel, the Nanjing Disputation illustrates Michel Serres's claim that "to hold a dialogue is to suppose a third man and to seek to exclude him."[25] This principle is of course central to German Idealism's discovery of dialectical reasoning; Fichte already stated, "Any pair of things to be distinguished must be related to a third thing."[26] If Ricci is engaging in a disputation with Buddhism, he is also specifically refraining from holding one with the Confucian literati. In a syncretic society with many religions, to distinguish

---

23. Haun Saussy has shown that Ricci's arguments against Buddhists coincided with a wider debate around the imperial court about mandarins who were perceived to have abandoned Confucian teachings; see his "In the Workshop of Equivalences: Translation, Institutions, and Media in the Jesuit Re-formation of China," in *Great Walls of Discourse and Other Adventures in Cultural China* (Cambridge: Harvard University Press, 2001), 24–29.

24. Matteo Ricci, SJ, *China in the Sixteenth Century: The Journals of Matthew Ricci (1583–1610)*, trans. Louis J. Gallagher (New York: Random House, 1953), 342.

25. Michel Serres, "Platonic Dialogue," in *Hermes: Literature, Science, Philosophy*, ed. Josué Harari and David Bell (Baltimore: Johns Hopkins University, 1992), 67, quoted in Bernhard Siegert, "Cacophony or Communication? Cultural Techniques in German Media Studies," trans. Geoffrey Winthrop-Young, *Grey Room* 29 (Winter 2008): 33.

26. J. G. Fichte, *The Science of Knowledge*, trans. Peter Heath and John Lachs (Cambridge: Cambridge University Press, 1982), 243.

between different teachings by criticizing only one of them is tanta-
mount to seeking an accommodation with another. While many
readers may have pondered the logical content of the disputation, the
most important aspect of Ricci's argument with Buddhism, the pagan
error that must be excluded, was his two-sided appeals to Confucians
within China and Catholics in Europe. As Ricci sought to draw a
connection between Christianity and Confucianism, he felt obliged
to block out the "noise" of Chinese idolatry, a cacophony that he labeled "Buddhism," but that included disparate practices.

Jesuit accommodation with Confucianism established a model
for European identification with elite Chinese culture. To the extent
that it was not just a strategy for delivering the Christian message
to the upper class, accommodation makes the case that Christianity and Confucianism have parallels both in terms of their teaching
and history. If modern scholars such as Karl Jaspers can marvel at
parallels between Europe and China, it is because the Jesuits first
put forward this position. At the same time, accommodation fosters identifications that often leave other Europeans wondering
whether the missionaries have given up their own culture and "gone
over." The suspicion asks whether the missionaries have themselves
been converted. This doubt about missionaries as having been se-
duced by the people they were supposed convert persists throughout
the Jesuit mission in China. The same accusation is made against
Protestant missionaries in India, such as Ziegenbalg, who see similarities between Christianity and Brahmin teachings. It is the charge
that Goethe toys with when he hints that he may have become a
Mohammedan as he announces the publication of *West-östliche Divan* (*West-Eastern Divan*). Accommodation with Confucianism is
decidedly not refutation; it did not attempt to measure a higher truth
on the basis of intellectual combat. Ricci was trained in disputations
as were all his colleagues, and there was almost no way to remain in
good standing within the mission and not refute idolatry. Instead,
Ricci's major maneuver was to shield Confucianism from the post-
Reformation desire to combat heresy. Ricci hoped to direct the urge
for forensic confrontation at Buddhism instead.

The banquet figures prominently in the early history of the Jesuit
mission because it shows clearly how Ricci aligned himself with a

magisterial elite by insisting on an interpretation of Confucianism that focused primarily on the early writings and that rejected later neo-Confucian syncretic appropriations of Buddhist teachings. Many historians have noted the Jesuit affinity for the polite scholarly conventions of the Confucian literati. Just as important is the story's rhetorical context. In most seventeenth-century texts, Ricci is presented within the conventions of early modern rhetoric as a subtle and understated master, capable of following long complex discussions with theological shadings while engaging in quick, witty one-upmanship, all in the company of the most educated men in Nanjing. Jesuits were trained in the conventions of classical rhetoric. Ricci makes a deliberate point of showing his skills in recollection by summarizing all the arguments that had been made during the dinner debate before offering his own concluding statement, a move anyone trained in classical rhetoric would have admired: "He began by making a detailed summary, from memory, of all that had been said on the question, after which he said: 'There is no room for doubt that the God of heaven and earth must be considered as infinitely good.'"[27]

As with many debates, the stakes were more complex than the arguments presented by the two speakers, and there were inevitably third and fourth parties looking on and who were implicitly addressed during the disputation. These onlookers included Catholic readers in Europe, who were supposed to acknowledge his confrontation with idolatry. Additionally, Ricci was also offering his Confucian audience a model of Christian metaphysics without directly engaging in an interpretation of canonical Chinese texts. To the extent that the first Jesuits in China suspected that the literati were not concerned with the afterlife or God as creator, Ricci may have been elaborating this principle for his Confucian listeners while arguing with a Buddhist with the hope that they too would be persuaded. The continued reception of the debate in Nanjing can be followed through its extended circulation throughout the early modern period, as it is retold by a succession of compilers and readers. The process allows the story to be recomposed repeatedly for the purposes of providing old material for new readers, while reconfirming

---

27. Ricci, *China in the Sixteenth Century*, 341.

established knowledge claims about China. The audiences and theological implications multiplied as the story of the Nanjing Disputation circulated in Europe, so that later radical philosophers and free-thinking poets would draw conclusions wholly at odds with Jesuit intentions—namely, that the Chinese were perfectly civilized and moral even without believing in a theistic creator and judge.

At the start of the debate, Ricci asks his opponent what he thinks of the creator of heaven and earth. His goal is to establish a first principle from which other conclusions could be drawn. Ricci feels that if he can demonstrate agreement that the world had been created by a single deity, then the rest of the debate will follow as he wishes. Anticipating the sequence of arguments that would flow from this claim, the Buddhist does not accept this appeal to first principles as decisive: "He did not deny the existence of a moderator of heaven and earth, but at the same time he did not believe him to be a god or endowed with any particular majesty."[28] In other words, the creator was no different than anyone else seated around the table. To show how common creation was, the Jesuit text states: "He then admitted that he could create heaven and earth." The original German translation of this passage includes the marginal gloss "Ungeschickte Sophisterey des Götzen Pfaffen" (the clumsy sophistry of the idolatrous priest), which implicitly draws the connection to Socratic dialogues. For all the warnings not to side with the Buddhist, Goethe is clearly drawn to his argument. Already in his youthful Sturm-und-Drang writings, he had extolled Promethean versions of the proposition that humans share in the ability to create the world, that the poet is a second creator. Ricci's response is to ask his opponent if he can grasp hold of a glowing stove like the one they had in front of them at the banquet—the point being that material things have their own reality apart from human representations. Consciousness alone cannot eliminate or ignore the heat of a glowing pot. Ricci claims that his commonsense refutation of Buddhist inwardness thoroughly flabbergasts Sanhoi. After some uproar—the Jesuit text refers to moments of vehement discussion without making clear exactly what was being said—Sanhoi offers

---

28. Ricci, *China in the Sixteenth Century*, 340.

an explanation of what he means by creating a universe. If an astronomer or a mathematician studies the heavens, he creates an image of the moon and the stars in his mind which he then can recall from memory." Ricci's text then has the monk state: "In other words, you have created a new sun, a new moon, and in the same way anything else can be created."[29] Goethe who so often described his own poetic creation as a process of drawing images from his storehouse of memory—a metaphor common to Roman rhetoric—would readily have identified with the Buddhist line of reasoning. Already in *Werther*, Goethe had coupled the proposition that reality is just a dream state with the conviction that an imaginative person could constitute an entire reality within his or her own mind. "Ich kehre in mich selbst zurück, und finde eine Welt!"[30] ("I look within myself and find a world") suggests a similar turning away from natural sensations to create a second version of that reality within consciousness. For Goethe this was the Idealist moment in the debate: that the human understanding of nature emerges only from subjective consciousness. Ricci responds by drawing a distinction between the reality of things and their representation in our minds—a move Goethe associates with Kantian epistemology.

On a general basis, Ricci's references to astronomy offer a shared intercultural form of knowledge, important to all earthbound observers. In the context of world literature and cultural comparison, astronomical observation provides a potential position of agreement. In an epistemological vein, Ricci insists that it must be obvious to everyone that there is not only a difference between a thing and its image, but also that it would be impossible to form an image of something that one had not seen—in other words that our mental representations are dependent on our perception of real natural things. Here again Ricci draws a distinction familiar to Kantian followers such as Reinhold. According to the Jesuit version, the debate descends into a chaotic string of arguments in which Sanhoi begins to quote mystical passages and Ricci responds by saying

---

29. Ricci, *China in the Sixteenth Century*, 340.
30. Johann Wolfgang Goethe, *Werke*, ed. Erich Trunz (Munich: C. H. Beck, 1982), 6:13; hereafter cited as HA.

that the debate can be carried out only through appeals to natural reason and not by each side quoting their own sacred writings. Ricci's account of the debate concludes with a summary statement about the wider flaws of the Buddhist arguments, which he sees as creeping into Confucian thinking as well—namely, the claim that "God and all things material are one and the same substance" so that even members of the literary class "imagine that God is the soul of the material universe, the one mind, as it were, of a great body."[31] This concluding statement tries to draw theological implications that reach far beyond the specific claims of the debate in order to make a broad criticism of pantheism. While Goethe does not refer to Ricci's summary statement in his letters, literary historians have assumed that he would have identified strongly with just the kind of pantheism Ricci denounced. Goethe's lifetime fascination with Spinoza is well documented, and the common scholarly assumption is that he would have found nothing wrong with the principle Ricci rejects.

Francisci's Retelling

The Reformation could be defined as a massive disputation, dividing North and South. Writing after the Thirty Years' War, Erasmus Francisci could not resist presenting the Nanjing Disputation in terms familiar to European readers, as a rhetorical duel or match. Readers would have known that Jesuit schools were famous for including public debates in the curriculum. The pedagogical presumption was that students were motivated to study and prepare their arguments out of an innate competitive desire to win in a forum of their peers and teachers. Even Protestants could acknowledge that Jesuits were highly skilled orators; indeed, Francisci's narrative frames the theological debate as a duel that allowed all Christians to cheer on the missionary. Buddhists are depicted as deceptive with a comical character, while the Jesuits are shown even to Protestants as honorable virtuosos defending the faith. The framework of a sociable conflict also allowed readers to recognize a moment of identity between Eu-

---

31. Ricci, *China in the Sixteenth Century*, 342.

ropean aristocrats and Chinese mandarins, for any respectable duel requires both participants to share the same rank. Yet in the end, the cultural differences were most important, for they made Ricci's triumph all the greater for having been managed under foreign rules.[32]

The theological details of the argument would have been familiar to European scholars, whether Protestant or Catholic. Thus Ricci's critique of Buddhism would have allowed a common agreement between European denominations. His logical demonstration of the existence of a God, in heaven apart from the universe he created, was also intended for Ricci's allies among the Confucian scholars, for his entire accommodationist synthesis between Christianity and Confucianism rested on his assertion that early Confucian writings also referred to a theistic god. By demonstrating logically that a divine Creator exists, Ricci was not only refuting Buddhism, but also advocating for his own rather speculative interpretation of Confucianism.

The original Jesuit text deliberately selects which heresy it addresses. Ricci specifically refrains from entering into a discussion of Buddhists writings. This reliance on logic rather than scripture in order to debate Jews and pagans can be traced back to St. Anselm's twelfth-century claim that reason alone could demonstrate God's existence. Joachim Kurtz points out that the Jesuit texts on China often stressed the superiority of European sciences in the paratext.[33] The Protestant Francisci follows a similar approach for recounting Ricci's conversation, for he frames the narration with a long paragraph explaining that Europeans have a better grasp of logical argumentation, in particular how to draw conclusions in a syllogism, than the Chinese. Natural reason is presented as a neutral, nonculturally

---

32. Baldesar Castiglione, *The Book of the Courtier*, trans. Charles Singleton (New York: AnchorBooks, 1959), 135: As Wayne Rebhorn states, "All the courtier's behavior . . . is designed to make people marvel at him." See his "Baldesar Castiglione, Thomas Wilson and the Courtly Body of Renaissance Rhetoric," *Rhetorica* 11.3 (1993): 249.

33. Joachim Kurtz, "Framing European Technology in Seventeenth-Century China: Rhetorical Strategies in Jesuit Paratexts," in *Cultures of Knowledge: Technology in Chinese History*, ed. Dagmar Schäfer (Leiden: Brill, 2011), 209.

specific mode of thinking, set in contrast to the interpretation of a region's myth and scripture, while at the same time, Francisci claims that the Jesuits have a superior skill—that is, that logical argumentation is a European trait. "The Jesuits excelled in sacred oratory: 'wisdom speaking copiously,' as Cicero defined oratory, putting eloquence and reason to serve the mysteries of the Christian faith."[34] Francisci gives the story a title, "Die ungeschickte Schluß-Künstler" (The clumsy deducers), and, in an appeal to European aristocratic readership, draws direct parallels between rhetorical debate, logical reasoning, and fencing. If Francisci crosses cultural boundaries to admire how clever the Jesuits are, Goethe does the same by admiring the Chinese, for he draws the exact opposite conclusion of Francisci by deducing that it is the Chinese who are cleverer than the missionaries. Jesuit reports were replete with examples of Chinese cleverness, yet both Jesuits and mandarins were known for their canniness, so that the one reputation burnished the other. In the overlapping claims to cleverness, Goethe suggests that the Buddhist monk was perhaps the most shrewd of all, for he put forward arguments that Ricci blindly believed he had refuted and therefore included in his report back to Europe, but that in the end were the more persuasive, at least to Goethe sitting in Weimar as he pondered Spinoza and the earliest formulations of German Idealism.

Francisci revises the Jesuit text so that the reader seems to be examining the narrative's unfolding with detachment. He conveys the sense that European reader is watching a distant spectacle, like a modern Olympic competition. For early modern German readers, it was necessary to provide a context and guidelines for understanding these Chinese encounters, and inevitably these foreign events were translated into familiar scenarios, sports among them, for a fencing match was one scenario that could be readily understood even if the motives for the fight and the combatant's utterances were unintelligible. Duels could bring in an audience that was entertained and excited by the contest, without requiring them to understand the theological expectations of the combatants. Fencing was but one

---

34. Hsia, *A Jesuit in the Forbidden City*, 12.

useful trope that helped structure a European readership. Not only was it presumed that armed personal conflict was universal, but the fencing metaphor was easily connected to other familiar tropes in rhetoric and politics.[35] By placing the reader out of bounds, the fencing metaphor allowed for an easy appropriation of the encounter without requiring knowledge of strange languages and religions. Fencing reduced foreign encounter to a simple visual denominator.

Whereas the Jesuit narrative differentiates between different forms of Chinese thought, Francisci makes perfectly clear that the primary motive for Europeans to study foreign cultures is so that they may know themselves better. The Other is quite explicitly the mirror against which Europe defines itself, according to Francisci: "To know ourselves in God remains the highest form of knowledge that man can achieve. . . . However, to reach the highest form of self-knowledge we are urged to study other people as much as ourselves, as they are civilized in manner, customs, and practices. Herein we can learn what we lack."[36] Further translating the Jesuit text into a courtly context, Francisci presents Ricci's conversations as a demonstration of superior skill. The Jesuit need to disprove heresy and reveal divine truth recedes in Francisci's telling. Trigault's original narration stresses Ricci's role in giving sermons on God's law. He emphasizes Ricci's campaign against the worship of false idols, which the story will demonstrate is practiced by Buddhists, not Confucian mandarins. Trigault's interest is to further the Jesuit policy of *approachement* with the Confucian elite by writing for an ecclesiastical audience in Rome, whereas Francisci emphasizes Ricci's skill in verbal combat. As much as Francisci admires Ricci's dexterity, his account stresses that he doubts, or says he cannot understand, the Jesuit claim that pictures of Confucius were treated

---

35. Dena Goodman draws a direct parallel between the forensic pedagogy of Jesuit schools and fencing in *The Republic of Letters: A Cultural History of the French Enlightenment* (Ithaca, NY: Cornell University Press, 1996). 94.

36. Erasmus Francisci, *Neu-polirter Geschicht- Kunst- und Sitten-Spiegel ausländischer Völcker fürnemlich Der Sineser, Japaner, Indostaner, Javaner, Malabaren, Peguaner, Siammer, . . . und theils anderer Nationen mehr: welcher, in sechs Büchern, sechserley Gestalten weiset . . .* (Nürnberg: Endter, 1670), n.p.

with respect as being of a human and not a god.[37] In other words, on the crucial question of idolatry, Francisci sides against the missionaries. For Goethe writing to Schiller, Ricci's preference for logic over scripture does not appear as a universal form of humanity; rather it is quickly reduced to a particular philosophical school. Indeed, the Buddhist challenges Ricci's reliance on abstract categories by arguing that they constituted a secondary mode of creation. To postulate abstract terms for the sun, moon, and heavens amounted to their recreation.

Goethe's Reversal

By the time Goethe read about Matteo Ricci, European interest in China had taken on a very different tone than when the missionaries were sending back reports about the court in Beijing. The Jesuits had been suppressed by papal decree in 1773, the China mission had been closed, and new ethnographic travelogues about more contemporary journeys to Peking, such as the failed British Macartney embassy, were filling the book market. Before Goethe sent his friend a copy of Francisci's report on the disputation, Schiller had already sent Goethe the first translated Chinese novel, originally published 1761 in London as *The Pleasing History* and then given a German makeover, entitled *Die angenehme Geschichte*, by Christian Gottlieb von Murr in 1766. Murr had sent Schiller a copy in 1794, which Schiller presumably passed along to Goethe.[38] Thus, in the 1790s, Goethe and Schiller were pursuing any number of Chinese sources, driven by a clear sense of having rediscovered a culture that had been ossified into rococo stereotypes. For them, China was a discovery made in the library rather than on a porcelain vase. Rejecting Francisci's inclination to perceive the dinner debate as an encoun-

---

37. Francisci, *Neu-polirter . . . Spiegel*, 1012.
38. Schiller mentions Goethe reading a Chinese novel in a letter dated January 24, 1796; *Briefwechsel*, 1:148. Goethe's diary entry from January 12, 1796, likewise mentions the Chinese novel—at this point only one had been translated. Commentators identify it as Murr's translation of the English *The Pleasing Story*; *Briefwechsel*, 3: 101–2.

ter between East and West, Christianity and paganism, Goethe sees the disputation as a contest between two types of thought that have their direct parallel in Weimar as well. He characterizes his interpretation of the debate in terms of two sets of antithetical couplings, one in China, the other in Germany, thereby suggesting a set of constellations that reoccur in different times and locations.

Given how assiduously German literary historiography distinguishes between what it has called baroque literature and the classical period of autonomy aesthetics, we should pause to consider what it means for the two luminaries to read through a seventeenth-century scribe such as Francisci in search of good material. In German literary history, Goethe and Schiller are the authors who define literature as a self-created reality, flowing from the internal genius of the author as a second creator. What does it mean that they have been caught poaching from an earlier, encyclopedic compilation about exotic places? Do we have to reconsider our awe for aesthetic autonomy? Schiller refers to Francisci's style as "gothic," a term Herder used decades earlier to describe ornate courtly style, what we call "baroque" or "rococo." Both Goethe and Schiller reassure themselves and each other that even as they read Francisci, they are detached from his convoluted style.

Goethe's rummaging through old collections looking for exotic stories is itself a seventeenth-century practice.[39] The late poetic works that led up to his notion of world literature emerged from reading around in oriental literature and scholarship looking for inspiration. The legend of his renewed poetic voice upon reading Hammer-Purgstall's translations of Hafez fits this pattern of searching through writing about non-European cultures for new material. This readerly gleaning of poetic material is by no means confined to the late Goethe, for *Faust* is also a product of long dives through seventeenth-century literature. In the end the discursive practices that Friedrich Kittler claims ended with Goethe's *Faust*, the constant borrowing and refurbishing of someone else's

39. See the introduction to Robert Folger, *Writing as Poaching: Interpellation and Self-Fashioning in Colonial relaciones de méritos y servicios* (Leiden: Brill, 2011), 3–12.

old stories, were indeed still at play in Weimar classicism. If we see Goethe as a complex writing-machine, then reading books intensively, in order to put them to use, drives its operation.[40] As Peter Bürger claims, "The organic artwork tries to make the facts of its having been produced invisible."[41] For his part, Walter Benjamin suspected that Goethe had burned the notebooks he kept while writing *Die Wahlverwandtschaften* (*Elective Affinities*) because he did not want his trade secrets revealed. The one difference between baroque practices and Goethe, of course, is that with his appropriation of the Faust legend or Hafez's *ghasels*, he composed poetry in his own distinctive voice—a point Hegel makes in his commentary on the *Divan* and one that Heine ignores deliberately when he tells Goethe of his own plans to write *a* Faust, as if the story were not uniquely bound to Goethe, but was available to anyone reading through old tomes. Heine, like Edgar Allan Poe pondering over some "quaint and curious volume of forgotten lore," reveals that one of his poetic strategies was to recast old compilations within a modern idiom, as opposed to commenting upon them with learned discourse:

> Yes, what I said is nothing new, and can be found in old, respectable folio and quarto editions of the compilers and antiquarians, in these catacombs of learnedness, where sometimes with a dreadful symmetry that is more horrifying still than the wildest arbitrariness, we find the heterogeneous bones of ideas are piled up—I admit as well, that modern scholars have also examined these topics; however they have entombed them in the wooden mummy caskets of their confusing and abstract scholarly language, which the general public cannot decode because they seem like Egyptian hieroglyphs. I have conjured up these thoughts from out of such crypts and ossuaries in order to bring them back to life through the magic power of commonly understood words, through the black art of a healthy, clear, popular style![42]

40.   Gilles Deleuze, "Letter to a Harsh Critic," *Negotiations* (New York: Columbia University Press, 1990), 7–8. Deleuze's notion of intensive reading differs substantially from Rolf Engelsing's *Lesegeschichte*; indeed, it aligns more with his "extensive" reading.

41.   Peter Bürger, *Theorie der Avantgarde* (Frankfurt: Suhrkamp, 1982), 97.

42.   Heinrich Heine, "Die Götter im Exil," in *Historisch-Kritische Gesamtausgabe der Werke*, ed. Manfred Windfuhr (Hamburg: Hoffmann and Campe, 1987), 9:125.

Goethe shares this black art of borrowing from forgotten collections with Friedrich Schiller, who in his correspondence about Ricci's disputation referred to the practice as searching for poetic spoils, "poetische Ausbeute."[43] The language of acquisition that Goethe, Schiller, and Heine use to describe the search for poetic inspiration—the borrowing of another text's images for one's own writing—becomes explicit in Goethe's "Harzreise im Winter" (Winter journey into the Harz mountains), where a soaring bird embodies the poet's constant search for new symbols to draw into his compositions.

Just as a raptor
with soft wings resting
upon heavy morning clouds
scans for prey,
may my song soar

Dem Geier gleich,
Der auf schweren Morgenwolken
Mit sanftem Fittich ruhend
Nach Beute schaut,
Schwebe mein Lied.[44]

As David Wellbery shows in his comprehensive reading of this poem, the hunting theme depicts the mediation between the poet and his long sought-for song. As far as finding the sources for poetic inspiration, "Harzreise" makes clear that the predatory poet's prey lies well off the path of established culture.[45] The poet must travel far afield away from the courts and the "comfortable crowd" to find plunder. The poetic object that breaks with convention and establishes a new vision possesses at first a degree of hiddenness and obscurity. It lies "abseits" and off to the side in the bushes as within

43. *Briefwechsel*, 2:11.

44. Johann Wolfgang Goethe, "Harzreise im Winter," in *Sämtliche Werke. Briefe, Tagebücher und Gespräche*, ed. Karl Eibl (Frankfurt: Deutscher Klassiker Verlag, 1987), 1: 322; hereafter referred to as FA.

45. David Wellbery, *The Specular Moment: Goethe's Early Lyric and the Beginnings of Romanticism* (Stanford, CA: Stanford University Press, 1996), 356–66.

the terms of "Harzreise's" hunting metaphor.[46] Hermeneutic excursions into unfamiliar texts would over time substitute for actual travel, though from the earliest Goethe was just as inclined to work through an esoteric book as to wander into the mountains in search of a poetic symbol. Reading foreign texts and traveling abroad were mutually reinforcing and eventually interchangeable avenues to an epiphany. By the time he turned to Asian literature, Goethe was too old to go there. His trips remained virtual all the better to actualize his writing.[47]

Goethe's relationship to Persian and Chinese literature entails borrowing stories for the sake of his own writing—a relation of influence that he acknowledges for Shakespeare and the Bible as well: "Does not everything accomplished by our predecessors and contemporaries belong by rights to the poet? Why should he refrain from picking flowers from where he finds them? A great work requires the appropriation of foreign treasures. With Mephistopheles did I not take from Job and Shakespeare?"[48] If Goethe and Schiller referred to themselves ironically as marauders and magicians, we can understand these allusions on several levels: first, as a witty contradiction to the polite public discourse about artists, second as an identification with their own critical representation of the construction of meaning in *Faust* or *Iphigenie* as trickery or exploitation, and thirdly as an acknowledgment of the fundamental intertextuality of all writing as derived from earlier reading. With these considerations, classical aesthetics emerges as the appropriation of ancient texts—that is, as a process of rewriting already established stories. As Eckermann puts it, "Everything is different with already *given* material and easier. Facts and characters are then already provided and the poet has only to enliven the whole. . . . Yes, I would advise to use objects that have already been worked upon. How often has Iphige-

---

46. Goethe, FA, 1:32.

47. Within this poetic framework reading is virtual, writing actual. For more on this Deleuzean distinction, see Matt Bluemink, "On Virtuality: Deleuze, Bergson, Simondon," *Epoché* (December 2020), https://epochemagazine.org/on-virtuality-dele uze-bergson-simondon-824e3742368e.

48. Johann Wolfgang Goethe, "Gespräch 17 Dezember 1824 mit von Müller und Eckermann," WA, 5:120.

nia been done and yet they are all different, for everyone sees and positions the situation differently, according to his own manner."[49] In the 1798 letter in which he describes Matteo Ricci's dinner debate, Goethe refers to "we poets" as magicians (*Taschenspieler*), who do not want anyone to see how their art is practiced.[50] If modern avant-garde works make a point of displaying the techniques used in their production, Weimar classicism preferred to hold them as a guild secret. Goethe's identification in this passage with the most notorious early modern magicians is but a turn of the hand away from the tricks Mephistopheles pulls off in the Auerbachs Keller scene, his *Taschenspielersachen*.[51] As an example of literary magic, Goethe cites, in his letter to Schiller, the Germans' enthusiastic reception of "Hermann und Dorothea," an epic poem whose original source was discovered only later in the nineteenth century. Rather than having been about the recent arrival of the French Revolution's refugees, Goethe's tale about a man who falls instantly in love with a woman fleeing her home derives from a 1732 account of Protestants driven from the Salzburg archbishopric.[52] Schiller shared Goethe's habit of roving through old chronicles and compilations for inspiration. His ballad "Der Kampf mit dem Drachen" (Battle with the dragon) was also based on a tale found in the Francisci collection. After Goethe praised the Jesuit compiler Athansius Kircher, Schiller was able to compose "Der Taucher" (The diver), based on a tale in several baroque compilations.[53] A key difference between scholars and poets lies merely in the manner in which they peruse libraries. Classical authors looked for material they could

---

49. Johann Peter Eckermann, *Gespräche mit Goethe in den letzten Jahren seines Lebens*, ed. Christoph Michel and Hans Grüters (Berlin: Deutscher Klassiker Verlag, 2011), 51–52 (September 18, 1823) (emphasis in original).

50. "Wen nuns als Dichtern, wie den Taschenspielern, daran gelegen sein mußte, daß niemand die Art, wie ein Kunststückchen hervorgebracht wird, einsehen dürfte, so hätten wir freilich gewonnen Spiel" (*Briefwechsel*, 2:9).

51. Goethe, *Faust I*, HA 3: 73, line 2267.

52. *Das Liebthätige Gera gegen die Salzburgischen Emigranten* (Franckfurt, 1732).

53. John Edwards Fletcher, *A Study of the Life and Works of Athanasius Kircher, "Germanus incredibilis"* (Leiden: Brill, 2011), 384.

transform into their own writing; scholars sought to understand in order to produce knowledge.

Friedrich Kittler argues that modern German literature was born as a subjective cry of despair sent out from a scribe caught within the baroque discourse of cutting and pasting earlier texts. The celebration of Goethe as the founding genius of German *Poesie* concentrates on this personal voice but by doing so overlooks Faust's intellectual labor as a translator, for it is in the intertextual transfer of a text from one language to the other that we can most readily recognize baroque literary practices. The two types of utterances—the poet's cry and his dictionary searches for the right word—are interdependent. Without the endless repetition of old stories in new bindings, Goethe's—or Faust's—personal shout of frustration and defiance would have never been made. The translation scene in *Faust*, far from showing the end of the baroque, hints at the poet's persistent return to familiar texts and forgotten tomes in search of his own voice. The interdependence between repetitive learning and personal revolt does not lead only to a synthesis of higher poetry and insight, but rather it starts the same process anew at a different register, so that after rereading old books so that you can find your own epiphany, and then start another such cycle of rereading old books to find your another version of that inner voice. As the legend of *West-Eastern Divan* suggests, the best Goethe can hope for is that the books change and the voice remains the same.

9

CHINESE-GERMAN PAIRINGS

The ability to draw analogies in the face of differences was a skill that the first Jesuits in Asia applied in their effort to reconcile Christianity with Confucianism. European monarchs in the early modern period flattered themselves that they too carried a Christian version of the Chinese emperor's mandate from heaven. Enlightenment cosmopolitans recognized a similarity between their own aspirations to rule as intellectuals and the literati administering China. Franz Kafka extended the analogy as a critical insight into the mythic irrationality of imperial structures. The inclination for elites to find similarities in their intellectual and administrative procedures continues to ease the expansion of capitalism's managerial class, even in the face of local resistances.

Goethe's letters to Schiller about Matteo Ricci's disputation in Nanjing draw a critical parallel to the philosophical debates that were then riling the university at Jena.[1] As he proposes to Schiller, Erasmus Francisci's account of a debate between the Jesuit and the Buddhist views on creation sounded very much like the disagreements between Karl Leonhard Reinhold's defense of Kantian limits to knowledge and Fichte's all-encompassing Idealist subject. Most notably, Goethe quietly aligned his own sympathies with a Buddhist position. Not only did he recognize the similarities between the epistemological quandaries in post-Kantian philosophy and Jesuit attempts to insert Christian theology into Chinese learned society, but he also identified himself with a line of argumentation that from almost any European perspective was the more radical and least familiar. Goethe's parallel suggests that we might read the two pairings in opposite directions: not only did Karl Leonhard Reinhold write like a Jesuit, but Matteo Ricci could be read as offering a position compatible with Reinhold's attempt to find a universally acceptable principle that grounds Kantian philosophy. Likewise, not only might Idealism reiterate Buddhist pantheism, but Buddhism may itself also be based on the principle of the Absolute Ego contemplating the world created by self-awareness. To the first comparison: Was the Jesuit reliance on a logic outside spiritual revelation a form of transcendental reasoning? In Goethe's response to Francisci's retelling of Ricci's Nanjing debate, we can trace out three major philosophical approaches to Chinese thought in early modern Europe: the Jesuit accommodation, which sought to recuperate early Confucianism as compatible with Christian teaching while dismissing Buddhism as idolatry, Francisci's dogmatic Christian suspicion that all Chinese belief systems, despite Jesuit assurances, amounted to pagan idol worship, and a radical Enlightenment pantheism that happily drew parallels between its own disavowal of theism and Chinese practices.

That the Nanjing debate correlated with Weimar contests also suggests a similarity between the classes of intellectuals in both sites.

---

1. My interpretation differs from that of the Heidelberg sinologist Günter Debon, who in the end remained undecided about how to draw the parallels between Nanjing and Weimar; see his *China zu Gast in Weimar. 18 Studien und Streiflichter* (Heidelberg: Brigitte Guderjahn, 1994), 175.

If the Jesuits could identify with the Chinese literati as a similar class of learned scholars ready to take on administrative assignments, Goethe could readily see himself in a similar role as the Duke of Weimar's *Geheimrat* (privy counsellor). Given that the German academic elite have been characterized as mandarins since the turn of the twentieth century, there is no question that Goethe, with his combination of administrative, scientific, and poetic modes of writing, became a model for this intertwining of intellectual and state functions.[2] Goethe's late poetry cycle, "Chinesisch-Deutsche Jahres- und Tageszeiten," ("Chinese-German Book of Hours and Seasons") makes this comparison explicit. In it Goethe assumes the voice of a mandarin, clearly aligning himself with the same literati Ricci addressed in offering a synthesis between early Confucianism and Christian metaphysics, though his appeal to Chinese poet-administrators came in the moment of retiring from politics in favor of writing poetry and drinking wine in the garden, rather than as an affirmative model of state power. By abandoning the functions of running a principality, the aged Goethe nevertheless concedes that he has served like the literati for much of his life. The idealization of the Chinese administrative class with its rigorous exam structure and lack of an aristocracy had been a staple of Enlightenment discourse. Voltaire was constantly flattering Frederick the Great that he should write poetry like the Emperor of China. Goethe's last poems have the ruler write poetry not as an ornament but as a substitution for politics. His identification follows the example of literati life depicted in Abel Rémusat's translation of the Chinese romance known in English as *The Two Fair Cousins* in which court politics is abandoned in favor of writing.

Goethe's recognition of a similarity between the two disparate debates reflects the intellectual tensions and transitions of Weimar at that very particular instance. Goethe's discovery comes at a moment in Weimar and Jena when Kantian philosophy is starting to give way to an Idealism that was just then beginning to emerge. Walter Benjamin describes how sudden insights arise in time: "The

---

2. Fritz K. Ringer, *The Decline of the German Mandarins: The German Academic Community, 1890–1933* (Cambridge, MA: Harvard University Press, 1969).

perception of similarity is in every case bound to a flashing up. It flits past, can possibly be won again, but cannot really be held fast as can other perception. It offers itself to the eye as fleetingly and transitorily as a constellation of stars. The perception of similarities thus seems to be bound to a moment of time."[3] While the inclination to draw correspondences between Europe and China was already a long-standing tradition, Goethe's insight is radically different, for it finds an affinity precisely where the Jesuits would not have wanted to find one: in Idealism's and Buddhism's rejection of a divine creator.

Goethe and Schiller had been following the development of Fichte's *Wissenschaftslehre* (*Science of Knowledge*) closely. While his lectures had already drawn a large audience, Fichte kept trying to reformulate his speculations more clearly. On February 27, 1797, Schiller writes to Goethe recommending that he read the (first) new introduction that Fichte just published.[4] By March the two men are reading all of Fichte's *Wissenschaftslehre* together.[5] Standing behind Goethe's correspondence with Schiller about China is the need to disguise the two thinkers' rejection of orthodox Christianity. Goethe always wrote diplomatically to Schiller about religious matters, and when the questions became too controversial, he often recommended that they speak discretely in person, with no paper trail. The accusations of atheism and Spinozism leveled at Christian

---

3. Walter Benjamin, "Doctrine of the Similar," in *Selected Writings*, ed. Michael Jennings (Cambridge, MA: Harvard University Press, 1999), 2:695–96; Johannes Endres, "Unähnliche Ähnlichkeit. Zu Analogie, Metapher und Verwandtschaft," in *Similitudo. Konzepte der Ähnlichkeit in den Künsten*, ed. Martin Gaier, Jeanette Kohl, and Alberto Saviello (Munich: Wilhelm Fink, 2012), 27–56.

4. Siegfried Seidel, ed. *Der Briefwechsel zwischen Schiller und Goethe* (Leipzig: Insel, 1984),1:310; hereafter cited as *Briefwechsel*. For an overview of the Weimar reactions to Fichte's additions to his lectures on the *Wissenschaftslehre*, see Johann Gottlieb Fichte, *Werke 1797–1798*, ed. Reinhard Leuth, Hans Gliwitzky, and Richard Schottky (Stuttgart: Friedrich Frommann, 1970), series 1, 4:169–82.

5. In a letter to J. H. Meyer, March 18, 1797, Goethe distances himself from speculative philosophy by writing that it represents a wrong direction for him as an artist: "Sodann gibt Fichte eine neue Darstellung seiner Wissenschaftslehre stückweise, in einem philosophischen Journal heraus, die wir den abends zusammen durchgehen" (*Goethes Briefe*, ed. Karl Robert Mandelkow [Hamburg: Christian Wegner, 1964], 2:259–60).

Wolff in 1723, along with his subsequent banishment from Prussia, all because he had compared Chinese ethics to his own rationalist system, were surely familiar to every intellectual in Weimar.[6] A year after Goethe's discovery of the Nanjing disputation, the Thuringian town would itself be embroiled in a scandal over whether Fichte, the newly arrived Idealist philosopher at the University of Jena, had been teaching atheism. Anticipating the danger, Goethe writes in veiled analogies about his own affinity for the Buddhist monk's argument with the Catholic priest. His attention to the 200 -year old theological debate, his eagerness to share his thoughts with Schiller, and his reticence to writing explicitly about what he saw in the analogy reflect the unrelenting pressure Christian institutions placed on radical thought.

In his first letter to Schiller about the Nanjing Disputation, Goethe also includes a copy of Schelling's *Ideen zu einer Philosophie der Natur* (*Ideas for a Philosophy of Nature*), lending further evidence that the aporias that frustrated the Nanjing debaters could also to be found in Weimar disagreements about the Kantian "thing in itself." Quite plausibly Goethe was reading the introduction to Schelling's *Ideen* when he stumbled across Ricci's disputation in Nanjing. After all, Schelling's description of the ideal philosopher sounds very much like a Romantic conception of Buddhism: "The greatest spirits have lived in their own world, undisturbed by the principles of their experience. What is the fame of the sharpest doubters compared to the life of a man that carried an entire world in his mind and all of nature in his imagination?"[7] The opposing arguments in the debates form a constellation that allows Goethe's philosophical discourse to weave between the two settings, combining Kantian terminology with Jesuit reasoning, so that one scenario illuminates the other: "The Idealist may ward off things as he will. Nevertheless he will knock into things outside of himself before he realizes it, and in the first encounter they get in his way much

---

6.   Daniel Purdy, "Chinese Ethics within the Radical Enlightenment: Christian Wolff," in *Radical Enlightenment*, ed. Carl Niekerk (Amsterdam: Ropodi, 2018), 112–30.

7.   Friedrich Wilhelm Joseph Schelling, *Ideen zu einer Philosophie der Natur*, 1st ed. (Leipzig: Breitkopf & Härtel, 1797), xvi.

like the glowing oven did for the Chinaman." Just because the Idealist has a valid point that consciousness can never know the thing in itself does not mean that all things are wholly dependent on consciousness and that material things do not exert a force on their own that confronts humans, sometimes in surprising and unexpected ways.[8] In describing the epistemological impasse in Weimar and Nanjing, Goethe prefers to avoid falling into either of the two epistemological camps, but instead to remain as long as possible in a natural state of consciousness, which Schelling claimed exists prior to philosophical inquiry, where subject and object are still inseparable.[9] Once torn out of this naïve state and dropped into philosophical inquiry, Goethe suggests, a person is frustrated either by the inability to escape the internal order of things, so that one cannot draw a connection from the empirical world to the subjective state of the mind, or one cannot find an explanation for how consciousness is able to know the empirical objects outside itself. The Weimar Idealist, Goethe maintains, is just as surprised by the externality of material objects as the Buddhist. In their introspective meditation on the universe, both are confronted by the painful otherness of the glowing hot stove.

The parallel Goethe draws involved the first two professors of critical (post-Kantian) philosophy at the University of Jena: Karl Leonhard Reinhold and Johann Gottlieb Fichte. These types of oppositions were not unusual: Fichte himself drew a distinction between Idealists, for whom "the object appears . . . as having first been created by the presentation of the intellect" (a position close to the Buddhist) and metaphysical dogmatists for whom the object exists in nature without the aid of the intellect (far too crude to be attributed to Jesuit thinking).[10] As his argument unfolds, Fichte adds a third position—critical philosophy (in other words,

8. *Briefwechsel*, 2:13.

9. For further elaboration on Goethe's caution, see John Noyes, "Eradicating the Orientalist: Goethe's 'Chinesisch-deutsche Jahres- und Tageszeiten,'" in *China in the German Enlightenment*, ed. Bettina Brandt and Daniel L. Purdy (Toronto: Toronto University Press, 2016), 157–60.

10. J. G. Fichte, "First Introduction," in *The Science of Knowledge*, trans. Peter Heath and John Lachs (Cambridge: Cambridge University Press, 1982), 10–12.

Kant). Goethe's opposition is more narrowly focused and nuanced, because, in writing to Schiller, he is simply suggesting a correspondence between debates in Weimar and Nanjing, rather than summarizing the central tenets of modern European philosophy.

Buddhism and Idealism seem alike because Fichte argues in the *Wissenschaftslehre* that empirical perceptions are knowable as facts only from a position within the self: everything that consciousness perceives as not being itself is itself the result of the self's own positing. According to Fichte, the empirical world is understood within consciousness as an intuition; only a dogmatist who is captured by the causality of things would argue that empirical perceptions originate outside self-consciousness. If we cannot know the thing in itself, then we are left with our own intuitions of the world, which occur in consciousness, not outside. The nicht-Ich is posited by an Absolute Ich. Fichte points to several passages in the *Critique of Pure Reason* in which Kant cautiously describes the self's sensation of external empirical perceptions—without declaring that they originate in some "thing in itself" that exists wholly and metaphysically by itself. Fichte argues that many of Kant's followers—and he considers Reinhold the most adept—still have a dogmatic view of the "thing in itself" as grounded outside the subject rather than recognizing that Kant himself often writes like an Idealist who holds that empirical perceptions are knowable only as intuitions within consciousness, therefore a (somewhat dialectical) product of the self's self-positing.

Goethe takes two steps back from this debate to draw an analogy between Fichte's claim that empirical perceptions occur within consciousness rather than originating from the outside and the Buddhist's claim that our idea of the sun is itself a (second) creation in the mind. Much as Goethe admires the Buddhist's maneuvering around Ricci's metaphysics, he also wishes the Buddhist had been able to physical demonstrate that empirical objects are solely mental images. Like any detached yet interested spectator, Goethe enjoys the deft maneuvers of both sides; he is not rooting for any particular position. Fichte and Reinhold are themselves well aware of the public nature of their debate, indeed they go out of their way to speak politely about each other. The two philosophers corresponded even as they held differing positions. They were hardly hostile to one another, though Fichte had plenty of sharp words and mockery for other members of the philosophical public. Reinhold comes very close to accepting the claim that Kant's *Critique of Pure Reason* and Fichte's *Science of Knowledge* agree on the fundamental point that empirical facts are intelligible only because they occur within consciousness. Reinhold understands this self as merely empirical, and not transcendental. Fichte then picks up on this new difference; Reinhold almost agrees with him, but then makes a further distinction that moves the debate forward. Fichte writes generously about Reinhold in his "Second Introduction to the *Wissenschaftslehre*," quoting the essay in which Reinhold equates and then distinguishes Kant from Fichte.[11] Goethe could track the dialectical unfolding of Fichte and Reinhold's debate better than the Nanjing Disputation, because he had only the Jesuit representation.

When he equated the Jesuit reliance on logic with the Kantian arguments of Karl Leonard Reinhold (1757–1823), Goethe was not just being whimsical. Reinhold had been born in Vienna, where he attended a school with Jesuit teachers from the age of seven. In 1772, he enrolled as a novice in the Jesuit church of St. Anna, but after a year of strict monastic discipline he was forced to leave when the Society of Jesus was suppressed by papal decree. A letter written by the fifteen-year-old Reinhold to his father testifies to how stricken he was by being forced to leave his devotional life.[12] A year later he entered the Barnabite Collegium at St. Michael, where he studied philosophy and theology. After six years, he was allowed to instruct the novices in the disciplines that comprised the philosophical curriculum: logic, metaphysics, ethics, spiritual rhetoric, mathematics, and physics.[13] By the time he was in his twen-

---

11. Fichte, "Second Introduction to the Science of Knowledge," in *The Science of Knowledge*, trans. Peter Heath and John Lachs (Cambridge: Cambridge University Press, 1982), 52–53. Carl Leonhard Reinhold, "Meine gegenwärtige Ueberzeugung vom Wesen der reinen Philosophie, Transcendentalphilosophie, Metaphysik," *Auswahl vermischter Schriften* (Jena: Mauke, 1797), 341–42.

12. Ernst Reinhold, *Karl Leonhard Reinhold's Leben und litterarisches Wirken* (Jena: Friedrich Frommann, 1825), 5–13.

13. Karianne J. Marx, *The Usefulness of the Kantian Philosophy: How Karl Leonhard Reinhold's Commitment to Enlightenment Influenced His Reception of Kant* (Berlin: De Gruyter 2011), 15–17.

ties, Reinhold had moved turned away from his youthful piety to participate in the new Enlightenment culture that had emerged in Vienna after Joseph II started introducing his progressive reforms in 1781. In time, he joined an Enlightenment club that was modeled on the Free Masons and dedicated to combatting superstition, *Schwärmerei* (raving fanaticism), and monasticism.[14] In 1783, with the assistance of the Leipzig professor of philosophy Christian Friedrich Petzold, Reinhold fled Vienna and his church obligations for Protestant Saxony. When news reached Vienna that Reinhold was now teaching and studying in Leipzig, his friends advised him to move to Weimar, where Christoph Wieland received him generously with the offer to help edit his journal, *Der Teutsche Merkur*, following the departure of his earlier assistant, Friedrich Bertuch. While working for the *Merkur*, Reinhold began publishing letters on Kantian philosophy (1786–1787), which helped make the issues in the *Critique of Pure Reason* more accessible and provided him with an appointment as the first philosophy professor at the University of Jena. Reinhold thereby inaugurated the Idealist project at Jena, enabling the university to attract a succession of young thinkers—Fichte, Schelling, Hegel—along with their enthusiastic students.

With his next publication, Reinhold distanced himself from Kant's arguments. Following Kant's architectural image of philosophical systems, Reinhold sought to demonstrate the existence of a foundation to reason that lay below Kant's epistemological constraints on human knowledge. In the preface to his *Vorstellungsvermögen* (Faculty of representation), Reinhold directly refers to finding philosophical principles that could be accepted by all sects, referring here to schools of philosophy, yet his purposeful use of the term "sect" draws a parallel between different religions as well as. "In order to consolidate the principles he seeks with all pre-existing systems, he must start with propositions that no sect can challenge."[15] Reinhold may have intended to draw Protestants and Catholics together to accept these new foundations for philosophy, but Goethe

---

14. Reinhold, *Reinhold's Leben*, 18.

15. Karl Leonhard Reinhold, *Versuch einer neuen Theorie des menschlichen Vorstellungsvermögens*, 2nd ed. (Prague: C. Widtmann and J. M. Mauke, 1795), 24.

recognized that this claim to a natural foundation to reason that precedes all dogmatic religion was much the same as the Jesuits' scholastic approach to disputing Asian religions.

While Jörg-Peter Mittmann suggests that Reinhold's search for a fundamental principle that grounds reason is an inheritance from the work of Leibniz and Wolff, the concern has older sources in Reinhold's training as a Jesuit.[16] Goethe's analogy between Ricci and Reinhold can be explained by this connection. Missionary work, when it is understood as the task of persuading interlocutors through philosophical demonstrations, requires a practical application of the theoretical claim that rational principles can be shared by all humans. As Wolff's lectures on Confucianism made clear to his Pietist colleagues, the trouble with this assumption for missionaries is that if all people share a basic form of rationality, which grounds their social and moral lives, then there is little need for Christian revelation.[17] In historical terms, a sceptic could have asked: Why convert other people to Christianity through logical arguments when they already have their own rational moral system? If Chinese philosophy, whether Buddhist, Confucian, or another syncretic mix is as rational as Christian metaphysics, then there would seem no justification, on a strictly philosophical level, for trying to convert the Chinese to Christianity. This problematic became obvious as Leibniz and Wolff adapted Ricci's accommodationist interpretation of Chinese thought, thereby turning the issue into one of most important scandals of the German Enlightenment.

The question of finding a rational principle that all sides can agree upon serves as the starting point for the Nanjing disputation as well as the succession of attempts by Jena Idealists to solve Reinhold's query.[18] Like the Idealists after Reinhold, Sanhoi, the sixteenth-century Buddhist in Nanjing, accepted the need for finding such a

---

16. Jörg-Peter Mittmann, "Das Prinzip der Selbstgewissheit. Fichte und die Entwicklung der nachkantischen Grundsatzphilosophie," PhD diss., University of Munich, 1992, 10.

17. Purdy, "Chinese Ethics."

18. Eckhart Förster describes Fichte's attempt at finding such a first principle in *Die 25 Jahre der Philosophie: Eine systematische Rekonstruktion* (Klostermann: Frankfurt, 2012), 187–88.

basic, intercultural, rational principle during his debate with Matteo Ricci. The philosophical difficulties quickly emerged in the next phase of the debate, which in Goethe's constellation entails the introduction of Buddhism and philosophical Idealism. While it is certainly beyond the scope of this book to explain how Buddhism and Idealism share similarities, an entry in Goethe's diary written years later does provide us a sense of why Fichte might have seemed to Goethe to be arguing in the Buddhist manner. Like Sanhoi, Fichte seems to claim that he can create a world in his mind. Goethe says as much when he summarizes the turbulent first years of Jena's philosophy chair during which Reinhold received the first appointment and left for a better job, only to be replaced by Fichte, who riled up the students and defied the duke with his writing and lecturing on religion. "After Reinhold's departure, which truly seemed a great loss for the academy, the bold, audacious step was taken to appoint Fichte, who had made grand but not quite respectable statements on the most important moral and political topics, in his place. He was one of the most able persons ever, and nothing could be said against his view when taken as a whole; yet how could he keep up with the world, which, after all, he considered to be a possession of his own creation?"[19] When Goethe writes that Fichte contemplated the world to be his own self-created possession, he is alluding to both the philosopher's egoism and Idealist speculation. In looking back, Goethe takes a detached view of the atheism scandal by describing Fichte's actions as "not quite respectable." Throughout the eighteenth-century German intellectuals feared monarchical suppression whenever they publicly attacked Christianity and its institutions. Any avowal of Chinese philosophies that suggested them as an alternative to Christian metaphysics was just as likely to invite extreme censure as simply attacking Christianity was. Goethe may have been intrigued by Sanhoi's metaphysics, but he was unlikely to let anyone other than Schiller know about it directly. Only later in life would Goethe express his Chinese sympathies through lyric

---

19. Johann Wolfgang Goethe, *Goethes Werke* (Weimar: Hermann Böhlaus Nachfolger, 1887–1919), 1, 35:31; hereafter cited as WA.

poetry, a genre that sought to avoid public contests by adopting a voice of interior reflection.

Goethe's interest in Matteo Ricci's debate with Sanhoi and his recognition of its similarities with the philosophical debates in Jena are hardly surprising given how important such disputations were in defining the Enlightenment. The university at Jena was the latest forum in Germany's culture of debate (*Streitkultur*). While Leibniz had been a consummate diplomat throughout his career, intellectual history in the previous century had hardly been a smooth unfolding of systematic ideas. Much of the eighteenth century was filled with long stretches of quiet rumination, punctuated by explosive disagreements. The debates around Gotthold Lessing, both during and after his life, were probably its most prominent representative, but Christian Wolff's scandalous lecture on the rationality of Confucian ethics had already shown how the Enlightenment's reception of Chinese thought could be turned against both Protestant and Catholic theology, in his case Pietist and Jesuit. When the aged Herder changed his mind about the Jesuits in China and published warm praise for their work, he cited the intense debates in the 1770s initiated by the Dutch writer Cornelius de Pauw, who published blanket denunciations of Jesuit writing about the Americas and Asia. Looking back on the debates between De Pauw and the Jesuits, Herder tried to find some value in the scandal by saying that even though De Pauw really was rude and ignorant, his writings were useful because they provoked comprehensive and convincing refutations from the Jesuits: "Even the debates about the Chinese that De Pauw provoked brought more light to the topic through the answer that the Fathers gave them."[20] Even stupid arguments served a purpose in the long run. For example, Voltaire had a lengthy correspondence with Frederick the Great about China, which was motivated, in large part, by the urge to deny De Pauw's negative account. On the question of representing China, Voltaire found himself on the Jesuits' side, even though he showed little love for the society in *Candide*. Enlightenment thinkers like

---

20.   Quoted in R. F. Merkel, "Herder und Hegel über China," *Sinica* 17 (1942): 6.

Herder and Voltaire still held the belief that public debates were decided by the better arguments, regardless of who made them.

This Enlightenment preference for the superior argument sometimes led to unexpected affinities. As Goethe well understood, the verbal gymnastics of religious debates often turned arguments on their head. While he claimed to avoid polemics himself, particularly concerning charges of atheism and pantheism, Goethe enjoyed watching experts attack each other in public.[21] When two prominent Vienna orientalists, Heinrich Friedrich von Diez in Berlin and Joseph von Hammer-Purgstall, entered into a raucous debate over who understood the Ottomans better, Goethe followed the public rebuttals as part of his studies in Persian poetry. In his notes to *West-Eastern Divan*, Goethe adopted Francisci's fencing metaphor, when he compared their orientalist one-upmanship to a duel, in which he as a spectator was trying to learn the moves from two masters.[22] As Joan-Pau Rubiés points out, disputations functioned as a means of transmitting knowledge from a private setting to wider and quite distant audience.[23] In public debates between skilled orators, knowledge moved through a sequence of exchanges as contradictions were exposed and then placed against each other for the sake of presenting the superior argument. These formal moves were fascinating in themselves.

That any European would be persuaded by Sanhoi's defense of Buddhism was not very likely because, as every modern scholar points out, the European record presents only the Jesuit side of the story. In their critical reinterpretation of the Jesuit narrative, Goethe and Schiller speculate on the deeper meanings that lay behind the Buddhist utterances, meanings that were not conveyed by the Jesuit

---

21. In *Dichtung und Wahrheit*, Goethe explains his aversion to theological controversies specifically in relation to debates over Spinoza; Johann Wolfgang Goethe, *Werke*, ed. Erich Trunz (Munich: C. H. Beck, 1982), 10:76; hereafter cited as HA.

22. Johann Wolfgang Goethe, *Sämtliche Werke. Briefe, Tagebücher und Gespräche*, ed. Karl Eibl (Frankfurt: Deutscher Klassiker Verlag, 1987), 3.1:273; hereafter cited as FA.

23. Joan-Pau Rubiés, "Real and Imaginary Dialogues in the Jesuit Mission of Sixteenth-Century Japan," *Journal of the Economic and Social History of the Orient* 55 (2012): 447–94.

narrative, but that tantalize any reader who does not believe that the Buddhist position could really be as foolish as the Jesuit story portrayed it. In their humanist mode, they attempt to find a hermeneutic or empathetic engagement with the strange Chinese figures, which for them means imagining or projecting motives and a psychology onto the foreigner. Goethe writes that he imagines any number of different responses the monk may have made to the missionary, to which Schiller adds his epistemological worry: Just how much depth can we attribute the surface statements of the Chinese monk? "I am just not certain . . . whether something smart or dull lies behind this Chinese rationalization."[24] In order to perceive Chinese figures as meaningful speakers, Schiller needs to move beyond the surface images of chinoiserie—which is to say he looks to find motives and reasoning that he can recognize in himself. The ability to identify with Chinese literary characters, what later might be called empathy, or *Einfühlung*, entails leading sympathy past the almost comical impressions of rococo images on porcelain so that they seem comparable with what Schiller understands to be human. This readerly maneuver entails ascribing depth behind the foreign surface by imagining oneself within the strange figure.

This problem of what thoughts lie behind enigmatic Chinese statements weighed on Schiller, who was just then rewriting Carlo Gozzi's *Turandot*, the rococo drama about a beautiful Chinese princess who executes her suitors one after the other because they cannot answer the riddles she gives them. Schiller's rewriting of the play thematizes the hermeneutic attempt to pass beyond frightening surfaces to perceive a hidden emotional interior that motivates them. *Turandot* was one of the popular representations of China that had been circulating through the eighteenth century. Schiller's drama would later serve as the libretto for Puccini's 1926 opera. In adapting the Italian play, Schiller worries about what could possibly have brought about such royal cruelty, a question that never arises in the Italian original, where Turandot's arbitrary tyranny is simply presented as normal by Chinese expectations. Out of Goethe's projection and identification with the Buddhist monk one can see how

---

24. *Briefwechsel*, 2:17.

both authors are trying to build identifications with Chinese characters. Schiller wants to get past the conventional Asiatic despot found in martyr plays, baroque tragic drama, fairy tales, and operas. As much as he admires Gozzi's version, he believes that modern audiences would not find Turandot a plausible character. Schiller writes to his friend Christian Gottfried Körner in Dresden, who also hopes to stage the play: "The figures look like marionettes controlled by a wire; the whole thing has a certain pedantic stiffness that must be overcome. I really have a chance to earn some honor and the six or seven weeks that will go into the business will not be lost."[25] For Schiller, the difficulty in understanding motivations lies both with Gozzi's stock characters and with the otherness of the Asian figures inherited from the original Persian tale. In order to answer his own hermeneutic concern to intuit the thoughts behind seemingly inscrutable actions, Schiller writes a monologue into the play that has Turandot explaining herself in a pseudo-feminist critique of how women are treated in Asia. Schiller lets Turandot describe the subjugation of women, yet in doing so, she is voicing the false consciousness of a Western anthropological critique. With her supposedly feminist version of the Asiatic despot role, she has assumed the position of the Caliph in *A Thousand and One Nights* who forces Scheherazade to tell a new tale every night, thereby reversing an established gender hierarchy. Schiller was of course not alone in wanting an Asian figure to explain Asians' seemingly tyrannical behavior to a German theater audience. At the same moment when he is writing *Turandot* for the Weimar theater, Schiller is also preparing a restaging of Goethe's *Iphigenie auf Tauris*, wherein Goethe projects a similar Asian inner monologue onto the Scythian king Thoas, who denounces the Greek tendency to steal treasures from barbarians, thereby gaining the sympathies of cosmopolitan (in the Kantian sense) audiences.

---

25. Schiller letter to Körner, November 16, 1801, in Friedrich Schiller, *Werke: Nationalausgabe* (Weimar: Verlag Hermann Böhlaus Nachfolger, 1943ff), 14:291; hereafter cited as NA. Karl Goedeke, *Grundrisz zur Geschichte der deutschen Dicthung aus den Quellen* (Hanover: L. Ehlermann, 1859), 2:989.

Because Goethe and Schiller were seeking continuities between cultures, the Jesuit hostility toward Buddhism appeared to them as an obstacle to sympathy. For, insofar as the missionaries were willing to accommodate their understanding of Confucianism, they sought to establish a clear difference between Christian and Buddhist cosmology. Indeed, Goethe selects the precise point were Ricci was least accommodating to Chinese philosophy. Goethe, an enthusiast for heresies in general, then also sides against the Jesuit, but for utterly different reasons than the pious Francisci. Since the nineteenth century, commentators on this passage in the Goethe-Schiller correspondence have speculated that the similarities between the Buddhist position and pantheism explain why Goethe would have read the story against the Jesuit side of the debate. Woldemar von Biedermann writes: "What seemed clear to Goethe was that the Chinese position, against which the Jesuit missionary Ricci was arguing, agreed with that of Spinoza, a philosophy that Goethe had long cherished and defended."[26] Spinoza has often stood as the third term in any comparison between European pantheism and Eastern philosophy. That Goethe would compare the Buddhist position with Idealism does not weaken the plausible connection to Spinoza. Indeed, Schelling had written to Hegel in 1795, just a few years before Goethe's encounter with the Francisci story (1798), that the poet had become a Spinozist. Contrary to Biedermann's assertion, Spinoza and early Idealism were however far from identical. In an effort to define his own focus on the transcendental subject, Fichte lumps Spinoza together with the dogmatic metaphysics who presume that objective reality lies fully outside the self.[27] Schelling makes much the same distinction when he explains that for Spinoza the world as absolute object is everything, whereas for him it is the "I" as absolute subject.[28] Goethe makes

---

26. Woldemar Freiherrn von Biedermann, "Goethe und das Schrifttum Chinas," *Zeitschrift für vergleichende Literaturgeschichte* N.F. 7 (1894): 383–401.

27. Fichte, *The Science of Knowledge*, 226.

28. Dalia Nassar, "Spinoza in Schelling's early conception of intellectual intuition," in *Spinoza and German Idealism*, ed. Eckart Förster and Yitzhak Y. Melamed (Cambridge: Cambridge University Pres, 2012), 136. See also Horst Lange, "Goethe and Spinoza: A Reconsideration," *Goethe Yearbook* 17 (2011): 12.

clear in *Dichtung und Wahrheit* (*Poetry and Truth*) that Spinoza was a profound source for his own pantheism, referring to him as "this spirit, which has so decisively changed me, and which has had an influence on my entire way of thinking."[29] Goethe's understanding of the divine in nature, which he attributes to Spinoza, denies the possibility of divine intervention into the world, much as the Buddhist monk rejects the supremacy Ricci attributed to God as creator: "Nature operates according to eternal, necessary, and therefore divine laws, so that the Deity himself could not alter anything about it."[30] Indeed, it is this adherence to Spinoza's cosmological position that allows Goethe to hold a pantheist view while still wishing that the Buddhist monk had a more realist view of objects in the universe.

Jonathan Israel has also argued that Chinese thought was often interpreted as a form of coded Spinozism—indeed that references to Confucianism were understood as a nod toward the scandalous material metaphysics of Spinoza. Israel portrays the Enlightenment interest in China as something of a code or masquerade: "Another favourite ploy was to stress the parallels between Spinoza and Confucius, classical Chinese philosophy having, ever since Isaac Vossius, been eulogized by Temple, Bayle, Saint-Hyacinthe, Lévesque de Burigny, Wolff, and others as an entirely 'natural' philosophy based solely on reason and steeped in moral ad metaphysical truth."[31] Leibniz recognizes the possibility but understands the link as a matter of the interpreter's intentions. A believer could just as well find a theistic God. Responding to a Franciscan critique of Chinese pantheism, Leibniz claims that such a reading is really only a matter of how one wants to argue the point: "Father [de Sainte Marie] adds that the Chinese are like the Stoics, who pictured a material God suffused throughout the universe to animate it. . . . But I see nothing that prevents us from finding here a spiritual God, author of matter itself, showing His wisdom and power in brute

29. Goethe, *Dichtung und Wahrheit*, HA 10:35 (book 14).

30. Goethe, *Dichtung und Wahrheit*, HA 10:79 (book 16).

31. Jonathan I. Israel, *Radical Enlightenment: Philosophy and the Making of Modernity (1650–1750)* (Oxford: Oxford University Press, 2001), 588.

things."[32] Hegel was also well aware of the tendency to equate Chinese philosophy with Spinoza.[33] Far from accepting the comparison as a necessary ruse for radical philosophers, he considered the analogy inappropriate because of the differing material character of some metaphysical unity posited in Chinese thought and by Spinoza's *Ethics*.[34] Just how slippery the comparisons between European and Chinese metaphysics were, is made clear when we recall that Goethe is drawing an analogy between undefined forms of Buddhism and Idealism. Clearly the inclination to cite parallels between Confucianism and Spinoza ran counter to the Jesuit assertion that early Confucianism was compatible with Christian teaching. At stake were two approaches to Confucian writings, each grappling with the other: radical rationalism and reformed Catholicism. Chinese philosophy became the third element in this European contest, the external referent that both sides cited as proof of their own intra-European validity. Because China presented such a well-respected and ancient civilization, both philosophical camps aspired to claim Confucianism as an ally.

Goethe is reversing Ricci's reversal. By attending a dinner and finding an opportunity to debate and then refute the Buddhist, Ricci has walked the thin line of hospitality. In arguing with the Buddhist, Ricci is demonstrating that he has acquired the skills of a mandarin, but he is also deploying them against an outside monk. The strategy was intended to draw a clear separation between Confucian and Buddhist links to Christianity. Where Francisci's text presumes and reinforces the expectation that the European reader will identify and agree with Ricci, Goethe reverses that expectation, pre-

---

32. Julia Ching and Willard G. Oxtoby, "Discourse on the Natural Theology of the Chinese," in *Moral Enlightenment: Leibniz and Wolff on China*, ed. Julia Ching and Willard G. Oxtoby (Nettetal: Steyler Verlag, 1992), 127; see also p. 131 for the link to Spinoza.

33. Georg Wilhelm Friedrich Hegel, *Vorlesungen über die Philosophie der Geschichte*, ed. Eva Moldenhauer and Karl Markus Michel (Frankfurt: Suhrkamp, 1986), 90. "Similarly the Chinese Philosophy, as adopting the One as its basis, has been alleged to be the same as at a later period appeared as Eleatic philosophy and the Spinozistic System" (Hegel, *The Philosophy of History*, trans. J. Sibree [New York: Dover, 1956], 66).

34. Hegel, *Vorlesungen*, 94–95, and *The Philosophy of History*, 70.

ferring instead to side with the Buddhist, so that his reading also turns against the rules of politeness.

Disputations and Letter Writing

This chapter moves backward in history from the late eighteenth to the late sixteenth centuries in order to outline three constellations of European reflections on China. These three pairings of Goethe-Schiller, Reinhold-Idealism, and Ricci-Buddhism are stretched out across four levels of textual commentary and recapitulation: the Goethe-Schiller correspondence, Erasmus Francisci's compilation, the official Jesuit history of the China mission in *De Christiana*, and Ricci's Italian manuscript. All these texts are of course embedded in oral communications that are not always repeated in writing: what was actually said over dinner in Nanjing, Ricci's instructions to Trigault, Goethe and Schiller's frequent chats. As we fill in the space between Goethe and Matteo Ricci, we will find additional German-Chinese constellations.

The debate in Nanjing has its own prehistory: the Chinese scene repeats earlier disputations in which Christian metaphysicians tried to incorporate another religion through the claim that both share a similar "foundation" in a monotheistic rationality. The debates varied of course, so that the theological stakes in medieval disputes with Judaism differed from those with East Asian Buddhism, yet the dialectic always sought a resolution through an ever more all-encompassing claim to a rational order that could also align itself with scriptural interpretation. These constellations became rhetorically visible over the course of theological disputations and theatrical performances that were written about and commented upon long after the initial scene had been completed. Thus, the terms of the Nanjing debate were retold and studied for at least two hundred years, just as the major disputations in German philosophical history resurface with renewed vigor long after the immediate historical context has disappeared. As Goethe noted, disputations reveal the ideas that had been on everyone's mind but had not yet found expression.

Matteo Ricci engages in a disputation with Buddhism because his primary interest is to avoid one with Confucianism. His overall strategy for establishing Christianity in China centers on finding an accommodation between his interpretation of Confucian thought and Christianity, one that reiterates the slow synthesis medieval Christianity undertook with Plato and Aristotle. Accommodation and synthesis are the inverse of disputation. Ricci presented himself as fighting Buddhist heresy because he needed to show his European audience that he had not abandoned his mission.

At every disputation there are some onlookers who seek out a diplomatic resolution. Goethe may have been attracted to them, but he carefully avoided becoming trapped among them. For much of his later career, Goethe maneuvered between institutions with much the same skill and detachment that Gottfried Leibniz had demonstrated a hundred years earlier as he tried to resolve the antagonisms between Protestant and Catholic princes. For Goethe, one challenge was to evade the charge of atheism as he wrote poetry on superstitious encounters with demons and learned reveries about Islam.

Disputations create a tension that appears to challenge the systematic operation of the different faiths. The regularized practices of a system are open to sudden change by the disputation, which allows the speakers to question publicly rituals and principles that have been accepted as valid without argumentation. They provide a shock to normality. They also reveal the limits of what can be said, the confines within which learned debate takes place, the point when state authority intervenes in academic reasoning.

The ability of disputations to reveal previously unrecognized arguments depends upon their circulation within channels of communication available to a wide audience. Matteo Ricci surely had many conversations with Chinese monks and administrators, but the inclusion of the Nanjing debate in the first history of the Catholic mission as a complex allegory depicting the multiple sides of Jesuit accommodation—its confrontation with Buddhism alongside its very particular approach to Confucianism—allowed it to move continuously through European discussions of China as an illustration of how the three religions intermeshed. Communication networks allowed short-lived oral debates to assume a representative function, so that commentators could mull over what had been said in a centuries-long *l'esprit de escalier* that revised the origin conversation as if it were a dream. Given how often these debates were retold, we must be sensitive to the possibility that what appears to be their original recitation is already itself a revision. Particularly in intercultural debates, there is no clear standard as to what had been said by whom at what point in the conversation. The more we compare the Buddhist-Jewish-Christian-Confucian versions of historical debates, the more dependent historians become on literary interpretation. Like tragedies, intercultural disputations set mythic forces in confrontation. Rhetoric and logic contain these forces by making them presentable to foreigners raised in another tradition, yet at some point in the proceedings, force, violence, and forgery replace persuasive appeals. Learned disputations are admired because unlike tragedies they claim to hold mythic forces at bay. Yet the potential for dialogue to turn into such a force and the need to choose words wisely are obvious whenever the potential for violence favors one side. In the heat of a disputation, however, participants state arguments they might not have otherwise, most notably positions that offend Christian orthodoxy. Medieval rabbis were not the only public speakers reluctant to offend church officials. Goethe avoided attacking the church more than it seemed appropriate for a poet, as he wrote to Schiller. Their correspondence has many passages where Goethe writes that he will elaborate his point in person; often these references to oral conversations suggest that one or the other writer does not want to commit his heretical view to paper—far better to discuss atheism or pantheism while strolling through the garden together. Goethe practices a rhetoric of silence, alluding to significant thoughts, then passing over them. Nietzsche suggests that Goethe maintained the fine art of keeping quiet all his life, for good reasons we will never learn.[35] Letters often include passages alluding to what was said outside the text, suggesting a complementarity between speaking and writing. Neither discourse completely subsumes the other. Goethe's walk-and-talk strategy was

---

35.   Friedrich Nietzsche, *Beyond Good and Evil*, trans. R. J. Hollingdale (London: Penguin, 1973), 155, #244.

particularly important in Weimar, for six months after his discovery of the Nanjing disputation, Fichte would become embroiled in a scandal about his supposed avowal of atheism in print and during lectures. Goethe's detached attitude toward Fichte and his acquiescence to the duke's pressure to have Fichte removed from his professorship reflect a diplomatic aversion to being labeled an unbeliever. Goethe and Schiller could easily have been implicated in the firestorm that fell on Fichte, for the philosopher cites both poets as allies in the essay that created the uproar; specifically Fichte quotes Faust's pantheistic answer to Gretchen's question, "Tell me, how to you stand on religion?" in the last pages of his controversial essay "Über den Grund unseres Glaubens an eine göttliche Weltregierung" ("On the Reason for Our Belief in a Divine World Order"), published later in 1798. Goethe may have written and spoken with Schiller about his sympathy for the Buddhist rejection of Christian theism, and Fichte may have been quite correct to bring in *Faust* in support of his own position, but Goethe was in no way inclined to follow Fichte's public self-destruction as an atheist. Even when he is discussing Milton's *Paradise Lost*, Goethe cuts his own critical comments off by saying that he will save them for a later conversation, when they can also discuss Reinhold's response to Fichte: "However, this may be best reserved for an oral conversation, just like Reinhold's explanation of Fichte's atheism."[36]

The "atheism controversy" was but one late manifestation of the Enlightenment practice of not attacking theism in print, but instead reserving such discussions for conversations with trusted friends. Jonathan Israel's detailed examination of the radical Enlightenment is predicated on the thesis that heterodox support for Spinoza's philosophy was widespread but unstated in any public forum. Reinhard Koselleck has shown how important it was for courtiers and intellectuals to keep their most critical beliefs hidden. In the heat of intellectual battle, disputations sometimes brought out statements that would otherwise have been self-censored and that after the fact were almost always revised, or "walked back" in American political parlance. Because of their formal structure,

---

36. *Briefwechsel*, 2:248. (July 31, 1799).

because they seemingly start with no assumptions, disputations raise the possibility that anything is possible, that the conclusion could be wholly unexpected, yet all too often their arguments unfold in a predictable fashion, so much so that cynics might assert that their conclusion was foregone. Under these circumstances, only the very open-minded audience member could find the antithetical thread that denies the foregone conclusion to the debate. Indeed, anyone who sides with the opposing side may be condemned as a perverse heretic; thus it behooves those listening for the counterargument to remain quiet about their conversion.

Disputations also have an inherent instability built into their origins. Many hinge on the question of what had someone actually said originally: What were the Buddhist arguments at the Nanjing supper? How fluently did Ricci speak the high language of court officials? What did Christian Wolff say in his lecture on Chinese philosophy that so offended his Pietist listeners? Did Lessing really tell Jacobi that he had accepted Spinoza's philosophy? How defiant was Fichte in his negotiations with the Weimar court? In reviewing these controversies, Goethe had an inclination toward the heretical position but a strong caution against letting his views be known beyond his most trusted friends.

My argument here is not just concerned with tracing out the historic ebb and flow of Christian-Confucian-Buddhist debates. In addition, I wish to consider how it is possible for members of the audience to switch sides. What justifications do the converts accept in defiance of their own community's principles? Whether by an inversion of logical arguments or by the transfer of emotions, my study asks how did Europeans come to identify with Chinese culture? I am interested in those who pass over to the other side, an accusation first leveled against Ricci by many European Christians for his accommodation with Confucianism, but then reiterated in a literary context by nationalists offended by Goethe's concept of world literature. Among academics in the twenty-first century, Ricci's accommodation and Goethe's world literature are accepted as the obviously superior positions, which only narrow-minded dogmatists would oppose, yet any historically ground review would show that these cosmopolitan positions were always quite tenuous, constantly challenged, and eventually dismissed by institutions opposed to their existence.

From Plato's symposium to the Algonquin Club, intellectuals have celebrated clever exchanges over dinner. Florentine humanists revived the ancient tradition of celebrating Plato's birthday with a banquet, as Marsilio Ficino's commentary on the *Symposium* announces on its first page.[37] Added to scholarly sociability was the cosmopolitan ceremony of inviting a foreigner to the table in order to hear him speak of himself. Expectations raised by European rules of hospitality, inherited from antiquity and refined in Renaissance courts, frame the Jesuit narrative. Ricci's memoir attributes the same tradition to the Chinese, making clear that in arguing over religion at dinner, Ricci was not violating the rules of politeness: "We have mentioned that it is customary with the Chinese to argue over their differences at the dinner table."[38] Early modern readers would have understood the dialogue as a refined scholarly duel performed rhetorically and without violating decorum. Even-handedness was an important requirement within the long rhetorical tradition of the theological dialogue, particularly if the narrative was going to pull in European readers. Jesuit narratives in Asia particular allow a somewhat fair distribution of rational arguments between contestants. Indeed, the plausible balance between Christian and Chinese arguments allows Goethe centuries later to reverse the decision in favor of the Buddhist. Scholars in our era, just like Goethe, have listened for what they imagine is the Buddhist voice speaking through the Jesuit representation. Joan-Pau Rubiés, for example, has argued that while "it is often difficult to obtain independent information about the alternative point of view of native speakers, . . . it is possible, in some cases, to read fruitfully between the lines."[39]

There were at least three academic responses to the rediscovery of Chinese culture in the early modern period. Each line of interpretation developed from a distinct form of writing though eventu-

---

37. Sears Reynolds Jayne, *Marsilio Ficino's Commentary on Plato's 'Symposium'* (Columbia: University of Missouri Press, 1944), 121.

38. Matteo Ricci, *China in the Sixteenth Century: The Journals of Matthew Ricci (1583–1610)*, trans. Louis J. Gallagher. New York: Random House, 1953), 339.

39. Rubiés, "Real and Imaginary Dialogues," 449.

ally the genres and types of books overlapped. The Jesuit approach was grounded in theological interpretation of classical texts, in this case the canonical works of early Confucianism. It was sharply focused on a specific tradition within Chinese thought that separated its own interests distinctly from other Chinese traditions such as neo-Confucianism or Buddhism. The conservative Christian response to accommodation appeared in second-hand compilations combining many different sources in a comparative manner that ultimately blurred the differences between cultures, languages, religions, or philosophical interpretations. The comparative approach of these collections eliminated differences so that all non-European beliefs were summarized as demonic, pagan idol worship. Peruvian practices were placed next to Chinese and African so that all three seemed identical in their difference from Christian dogma. The third line of analysis was more secretive and therefore most scholarly. It sought to recuperate Confucianism, with an ear to other Chinese traditions, for the sake of formulating a rationalist critique of Christianity. Like the conservative Christian compilations, the rationalists interpreted Jesuit accounts critically, also questioning the compatibility of Confucianism and Christianity but in their case with an eye toward mobilizing Chinese ethical thought as an argument against Christian revelation.

The alliances between these three approaches shifted unexpectedly, so that rationalists and Jesuits could find themselves positioned against conservative Christians, as when Christian Wolff found unexpected support from Jesuits in his debate with Halle Pietism over the value of Confucian thought. On the other hand, Jesuits would make a point of denouncing Chinese idolatry when it was ascribed to Buddhism or neo-Confucianism. If the Jesuits and the rationalists made subtle distinctions between theological camps, the conservative Christians were broadly defined, often encompassing Protestant and Catholics arguments. Later scholarship has treated the Jesuit position as the most noble and sophisticated form of early modern cosmopolitanism, with rationalists such as Leibniz and Wolff as sympathetic travelers. However, we must consider that eighteenth-century anthropological approaches to China emerged out of the heresy-hunting practices of conservative Christians, whose roving comparisons sought broad categorical statements about non-European culture based on eye-witness accounts as opposed to the philological interpretation of canonical philosophical texts proposed by the Jesuits and the rationalists. The earliest forms of the comparative approach were far from cosmopolitan in their aims; they were much more concerned to show that many different practices of the non-European world shared one fundamental problem—namely, paganism—which ultimately was summarized as an alliance with the devil.

If the European understanding of China was shaped by the disputation as a rhetorical practice, it was also conditioned by the effect that the operation of communications networks had on the content of their transmissions. Goethe and Schiller wrote to each other frequently: every two or three days a letter passed between them. The distance between Weimar, where Goethe composed near the court, and Jena, where Schiller taught, was not great, even for eighteenth-century travelers. Any misunderstandings or elisions in their correspondence could be supplemented by conversations when they next saw each other. The letters testify to the practice of leaving the most important ideas unwritten because it was safer to express controversial and unorthodox thoughts in conversations that evaporated once they were finished, rather than in letters that could fall into unfamiliar hands long after they had been written. Throughout their correspondence, there lingers the danger that someone unexpected might read the letters—and it was not posterity the two men feared. Letters needed to be burned sometimes, as Goethe did with his father's correspondence, thereby leaving behind little record of their relationship.

As they sought to integrate into elite Chinese society, the Jesuit missionaries were intensely aware of the complexities involved in depicting their lives in letters sent back to Europe. For them, the distances and the delays were immense. No writer in Asia could be certain that his letter would arrive in Europe, though he could be sure that any that did would be read by many unfamiliar people. Missionary letters circulated widely first within the Society of Jesus, then within the church, and then, with any luck, across Europe's network of learned and curious readers. Jesuit correspondences were written with an appreciation of the many messages and meanings that needed to be sent and that would be adduced from their texts. As always, there would be unintended interpretations, but the letters would also strive to make these positive and inspirational, so as to reinforce faith and recruit new participants.

Both sets of correspondences display an awareness of time and distance—the very near and the unimaginably far away. The writers recognize the risks of committing their thoughts to paper, and they take advantage of the spatial relations within their respective postal systems. Distance and delay are always described as unfortunate burdens, yet each set of writers operate within these spatial relations. They take advantage of the distances even as they complain about them. Goethe and Schiller sometimes prefer to write to each other when they could visit each other—their correspondence maintains a distance between them which they regularly suspend by speaking in person. Like the poets, the Jesuits maneuver within the space that letter writing creates between the sender and receiver, between the text and what it describes. They write honestly to each other, for their spirits need to share their experiences with a kindred soul, but they also understand that postal delivery leaves an opening for delay, reflection, second thoughts, manipulation, and ambiguity. The difference between these two sets of correspondents was their attitude toward Christianity. While the missionaries wrote letters and reports affirming church doctrine and dispelling the assumption that the Chinese were all unbelievers, Goethe writes to Schiller about Buddhism in order to convey cautiously his own eagerness to escape Christian doctrine. In both sets of correspondences, anything too foreign, pagan, or atheistic is left unarticulated and unassimilated even as it structures the text.

WORLD LITERATURE AND GOETHE'S CHINESE POETRY

Another winter in Weimar finds Goethe immersed again in Chinese literature. His best correspondent and friend, Friedrich Schiller, has long since died, yet the urge to hold forth on the books he has just been reading persists. On January 31, 1827, over dinner, Goethe lists them off to a new conversation partner, Johan Peter Eckermann. Among the group, a Chinese novel. In response to his companion's astonished reaction that a Chinese novel must seem very strange, Goethe offers one of the first, and best, accounts of world literature: "Not as much as one expects to believe. The people think, act and feel almost just like us and it does not take long before one feels oneself to be their equal."[1] Goethe's identification with Chinese figures does not require the emotional shock of martyr dramas or

---

1. Johann Peter Eckermann, *Gespräche mit Goethe in den letzten Jahren seines Lebens*, ed. Christoph Michel and Hans Grüters (Berlin: Deutscher Klassiker Verlag, 2011), January 31, 1827; hereafter cited by date of entry.

earthquake news reports; instead he focuses on the quiet particulars of scholarly retirement: gardens, poetry, wine, memories of past love. Just as he was quick to recognize correspondences between metaphysical debates in Nanjing and Weimar, he now draws parallels between Chinese and European narrative fiction: "There is a strong resemblance to my 'Hermann and Dorothea,' as well as to the English novels of Richardson." Yet similarities in plot events are less important to Goethe than the interpenetration of human and natural environments in the descriptive language: "You always hear the goldfish splashing in the pond, the birds are always singing on the bough, the day is serene and sunny, the night is always clear. There is much talk about the moon . . . and the interior of the houses is as neat and elegant as their pictures."[2]

If the report of Matteo Ricci's Nanjing Disputation contains augmentations and revisions, then surely Eckermann's conversations with Goethe do as well. Both present rhetorical occasions allowing their protagonists to explain their agendas. Goethe is eager to find similarities with Chinese figures, but he is confident that he will not lose his orientation in the process. While speaking with Eckermann, Goethe offers a balance. In its novels, China appears strange and curious yet not alienatingly foreign. Its otherness is heightened by the absence of any colonial or missionary connection between Weimar and China. The relationship is strictly a readerly one, mediated by a text that seems to have an autonomous existence. The genealogy of cosmopolitan reading practices and the circuitous route the novel took to arrive in Weimar are not mentioned in this conversation. In recounting the noteworthy features of the Chinese novel, Goethe cannot help but revive the fable of China's ideal character. His answer to Eckermann alternates between explaining how China is knowable, while distinctly wonderous. The notion that all people are fundamentally the same remains the starting point for his approach to Chinese literature, though in explaining himself, Goethe adds a singular quality that is perhaps supposed to motivate his interlocutor to read a Chinese novel as well. Goethe, the old raconteur, cannot resist the opportunity to bedazzle his listener: "The

---

2. Eckermann, January 31, 1827.

people [in Chinese novels] think, act, and feel almost just like us and one soon senses to be their equal, except that with them everything proceeds more clearly, purely, and morally."[3]

As Michel Serres argues, a dialogue between two interlocutors always involves the implicit exclusion of a third person.[4] In this case, Goethe's advocacy for world literature establishes multiple dialogues between his own writing and foreign literature, while implicitly rejecting nationalist Romantic poetry. Because Goethe understands the logic of exclusion inherent to dialogues, he goes out of his way to tell Eckermann that just because one can find compatibility with foreign cultures does not mean that Europeans, and especially German classicists like himself, would therefore abandon Greek antiquity, which, Goethe argues, will always be the foundation from which Europe seeks dialogue with others. Rather than disavowing antiquity, Goethe prefers to reject the newly emerging nationalist literary cultures. In many forms of intercultural dialogues—accommodation and world literature—the cosmopolitan positions turn away from domestic cultural forms that are perceived as irrational, superstitious, and incapable of reaching out beyond local norms. Since cosmopolitan thought seeks to transport cultural forms beyond the site of their first articulation, its dialogues always brush aside or stamp out those aspects of indigenous culture that cannot be adapted to new settings. If Goethe has a local allegiance, it is to classical antiquity, not German nationalism.

When Goethe tells Eckermann that the Chinese are the same as we are, he is not invoking an abstract ideal so much as a pantheist eternal recurrence of common human qualities—poetry being one. Goethe's enthusiasm for Chinese novels quickly turns into one of his earliest formulations of world literature, so that his reading serves as a paradigm for many more to follow. Contemporary scholars of world literature who seek to connect Goethe's term with our own globalized networks often start with this important dia-

---

3. Eckermann, January 31, 1827.
4. Michel Serres, "Platonic Dialogue," in *Hermes: Literature, Science, Philosophy*, ed. Josué Harari and David Bell (Baltimore, MD: Johns Hopkins University Press, 1992), 67.

logue.[5] "I see more and more," Eckermann reports Goethe as having said, "that poetry is the common good of humanity and that it appears everywhere and at all times among hundreds and hundreds of people."[6] Goethe's appreciation for the repetition of human actions across cultures derives from his distinctive adaptation of Spinoza. To quote again the passage from *Dichtung und Wahrheit* (*Poetry and Truth*) in which Goethe summarizes his understanding of Spinoza's metaphysics: "Nature operates according to eternal, necessary, and therefore divine laws, so that the Deity himself could not alter anything about it. All people are thereby unknowingly completely united."[7] This sense of universal, unchangeable oneness allows the poet to treat subjective experiences as externally generated even though they are so often held to be uniquely individual. Sympathies can thus reflect larger unities rather than just individual passions.

As Walter Benjamin elaborated in his essay on Goethe's *Elective Affinities*, the recognition of sudden, unexpected similarities emerges from a hidden substrate of mythical dynamics. Goethe had already expressed this archaic understanding of human existence in a letter to Zelter while working on his other great orientalist project, *West-östliche Divan* (*West-Eastern Divan*), in which he attributed his freedom to emulate and compose with Hafez to his own aged sense that all things moved in a cycle: "Meanwhile I am collecting new poems again for the Divan. The Mohammedan religion, mythology,

---

5. Hendrick Birus, "Goethes Idee der Weltliteratur, Eine historische Vergengwärtigung," in *Weltliteratur Heute*, ed. Manfred Schmeling (Würzburg: Königshausen & Neumann, 1995), 1–28; Ritchie Robertson, "*Weltliteratur* from Voltaire to Goethe," *Comparative Critical Studies* 12.2 (2015): 163–81; David Damrosch, "Goethe Coins a Phrase," *What Is World Literature?* (Princeton, NJ: Princeton University Press, 2003), 1–36. Damrosch emphasizes the monumentality of the concept. By approaching the topic through his biographical tale of Eckermann's humble origins, he only elevates the term. Better to see how fragile Goethe's concept is, how much it depends on translators' prefaces. For a more critical reading of this primal scene, see B. Venkat Mani, *Recoding World Literature: Libraries, Print Culture, and Germany's Pact with Books* (New York: Fordham University Press, 2017), 53–65.

6. Eckermann, January 31, 1827.

7. Johann Wolfgang Goethe, *Werke*, ed. Erich Trunz (Munich: C. H. Beck, 1982), 10:79; hereafter cited as HA.

mores allow room for a poetry that suits my age. Unconditional acquiescence to the unfathomable will of God, cheerful overview of
the mobile ever circling and spiraling recurrent earthly drives, love,
inclinations between two floating worlds, everything real purified,
dissolving into symbol. What more could a grandpapa want?"[8]
He offers a similar viewpoint in a letter to Wilhelm von Humboldt
on December 1, 1831, wherein he again invokes his old age: "If I
may, my revered friend, express myself in our old confidence, then I
would gladly confess that, in my advanced years, everything has
become more and more historical for me: whether something occurred in a past era, in a distant kingdom or whether it just happened nearby is all the same to me. In fact I appear to myself ever
more and more to be historical."[9] For Goethe, the past and the
distant are grasped as moving together into an extended historical
present. All things, the near and far, the immediate and the ancient,
are perceived with detachment, with an observer's eye, such that
any intellectual participation requires an emotional reach because
there is little that comes across with urgency.

Anil Bhatti cites a letter the poet writes but does not send to his
editor Cotta, wherein he spells out his intentions too clearly for his
own liking. "I have quietly busied myself with *oriental literature*,
and in order to understand it more deeply, composed much in the
in the sense and style of the Orient. My intention is to connect, in
a cheerful manner, West and East, the past and the present, Persian
and German and to allow each side's mores and thinking to reach
into the other."[10] Goethe reads oriental literature in *secret* in part
because he long had the habit of not revealing his creative intentions to others, and this explains largely why he never sent the
letter—for it provides an all-too clear and confident statement of
purpose. Bhatti emphasizes Goethe's desire to tie two poetic traditions together, *verknupfen*, in a cheerful manner, *heiter*, to call attention to the *Divan*'s playful-performative quality, which avoids

8.   *Goethes Briefe,*ed. Karl Robert Mandelkow (Hamburg: Christian Wegner,
1965), 3:477, May 11, 1820.
9.   *Goethes Werke* (Weimar: Hermann Böhlaus Nachfolger, 1887–1919),
4.49:165; hereafter cited as WA.
10.   *Goethes Briefe*, 3:306, to Cotta, May 1815 (emphasis in original).

colonial logic in its spatial (East, West), temporal (past, present) or cultural (Persian, German) structures.[11]

World literature, as Goethe proposes it, is driven by an inclination to recognize resemblances between disparate forms of writing. The search for resemblances between literary texts and traditions guided his own interpretation of foreign cultures. He was not interested in organizing knowledge as literary historians do, so much as driving his own creative ability to write poetry. Johanna Schopenhauer provides an example of the Weimar world literature milieu in her salon in which his reading turns into poetic composition: "For the last few evenings, Goethe himself has been reading aloud for us, and to see and hear him is magnificent. Schlegel sent him a translated drama by Calderón in manuscript form; it is all a sound and light show, yet in an evening he cannot read three pages without his own poetic spirit springing to life, so that he interrupts himself with every line and a thousand wonderful ideas emerge and stream out in rampant abundance, so that one forgets everything and just listens to him."[12] More than positing an overarching concept of humanity and poetry, his readings were focused on detecting resemblances.[13] To the extent that these similarities were then understood as belonging to a larger unity, Goethe did share in the premodern presumption of an organic wholeness to human existence. He was more concerned with how texts overlapped and intersected than in the application of a single universal concept to diverse forms of writing. Similarities could come into being without having to assert some complex causal connection between themselves, yet the act of recognition was greatly enhanced by the increased circulation of texts through expanding international media circuits.

---

11.   Anil Bhatti, "Der Orient als Experimentierfeld. Goethes *Divan* und der Aneignungsprozess kolonialen Wissens," in *From Popular Goethe to Global Pop*, ed. Ines Detmers and Birte Heidemann (Amsterdam: Rodopi, 2013), 22 (emphasis in original).

12.   Reinhart Meyer-Kalkus, *Geschichte der literarischen Vortragskunst* (Berlin: Metzlar, 2020), 137.

13.   John Noyes distinguishes Goethe's individualistic focus on aesthetic perception from Herder's communal understanding of culture in "The World Map and the World of Goethe's *Weltliteratur*," *Acta Germanica* 38 (2010): 128–45.

Goethe apprehends foreign literature by drawing analogies with familiar writing, thus allowing for a loose encounter with the text that generates a series of further associations. While scholars usually cull Goethe's reflections on analogic thinking from his morphology, they also clearly describe his comparative reading habits as a means of inspiring his own creativity.[14] The epistemological status of an analogy in Goethe's account is itself quite similar to fiction. Reading a foreign text as in Schopenhauer's salon suggests analogies, in this case between cultures. "Communicating through analogies I consider to be as useful as it is pleasant; the analogy does not want to impose itself nor prove anything; it seeks to engage with others without incorporating them. Multiple analogies do not form closed ranks; rather they are like good company that inspires more than it gives."[15] Analogic thinking hovers between identity and difference; it allows for the possibility of similarity by bridging difference. Analogies posit equivalences only contingently, preventing thereby the assertion of any over-arching principle. Anyone can point in both directions without following either to a conclusion. The analogy mediates between positions, such as the individual and the universal, without insisting on a dialectical relation between them. "Every existing entity is an analogue to everything else; thus, existence appears to us as both separate and connected. If one follows an analogy too closely, then everything collapses into the identical; if one avoids analogy, then everything becomes scattered across infinity."[16] Because they are open-ended and do not make absolute assertions, analogies can avoid polemics—an important goal for Goethe, who sought to elude rhetorical confrontations whenever possible. "To think according to analogies means to not scold: the analogy has the benefit that it does not close off and really does not desire anything final."[17] Analogies are particu-

---

14. Eva Geulen, *Aus dem Leben der Form: Goethes Morphologie und die Nager* (Berlin: August, 2016), 87–98. Hermann Schmitz interprets Goethe's analogic thinking in relation to logical categories (Aristotle, Kant) and theology in *Goethes Altersdenken im problemgeschichtlichen Zusammenhang* (Bonn: Bouvier, 1959), 245–50.

15. HA, 12:368.

16. HA, 12:368.

17. HA, 12:368.

larly suited for literary interpretation and creation, for they allow one to recognize similarities without insisting on their being subsumed under a philosophical principle.

Goethe's comparisons have an unavoidably historical and psychological origin; they are formed by an obvious subject, yet they encourage a detached examination. Within any juxtaposition there is considerable room for illusion: a reader could easily over-identify with one, so that it becomes omnipresent, creating a poetic atmosphere wherein one element flows into another, as well as errors that any knowledge-producing discipline would reject. Within the field of world literature, analogical thinking reintroduces the sympathetic relations of early modern cosmology as readerly epiphanies about intertextual affinities, rather than as universal harmonies. Thus, Goethe's identification with Chinese fiction takes a more subjective position than Leibniz's claim that fate has placed the two refined civilizations, Europe and China, at opposite ends of the same continent.[18] However, this subjectivity is not just personal or psychological. Goethe's acknowledgement of Chinese characters as analogous to himself and to those found in European novels entails a philosophical transfer from the earlier, Sturm-und-Drang insistence on the speaking subject's singularity to a more general sense of ego that vacates the willfulness of the empirical self.

Goethe's appreciation for Asian literature was at odds with the dominate inclination in nineteenth-century Germany and Austria to hierarchize cultures with terms borrowed from *Weltliteratur*, such as the notion of a cultured language (*Kultursprache*), an ideology strongly reinforced by Hegel's account of the world spirit moving from Asia westward to Europe. Goethe's attempts to establish an emotional parity with Chinese figures came just a few years after Hegel depicted China as a civilization that the spirit of reason had left behind. While Hegel's position is often taken as reflecting a European sense of superiority over China and thus as a representative of racist colonialism, Goethe's sympathetic approach to Chinese literature is too often overlooked. Hegel's account is conveniently

---

18. Gottfried Wilhelm Leibniz, *The Preface to Leibniz' Novissima Sinica*, trans. Donald Lach (Honolulu: University of Hawaii Press, 1957), 68.

placed within the larger arc of a turn from early modern fascination with China (Sinophilia) to a nineteenth-century aspiration to force colonial concessions upon a backward empire (Sinophobia). Goethe's literary aspirations to find similarities with Chinese figures stand directly at odds with this larger narrative. We should not presume that Goethe's view balances out Hegel's, for, over the stretch of the nineteenth century, the identificatory idealism of world literature was overwhelmed, indeed subsumed, by colonialist assertions of a hierarchy of civilizations.

Goethe's final collection of poems reflects the cyclical intersection between space and time in the form of Chinese-German rotations moving through the spans of a day and a year. "Chinesisch-deutsche Jahres- und Tageszeiten" ("Chinese-German Book of Hours and Seasons") refers to media forms such as the daily newspaper and the annual journal, allowing thereby the mythic to acquire the connotation of information passing in and out of a temporal rotation. Media information rolls past just like the day or the seasons. An easy elision of temporal terms allows the names of newspapers and journals to blend in with pastoral seasons, as becomes apparent in Goethe's letter to Carlyle explaining the importance of media channels in connecting different national literatures together: "You will see . . . that we Germans are also busy reading foreign literature. Through express post and steam ships, the nations' daily, weekly, and monthly journals are moving closer together." Goethe declares his intention to use these communication lines as much as possible: "So long as I am capable, I will turn my attention to this reciprocal exchange." He urges his English correspondent to do the same: "Let us make ever more free use of the newly opened communications."[19] "Reciprocal exchange" operates not only within the communication channels, but also across discourses, from media to poetry. By hyphenating German and Chinese in the title of his poetry cycle, Goethe also returns to the parallels he recognized between the Weimar and Nanjing disputations, for the title indicates that the rotations are much the same in both cultures. Indeed, they may well be synchronized. Astronomy, with its mythic forebear, as-

---

19. Goethe letter to Carlyle, August 8, 1828, WA, 4.44:257.

trology, appears as a second connotation offered by the complicated title. The seasons and times of day are measured and understood through the movement of heavenly bodies. To the extent that pre-industrial humans the world over oriented themselves according to the stars, the title suggests that astronomy can serve as an intercultural form of knowledge.

This last collection revives a model of aesthetic imagination and mediation already familiar from Goethe's youthful novel, *The Sorrows of Young Werther*. Much as Goethe characterized his sympathetic affinity as a new insight due to his advanced age, his correspondence in the last years of his life echoes an implied dialogue from his first novel, when Werther writes to his friend on May 17: "If you ask, how the people here are, I must tell you: like everywhere else! Humans are a uniform species."[20] Before long, of course, Werther goes on to describe his fateful encounter with the singular Charlotte. When Charlotte states that she prefers reading books in which she can discover her own world once more, where the characters behave as she would and whose fates are as sincere as her own domestic life, Werther turns the conversation to Oliver Goldsmith's *The Vicar of Wakefield*.[21] In *The Sorrows of Young Werther*, the range of identifications extended as far as the British Isles, but by the time of his work on *West-Eastern Divan*, they extended into Central Asia. Goethe's inclination to integrate foreign literature into his own writing shows itself already in *Werther*. The passages from *Ossian* sounded to German readers as a strange alternative to the canon of classical and courtly French literature. The second-to-last section of *Werther*, when the would-be lovers read aloud to each other, represents an early attempt to display the correspondences between familiar passions and a newly discovered foreign literature. If readers were willing to accept the strange names of Ossian, then old-man Goethe expects they might tolerate his Muslim and Chinese references.

Paradoxically, the notion that all people share the same traits can require the reader to become transformed into a stranger, or at the

---

20. HA, 6:11.
21. HA, 6:23.

very least, to learn the foreign language. In his notes to the *Divan,* Goethe instructs the reader: "If we want to join in with the productions of these most wonderful spirits, then we must orientalize ourselves because the Orient will not come over to us." As accommodating Jesuit missionaries well understood, learning the language is central to this transformation: "And while translation is highly praiseworthy as a way of attracting and introducing us, it is evident that in this literature the language as language plays the foremost role."[22] If learning the language is the means to become like another, it also is the means by which this role of being different can be played. Far from expressing a rule for excluding difference, Charlotte's preference for characters that are much like herself reflects Goethe's lifelong tendency to leave his own security in order to better perceive similarities with others. Underlying Goethe's storytelling is the principle that "humans are much the same everywhere, yet the ones I am telling you about now have a special quality." His addendum to Eckermann, that among the Chinese everything is done more clearly, cleanly, and ethically, turns back on itself to show perhaps more than just the continuing influence of the Jesuit view that China was an ordered society guided by literary administrators—an image that Eckermann's *Conversations with Goethe* established for many in the long nineteenth century.

Three Chinese Romances

By the last decade of Goethe's career, three novels had been translated into European languages. All evidence indicates that he had read them intensely in search of material and inspiration for his own poetic creativity. These translations appeared during two distinct phases of interest in China: *The Pleasing History* (1761), *Chinese Courtship. In Verse* (1824), and *Les deux cousines* (The two fair cousins, 1826). In between lay a string of memoirs published in the

---

22. This passage appears in the section "Übergang von Tropen zu Gleichnissen" in *Noten und Abhandlungen* zu besserem Verständniß des *West-östlichen Divans,* WA, 7:106.

1790s recounting Lord Macartney's failed embassy for the British government to Beijing. The first novel was published under the great weight of Jesuit erudition about China while the last two were offered up as autonomous works intent on conveying poetic beauty within the discourse of their own narrative. Until recently, practically no Goethe scholar has been able to lay hands on all three. Now, however, they are readily available on the internet, including many additional translations. Today it is possible to formulate close readings and comparisons of these earliest examples of world literature.

All three of the novels can be classified as "beauty-scholar" romances, which entail a young man studying and taking exams, traveling to the capital for further exams, and meeting lovely, learned women along the way with whom they develop relationships. In the case of *The Pleasing History*, the scholar and the beauty go out of their way to remain chaste even though, contrary to respectable custom, they share a household together.[23] All three novels, highlight the importance of the imperial postal system by having the plots depend upon characters who send petitions and letters to and from the court.[24] In the latter two romances, the scholar protagonist becomes betrothed to two different women during the course of his adventures and in the end is allowed to marry them both in such a manner that they share equal status as wives. Writing poetry and displaying learnedness are important in all the novels, but really only *The Two Fair Cousins* depicts a sophisticated poetic community. Although the second romance, *The Chinese Courtship*, is written in verse, it is only *The Two Fair Cousins* that repeatedly valorizes poetic genius—the ability to compose verse immediately when a situation requires it—a skill Wilhelm Meister displays repeatedly. The novel's atmosphere, its garden settings, and its special

---

23. Robert Hegel provides a comprehensive characterization of the genre in *Reading Illustrated Fiction in Late Imperial China* (Stanford, CA: Stanford University Press, 1998), 48.

24. Ning Ma notes in that while Chinese romances do not adopt the first-person voice of epistolary fiction, the dramatic plot shifts brought on by the arrival of crucial news nevertheless direct attention to how much personal lives of the administrative elite were entwined with the postal system; *The Age of Silver: The Rise of the Novel East and West* (New York: Oxford University Press, 2016), 172.

attention to the connotations associated with specific types of flowers correspond closely to the mood of Goethe's "Chinesisch-deutsche Jahr- und Tageszeiten." The novel not only pairs the scholar with two beautiful, brilliant women, it also establishes an affinity between the young poet and the aged, retired mandarin, clearly marking each as standing at opposite ends of the imperial career circuit. Goethe uses temporal biographical markers in his titles—most notably *Wilhelm Meisters Apprenticeship* and then his *Journeymanship*. The title of his last poetry cycle again calls attention to marking the passage of time, with Goethe voicing himself from the position of an old mandarin contemplating his past life as he reviews the flowers in his garden. When Goethe's poetic cycle is read in relation to *The Two Fair Cousins*, its Chinese character becomes evident.

The first novel appeared in London 1761 with the title *Hau Kiou Choaan, or The Pleasing History. A Translation from the Chinese Language in Four Volumes with Notes.* Those footnotes will prove important for they provide the reader an abundance of encyclopedic annotations drawn from Jesuit sources, particularly Du Haldes's *Lettres edifiante et curiouse.*[25] This first English edition and the subsequent German translation belong to an era when novels served as the bearers of information. The original Chinese author remains unknown, though it is presumed that the book was composed during the early Qing period.[26] The English translation was published by the Anglican pastor Thomas Percy, who received the manuscript from the descendants of James Wilkerson, a merchant with the English East India company who resided in Canton. In its original form, the first three-quarters of the novel had been translated into English with the remainder written in Portuguese. Given the manuscript's many interlinear corrections, Percy surmises that the translation was presumably undertaken as a language-learning exercise with the guidance of a Chinese teacher. The footnotes were

---

25. *Hau Kiou Choaan, or The Pleasing History. A Translation from the Chinese Language in Four Volumes with Notes* (London: Dodsley, 1761).

26. Kai-chong Cheung, "The *Haoqiu zhuan*, the First Chinese Novel Translated in Europe: With Special Reference to Percy's and Davis's Renditions," in *One into Many: Translation and the Dissemination of Classical Chinese Literature*, ed. Leo Tak-hung Chan (Amsterdam: Rodopi, 2003), 29–37.

not part of the original translation; they are offered, Percy explains sheepishly, so as to facilitate the English reader's understanding of Chinese society. "It remains that something be said concerning the Notes, if it be only to apologize for their frequency and length. It was at first intended to have incumbered the page with as few of these as possible: but it was soon found necessary to depart from this plan."[27]

In his role as editor, Percy relies much on Du Halde—the title page includes a quotation in French explaining that there is no better way to learn about the Chinese (people and language) than from them directly.[28] Thus, from the very first page of the first translated novel, the argument is presented that Chinese texts written for domestic consumption are the most reliable source of information, thereby setting up in adumbrated form the thesis that fiction provided the clearest and least biased insight into Chinese thought and manners. This argument echoes Ricci's and Trigault's claim that the best way to reach into the private life of the Chinese was to publish books that they will read at home rather than to preach in the streets. The appeal of reading Chinese literature was precisely that it was not written for Europeans. These texts made no appeal to Western Christians, but were wholly absorbed with their own concerns. Precisely because of its monadic isolation from outsiders, Chinese literature seemed to promise insight into the authentic relations of Chinese family life. In his preface, Percy explains that while the Jesuits have summarized and translated many moral and philosophical works, they have provided only a few, short pieces of literature.[29] We now know that the first Jesuit to learn Chinese, Michele Ruggieri, did write Chinese poems, but these works were never published.[30] As scholars trained in literati culture, the missionaries would have well understood the high value placed on good poetic style. The titles of Ruggieri's first poems suggest not only that they

---

27. *Pleasing History*, 1:xxiv.

28. *Pleasing History*, title page: "Il n'y a pas de meilleur moyen de s'instruire de la Chine, que par la Chine même: car par la on est sûr de ne se point tromper, dans la connoisance du genie et des usages de cette nation."

29. *Pleasing History*, 1:xi.

30. Albert Chan, "Michele Ruggieri, S. J. (154–1607) and His Chinese Poems," *Monumenta Serica* 41 (1993): 129–76.

were dedicated to introducing Christianity but that they also observed the rituals of exchanging poems between scholars, traditions that all three of the translated Chinese novels affirm. The contrast between literature and ethnography will visibly consume the translation's page as a struggle between narrative and footnote. Compilations have their merit, Percy allows, but "the true character of a living people will hardly be learnt from them."[31]

The argument that novels provide foreign observers insights into the domestic morality of a culture that they would otherwise never acquire was used repeatedly by subsequent translators. Abel Rémusat extends this thesis in the preface to his 1827 translation of *The Two Fair Cousins* to assert also that Chinese and European novels share many features in common, thereby making it easy for European readers to understand. In his comments about world literature to Eckermann, Goethe is clearly reiterating Rémusat's point. Out of the claim that novels provide privileged ethnographic information about Chinese private lives, Goethe asserts further that European novel readers can recognize similarities between the two cultures, thereby allowing them to develop much the same kind of emotional bond with Chinese fictional characters as they do with those in their own literary tradition. This claim to fiction's ability to convey private information is first understood in ethnographic terms, but then in the context of Goethe's world literature discussion, translated novels become a means of expanding the reader's ability to recognize shared traits with foreigners. More than treatises and travelogues, novels encourage readers to extend their sympathies to previously unfamiliar strangers. The knowledge that novels provide is not instrumentalized. Recognizing the mimetic qualities of European novels, Goethe, Rémusat and other orientalists attributed the same function to Chinese novels: namely, that they reflect society's larger conflicts and organization within their own aesthetic order. This approach to the novel did not treat the text as a collection of facts to be explained with footnotes, but instead it presumed that social tensions appeared within the novel as formal distinctions. As the novel elucidated and resolved these con-

---

31. *Pleasing History*, 1:xvi.

flicts, it also revealed structures inherent in the world outside fiction. In order to analyze Chinese works as if they were European novels, they obviously had to be translated in a manner that made this recognition possible. This additional form of mediation layered new European meanings onto these works. Not only were Chinese novels expected to depict the relations common to the society in which they were written, but as translated works they also had the task of mediating between cultures. Translations seek out and construct analogies between languages thereby facilitating the readers' incorporation of the strange into the already known. In performing this diplomatic transfer, translated Chinese novels allowed Goethe and other sympathetic readers to conclude that the foreign is actually quite familiar, not merely because of the translator's work, but also because of a commonality discovered through the reading process, which constantly stirs up comparisons and identifications. For Goethe, the ultimate purpose in reading Chinese novels was to write poetry, in his own Chinese manner. The slim collection of his last years, "Chinesisch-Deutsche Jahres- und Tageszeit," emerges only after he has read the available library of Jesuit treatises, merchant travelogues, translated poems, together with the three Chinese novels available in Europe.

In building a case for why Europeans should read Chinese literature, Thomas Percy commences critically by first calling attention to the smallness, the lack of innovation, and the servile genius of Chinese poems. Only after having established his own nonpartisan detachment does he praise them for not indulging in the extravagant flights of marvel and fantasy common to other Eastern nations.[32] "They pay a greater regard to truth and nature in their fictious narratives, than any other of the Asiatics."[33] If Chinese poetry does not fascinate for its literary forms, Percy offers the novel as a more accurate means of conveying information otherwise hidden to foreign observers. Positing a further intermedial relation between the arts that goes beyond his proposed competition with Jesuit ethnography, Percy asks that his work "may be considered . . . as a faithful

---

32. *Pleasing History*, 1:xii.
33. *Pleasing History*, 1:xiv.

picture of Chinese manners, wherein the domestic and political economy of that vast people is displayed with an exactness and accuracy to which none but a native could be capable of attaining."[34] By asking that the reader "see" the novel's narration, Percy is also implicitly acknowledging the enormous appeal of images of China in travelogues or chinoiserie commodities. The analogy to visuality extends to Percy's critique of compilations that provide a stiff, lifeless portrait of a people compared with novels, which show "every passion in play and every part . . . in motion."[35]

By offering the novel, Percy extends a critique of Jesuit writing about China. Like most northern European scholars, Percy states that he cannot challenge the Jesuits' claim to knowledge, though in his first long footnote summarizing the Rites Controversy, he notes that other Catholic missionaries have done exactly so. Without questioning the Jesuits' language skills and their access to the highest classes, Percy suggests that "the very gravity of their character would prevent them from being ocular witnesses (not only of the idolatrous ceremonies, but) of many particulars of the interior conduct of the Chinese."[36] In other words, the novel promises the reader access to domestic passions, courtship done properly and poorly. The hope is that the Chinese will no longer appear only as opaque exterior surfaces, but that novel reading will provide a route from the interiority of the European reader to the interiority of the Chinese. This readerly connection offers the aesthetic appearance of intimacy, which softens the hard shell thrown up by distance and alterity and allows for formal interconnections between Germany and China, or in the late Goethe's case, for the poetic merging of a garden in Weimar with one outside Nanjing—a conjunction I will consider below.

Percy expects that the Chinese offer a new virtue to the European bourgeois reader: their exquisite sense of privacy and reserve. Just as the original manuscript was written as a personal exercise, so too the stories it relates were not intended for the European pub-

---

34. *Pleasing History*, 1:xv.
35. *Pleasing History*, 1:xvi.
36. *Pleasing History*, 1:xix.

lic. As editor, Percy mediates between the messy manuscript and the English reader, so that the public may learn about Chinese private behavior. Intimate questions drive the novel's plot in a manner that no Jesuit would ever convey: much of the story revolves around precisely the question of whether the male and female protagonists have had sex with each other. That they persistently deny having done so while living together and refuse even after formal marriage in order to preserve what they consider to be honor leads the reader on through the long story in fascinated frustration.

In 1766, Christoph Gottlieb von Murr published a German rendition of *The Pleasing History* based on the English translation.[37] In reworking his source, Murr immediately points out that the English translator mistook "Hao Kiu Tschuan" as the work's title, when it is actually the author's name. Faced with an English text that offered the curious reader an overwhelming array of citations to Jesuit authorities, Murr rose to the pedantic challenge by offering his own additional emendations to these notes, placing them at the bottom of the page, so that the German reader was often faced with a slim line of narration at the top of the page while a three-page footnote took up the remainder. In addition to the Jesuit sources, which he knew thoroughly, Murr added references to the work of Étienne Fourmont, a professor of Arabic at the College de France, who had studied Chinese for thirty years and worked so closely with Arcade Huang, a Chinese Catholic convert living in Paris, in cataloguing the Chinese books in the royal collection that he was later accused of plagiarism. In his preface, Murr also provides an overview of Chinese grammars and dictionaries available in Europe. Furthermore, he makes a point of writing Chinese names in a German spelling, so that Germans can pronounce them, rather than relying on French.[38] Murr asserts that "after Portuguese, I consider the German language in most cases as the most adept among

---

37. Christoph Gottlieb von Murr, *Haoh Kjöh Tschwen, d.i. Die angenehme Geschichte des Haoh Kjöh, Ein chinesischer Roman in vier Büchern, Aus dem Chinesischen in das Englische, und aus diesem in das Deutsche übersetzt* (Leipzig: Johann Friedrich Junius, 1766).

38. Murr, *Angenehme Geschichte*, xvii.

the European languages for expressing Chinese words."[39] Echoing
the English preface, Murr agrees that the missionaries provided too
few examples of Chinese literature. This absence of Chinese literature thus justifies multiple translations of the same novel.[40]

As Goethe and Schiller were corresponding about Matteo Ricci's Nanjing Disputation, they were also discussing Murr's Chinese
novel. Their conversations would have a long after effect. Günther
Debon has shown that Goethe continued his Chinese studies years
after Schiller died.[41] Three years after the two poets first corresponded about it, Schiller started urging Jacob Friedrich Unger to
publish a new version, focused on the protagonists' drive for justice. Schiller sensed a much more dramatic story underneath the ethnographic details of the first translations. He concentrated on the
story as an aesthetic process to be rescued from its scholarly exege-
sis. Rather than peppering the narrative with footnotes to historical sources to demonstrate its accuracy, classical aesthetics presumed
that knowledge constituted within the totality of the work reflected
social reality. To be certain, Schiller intended to reinterpret the earlier
translation by concentrating on what he understood to be it aesthetic core as opposed to its many ethnographic details: "There exists a Chinese novel under the name of Hao Kioh Tschuen, or *The
Pleasing History* that was translated in 1766 from the English by
Mr. von Murr of Nuremberg. The translation is, as you can imagine, outdated and the book forgotten. However, it has many excellent qualities and is such a singular product of its age, that it
deserves to be revived. I would venture to condense the spirit of the
work to 15 folio volumes and to raise a higher degree of interest
with this practical abbreviation, for at times the story is too drawn
out."[42] Schiller clearly felt that the earlier translations were both too
literal and over-freighted with commentary. Murr had been the per-

---

39.   Murr, *Angenehme Geschichte*, xviii.

40.   Murr, *Angenehme Geschichte*, xx.

41.   Günther Debon, "Goethe erklärt in Heidelberg einen chinesischen Roman," in *Goethe und China—China und Goethe*, ed. Günther Debon and Adrian
Hsia (Bern: Peter Lang, 1985), 51–62.

42.   Schiller to J. F. Unger, August 29, 1800, Friedrich Schiller, *Geschäftsbriefe
Schillers*, ed. Karl Goedeke (Leipzig: Veit and Co. 1875).

fect German scholar to deliver a massive editorial apparatus, for he belonged to the same class of Nuremberg polymath historians as Erasmus Francisci and was completely familiar with Jesuit writings.[43] Yuan Tan speculates that Schiller's attention turned to the novel because of the appearance of many books related to the Macartney embassy of 1792–1794. The official account was published in London in 1797 with at least five German versions hitting the market thereafter.[44] Unlike Goethe, Schiller depended on selling books in order to earn his living. He left only a fragment at the time of his death, yet it shows how he intended to distill a plot driven by the urge to defend the weak through revenge and the imposition of justice. His opening lines echo the Sturm-und-Drang of *Die Räuber* (The Robbers): "Near Tahmin, a large city in the Chinese empire, there lived a noble young man, named Tiebtschongu, dedicated to learning. His figure was beautiful, his soul magnanimous and noble. He loved justice with a passion and his joy was to fight for the oppressed. In such cases, he was bold and daring and shied away from nothing; nothing could cool his ardor when he was avenging a crime."[45] Within two pages, Schiller's protagonist has found a helpless villager in need of defending against a corrupt mandarin, who has kidnapped his fiancée. Schiller died before he finished his revision, and as the peculiarities of the publishing world would have it, the novel was retranslated in 1829 from the Chinese by John Francis Davis as *The Fortunate Union*.[46] Clearly writers and translators sensed a potential in the story that had not been rendered in the first attempt. Nevertheless, one anonymous reviewer in the *Asiatic Journal* noted in 1830: "I regret that Mr. Davis, amongst so many

43.   Peter Wolf, "Protestantischer 'Jesuitismus' im Zeitalter der Aufklärung: Christoph Gottlieb Murr (1733–1811) und die Jesuiten," *Zeitschrift für bayerische Landesgeschichte* 62 (1999): 99–137.

44.   Yuan Tan, *Der Chinese in der deutschen Literatur, Unter besonderer Berücksichtugung chinesischer Figuren in den Werken von Schiller, Döblin und Brecht* (Göttingen: Cuvier, 2007), 47–48.

45.   Friedrich Schiller, *Werke: Nationalausgabe* (Weimar: Verlag Hermann Böhlaus Nachfolger, 1943ff.), 16:361; hereafter referred to as NA.

46.   *The Fortunate Union*, trans. John Francis Davis (London: Oriental Translation Fund, 1829).

novels as are contained in the literature of China, did not choose one which had not been before translated."[47]

As the title of the second Chinese literary work translated into English makes clear, *Chinese Courtship. In Verse* was really a poetic narrative, not a novel in the strict sense, although Abel Rémusat refers to it repeatedly as such. In his notes, Goethe refers to it as "a long poem" but it clearly enters into his conversation with Eckermann about the Chinese novel, as does Goethe's own idyll, "Hermann and Dorothea."[48] The translator, Peter Perring Thoms (1790–1855), a printer employed by the East India Company, published the work 1824 in Macao.[49] We have a record of Goethe checking it out from the Grand Ducal Library on January 29, 1827—two days before Eckermann's date for his conversation about Chinese novels.[50] The *Chinese Courtship* was notable immediately because it offered a bilingual text. A glance at almost any page finds three distinct print blocks: Chinese script, alphabetic script, explanatory English footnote. Each page contains one complete poem: twelve lines of Chinese characters, above twelve lines of English translation. In his preface, Thoms tries to present a general description of Chinese poetry, again because very little has been translated, leaving Europeans unaware of its excellent qualities. Thoms acknowledges that the original is unusual because most Chinese poems are very short; they do not depict epic stories. He comes around to the question of idol worship indirectly when he states that unlike the Greeks and Romans, the Chinese do not

---

47. "On Translation of Chinese Poetry," *Asiatic Journal* 2 (May 1830): 37.

48. Patricia Sieber, "Location, Location, Location: Peter Perring Thoms (1790–1855), Cantonese Localism, and the Genesis of Literary Translation from the Chinese," in *Sinologists as Translators in the Seventeenth to Nineteenth Centuries*, ed. Lawrence Wang-chi Wong and Bernhard Fuehrer (Hong Kong: Chinese University of Hong Kong, 2015), 148n63; Eric Blackall, "Goethe and the Chinese Novel," in *The Discontinuous Tradition: Studies in German Literature in Honour of Ernest Ludwig Stahl*, ed. P. F. Ganz (Oxford: Clarendon Press, 1971), 51.

49. *Chinese Courtship. In Verse. To Which Is Added an Appendix, Treating the Revenue in China*, trans. Peter Perring Thoms (Macao: East India Company and London: Parbury, Allen, and Kingsbury, 1824).

50. Günther Debon, "Goethes Berührung mit China," *Goethe Jahrbuch* 117 (2000): 48.

have a pantheon of gods racing about on adventures. Hence, the absence of an epic form. What speaks for the *Chinese Courtship*, Thoms argues, is its popularity among domestic readers. Like most early translators, Thoms takes a modest stance, apologizing in advance for mistakes by explaining that the language is very difficult.[51] In the same manner as Percy, he begins by explaining why English readers might not find Chinese poetry appealing. Like Percy sixty-nine years earlier, Thoms cites Du Halde as the most important European commentator on Chinese literature available, but he does so only to replace his judgments with those of Chinese editors and critics. Thoms's preface stands out because he translates Chinese assessments of poetry into English; he is one of the first Europeans to do so. Overall, the degree to which Thoms relies on Jesuit sources has diminished enormously compared with his predecessors. Most of his explanations of Chinese poetry arrive without footnotes, as if he were writing based on his own familiarity with the genres. Indeed, Thoms is mocked for having studied Chinese languages too long. In response to his mistakes in the English text, reviewers suggested that he had immersed himself so thoroughly into Chinese that he had gone over. "Mr Thoms, from his long residence in China, seems to have forgotten somewhat of the construction and orthography of his native tongue."[52] A second review confirmed the impression that novels provided more complete insights into Chinese society than travelogues: "It places us on very familiar terms with the Mandarins and their wives; and, by describing the offices and occupations, the friendships and social intercourse, of the persons whose story is related, conveys a clearer notion of what Chinese society really is, than all the descriptions we have ever seen of the Celestial Empire."[53] If the Jesuit's claim to legitimacy lay in their ability to have integrated into literati society, then the translated Chinese novels provided Europeans an alternative entry.

51. For a modern enumeration of Thoms's translation mistakes, see K. C. Leung, "Chinese Courtship: The Huajian Ji in English Translation," *CHINOPERL: Journal of Chinese Oral and Performing Literature* 20.1 (1997): 269–88.

52. Review of *A Chinese Courtship*, *Monthly Review* 1 (1826): 544.

53. *Oriental Herald* 9 (April–June 1826).

Chinese Courtship has only a few scenes in which poetic talent determines the protagonist's advancement, though one early exchange of odes in a garden is vital to establishing the lead male character's romantic desire for his beloved. When the novel's protagonist, Leang, moves into his new mansion, he is told not only that his uncle, General Yang, is his neighbor, but that his library is separated from his uncle's by only a thin wall.[54] Leang takes his cousin Heaou along to visit his uncle, where he learns that he once had had an intimate bond with his father: "While young, the friendship that existed between us, was that of brothers."[55] Yang failed his exams and threw his books into the river before starting on a military career, while Leang's father became an important magistrate. While not a scholar, the uncle still understands the importance of poetic composition as a test for a potential suitor's worthiness. The general's garden offers Leang a beautiful landscape with a corresponding poem:

> While looking at the fishpond and gallery, which had a splendid appearance,
> They saw, in the Hopeful-spring summer house, some lines of poetry.
> The verses, it appears, had just been written and pasted against the wall.[56]

This scene in *Chinese Courtship* provides evidence for Goethe's remark to Eckermann about the familiar tropes of Chinese poetry involving goldfish, birds, and the moon. Goethe's larger point here is not to reiterated chinoiserie conventions, but to show that the vision of the garden pond corresponds to the ode hung on the wall. Leang's visit to his uncle's garden in *Chinese Courtship* is one probable source for Goethe's observation.[57] The uncle's pond and the ode on

---

54. *Chinese Courtship*, 43.
55. *Chinese Courtship*, 44.
56. *Chinese Courtship*, 46.
57. Woldemar von Biedermann relies on similar plot moments to argue that *Chinese Courtship* was Goethe's source for his poetry cycle, though Biedermann gives no indication of being familiar with Rémusat's publication of *Les deux cousines*. See his "Chinesich-Deutsche Jahres- und Tages-zeiten," in *Goethe Forschungen*, ed. Woldemar von Biedermann (Leipzig: Metzger and Wittig, 1886), 426–46. This discrepancy once again shows the advantage of internet research in which

the wall are aligned: "As the elegant pencil had been used in praise of the fish pond and willows, / The two youths approached to examine it more minutely."[58] The parallel between the willow beside the pond and the poem hung on the garden wall is underscored by the question of who is responsible for both compositions (garden scene, poem). The first two lines of the poem ask: "Who could it be that planted the drooping willow within the pond, / For the spring breeze, causes its delicate branches to agitate the water's bosom."

While the gardener's name is never revealed, the uncle explains: "Those lines are the composition of my little daughter." The general then invites Leang to compose some lines on the garden's flowers, thereby expanding the correspondence between landscape and poetry:

> What a happy occurrence, that a person of talent has entered my garden,
> For all the flowers and shrubs are now in full bloom,
> May I request, that your elegant pencil will leave a bewitching stanza.[59]

Precisely just such an invitation stirs Goethe to write the "Chinese-German" cycle. As with Goethe, the garden in *Chinese Courtship* provides codes for expressing desire. "In this ode," Leang announces, "I will detail the anguish I feel on being separated, / And thus excite the sympathy of the beautiful maid."[60] His reply intensifies the erotic connotation of the willow hanging over the fish pond:

> I have heard that the spring breeze causes a ripple in the green pond,
> And that the slender and pendant branches dance in the pure stream.
> Having been informed, that within this garden, grows a tree of that
>   description.
> Can it be insensible to the distress and feelings of those who are deserted?[61]

---

copies of all three translated Chinese romances are available, whereas earlier scholars struggled to find copies of the novels Goethe read.
58. *Chinese Courtship*, 46.
59. *Chinese Courtship*, 47.
60. *Chinese Courtship*, 48.
61. *Chinese Courtship*, 48.

With Leang unable to speak directly with his uncle's daughter and having only a fleeting vision of her in the garden, the two poems form the only means for conversing—a ritual the old general well understands, for he has Leang's poem pasted on the garden wall, next to his daughter's.

These scenes refer to earlier poems that are even more famous. Through these allusions, the translations allow for an entry into the history of Chinese literature more vivid than the encyclopedic essays that list off the lineages of poets. By comparing a character or a poem to the classics, these stories show how vitally present the ancient works are in the minds of literary Chinese. The frequent references to earlier poets, many of them wholly unfamiliar to the European reader, provide a sense of historical depth to Chinese literature even if particulars remain mysterious. In *Chinese Courtship*, the ancients are invoked more as rhetorical gestures as characters maneuver through potential marriage proposals, whereas in *The Two Fair Cousins* they embody the ideal of poetry to which the protagonists aspire. The challenge of understanding and translating Chinese poetry could become an argument for its similarity to Western traditions. Precisely because of the poems' complexity, they seem as sophisticated as anything written in Europe.[62] Although the *Chinese Courtship* is written in verse, it does not celebrate the culture of poetry: the favored father-in-law is a general, and the father is a scholar, whose retirement leads to the lovers' separation. Eventually, Leang also wants to throw his books into the river—the same phrase the general used to describe his reaction to failing his exams.[63]

---

62. Thoms quotes George Staunton, secretary to Macartney on the ill-fated British embassy: "The great difficulty of Chinese poetry has not been over-rated, though it seems to have been imputed to wrong causes. The structure of their poetry is on fact much the same in principle as that of ours. Their stanzas are measured as with us, and the order of the characters, that is of the words, is regulated by what we term their accent or intonation, just as our syllables and words when monosyllabical are chosen and placed according to quantity. The beauty as well as difficulty, arising likewise from much the same causes—namely, the use of images, metaphors and allusions, and sometimes of individual words, which though not trite or universally obvious, at once strike the intelligent reader as happy and appropriate" (*Chinese Courtship*, xi–xii).

63. *Chinese Courtship*, 129.

The third Chinese novel to be translated into a European language was Abel Rémusat's French rendition, *Iu-Kiao-Li, ou Les deux cousines* (1826). German and English translations followed immediately, in Vienna as *Die beyden Basen*, in London as *The Two Fair Cousins*.[64] Not only did the novel provide scenarios of literary composition strikingly similar to Goethe's early lyric poetry, but Rémusat's preface expounded a comparative analysis that placed his translation in relation to the newly established lineage of European novels. Rémusat's theoretical reflections encourage Goethe's thoughts on world literature.

As he was chatting with Eckermann, Goethe probably had Thoms's *Chinese Courtship* nearby, but his musings on the similarities between European and Chinese novels reflect Rémusat's long preface to *The Two Fair Cousins*. Even though Goethe does not mention Rémusat's work in his diaries until May of the same year, he would have been familiar with the translator's claims to its importance, for he was a careful reader of Parisian literary journals. Rémusat's translation had just been reviewed in *Le Globe, Journal Philosophique et Littéraire*, an auspicious title.[65] Goethe received a copy of *Le Globe* with every postal day (*posttäglich*) in Weimar.[66] He described himself as almost having become a slave to reading the journal.[67] The review of Rémusat's translation begins by declaring with amazement that novels exist in China and that they parallel those in Europe. "Il y a donc des romans à la Chine, et des romans qui peuvent soutenir le parallèle avec de l'Europe!"[68]

---

64. *Iu-Kiao-Li: or, the Two Fair Cousins, from the French version of M. Abel-Remusat* (London: Hunt and Clark, 1827); *Ju-Kiao-Li, oder die beyden Basen, Ein Chinesischer Roman übersetzt von Abel Rémusat* (Vienna: Schade, 1827).

65. Eric Blackall, "Goethe and the Chinese Novel," concludes that in his statements to Eckermann Goethe is speaking primarily about the *Chinese Courtship* but also recalling *The Pleasing History* as well as the review he read in *Le Globe* about Rémusat's translation, *Les deux cousines*. Blackall follows the editors of the Weimar edition (WA, 42:232) in maintaining that Goethe was familiar with this review.

66. WA, 9:232–33.

67. David Barry, "Faustian Pursuits: The Political-Cultural Dimension of Goethe's Weltliteratur and the Tragedy of Translation," *German Quarterly* 74.2 (2001): 171.

68. *Le Globe, Journal Philosophique et Littéraire*, 4.57 (December 23, 1826): 299.

The marginal marking on Goethe's personal copy of the journal shows his attention to this passage.[69] The reviewer goes on to make the same basic claims about the abundance and antiquity of Chinese literature that Goethe provides Eckermann. They used printing presses five centuries before Gutenberg and the emperor's collection of noteworthy books contains more than 180,000 books. For too long Europeans have been forced to rely on the incomplete and contradictory accounts of travelers, whose information leaves readers filled with doubt and confusion. The review enthusiastically recapitulates the arguments Rémusat offers in his preface to *The Two Fair Cousins* that novels are far more effective in revealing the foibles of Chinese society in much the same manner as Fielding and Burney have done in England. It is of course fitting that in formulating his paradigmatic statement about world literature, Goethe would receive his inspiration from a foreign journal sent through the mail. The fleeting, incomplete, discontinuous appearances of Goethe's world literature statements reflect their origins in newspapers, journals, paratexts, and before dinner conversations with friends. The dispersed and irregular arrival of news that Goethe patches together into statements demonstrates that his happenstance utterances on world literature are not just a failure to deliver a systematic formulation; they are the preferred formats of the information circuits he credits with reviving international literary relations. We should not bemoan that Goethe did not get around to writing a fully composed essay on the subject, but instead appreciate that he was participating in the diffuse, new media forms he admired when he made his comments. The study of Asian literature did not belong to a new aesthetic agenda that he sought to impart to the German public, like his classicist aspirations with Schiller. His remarks were somewhere between a trade secret and a hope that the nationalism enflamed by the French Revolution was now over. His comments to Eckermann are half revelations of an esoteric poetics

---

69. Heinz Hamm provides a thorough investigation of Goethe's private edition of *Le Globe*, particularly the articles that he marked up, in *Goethe und die französische Zeitschrift Le Globe: Eine Lektüre im Zeichen der Weltliteratur* (Weimar: Hermann Böhlaus Nachfolger, 1998), 376–77. Hamm's introduction establishes the journal's importance for Goethe's interest in French literary culture.

to guide sympathetic readers. If it were not for the posthumous, best-selling success of *Conversations*, the idea might have remained an arcane scholarly observation, rather than becoming a cosmopolitan agenda.

Far from being an obscure work in China, as Goethe and most German researchers since have assumed, *Yu Jiao Li* was the second most printed work of fiction during the early Qing era, running through fifty-three editions.[70] Considered a clear example of the "scholar-beauty" genre of novels, *Yu Jiao Li* was included one of the ten "books of genius"—an alternative canon to the classical one.[71] Chinese novels did not date back nearly as far as Goethe imagined. The Ming-Qing period brought about new genres, such as romances, that had previously not been held in esteem. In her model of a horizontal, transcultural literary history, Ning Ma suggests that Chinese beauty-scholars romances emerged parallel to European sentimental novels.[72] Both genres suggest that protagonists can advance themselves to self-authenticity by going around the established rules.[73]

Rémusat was not the first person in Paris to work on a translation of *Yu Jiao Li*. The Chinese Christian from Xinghua, Huang Jialüe (1679–1716), who became known in salons by his European name, Arcade Houange, had attempted to translate the novel. His fragment remained in the royal library, along with copies of the original novel.[74] Houange was said to have spoken often about the novel.[75] While much of commentary on the novel focuses on the

70. Robert Hegel, *Reading Illustrated Fiction in Late Imperial China* (Stanford, CA: Stanford University Press, 1998), 65.

71. Patricia Sieber, "Translation as Self-Invention: Jin Shengtan (1608–1661), Arcade Houange (1679–1716), and the Fashioning of a Transcultural Discourse of Scholar-Beauty Ideals," in *Towards a History of Translating: In Celebration of the Fortieth Anniversary of the Research Centre for Translation*, ed. Lawrence Wang-chi Wong (Hong Kong: Chinese University of Hong Kong, 2013), 13.

72. Ning Ma, *The Age of Silver*, 13.

73. For the Chinese side of this comparison, see Maram Epstein, *Competing Discourses: Orthodoxy, Authenticity, and Engendered Meanings in Late Imperial Chinese Fiction* (Cambridge, MA: Harvard University Press, 2001), 229.

74. Sieber, "Translation as Self-Invention," 39.

75. Sieber, "Translation as Self-Invention," 50; Jonathan Spence, "The Paris Years of Arcadio Huang," *Granta* 32 (1992): 123–32.

plot as it leads to the double marriage, the novel is also important for its depiction of poetic scenes and its insertions of poetry in the narration. For Goethe seeking to adopt a new poetic idiom, these scenes of composition in gardens, with accompanying texts, would have been most inspirational. Keith McMahon focuses on the types of characters and plots in scholar-beauty novels, particularly as they lead to a happy polygamous conclusion.[76] Without a doubt, European translators and readers were curious about understanding how polygamy was structured in China. Ever since Leibniz, readers of Jesuit histories had understood that the major obstacle to converting the mandarin elite was the Christian demand that they disavow their multiple wives. *The Two Fair Cousins* and the *Chinese Courtship* both end with a double marriage, in which the male protagonist harmoniously marries two women at the same time. Rémusat draws comparison between his Chinese translation and European works, such as Goethe's *Stella,* that also hint at polygamy or bigamy. European readers' evident fascination with polygamous Chinese romances went beyond the characters' demonstrations of their Confucian virtue, much like the heroines in sentimental novels, to focus on the larger question of how a stable, civilized society could organize complex sexual relationships without immorality and the destabilization of authority. Beauty-scholar romances such as *The Two Fair Cousins* lend explicit approval to gender fluidity and multiple sexual partners within marriage, while Romantic literature was confined to offered veiled allusions to acknowledging such relationships.

Much as Goethe appreciated the similarities between *The Two Fair Cousins* and his own early, scandalous fiction, plot analogies alone would not have been the most important catalyst for Goethe's late Chinese poems. Rather, the convergence of desire with landscape as an atmosphere wherein learned mandarins retire to the garden to write and drink provided a much more important motivation to emulate Chinese aesthetics. When he remarks to Eckermann that the Chinese differ from Europeans because "with them external nature is always associated with the human figures," he is

76. Keith McMahon, "The Institution of Polygamy in the Chinese Imperial Palace," *Journal of Asian Studies* 72.4 (2013): 917–36.

identifying the rare quality that attracts him to read so that he may write in a similar manner. Chinese novels offer Goethe distinct atmospheres, *Stimmungen*, that his own nature poems often embody.

The novel is set in the early crisis years of the Ming dynasty, when the emperor Yingzong was being held hostage by the Mongols after the disastrous military defeat in the Battle of Timu. The first scene is set in the garden of a high official in the imperial court, named Pe Thaihouan.[77] He is regarded as both a moral and learned scholar. His respected position at court stems from the fact that during the earlier corrupt regime of the eunuch Wang chin, Pe had given up his political position so that he might retire to his estate in the south, near a small village outside Nanjing. One twenty-first-century historian of China referred to the "toxic court life and corrupt eunuch-dominated politics" that alienated late Ming elites from the state bureaucracy.[78] Now that the earlier emperor has been captured by the Mongols and his corrupt advisors dispersed, Pe has been recalled to Beijing as a trusted magistrate. While living in retirement, Pe enjoyed a quiet life as a man of letters and local official. He embodies the virtues of a Confucian scholar; the one thing that troubles him is that at the age of forty he has not yet produced a son. Here the complexity of marriage rituals emerges, and Western readers receive a first explanation for polygamy among the Chinese elite. Pe has several wives of the second rank in his household, yet he is disappointed in establishing an heir. At last, his first wife, who has been dutifully praying and carrying out fertility rites, gives birth to a daughter when she is forty-four. Husband and wife are delighted by the beauty and intelligence of their child, yet when the daughter is eleven, the mother dies prematurely, leaving Pe to educate his daughter in his own scholarly tradition. The young daughter, Houngiu, grows up to learn from her father the nuances of classical Chinese literature. After the death of his first wife, Pe retires from sexual relations and dismisses his second ranked wives, who go on

---

77. My references are to the English translation: *Iu-Kiao-Li: or, The Two Fair Cousins, from the French Version of M. Abel-Remusat* (London: Hunt and Clark, 1827).

78. Yulian Wu, *Luxurious Networks: Salt Merchants, Status, and Statecraft in Eighteenth-Century China* (Stanford, CA: Stanford University Press, 2017), 19.

to bear children in other marriages. Henceforth, he devotes himself to poetry and drinking—though the translation is very intent on explaining that the literati drank from very small cups that held only a spoonful or two.

In the first chapter, Pe and two friends, all mandarins, gather one spring day in a garden to drink wine and write poetry about the flowers just beginning to bloom there. Pe serves as host to old classmates: Sse, who is referred to as an inspector general in the English translation, and Gou, the brother of his deceased wife, a doctor in the imperial academy. Their entertainments are interrupted by the arrival of Yang, another inspector general. Yang appears to disturb the poetic moment, but he also enters to acknowledge his gratitude to Gou for helping him revise a poem that he then presented to the imperial viceroy. Yang's urgent need for editorial advice on a poem makes clear that the exchange between court officials went beyond simple pleasantry, but instead served as an offering that reaffirmed the hierarchies of their offices. Yang explains his position in presenting a poem to the viceroy: "This composition was rather a tribute due from my office, than a simple offering of courtesy."[79] He thanks Gou for having improved his writing so much so that the viceroy was enchanted by his lines, telling him "You have, I must say, converted 'iron into gold.'"[80]

In Europe, the novel was read with curiosity and attention to those details that would have seemed obvious to its original audience in early Ming China, but which to Europeans were revelations. It was precisely the sense that the novel shows what every member of the Chinese elite already knew that made *The Two Fair Cousins* so fascinating to Western readers. This impression of entering China's forbidden places was reinforced by the novel's own construction of space. The events take place in exclusive locations that only very select personages are permitted to enter. Mandarin society was walled off from the outside world already within China, and even more so for Westerners. The narration seemed to reveal what happened within the seclusion of literati's walled enclosures—their gar-

---

79. *Two Fair Cousins*, 1:13.
80. *Two Fair Cousins*, 1:13.

dens, libraries, inner and outer apartments. Moreover, the way that *The Two Fair Cousins* organizes space coincided with bourgeois notions of inward subjectivity and privacy.[81]

The novel provides a micro-economy of poetry composition and the political implications of their exchange between courtiers. The European reader thereby receives a glimpse into the literary interchange among imperial administrators, the exclusive milieu into which Matteo Ricci ingratiated himself. As settings, the garden and the library become microcosms of retirement; each allows court administrators to remove themselves from their political offices; each space has implicit rules about how to behave and which topics may be discussed. For Pe and his friends, an invitation into the garden brings with it an obligation not to act or speak about politics or careers.

Nevertheless, Yang's visit to the friends soon shows itself to have a political motive: he asks Sse to help him suppress a lawsuit in which local officials are defending their lands from a rising courtier intent on seizing them. Yang explains that as a court appointee, one is occasionally obliged to perform such underhanded deeds for politically connected members of the imperial court. The friends chide Yang for participating in a political maneuver that ought to be denounced.[82] They then decide that everyone should return to drinking and refrain from any further mention of court politics in to order to draft poems about the garden's blooming marguerites. Yang, who has already acknowledged his colleagues' superior lyrical grace, tries to beg off. Furthermore, in violation of good manners and the rules of the poetic game, Yang repeatedly returns to political topics, mention of which is punished in this company by requiring the speaker to drink a cup of wine. Drinking here to the

---

81. European languages readily incorporated Asian spatial terms, as with the modern English "compound," derived from the Malay word "kampong," which generated the Dutch "kampoeng" and the Portuguese "campon"; Henry Yule and A. C. Burnell, *Hobson-Jobson, A Glossary of Anglo-Indian Colloquial Words and Phrases and of Kindred Terms* (London: John Murray, 1903), 240–42.

82. Such illicit appropriations of property were one of the major accusations made against the court eunuch, Wang Chin, mentioned as the reason why Pe retired from the court; L. Carrington Goodrich and Chaoying Fang, *Dictionary of Ming Biography, 1368–1644* (New York: Columbia University Press, 1976), 2:1363–64.

point of becoming drunk is a punishment for it prevents one from composing elegantly. Yang never ceases speaking of politics, yet after several rounds of drinking penalties, it is the host, Pe, who becomes so drunk that he crawls behind a flowering shrub to sleep off his stupor. At this point, when he is at risk of losing face, while his friends are busy writing poetry, Pe's daughter, the young, clever, and beautiful Houngiu, comes to her father's rescue by writing an ode to the daisies, which a loyal servant then places besides his passed-out master. The friends presume the verses were composed by Pe even though he was delirious. "You have effected a miracle," cries Sse. "Not only have you written with wonderful dispatch, but your phrases are so well selected; they are marked by care, purity, elegance, and strength. It is certainly a most brilliant effusion; how different from what we are in the habit of reading daily! This is admirably perfect, and should make us blush to take a pen again in our hands."[83] Yang, the careerist, grows suspicious, so that when Gou rereads the poem, he recognizes that his niece, Houngiu, must have written the verses. At this point the old men learn that the sixteen-year old daughter is so skilled in poetry that she could marry into the court's highest class, a prediction that immediately sets Yang to arranging her marriage to his son.

While the first chapter distinguishes between careerist magistrates who maneuver in the imperial court and those who eschew politics in favor of literary studies, the second chapter introduces a dubious character, who gains his position within administrative circles through underhanded tricks. Mandarin culture had a clear sense of such imposters, who dress in the proscribed style but who lack composure: "He had on a square cap, and affected the deportment of a man of letters; but there was something rustic in his attire. He might have been taken for a hermit issuing from his cell. His beard and mustaches were short, but thick and disordered; his eyes, wild and startling, almost resembling a pair of bouncing balls. . . . When he commenced speaking, he turned his head one way; and his eyes were directed in another. . . . He pretended to be an astrologer, but in fact

---

83. *Two Fair Cousins*, 1:5.

his real character was that of a parasite."[84] An outsider who was such an imposter would not find acceptance among the literati. Matteo Ricci helped establish his legitimacy among his Confucian dinner companions by painting Sanhoi in the style of just such a comical and fraudulent rustic. The novel also takes a skeptical stance vis-à-vis superstitious practices, as shown by the astrologer's constant need to demonstrate that he is not an imposter by accurately predicting other people's future. Literary taste and expertise are thus juxtaposed with astrology. As the astrologer maneuvers Yang's son into Pe's good graces, he concedes: "Why, as to literature, I confess I do not pretend to any great judgment respecting it; but if I may believe his horoscope and the aspect of the stars, I should say that he possesses a degree of merit not very common amongst scholars."[85] The astrologer's goal is to supplant Pe's literary judgment of Yang's son with his own fraudulent fortune telling. The clearest sign that a character fails to live up to literary standards is his or her own inability to recognize the mistakes he or she has made in understanding a text. Any number of failed literary scholars are revealed by the narration, but the other characters refrain from pointing out these errors. The novel leaves it to the reader to recognize what the pretend scholar has misunderstood. Occasionally the translation will provide a footnote to explain a character's error as one based on Chinese pronunciation or character drawing, but often enough the translation replicates the practice of letting the reader figure out for themselves the mistakes that go uncorrected in the narration. Pe and his two friends are shown as ideal readers who recognize the failings of outsiders and draw the necessary conclusions about their suitability as a potential husband for Houngiu. Literati in the know share their nodding agreement and pleasure in not revealing to the pretender that they have seen through his guise.

In effect, the novel explains distinctions within literati society that would not have been available to traveling merchants. Aside from accommodationist Jesuits, no Europeans had gained entry to these imperial circles. Matteo Ricci described the disdain directed at him

---

84. *Two Fair Cousins*, 1:31–32.
85. *Two Fair Cousins*, 1:40.

as an outsider: "The Chinese look upon all foreigners as illiterate and barbarous, and refer to them in just these terms. They even disdain to learn anything from the books of outsiders because they believe that all true science and knowledge belongs to them alone. . . . Even the written characters by which they express the word foreigner are those that are applied to beasts."[86] Most every Dutch and English embassy to Beijing reported the same cold treatment from high administrators that Ricci first recounted: "One would scarcely believe how suspicious they are of a legate or an ambassador of a neighboring country. . . . The fact that China may have been on friendly terms with the kingdom of the visiting legates, from time immemorial, does not exempt the visiting dignitaries from being conducted along their entire route within the realm as captives or prisoners and permitted to see nothing in the course of their journey."[87]

Novels written expressly for a Chinese literary audience related all those social practices, knowledge unavailable from first-hand travel accounts. Translated in the nineteenth century, the novel turned the European audience back to the environment described by the first Jesuit missionaries, but without the Jesuits' religious apparatus. Goethe and the novel's many other nineteenth-century readers were fascinated by the narration's apparently unmediated access into elite Chinese classes. Readers could observe the literati rule of politeness: when to speak and what to say; how to greet and how to chide; how filial piety is observed properly and when it is used as a guise; what topics remain unspoken; how to drink and how to address the host. The translated novels provided detailed illustrations of that fine points of etiquette that guided Matteo Ricci's conversations but that the Jesuits kept hidden in the folds of their gowns. The Jesuits leveraged their understanding of Chinese social conventions so as to have the rituals of friendship extended to a handful of learned Westerners such as themselves. Ricci de-

---

86. Matteo Ricci, *China in the Sixteenth Century: The Journals of Matthew Ricci (1583–1610)*, trans Louis J. Gallagher (New York: Random House, 1953), 88–89.
87. Ricci, *Journals*, 89.

scribes just such distinctions in a recently uncovered 1595 letter written in Chinese:

> It was my good fortune that the Prince, instead of disdaining me, received me with appropriate guest ritual, permitting me to greet him with a deep bow. He served wine, over which we chatted happily. In the midst of our conversation, the Prince drew his chair close to mine and, while holding my hands, said to me: "I never failed to befriend, and show my respect to, gentlemen of virtue and merits whenever they honor my fief with their visit. Since the West is a place of righteousness and morality, I would like to know how people there think of friendship." On my return, I wrote down what I had learned in the past and my writing forms a volume of *A Treatise on Friendship* that follows [in a later letter].[88]

As he explains, Ricci composed an anthology of European aphorisms on friendship after having been accepted into literati society by early converts. If translating Latin sayings on friendship into Chinese helped Matteo Ricci gain entrée into literati society, translating these same conventions through novels allowed Western audiences to identify with Chinese manners. The feelings and expectations of friendship, particularly among male scholars and administrators, were a familiar concern for Goethe and most any other writer in Romantic era.

From the vantage point of autonomy aesthetics, *The Two Fair Cousins* offers an extended justification for privileging literature above and apart from other goal-oriented discourses. The literati gather over meals and wine to play complex games composing verse while passing a cup between themselves. In sociable terms, the aim is not just to establish a hierarchy of poetic skill, but also to sort out the literary imposters. The system of poetic composition runs parallel with but apart from the court's political network; not all careerists compose well. The limits of Rémusat's translation emerge as the literary games turn on the multiple connotations and pronunciations of Chinese figures. Rémusat provides footnotes to explain a pun or a faux pas by drawing analogies to Latin classics. So

---

88. Dongfeng Xu, "The Concept of Friendship and the Culture of Hospitality: The Encounter between the Jesuits and Late Ming China," PhD diss., University of Chicago, 2011, 109.

that when old Yang's son stumbles in a word game, the translations notes: "The ignorance of Yang Fang on this occasion, is as bad as that of an under-graduate would be, who, if called on to read a quotation from Horace or Vergil, should in the first place be unable to tell the author, and next should perpetrate a false quantity."[89] That the European bourgeoisie played literary games very similar to those depicted in *The Two Fair Cousins* is shown by the Viennese dinner party in Heimito von Doderer's *Die Studelhofstiege* (The Strudelhof Steps), where the guests are asked to translate a Latin verse on the spot and explain whether it was taken from a Classical or medieval source.[90]

If the Jesuits latinized the mandarin's philosophical canon, Rémusat rendered their social life into the familiar relations of the European novel. The Jesuits were concerned to show the compatibility of early Confucian ethics and metaphysics with Christianity, while later bourgeois readers of Chinese novels sought to understand the literati's family romances and class politics. Both translation projects created two new sets of linguists who sought to comprehend the Chinese language. The fluency of the missionaries was replaced by the linguistic systems of the first Sinologists.

Pe's virtue as a magistrate has earned him a high office but it also allows others, in particular the resentful Yang, to manipulate him. Yang recommends that Pe be sent to negotiate with the Mongols for the kidnapped emperor's release. Clearly, he hopes that the venerable old father will never return from his mission, thereby allowing Yang to force Pe's daughter to marry his son. Pe does not want Yang's son to marry his daughter because the son has weak skills as a poet and scholar. Pe holds to his position even though Yang demonstrates, through a series of threats, that he has long political connections that would make the match politically successful. Yang's attempts to compel a marriage would remind European readers of Richardson's novels, as well as the pressure felt by the heroine in Sophie Laroche's *Fräulein von Sternheim*. Before leaving for Mongolian territory, Pe entrusts his daughter's future to her uncle, Gou, who secretly leaves the capital for Nanjing with his niece to search

89. *Two Fair Cousins*, 1:52.
90. Heimito von Doderer, *Die Strudlhofstiege* (Munich: DTV, 1951), 140–44.

for a true poet worthy of marrying Houngiu. The answer is found relatively quickly. As Gou walks through a Nanjing park admiring the plum trees, he discovers lines of verse written in chalk that were obviously produced by a poet of some distinction, named Sse Yeoupe. The uncle sends intermediaries to the young scholar, who needless to say rejects the marriage broker because he is busy studying. Soon the suitor is called away by an uncle, but as he sets off on his journey, he of course encounters Houngiu. Poetic challenges are made, and Sse Yeoupe demonstrates his dexterity by composing brilliant extemporaneous poems. Houngliu requires Sse Yeoupe to compose a poem on the spot drawing together two specific themes in the mandarin's garden: "the first is the *Farewell to the crane*, and the second, the *Welcoming of the swallow*. The farewell to the crane must rhyme with the word *nothing* and the welcoming of the swallow with the word *nest*. Each stanza must be written in verses of seven syllables."[91] Sse Yeoupe recognizes the allegory implied by the test: namely, that Houngliu desires to dismiss another suitor and welcome him, a man with nothing to his name, so that they might establish a household together—a nest. Of course, the novel preserves its ironic suspense. Sse Yeoupe does not realize that Houngliu is the very same woman who was offered to him in marriage earlier.

Sse Yeoupe impresses Houngliu that he is the right husband for her, but is obliged to continue his journey, where, along the way, he meets other would-be suitors of Houngiu, who plagarize his poetry as their own. For much of the story, Sse Yeoupe is challenged to preserve the connection between his poetry and his authorship—to not have the poems stolen, used by anyone else, to not have them alienated or estranged. The story provides glimpses into an economy of poetry, wherein the poems that circulate are accredited to other people and have no link with their original author.

As Sse Yeoupe's obligatory travels make clear, administrative advancement in China required an itinerate life. The Chinese empire required an administration in constant motion. Eventually the old officials retire to be replaced by younger travelers, as the inspector Sse tells his nephew: "I am old; I have no children; besides, I am

---

91. *Two Fair Cousins*, 2: 227–28.

tired of travelling: the career which I pursue must have a termination. I see in you, my dear nephew, a young man in the flower of his age, and fitted for anything. You are one of those couriers who go a hundred leagues a day."[92]

In the course of his journey, Sse Yeoupe meets a delicate young man, Mengli, who in reality is a girl in disguise.[93] They become close friends, and promises are made that Sse Yeoupe will marry his new friend's sister, who of course will turn out to be his friend without masquerade. All along, the poet protagonist is being pursued as the only suitable husband for Houngiu. The introduction of androgyny and queer sexual attractions complicates the plot in a manner reminiscent of Goethe's *Bildungsroman*. By the fifteenth chapter, the reader senses that a hidden hand has been guiding Sse Yeoupe's travels and romances, while his poetic compositions look very similar to the relationship between Wilhelm Meister and the *Turmgesellschaft* (Society of the tower).

The novel shows the family and academic connections that bind the literati together. As with many romances, it is revealed over time that the various characters, and lovers, have complex genealogical relations with each other. While this makes for an intriguing romance, it also shows the continuity of elite classes as they reproduce themselves. "Networking was intertwined with the career of literati at various stages. It was essential when preparing and sitting examinations, when seeking appointment and reappointment, or when obtaining patronage for other types of employments. Networking involved literati in political coalitions."[94] To tie the knot together neatly, the two women are revealed to be cousins. As the plot steers toward a resolution in which Sse Yeoupe will marry the ideal beauty, Houngiu, along with the clever Mengli, queer desire becomes entwined with heterosexuality, friendship, and family obligations in an equal romance between two women and one man.

---

92. *Two Fair Cousins*, 2:106.
93. *Two Fair Cousins*, 2:80.
94. Hilde De Weerdt, Chu Ming-Kin, and Ho Hou-leong, "Chinese Empires in Comparative Perspective: A Digital Approach," *Verge: Studies in Global Asias* 2.2 (Fall 2016): 64–65.

Mengli is a sexually ambiguous figure who first establishes a male-male friendship with Sse Yeoupe by dressing up as a boy, though retaining feminine features.[95] Later, when Mengli joins Houngliu in her father's household, she speaks of her affection for her cousin even as she explains how she developed the plan for all three to marry. Mengli evokes desire both by cross-dressing as a man and by insisting on her femininity. If the text goes out of its way to explain how Sse Yeoupe could fall in love with two women at the same time, it also provides Mengli with two separate scenes when she elaborates her very distinct desires for both Houngliu and Sse Yeoupe. In this configuration Houngliu consistently appears as the supreme beauty, the goal of all desire, while all three characters share profound admiration of reach other's poetic talents. The two women become close after they have both completed one of the many poetry composition challenges that Pe assigns his guests. In the competition, the two women are shown to have identical abilities: "Both young girls finished their pieces of verse exactly at the same moment, and presented them simultaneously to Pe, who was a little surprised at observing that Miss Lo had written without the slightest hesitation, and finished as soon as Miss Pe."[96] The poetry competition in which both women excelled "increased the esteem and affection which these two young girls felt for each other as relations."[97] The text offers a poem to announce that, compared with their familial connection, shared poetic understanding was the more important bond:

When talent meets with talent,
Friendship soon springs up between them.
Deep as may be the attachment of relatives,
It is at bottom only relationship.[98]

---

95. Menjun Li discusses homoerotic qualities in these relationships in "Master of Heavenly Flowers Scripture—Three Personae as Publisher, Commentator, and Writer of Scholar-Beauty Fiction," MA thesis, Ohio State University, 2009, 103.

96. *Two Fair Cousins*, 2:138.

97. *Two Fair Cousins*, 2:141.

98. *Two Fair Cousins*, 2:142.

Such poems are constantly interrupting the prose narrative as they are read aloud after having been composed within the diegesis. Other times short couplets are inserted as commentary offered by some minor character in the novel. Mengli's amorous inclination toward her cousin reemerges through another poetic situation. Mengli walks in on Houngliu as she is completing her morning toilette, "dressed in a simple robe, whose colour corresponded with the tints of the spring."[99] Mengli immediately recognizes that the sight of her cousin is itself an object worthy of poetry: "This very spectacle itself would furnish a fine subject." Mengli places herself as the poet watching the beautiful woman dress. Striking the pose of an amorous suitor, Mengli dares not write her verse, for it would draw her eyes from the beautiful woman who inspires her, namely, her half-dressed cousin. Houngliu remains the most beautiful figure in this triad of beauty. But then Mengli of course grabs paper and pen to compose a poem entitled "Upon a Beautiful Woman." Houngliu senses the role she has been assigned, and answers Mengli, "Sister, if you were a young man, I should wish to have you, all my life, as near as my cap and my comb." Chloe Starr explains that the idiom in the original translates as "to hold his towel and comb," which is to say become his concubine.[100] Here it becomes clear that *The Two Fair Cousins* is not presenting a simple heterosexual arrangement of a man with two wives, but a triad in which desire flows in a circuit between the members. Still, the relations between the women grow more complex. Mengli fears that Houngli holds her at a distance when she compares her to a boy, for although Mengli dressed as one when she approached Sse Yeoupe, in front of her beautiful cousin Houngliu, she wants to be clear that she is not one. Mengli complains, "Then because I am not a young man, you wish me far away from you. This expression announces on your part an affection of little depth." In response to this charge that she does not have deep affection for Mengli, the ever-confident Houngliu responds by saying that she hardly would want Mengli to become a boy and that perhaps it is Mengli herself who is afraid of such de-

---

99. *Two Fair Cousins*, 2:143.
100. Chloe Starr, *Red-Light Novels in the Late Qing* (Leiden: Brill, 2007), 42.

sires. The two women resolve to let their feelings decide how their double marriage should be configured. Mengli declares heroically: "It entirely depends upon ourselves to pass our lives together. . . . It must be our own wishes that will decide it. If we both desire it, who can prevent us? What makes you suppose it impossible?"[101]

As Keith McMahon notes, all polygamous marriages require an extra degree of legitimation to justify their social acceptance,[102] yet it is the polyamorous Mengli who quietly consolidates these pretensions to mandarin virtue with her very intimate, multivalent emotions. Without her puckish attachments, the novel's double marriage would never have seemed desirable to the three participants. The consolidation of family alliances through marriage is certainly an explicit justification for the double marriage, but Mengli's circuit of desire provides its emotional urgency. First, as a crossed-dressed boy, she draws out such a warm response from Sse Yeoupe that he quickly agrees to the homosocial arrangement of marrying his new best friend's (imaginary) twin sister, only to discover at the end of the novel that she is Mengli herself. Then sometime later in the whirl of emotions brought on by a poetry competition with her cousin, Mengli begins to write about Houngliu's beauty, allowing desire to manifest itself as a poetic trope that begs for fulfillment. If poetic genius is judged in terms of the speed with which elegant verses are put down on ink and paper, Mengli's artistry includes the ability to express amorous desire suddenly and with unexpected turns. On the wedding day, Sse Yeoupe has still not been told that his second bride is in fact the cross-dressing Mengli. During the middle of the ceremony, he stares at her marveling at how much she resembles his friend. Only after the ceremony, on the night when they first sleep together, are the details revealed to the husband: "It was in the apartment of Miss Lo [Mengli] that Sse Yeoupe passed the second night. It was upon the pillow that she related to him the particulars of her adventure, when she had quitted the dress of her sex. This account augmented still more Sse Yeoupe's tenderness."[103]

101. *Two Fair Cousins*, 2: 145.
102. McMahon, "The Institution of Polygamy."
103. *Two Fair Cousins*, 2:279.

The decision, early on in the novel, to arrange a marriage between Sse Yeoupe and Houngliu based a single reading of poems the young man had chalked on a garden wall is affirmed by the novel's end, demonstrating the wisdom of fathers, uncles, and virtuous magistrates. The imperial administrative system of examinations and imperial appointments is affirmed as a meritocracy in which excellence overcomes corruption, ignorance, and sloth. Pe summarizes this conclusion to his daughter as he prepares to announce her betrothal to young Sse Yeoupe, who has passed all his exams and received a high office: "Your uncle made no mistake in becoming his go-between; nor was your father mistaken in the choice he made of a son-in-law. There was no error when he was put at the head of the list, when he was distinguished at the examination, and when he was appointed to an office. You see that upon all occasions they who have real merit receive recompense."[104] What surprises the paternal mandarins most is that two young women would have quickly come to the same conclusion about the merits of their future husband.

The novel incorporates formal networks and personal communications into the plot. It depicts the same administrative literary channels that Matteo Ricci hoped would spread Christianity. If the missionaries perceived these imperial and intimate linkages from the outside, the novel shows how they integrate themselves into the most intimate relations. Rather than speculating in sweeping terms about the administrative operations of the empire, the novel draws out the emotional implications of a missed delivery, a letter gone astray. Marco Polo and the Jesuits perceived the large-scale implications of the Chinese postal system, while the Chinese romance writer, along with Kafka, settle into micro-analysis. As the romance unfolds, the elder Pe remains fully informed on the lists of candidates for examination in both the north and the south because they are published in the gazettes issued by the imperial court. At key moments, conversations are interrupted by the arrival of the latest gazette, which brings crucial news. The magistrates themselves go on inspection tours wherein they collect and distribute orders, mandates, laws, administrative news, thereby extending the operation of the empire into the

---

104. *Two Fair Cousins*, 2:269.

distant provinces. More than once the characters find themselves in far-off rural settings with no hope of connecting with a higher literary and administrative society, when one of the novel's main magistrates happens to be passing along the road or down the river—a circumstance that makes it clear that their circuits were vital to providing updates from the capital. Hung-tai Wang argues that in the Ming-Qing period, the novel could serve as an elaboration of the gazette, in which the relatively succinct bulletin from the capital was filled in through a novel's more elaborate explanation of behind-the-scenes motives and actors.[105]

Recent digital network analysis reinforces the impression that European and Chinese scholars relied upon similar letter-writing networks to develop intellectual and political alliances beyond their immediate locality.[106] The networks of Han literati under Mongol rule appear to be quite similar to the republic of letters, particularly when they are mapped according to the exchange of letters. The digital methods in this essay produce graphic images that suggest a clear parallel to the epistolary networks that have been traced for Jesuit missionaries or Enlightenment *philosophes*.

By comparing Chinese novels with European, Rémusat and Goethe treated the genre as self-evident and completed. The novel serves a representative function for both Europe and China, for it allows for hermeneutic entry into the other's consciousness. It is a pathway to seeing the world as others do—a fantasy already proposed in Montesquieu's *Persian Letters*. In Goethe's writing, the Chinese novel becomes a means to another end, poetry, by portraying the spatial setting and subjective desires that constitute an atmosphere or mood (*Stimmung*). *The Two Fair Cousins* repeatedly describes when, where, and why poetry was being written, for noble and base aims. Through its shifting plots and many tests, the novel establishes a Chinese standard for poetic genius. Although Goethe could never learn the language well enough to read Chinese poets

---

105. Hung-tai Wang, "Information Media, Social Imagination, and Public Society during the Ming and Qing Dynasties," *Frontiers of History in China* 5.2 (2010): 189.

106. De Weerdt, Ming-Kin, and Hou-leong, "Chinese Empires," 58–69.

in the original, Rémusat's translation allows him to recognize his own imaginary Chinese scene, a garden to which one retires in order to write poems on the theme of flowers. The perception of atmospheres or moods emerges from a particular kind of aesthetic education that Goethe recognizes he shares with Chinese poets. The "Chinese" quality in Goethe's last poems lies not in any specific allusions or phrases, so much in the overlapping understanding of poetic moods, which have the effect of demonstrating that modes of perception can themselves be forms of intercultural exchange.

In explaining what he finds so strangely interesting about Chinese literature, Goethe does not just talk about humanity and sympathy, but also isolates a distinct aesthetic feature in reading the texts he has available. In the Chinese novels he has read, external nature appears in conjunction with the experiences of novel's protagonists. The novel distinguishes itself again in that for them external nature always lives together with the human figures. Within the German context, the passage from Eckermann's *Conversations* discussed at the start of this chapter provides a definition of *Stimmung*, or mood, a term that later critics such as Emil Staiger elaborate upon as the lyric poem's integration of interior feeling and external nature into a totalized whole that joins self and world together in an suspended unity.[107] The voice of lyric poetry hovers between the perceiving subject and its natural surroundings, creating a convergence between the two, so that any opposition between subject and objects is suspended within the experience of reading the poem. The *Stimmung* of a lyric poem supersedes the presumption that emotions are housed within an imagined interior of the subject by representing moods as a spatial reality passing through the subject from the exterior. Charles Taylor argues that the localization of mental states within the subject "is a function of a historically limited mode of self-interpretation, one which has become dominant in the modern West and which may indeed spread thence to other parts of the globe, but which had a begin-

---

107. Emil Staiger, *Basic Concepts of Poetics*, trans. Janette C. Hudson and Luanne T. Frank (University Perk: Pennsylvania State University Press, 1991), 81.

ning in time and space and may have an end."[108] To the extent that poetic *Stimmung* suspends the modern distinction between subject and object, culture and nature, it offers an unnerving turn to a mythic state in which the human does not stand above or apart from the world.

Romanticism is most often credited with expanding the discourse of interiority, yet the poetics of *Stimmung* around 1800 make clear that this attribution requires some inattentive revisions of literary history. Specifically, Hegel's critique of Romantic lyric poetry insisted that Romantic lyricism was "merely" an interior state projected outward. Chinese poetics lays great value on a poem's ability to portray the interpenetration of the material landscape and subjective feeling through a detached and contemplative voice. Within traditional poetics, the harmonious interactions and cross-references between subject and object are gathered under the concept of *yijing*, which "refers to an ineffable and meaning-laden artistic space that the poet constructs through a combination of his thoughts and feelings with the objects of scene he depicts in his poem."[109] *Yijing* constitutes the terrain of poetry, a space in which transcendence seems possible as perception and things reinforce each other's meanings.[110] Classical Chinese nature poems consolidate around specific images, laden with portent.

Chinese poems rely on familiar figures that repeat themselves in variations. Thoms's translation, *Chinese Courtship. In Verse*, provides a lengthy scene in which the young Leang, having caught a first glimpse of his beloved, leaves an evening garden to dream restlessly. Such familiar motifs can appear as universal references providing readily accessible metaphysical depth, or they can come across as unreflective stereotypes. Clearly drawn by their harmonious potential, Goethe offers Eckermann a list of such images teasingly, aware that outside of the text they may sound like chinoiserie.

108. Charles Taylor, *Sources of the Self: The Making of Modern Identity* (Cambridge: Cambridge University Press, 1989), 111.

109. Yanfang Tang, "Translating across Cultures: Yi Jing and Understanding Chinese Poetry," *Intercultural Communication Studies* 23.1 (2014): 188.

110. Bai Li-bing, "On *Yijing* in Chinese and English Nature Poetry: The Case Study of Wordsworth and Wang Wei," *US-China Foreign Language* 12.5 (2014): 416.

In recounting these literary features, Goethe recreates the utopian fable of China, so that with a few lines Eckermann has Goethe telling us how extraordinary the country is.

Goethe's interest in how Chinese texts create a mood of lyrical retreat has little to do with acquiring scientific knowledge about the place but everything to do with Goethe's own writing. From the opening chapter on, *The Two Fair Cousins* depicts many scenes of poetry writing, which, of course, allow readers to draw analogies to their own desire to escape political intrigue and oppression by withdrawing into a quiet, safe haven, but which also provide an impetus for writing poetry. Between the novel's many garden scenes and its repeated challenge to enter into writing contests, *The Two Fair Cousins* offered the aging, isolated Goethe a new impetus and literary form within which to compose. In *The Two Fair Cousins* and in Goethe's Chinese poems, the atmosphere depends on the cloistered space of a garden. Atmospheres occur across cultures: it matters little that the particular flowers in Nanjing and Weimar are different; the similarity lies in the intersubjective quality instilled by both sets of writing. Because the poems' Asian-German identity rest on the shared sense of atmosphere, they can never have a clear determinate code that allows us to map China onto Weimar. They construct a symbolic, nonrepresentational space. Critics who worry about the absence of overt Asian references in Goethe's Chinese-German poems are overlooking the gardens' shared aesthetic conditions. Atmospheres help inspire poetic production. In turn, the circular relations between reading translations, composing poetry, and contemplating a garden enact an imaginative Chinese-German space, which is not yet transnational, because of the limited physical mobility between the cultures, but which does assert a parallel identity.

Every text that describes the sacred places where the poet discovers the harmony between feeling and nature also includes an implicit contrast to sites where such experiences cannot be found. Like the young poet, the retired mandarin, and his daughter in *The Two Fair Cousins*, the aged Goethe favors his own country garden over cities and palaces. Already in his first writing about poetic atmosphere, Goethe insists that it cannot be found in and around aristocratic palaces.[111] Not only do the machinations of state power vitiate poetic insight, but the interpenetration of personal vision and natural environment is quite distinct from the pleasure-seeking drive of urban readers and theater audiences.[112] During a visit to his native Frankfurt, Goethe wrote to Schiller about the complete absence of poetic mood among the urban populace.[113] Unsettled by the shock and sensory overload of the walking through a busy urban market, Goethe perceived a nervous energy that produces a disharmonious integration of space and subjects. Modernists poets might easily recognize Goethe's perception of commercial cities, though without seeking a rural respite to restore a lost symbolic unity. By referring to "that which we call 'Stimmung,'" Goethe makes clear that he and Schiller shared a common understanding of the term as an aesthetic effect.[114] Given how much of their correspondence focused on the craft of writing, Goethe makes clear that in his trip to Frankfurt he is looking for objects that induce a symbolic *Stimmung* that he can then describe in his own writing. Goethe often sought a symbolic person, text, or setting that then became the basis for his poetic description. Find the right object and the poem can be written. Traveling through Italy provided just such an abundance of symbolic objects, which Goethe gathered up to preserve in memory, or what the Roman rhetorical tradition would have called the treasure house of the mind.[115] The hassle of travel went by unnoticed

---

111. "Ach dieser Zauber ist's, der aus den Sälen der Großen und aus ihren Gärten flieht, die nur zum Durchstreifen, nur zum Schauplatz der aneinander hinwischenden Eitelkeit ausstaffiert und beschnitten sind" (HA, 12:25).

112. Modernist poets have of course written extensively about urban *Stimmung*. See Burkhard Meyer-Sickendiek, "Die Stimmung einer Stadt. Urbane Atmosphären in der Lyrik des 20. Jahrhunderts," *Weimarer Beiträge* 59.4 (2013): 558–79.

113. Goethe to Schiller, August 8, 1797, Siegfried Seidel, ed., *Der Briefwechsel zwischen Schiller und Goethe* (Leipzig: Insel, 1984), 1:376.

114. David Wellbery notes that in his earliest formulations of the term, Goethe did not have a readily available aesthetic definition within eighteenth-century discourse; see his, "Stimmung," in *Historisches Wörterbuch Ästhetischer Grundbegriffe*, ed. Karlheinz Barck, Martin Fontius, Dieter Schlenstedt, Burkhard Steinwachs, and Friedrich Wolfzettel (Stuttgart/Weimar: Metzler, 2003), 5:706.

115. WA, 31:202.

because he experienced Italy in a state of attunement with his surroundings, which thereby allowed him gather up the individual moments in order to preserve them as memory objects for later writing. The trouble was that as he grew older, Goethe felt he had emptied his store house of symbolic experiences and therefore needed to search out for new moments. Precisely for this reason, he found Persian and Chinese literature so fulfilling.

In his remarks to Eckermann, Goethe does not rely on the metaphorical shorthand for poetic creation that he used when writing Schiller, but instead described in very simple terms the correlation between subject and natural objects, reinforcing the impression that he was thinking functionally as a writer trying to produce an effect in the reader. In writing about *Stimmung*, Goethe was not just concerned with his own symbolic experiences; he was more concerned with replicating the poetic maneuver that produced the mood. The Chinese novels he described to Eckermann offered a schema for writing that Goethe sought to elucidate in order to compose his own poetry. The list of chinoiserie effects in Chinese novels that Goethe provides Eckermann reflects the craftmanship of writing rather than an historical-critical analysis.

A poem's *Stimmung* does not itself depict a subject in search of an object to satisfy its desires, but rather a suspension of this dualism within a unity that maintains both. In such a poetic space, the subject does not seek to possess or overcome the other through struggle, acquisition, or seduction, but rather is portrayed as having joined together in a balance that grants neither extreme supremacy over the other. Desire within such a poem does not consume the otherness of the other; rather, it is held in suspense with the strange. If poetry does entail the spontaneous outpouring of feeling and thoughts, it does so only after the proper object for concentrated writing has been found. Goethe as artist did not invent poetic objects out of thin air; he encountered them before he wrote. In his *Italian Journey*, he underscores how important remains for the poet to first discover a person, story, or thing worth creating. The primacy of the found object was an old theme for him: "I always come back to my old principle. If the artist is presented with an authentic object, then he can accomplish something real."[116] If it cannot be perceived directly, that symbolic object may be found in the images created by reading, which in the case of *The Two Fair Cousins* includes the figure of the poet. Just as Goethe stumbled across the Nanjing Disputation in search of poetic booty, he consumes Rémusat's translation.

In finding a foreign source, Goethe transforms it into his own idiom. His Persian and Chinese poems do not imitate foreign meter and rhyme or ventriloquize another voice; instead they recognize their own affinity with the distant companion. The poetics of *Stimmung* enable intercultural commingling; the mood of the poem makes it possible for two antithetical or simply unrelated symbols to coexist within aesthetic experience. As many critics point out, the poetics of *Stimmung* are very different from what Hegel took to be Romanticism's projecting its own confused interior feelings out on to the world. Even though Romantic writers such as E. T. A. Hoffmann ironically show how emotionally young men often project their desires onto others, the poetics of *Stimmung*, in the mature Goethe particularly, are not always just the expansive residue of an emotional subject, but rather the expression of a point of union with nature and the foreign.

As the many writing scenes in *The Two Fair Cousins* show, the invention of a poem is itself filled with social tensions. The expectations and consequences for the poet after delivering his or her verse drive the Chinese novel's plot. Given the importance that understanding and composing classical poetry has for the Chinese novel's administrators, the idyllic garden where becomes the stage on which the drama of composition—the ability to write beautiful poetry on the spot—unfolds.

Chinese-German Atmosphere

Goethe was reading Rémusat's *The Two Fair Cousins* in May 1827, when he retreated to his garden house to escape into the beautiful

---

116. Goethe, *Italienische Reise*, October 5, 1786, HA, 11:80.

spring weather, so that he could work on his most important poetic engagement with Chinese literature, "Chinesisch-deutschen Jahres- und Tageszeiten," a work very much in the synthetic, cross-cultural mode of *West-Eastern Divan*.[117] Organized into fourteen short poems that do not reflect any particularly Chinese lyrical structure, the "Chinesisch-deutschen Jahres- und Tageszeiten" presents a two-sided temporal awareness of the beautiful day in the moment and at the end of a long lifetime.[118] Although the confusing title sounds as if it could have been yet another result of the nineteenth century's many quickly printed journals and almanacs, it also concentrates the poem's temporal sense on the present in order to contemplate the duration of a biological lifespan. Goethe used a similar clunky construction when he began in 1816 to organize his recollections in a chronology he called *Tag- und Jahres Hefte als Ergänzung meiner sonstigen Bekenntnisse* (Daily and annual notebooks as a supplement to my other confessions).[119] The title of the poems suggests an administrative, secretarial archiving of events, while the poems themselves speak with the diffuse immediacy of first-person recollection.

The poetry cycle enacts precisely that interdependence of inner thoughts with natural description that he ascribes to Chinese poetry in his chat with Eckermann.[120] The Chinese quality in these last poems shows itself very differently than the Persian does in *West-Eastern Divan*: the Chinese-German relation is announced in the title, but not performed lyrically. After identifying himself as belonging to the class of mandarins, Goethe does not adopt Chinese costume or the language as the Jesuit missionaries did. Rather, his poems challenge us to recognize the affinities between the poetic traditions without overtly emulating one another. Recent scholars,

---

117. On the place of Chinese gardens in Goethe's work, see Ingrid Schuster, *Vorbilder und Zerrbilder: China und Japan im Spiegel der deutschen Literatur, 1773–1890* (Bern: Peter Lang, 1988), 143–61.

118. Meredith Lee, "Goethes Chinesisch-Deutsche Jahres- und Tageszeiten," in *Goethe und China—China und Goethe*, ed. Günther Debon and Adrian Hsia (Bern: Peter Lang, 1985), 37–50.

119. WA, 35:277–78.

120. Christine Wagner-Dittmar, "Goethe und die chinesischer Literatur," in *Studien zu Goethes Alterswerken*, ed. Erich Trunz (Frankfurt: Athenäum, 1971), 222.

such as Arne Klawitter, have read the cycle as a poetic actualiza-
tion of Goethe's world literature paradigm insofar as the poems
show how the very distant Chinese also appears as the already
well-known, almost to the point of seeming conventional.[121] Just
about every commentator has noted how very German the poems
seem—indeed, that they fit comfortably in Goethe's long oeuvre.
While Goethe sought out the unfamiliar, his identification with the
new poetic forms transformed them into the well-known patterns
of his own writing. As Georg Simmel might argue, whereas the oriental work of art is marked as possessing a style because it appears
foreign, Goethe's poetry appears to many German readers as fully
identical with his person, as universal, and as in no way foreign.[122]
Of course, the fully familiar tone and themes of the poems confirm
the parallel between Chinese and German gardens with their poets
contemplating flowers as coded memories. As Chunjie Zhang has
shown, the earlier erotic connotations of the chinoiserie garden still
linger in Goethe's poems.[123]

In the eyes of most eighteenth-century Europeans, the single most
impressive feature of Chinese civilization was its antiquity. Thus, in
the opening lines Goethe associates his own old age with that of a
weary mandarin, for he too has become an ancient figure. In this
way Goethe is also starting with the same class that attracted the
Jesuits, the literati:

> Say, what remains for us mandarins
> finished ruling, tired of serving,
> Say, what can remain for us
> On such spring days
> to leave the north

---

121. Arne Klawitter, *Ästhetische Resonanz, Zeichen und Schriftästhetik in der deutschsprachigen Literatur und Geistesgeschichte* (Göttingen: V and Runipress, 2015), 234–37.

122. Georg Simmel, "The Problem of Style," trans. Mark Ritter, *Theory, Culture, and Society* 8.3 (1991): 63–71.

123. Chunjie Zhang, "Goethe's *Chinesisch-deutsche Jahres- und Tageszeitung*: Vernacular Universal, *Erotica Sinica*, and the Temporality of *Nachträglichkeit*," in *Receptions: Reading the Past Across Space and Time*, ed. Brenda Schildgen and Ralph Hexter (New York: Palgrave Macmillan, 2017), 245–64.

for the water and the garden
cheerfully drinking, spiritedly writing,
bowl after bowl, line upon lines

Sag', was könnt' uns Mandarinen,
Satt zu herrschen, müd zu dienen,
Sag', was könnt uns übrigbleiben,
Als in solchen Frühlingstagen
Uns des Nordens zu entschlagen
Und am Wasser und in Garten
Fröhlich trinken, geistig schreiben,
Schal auf Schale, Zug in Zügen.[124]

What is left to us mandarins after we are tired of ruling, tired of serving? The answer lies in writing poetry about flowers in the garden, a very specific scene common to both chinoiserie representations and the three translated novels, a feedback loop within which Goethe's Chinese-German poems appear. As John Noyes points out, these lines place Goethe's lyric voice in dialogue with other mandarins: Kant, Herder, Leibniz, and certainly the characters in the Chinese novel he was just reading, *The Two Fair Cousins,* which also opens with three learned friends retired to a garden to write and drink.[125]

By identifying as a mandarin, Goethe revives the parallel between the Chinese and the Holy Roman Empire. Most certainly, the phrase "us mandarins" recalls Goethe's first reading of the Nanjing Disputation as Matteo Ricci ingratiates himself at the literati dinner party. If the Jesuits perceived a similarity between their own office and those of the literati, and Goethe then draws the connection to include the intellectual scene in Weimar, then the European sides of this constellation are drawing to a close in 1827. Only the Chinese administrators would continue. The analogies operate on the level

---

124. Goethe, HA, 1:387.
125. John Noyes also reads the cycle in relation to Kant in "Eradicating the Orientalist: Goethe's 'Chinesisch-deutsche Jahres- und Tageszeiten,'" in *China in the German Enlightenment,* ed. Bettina Brandt and Daniel L. Purdy (Toronto: Toronto University Press, 2016), 146.

of textual production as well as historical institutions.[126] Goethe's 1798 letter to Schiller refers to the back-stage secrets of composition favored by poets, or "we, magicians"; then in 1827 he enacts his earlier insight in a broader invocation "us mandarins," leaving open to whom he is actually speaking. To refer to himself as a mandarin, the poet has arrived at a far extreme from his Werther—no longer the emotional outsider, Goethe acknowledges his privileged position. Yet this poetry cycle describes the inclination to abandon the position of the mandarin—the administrator and diplomat—in order to revive the memory of an earlier ease with nature and desire. By naming the mask, Goethe hopes to let it drop. This wearied stance is of course assumed many times by Chinese figures in the three translated novels, and it is one found in sentimental and rococo writing, figured as the desire to escape the intrigues and maneuvers of the political court in favor of an imagined rustic innocence. Exhaustion and exasperation at one's own engagement with power create yet another position from which to begin writing poetry. Andreas Angelet compares the opening to the *Divan*, where the poet seeks to flee after the collapse of empire, with the opening of the Chinese poem, where he announces himself a government official exhausted by ruling. If the *West-Eastern Divan* opens with a flight from the destruction of the Holy Roman Empire, the "Chinesisch-deutschen Jahres- und Tageszeiten" speaks of retirement from service to the state.[127] The question "was bleibt uns übrig" ("what remains for us") seeks to find what fragments of

---

126. Fritz K. Ringer in his influential study of the German academic elite states that the name "mandarin" has no particular importance for it draws no meaningful reference. My point here is not to disagree with his assessment of German professors, but to make the case that the German relation to the Chinese elite was indeed based on a perceived analogy, and thus the name applied to European intellectuals had a real historical basis in comparative self-justifications. See Ringer's *The Decline of the German Mandarins: The German Academic Community, 1890–1933* (Cambridge, MA: Harvard University Press, 1969), 5. As a German mandarin himself, Max Weber was far more open to the similarities between the two classes. See his *Economy and Society*, ed. Guenther Roth and Claus Wittich (Berkeley: University of California Press, 1978), 1047–51.

127. Andreas Anglet, "Die lyrische Bewegung in Goethes 'Chinesisch-Deutschen Jahres- und Tageszeiten,'" *Goethe Jahrbuch* 113 (1996): 182.

personal experience have survived being covered by the façade of officialdom. What remains after we drop the public mask? Goethe's view of the mandarin, enabled by the novels, looks beyond the idealized Confucian intellectual lauded by the Jesuits to consider hidden domesticity after all the proper ceremonies have been performed.

Most readers agree that the cycle revolves around the central, eighth poem. Meredith Lee refers to it as the collection's key. [128] Still, many find no particularly Chinese quality therein. In a volume dedicated to Emil Staiger, Wolfgang Bauer underscores how the late Goethe's interest in Chinese literature coincides with his retreat from the enthusing inwardness of his youthful, sentimental writing. Bauer finds that few poems in German come closer to a Chinese harmony between person and nature than the famous "Abendgedicht" (Evening Verse)—a poem without any overt Asian reference, or "costume." [129]

> Twilight descends from above
> Everything close seems already far;
> Though first the evening star
> raises its lovely light!
> Everything sways in uncertainty,
> Mist creeps into the heights;
> The sea quietly reflects
> the gloom's deepening darkness.
>
> Now in the eastern regions
> I sense the moon's glow and glance
> Slender willows' tangled hair
> Frolic in the nearby stream
> Through the moving shadow play
> Shimmers Luna's magic glow
> And through the eyes slides
> the cool that calms the heart.

---

128. Meredith Lee, "Goethes Chinesisch-Deutsche Jahres- und Tageszeiten," 40.

129. Without drawing his own conclusion, Günther Debon offers a summary listing of the many critical judgements rendered by Goethe scholars to the question of how Chinese the poem is: "Die 'Chinesische-Deutschen Jahres- und Tageszeiten,'" *China zu Gast in Weimar, 18 Studien und Streiflichter* (Heidelberg: Brigitte Guderjahn, 1994), 224–29.

Dämmerung senkte sich von oben,
Schon ist alle Nähe fern;
Doch zuerst emporgehoben
Holden Lichts der Abendstern!
Alles schwankt ins Ungewisse,
Nebel schleichen in die Höh';
Schwarzvertiefte Finsternisse
Widerspiegelnd ruht der See.

Nun am östlichen Bereiche
Ahn' ich Mondenglanz und -Glut
Schlanker Weiden Haargezweige
Scherzen auf der nächsten Flut
Durch bewegter Schatten Spiele
Zittert Lunas Zauberschein
Und durchs Auge schleicht die Kühle
Sänftigend ins Herz hinein.[130]

The verses thematize the inability to distinguish far and near distances with the arrival of nightfall—another way of alluding to his old age—such that things lying close by seem far removed: in blunt, unpoetic terms, a Weimar garden can appear Chinese. In the first verse, Western perspectivism with its delineations of distant lines disappears in the night garden, allowing another medium of lunar shadow play to replace it in the second verse. Darkness acquires an agency of its own; rather than just manifesting itself as the absence of light, it instead descends from above. Between the two modes of appearance, identities slide into a state of indeterminacy, not just for the observer, but for the cosmos as a whole. Fog rises up to the heights while the sky's darkness is reflected down onto a lake. The poem depicts the mutually mirrored relations in the landscape as harmonious, rather than in conflict. Much like Kant's confused rational subject in "What Does It Mean to Orient Oneself in Thinking?," the second verse opens with a subject intuiting an orientation by looking toward the east even as the ability to measure space has become meaningless. The appearance of some diffuse light in the east

---

130. Goethe, HA, 1:389.

serves as an initial marker. If Kant's subject orients itself through the eastern rise of the sun, the poetic observer here sees the moon rising from the same direction. While Kant's subject seeks to rise out from disorientation through abstract reasoning, Goethe's lyric voice allows the subject to descend upon its prey from above. Emil Staiger described this pleasant confusion in terms of Kantian epistemology when he introduced the poems in 1949: "A tender dizziness arises, that vertigo takes over our heads, whenever, approaching the upper limits of humanity, we try to comprehend simultaneity and successiveness as one."[131] In these late poems, Goethe can no longer position himself as a bird of prey looking at the earth from a height, as he did in "Harzreise im Winter." Instead, Goethe's poem sits contentedly in the condition Kant sought to overcome. Seeing the moon between the shadows cast by tall grasses or willows, the poetic subject's momentary apprehension of direction is recast into a sensory reversal in which a feeling of coldness enters the body through the eye, by mere looking alone. Goethe combines the haptic sense of sight and touch, though most importantly without any other person returning his gaze. The poem conveys isolation through the wavering recognition of the moon. By naming it "Luna," the poem places the astrological body within a Latin mythic tradition, even though the subjective state of finding the moon on a dark night is another feature of poetry shared the world over. Goethe invokes the ancient definition of sympathy as the relation between bodies on earth and in the heavens when the poem refers to the moon's magical appearance.[132] The poem couples astronomy with sympathetic medicine when it explains that the moon's cooling effect—in contrast to the sun—enters the body through the eye. The *laterna magica* of the moon shining through the willows (*Weiden*) reveals nature to be an optical medium, known in eighteenth-century

131. Emil Staiger, "Einführung," *Johann Wolfgang Goethe Sämtliche Gedichte* (Zürich: Artemis Verlag, 1953), 611.

132. "Urworte. Orphisch" is the late poem that has attracted the most commentary about Goethe's lifetime interest in astrology. See Johannes Klein, *Geschichte der deutschen Lyrik* (Wiesbaden: Frank Steiner, 1960), 57, and Herbert Anton, "Orakel der Existenz," in *Gedichte von Johann Wolfgang Goethe*, ed. Bernd Witte (Stuttgart: Reclam 1998), 170–85.

theater-goers as Chinese shadows, *ombres chinoise*. Without announcing the metaphor, the poem suggests that the moon's light turns the landscape into a darkened theater. Nature operates thus as a medium.

Chinese poets and many others write about the moon as much as any German. Thoms's *Chinese Courtship* abounds with references to willows in gardens, among them a comparison that links the drooping tree branches with aging: "I think mankind in general, resemble those delicate willows, / For on attaining manhood their autumn commences."[133] Goethe could well have published his cycle of poems without mention of any Chinese source, and they would well have been understood as his late creation. The title then is a specific gesture to draw the reader to possible Chinese comparisons: "The blighted willows will again experience the return of Spring, / But man, as yet, when old has never become young."[134] The underlying though unarticulated discrepancy is in Goethe's garden: plants will regenerate in the next year's seasons but the old poet does not know whether he will encounter another spring.

Astronomy serves as a point of orientation not only in a geographical and epistemological sense, but also as a shared motif within the eternal return of cross-cultural poetics. Bauer concludes, "There exist few poems in western literature, whose language and content come closer to the Chinese tradition than these."[135] His conclusion stands in direct opposition to Kommerell, who misses the point by claiming that "the most beautiful of all Goethe's evening verses" is "is totally unChinese."[136] Bauer goes on to cite the translator Kuo Mo-jo, who speculated that Goethe must have been familiar with a lost poem by the great Li-Po (699–762), famous for his shimmering drinking poems in nature, an impossibility given that he was not yet known in Europe.

---

133. *Chinese Courtship*, 78.
134. *Chinese Courtship*, 78.
135. Wolfgang Bauer, "Goethe und China: Verständnis und Misverständnis," *Goethe und die Tradition*, ed. Hans Reiss (Frankfurt: Athenäum, 1972), 189.
136. Max Kommerell, *Gedanken über Gedichte*, 4th ed. (Frankfurt: Klostermann, 1985), 112–13.

To the extent that critics have always wondered how Chinese these poems are, for they seem just like his other poems, the title suggests that Goethe's poems have always already had an affinity with Chinese literature. When Max Kommerell provides a list of eight nuanced answers to this challenge, the motifs and features he isolates are hardly uniquely Chinese, yet they do describe the overlapping motifs and moods that Goethe's poems share with the "scholar-beauty" romances he read.[137] Goethe's sense of human existence as an eternally recurring cycle allows him to perceive the supposedly foreign and strange qualities of Chinese literature as having been continuously present in his writing—they simply have not been called such. That which remains for exhausted mandarins is the same as that which they desired and which inspired them from the first. The temporal orientation—anticipating or recollecting—has simply shifted. The new insight offered by Goethe's last poems manifests itself as a creative recognition of the fundamental similarities between the two literary and administrative traditions, a statement made in the collection's title most explicitly. Along with the wonder of discovering Chinese culture comes the realization that it has always already been there.

---

137. Kommerell, *Gedanken*, 112.

BIBLIOGRAPHY

Albrecht, Andrea. *Kosmopolitismus: Weltbürgerdiskurse in Literatur, Philosophie und Publizistik um 1800*. Berlin: De Gruyter, 2005.

Alliston, April. "Transnational Sympathies, Imaginary Communities." In *The Literary Channel*, edited by Margaret Cohen and Carolyn Dever, 133–48. Princeton, NJ: Princeton University Press, 2009.

Anglet, Andreas. "Die lyrische Bewegung in Goethes 'Chinesisch-Deutschen Jahres- und Tageszeiten.'" *Goethe Jahrbuch* 113 (1996):179–98.

Anton, Herbert. "Orakel der Existenz." In *Gedichte von Johann Wolfgang Goethe*, edited by Bernd Witte, 170–85. Stuttgart: Reclam 1998.

Aravamudan, Srinivas. *Enlightenment Orientalism: Resisting the Rise of the Novel*. Chicago: University of Chicago Press, 2012.

Archenholtz, Johann Wilhelm von, ed. "Fragmente aus der Reisegeschichte des Marco Polo, eines berühmten Reisenden des dreyzehnten Jahrhunderts." In *Literatur- und Völkerkunde*, 3:93–107. Dessau und Leipzig, 1783.

Aristotle. *Aristotle's Theory of Poetry and Fine Art*. Translated by S. H. Butcher. New York: Dover, 1951.

Avvisi della Cina et Giapone del fine dell'anno 1586. Antwerp: Plantin, 1588.

Bachelard, Gaston. *The Poetics of Space*. Boston: Beacon, 1994.

Barthes, Roland. *Sade-Fourier-Loyola*. Translated by Richard Miller. New York: Hill & Wang, 1976.

Barry, David. "Faustian Pursuits: The Political-Cultural Dimension of Goethe's Weltliteratur and the Tragedy of Translation," *German Quarterly* 74.2 (2001): 164–85

Bauer, Wolfgang. "Goethe und China: Verständnis und Missverständnis." In *Goethe und die Tradition*, edited by Hans Reiss, 177–97. Frankfurt: Athenäum, 1972.

Baumgartner, Alexander. *Joost van den Vondel, sein Leben und seine Werke*. Freiburg: Herdersche Verlagshandlung, 1882.

Begheyn, Paul. "The Jesuits in the Low Countries, 1540–1773: Apostles of the Printing Press." In *The Jesuits of the Low Countries: Identity and Impact (1540–1773)*, edited by Rob Faesen, 129–38. Leuven: Peeters, 2012.

Behrmann, Caroline. "'Le monde est une peinture': Zu Louis Richeômes Bildtheorie im Kontext globaler Mission." In *Le monde est une peinture: Jesuitische Identität und die Rolle der Bilder*, edited by Elisabeth Oy-Marra and Volker R. Remmert, 15–44. Berlin: Akademie Verlag, 2011.

Bell, Michael. *Sentimentalism, Ethics and the Culture of Feeling*. Basingstoke, Hampshire: Palgrave, 2000.

Benjamin, Walter. *Gesammelte Schriften*. Edited by Rolf Tiedemann and Hermann Schweppenhäuser. Frankfurt: Suhrkamp, 1985.

——. *The Origin of German Tragic Drama*. Translated by John Osborne. London: Verso, 1985.

——. *Selected Writings*. Edited by Michael Jennings. Cambridge, MA: Harvard University Press, 1999.

Berensmeyer, Ingo. "Empfindsamkeit als Medienkonflikt: Zur Gefühlskultur des 18. Jahrhunderts." *Poetica* 39.3/4 (2007): 397–422.

Berger, Willy Richard. *China-Bild und China-Mode im Europa der Aufklärung*. Cologne: Böhlau, 1990.

Berman, Russell A. *Enlightenment or Empire: Colonial Discourse in German Culture*. Lincoln: University of Nebraska Press, 1998.

Bhatti, Anil. "Der Orient als Experimentierfeld. Goethes *Divan* und der Aneignungsprozess kolonialen Wissens." In *From Popular Goethe to Global Pop*, edited by Ines Detmers and Birte Heidemann, 21–39. Amsterdam: Rodopi, 2013.

Biedermann, Woldemar von. "Chinesisch-Deutsche Jahres- und Tages-zeiten." In *Goethe Forschungen*, edited by Woldemar von Biedermann, 426–46. Leipzig: Metzger and Wittig, 1886.

——. "Goethe und das Schrifttum Chinas," *Zeitschrift für vergleichende Literaturgeschichte* N.F. 7 (1894): 383–401.

Birus, Hendrick. "Goethes Idee der Weltliteratur, Eine historische Vergengwärtigung." In *Weltliteratur Heute*, edited by Manfred Schmeling, 1–28. Würzburg: Königshausen and Neumann, 1995.

Blackall, Eric. "Goethe and the Chinese Novel." In *The Discontinuous Tradition: Studies in German Literature in Honour of Ernest Ludwig Stahl*, edited by P. F. Ganz, 29–53. Oxford: Clarendon Press, 1971.

Blaeu, Willem Janszoon, Joan Blaeu, Martino Martini, and Jacobus Golius, eds. *Novus Atlas Sinensis Das ist ausfuhrliche Beschreibung des grossen Reichs Sina*. Vol. 6 of *Novus Atlas, Das ist, Weltbeschreibung: Mit schönen newen außführlichen Land-Taffeln in Kupffer gestochen, vnd an den Tag gegeben*. Amsterdam, 1655. http://digi.ub.uni-heidelberg.de/diglit/blaeu1655bd6.

Blondheim, Menahem. "Prayer 1.0: The Biblical Tabernacle and the Problem of Communicating with a Deity." Paper presented at the Sixty-Second Annual Meeting of the International Communication Association, Phoenix, AZ, May 28, 2012. https://www.academia.edu/5915336/Prayer_1.0_The_Biblical_Tabernacle_and_the_Problem_of_Communicating_with_a_Deity.

Bluemink, Matt. "On Virtuality: Deleuze, Bergson, Simondon." *Epoché*, December 2020. https://epochemagazine.org/on-virtuality-deleuze-bergson-simon don-824e3742368e.

Bod, Rens, Jaap Mat, and Thijs Weststeijn, eds. *The Making of the Humanities*. Vol. 2 of *From Early Modern to Modern Disciplines*. Amsterdam: Amsterdam University Press, 2012.

Börne, Ludwig. *Gesammelte Schriften*, 3rd ed. Stuttgart: Fr. Brodhag'sche Buchhandlung, 1840.

Boswell, Grant. "Letter Writing among the Jesuits: Antonio Possevino's Advice in the *Bibliotheca Selecta* (1593)." *Huntington Library Quarterly* 66 (2003): 247–62.

Botero, Giovanni. *The Reason of State*. Translated by P. J. and D. P. Waley. New Haven: Yale University Press, 1956.

Boxer, C. R. "Review of *Jesuit Letters and Indian History* by John Correia-Afonso." *Bulletin of the School of Oriental and African Studies* 19 (1957): 189–90.

Bucher, Otto. "Der Dillinger Buchdrucker Johann Mayer (1576–1614)." *Gutenberg Jahrbuch* (1955): 162–69.

Bürger, Peter. *Theorie der Avantgarde*. Frankfurt: Suhrkamp, 1982.

Burke, James. *The Speeches of the Right Honorable Edmund Burke*. Dublin: Duffy, 1854.

Burnett, Charles. "The Freising Titus Play." In *Mission und Theater: Japan und China auf den Bühnen der Gesellschaft Jesu*, edited by Adrian Hsia and Ruprecht Wimmer, 413–67. Regensburg: Schnell and Steiner, 2005.

Burrus, Ernest J., SJ, ed. *Kino Writes to the Duchess: Letters of Eusebio Francisco Kino, S.J., to the Duchess of Aveiro*. Rome: Jesuit Historical Institute, 1965.

Burschel, Peter. *Sterben und Unsterblichkeit. Zur Kultur des Martyiums in der frühen Neuzeit*. Munich: Oldenbourg, 2004.

Bush, Christopher. *Ideographic Modernism: China, Writing, Media*. Oxford: Oxford University Press, 2010.

Caracciolo, Carlos H. "Natural Disasters and the European Printed News Network." In *News Networks in Early Modern Europe*, edited by Joad Raymond and Noah Moxham, 756–78. Leiden: Brill, 2016.

Carruthers, Mary. *The Craft of Thought: Meditation, Rhetoric, and the Making of Images, 400–1200*. Cambridge: Cambridge University Press, 1998.

Castiglione, Baldesar. *The Book of the Courtier*. Translated by Charles Singleton. New York: Anchor Books, 1959.

Certeau, Michel de. *The Writing of History*. Translated by Tom Conley, 147–205. New York: Columbia University Press, 1988.

Chakravarti, Ananya. *The Empire of Apostles: Religion, Accommodation, and the Imagination of Empire in Early Modern Brazil and India*. Oxford: Oxford University Press, 2018.

Chan, Albert. "Michele Ruggieri, S.J. (154–1607) and His Chinese Poems." *Monumenta Serica* 41 (1993): 129–76.

Chan, Wing-Tsit, ed. and trans. *A Source Book in Chinese Philosophy*. Princeton, NJ: Princeton University Press, 1963.

Chandler, James. *An Archeology of Sympathy: The Sentimental Mode in Literature and Cinema*. Chicago: University of Chicago Press, 2013.

Cheung, Kai-chong. "The *Haoqiu zhuan*, the First Chinese Novel Translated in Europe: With Special Reference to Percy's and Davis's Renditions." In *One into Many: Translation and the Dissemination of Classical Chinese Literature*, edited by Leo Tak-hung Chan, 29–37. Amsterdam: Rodopi, 2003.

China und Europa: Chinaverständnis und Chinamode im 17. und 18. Jahrhundert, Ausstellung vom 16. September bis 11. November 1973 im Schloß Charlottenburg, Berlin. Berlin: Verwaltung der Staatlichen Schlösser und Gärten, 1973.

Chinese Courtship. In Verse. To Which Is Added an Appendix, Treating the Revenue in China. Translated by Peter Perring Thoms. Macao: East India Company and London: Parbury, Allen, and Kingsbury, 1824.

Ching, Julia, and Willard G. Oxtoby. "Discourse on the Natural Theology of the Chinese." In *Moral Enlightenment: Leibniz and Wolff on China*, ed. Julia Ching and Willard G. Oxtoby, 87–141. Nettetal: Steyler Verlag, 1992.

Clossey, Luke. *Salvation and Globalization in the Early Jesuit Missions*. Cambridge: Cambridge University Press, 2008.

Confucius Sinarum philosophus. Translated by Prosperi Intorcetta, Christian Herdtrich, Francisci Rougemont, and Philipp Couplet. Paris: Daniel Horthemel, 1687.

Conway, Charles Abbot, Jr. *The Vita Christi of Ludolph of Saxony and Late Medieval Devotion Centred on the Incarnation: A Descriptive Analysis*. Salzburg: Analecta Cartusiana, 1976.

Correia-Afonso, John, SJ. *Jesuit Letters and Indian History, 1542–1773*. Oxford: Oxford University Press, 1969.

Cosmo, Nicola di. "The Manchu Conquest in World Historical Perspective: A Note on Trade and Silver." *Journal of Central Eurasian Studies* 1 (2009): 43–60.

Cowan, Alex. "Nodes, Networks and Hinterlands." In *Cultural Exchange in Early Modern Europe,* edited by Donatella Calabi and Stephen Turk Christensen, 2:28–41. Cambridge: Cambridge University Press, 2007.

Damrosch, David. *What Is World Literature?* Princeton, NJ: Princeton University Press, 2003.

Das ärgerliche Leben und schreckliche Ende des viel berüchtigren Ertz-Schwartzkünstlers D. Johannis Fausti . . . und einem Anhang von den Lapponischen Wahrsager-Paucken wieauch sonst etlichen zauberischen Geschichten. Nürnberg: Endters, 1717.

Das Liebthätige Gera gegen die Salzburgischen Emigranten. Frankfurt, 1732.

Davids, Karel. "Dutch and Spanish Global Networks of Knowledge in the Early Modern Period: Structures, Changes and Limitations." Paper presented at the Iberian-Netherlandish Knowledge Exchange, Barcelona, November 27–29, 2009.

Debon, Günther. "Goethe erklärt in Heidelberg einen chinesischen Roman." In *Goethe und China—China und Goethe,* edited by Günther Debon and Adrian Hsia, 51–62. Bern: Peter Lang, 1985.

——. *China zu Gast in Weimar. 18 Studien und Streiflichter.* Heidelberg: Brigitte Guderjahn Verlag, 1994.

——. "Goethes Berührungen mit China," *Goethe Jahrbuch* 117 (2000): 46–55.

Dekoninck, Ralph. "On the Threshold of a Spiritual Journey: The Appealing Function of a Jesuit Frontispiece (Antwerp, 1593–1640)." In *Le Monde est une peinture: Jesuitische Identität und die Rolle der Bilder,* edited by Elisabeth Oy-Marra and Volker R. Remmert, 71–84. Berlin: Akademie Verlag, 2011.

Deleuze, Gilles. *Negotiations.* New York: Columbia University Press, 1990.

Demarchi, Franco. "Martino Martini und die Chinamission der Jesuiten im 17. Jahrhundert." In *Martini Martini (1614–1661) und die Chinamission im 17. Jahrhundert,* edited by Roman Malek and Arnold Zingerle, 25–49. Sankt Augustin: Institut Monumenta Sinica, 2000.

Dharampal-Frick, Gita. *Indien im Spiegel deutscher Quellen der Frühen Neuzeit (1500–1750): Studien zu einer interkulturellen Konstellation.* Tübingen: Max Niemeyer, 1994.

Diderot, Denis. *Rameau's Nephew—Le Neveau de Rameau: A Multi-Media Bilingual Edition,* edited by Marian Hobson, Kate E. Tunstall, and Caroline Warman. N. p.: Open Books Classics, 2016.

Ditmanson, Peter. "Venerating the Martyrs of the 1402 Usurpation: History and Memory in the Mid- and Late Ming Dynasty." *T'oung Pao* 93.1/3 (2007): 110–58.

Dodds, Phil. "'One Vast Empire': China, Progress, and the Scottish Enlightenment." *Global Intellectual History* 3.1 (2018): 47–70.

Doderer, Heimito von. *Die Strudlhofstiege.* Munich: dtv, 1951.

Dohm, Burkhard. "Radikalpietistin und 'schöne Seele': Susanna Katharina von Klettenberg." In *Goethe und der Pietismus,* edited by Hans-Georg Kemper and Hans Schneider, 111–34. Tübingen: Franckesche Stiftung and Niemeyer Verlag, 2001.

Donnelly, John Patrick, SJ, ed. *Jesuit Writings of the Early Modern Period, 1540–1640.* Indianapolis: Hackett, 2006.

Doody, Margaret Ann. *A Natural Passion: A Study of the Novels of Samuel Richardson.* Oxford: Clarendon Press, 1974.

Doyle, Laura. "Inter-Imperiality." *Interventions: International Journal of Post-colonial Studies* 16.2 (2014): 159–96.

Dryden, John. *The Indian Emperour.* London, 1667. http://ezaccess.libraries.psu.edu/login?url=https://www-proquest-com.ezaccess.libraries.psu.edu/books/indian-emperour-1667/docview/2138574641/se-2?accountid=13158.

Duhr, Bernhard, SJ. *Deutsche Auslandsehnsucht im achtzehnten Jahrhundert, Aus der überseeischen Missionsarbeit deutscher Jesuiten.* Stuttgart: Ausland und Heimat Verlag, 1928.

Dünnhaupt, Gerhard. "Erasmus Francisci, ein Nürnberger Polyhistor des siebzehnten Jahrhunderts. Biographie und Bibliographie." *Philobiblon* 19.4 (1975): 272–303.

Duyvendak, J. J. L. "Early Chinese Studies in Holland." *T'oung Pao* 32.1 (1936): 293–344.

Eckermann, Johann Peter. *Gespräche mit Goethe in den letzten Jahren seines Lebens.* Edited by Christoph Michel and Hans Grüters. Berlin: Deutscher Klassiker Verlag, 2011.

Eco, Umberto. *The Book of Legendary Lands.* Translated by Alastair McEwen. New York: Rizzoli, 2013.

Eichendorff, Joseph von. *Eichendorff Werke: Geschichte der Poesie, Schriften zur Literaturgeschichte.* Edited by Hartwig Schultz. Frankfurt: Deutscher Klassiker Verlag, 1990.

"Edmund Burkes Schilderung der gegenwärtigen Lage der Englisch-Ostindischen Gesellschaft." *Historisches Portefeuille* 3.7 (July 1784): 75–101.

Endean, Philip. "The Spiritual Exercises." In *The Cambridge Companion to the Jesuits,* edited by Thomas Worcester, 52–68. Cambridge: Cambridge University Press, 2008.

Endres, Johannes. "Unähnliche Ähnlichkeit. Zu Analogie, Metapher und Verwandtschaft." In *Similitudo. Konzepte der Ähnlichkeit in den Künsten,* edited by Martin Gaier, Jeanette Kohl, and Alberto Saviello, 27–56. Munich: Wilhelm Fink, 2012.

Enns, Anthony. "Introduction: The Media Philosophy of Sybille Krämer." In Sybille Krämer, *Medium, Messenger, Transmission: An Approach to Media Philosophy,* translated by Anthony Enns. Amsterdam: University of Amsterdam Press, 2015.

Epstein, Maram. *Competing Discourses: Orthodoxy, Authenticity, and Engendered Meanings in Late Imperial Chinese Fiction.* Cambridge, MA: Harvard University Press, 2001.

Erlin, Matt. *Necessary Luxuries: German Literature and the World of Goods, 1770–1815.* Ithaca, NY: Cornell University Press, 2014.

Ettinghausen, Henry. *How the Press Began: The Pre-Periodical Printed News in Early Modern Europe.* Coruña: Janus, 2015.

Feder, Johann Heinrich Georg. [Review of *Wealth of Nations*]. *Göttingischen Anzeigen von gelehrten Sachen* (March 10, 1777): 234–40.

Fenger, J. F. *History of the Tranquebar Mission*. Tranquebar: Evangelical Lutheran Press, 1863.

Festa, Lynn. *Sentimental Figures of Empire in Eighteenth-Century England and France*. Baltimore: Johns Hopkins University Press, 2006.

Fichte, Johann Gottlieb. *Werke 1797–1798*. Edited by Reinhard Leuth, Hans Gliwitzky, and Richard Schottky. Stuttgartt: Friedrich Frommann, 1970.

———.*The Science of Knowledge*. Translated by Peter Heath and John Lachs. Cambridge: Cambridge University Press, 1982.

Fleischacker, Samuel. "Philosophy in Moral Practice: Kant and Adam Smith.' *Kant-Studien* 82.3 (1991): 249–68.

Fletcher, John Edwards. *A Study of the Life and Works of Athanasius Kircher, "Germanus incredibilis."* Leiden: Brill, 2011.

Fletcher, Joseph. "Integrative History: Parallels and Interconnections in the Early Modern Period, 1500–1800." *Journal of Turkish Studies* 9.1 (1985): 37–57.

Florenius, Paulus, and Christianus Francken. *The Doctrines and Practises of the Societies of Jesuites*. London: George Gibbs, 1630.

Foertsch, Henrike. "Missionare als Sprachensammler, Zum Umfang der philologischen Arbeit der Jesuiten in Asien, Afrika und Lateinamerika. Auswertung einer Datenbank." In *Wege durch Babylon: Missionare, Sprachstudien und interkulturelle Kommunikation*, edited by Reinhard Wendt, 43–73. Tübingen: Gunter Narr, 1998.

Folger, Robert. *Writing as Poaching: Interpellation and Self-Fashioning in Colonial relaciones de méritos y servicios*. Leiden: Brill, 2011.

Forman-Barzilai, Fonna. "Adam Smith as Globalization Theorist." *Critical Review* 14.4 (2000): 391–419.

———. *Adam Smith and the Circles of Sympathy: Cosmopolitanism and Moral Theory*. Cambridge: Cambridge University Press, 2010.

Förster, Eckhart. *Die 25 Jahre der Philosophie: Eine systematische Rekonstruktion*. Klostermann: Frankfurt, 2012.

The Fortunate Union. Translated by John Francis Davis. London: Oriental Translation Fund, 1829.

Foucault, Michel. *The Archeology of Knowledge and the Discourse on Language*. Translated by A. M. Sheridan Smith. New York: Pantheon, 1972.

———. *The Order of Things: An Archeology of the Human Sciences*. New York: Vintage, 1973.

———. "Of Other Spaces." Translated by Jay Miskowiec. *Diacritics* 16.1 (1986): 22–27.

Francisci, Erasmus. *Neu-polirter Geschicht- Kunst- und Sitten-Spiegel ausländischer Völcker fürnemlich Der Sineser, Japaner, Indostaner, Javaner, Malabaren, Peguaner, Siammer, . . . und theils anderer Nationen mehr*. Nürnberg: Johann Andreae Endters und Wolfgang des Jüngern Erben, 1670.

Francken, Christian. *Ein Gesprech von Jesuiten: allen frommen Christen, die Jesuiter und ihre Religion recht zu erkennen, vast nützlich zu lessen*. Basel, 1581.

Francken, Gotthilf August, founding editor. *Der Königlich Dänischen Missionarien aus Ost-Indien eingesandter Ausführlichen Berichten.* Halle: Waysen Hauses, 1735–1772. https://digital.francke-halle.de/fsdhm.

Freedberg, David. *The Power of Images: Studies in the History and Theory of Response.* Chicago: University of Chicago Press, 1989.

Frevert, Ute. *Emotions in History—Lost and Found.* Budapest: Central European Press, 2011.

Friedrich, Markus. "Communication and Bureaucracy in the Early Modern Society of Jesus." *Zeitschrift für Schweizerische Religions- und Kirchengeschichte* 101 (2007): 49–75.

——. "Circulating and Compiling the *Littrerae Annuae*. Towards a History of the Jesuit System of Communication." *Archivum Historicum Societatis Iesu* 77 (2008): 3–39.

——. *Der lange Arm Roms: Globale Verwaltung und Kommunikation im Jesuitenorden 1540–1773.* Frankfurt: Campus Verlag, 2011.

——. "Organisation und Kommunikationsstrukturen der Gesellschaft Jesu in der Frühen Neuzeit/Organization and Communication in the Society of Jesus (1540–1773)." In *Etappen der Globalisierung in christumsgeschichtlicher Perspektive/ Phases of Globalization in the History of Christianity*, edited by Klaus Koschorke, 83–104. Wiesbaden: Harrassowitz, 2012.

Galli, Barbara E. *Cultural Writings of Franz Rosenzweig.* Syracuse, NY: Syracuse University Press, 2000.

Gellert, Christian Fürchtegott. "Praktische Abhandlung von dem guten Geschmack in Briefen." *Sämtiche Schriften.* Berlin: Weidmann, 1867.

Geulen, Eva. *Aus dem Leben der Form: Goethes Morphologie und die Nager.* Berlin: August, 2016.

Gillet, Joseph Eugene. "De Nederlandsche letterkunde in Duitschland in de Zeventiende eeuw." *Tidjschrift voor Nederlandsche Taal- en Letterkunde* 33 (1914): 1–31

Göchhausen, Ernst August Anton. *Enthüllung des Systems der Weltbürger-Republik, In Briefen aus der Verlassenschaft eines Freymaurers.* Rome 1786.

Goebel, Rolf J. *Constructing China: Kafka's Orientalist Discourse.* Columbia, SC: Camden House, 1997.

Goedeke, Karl. *Grundrisz zur Geschichte der deutschen Dichtung aus den Quellen.* Hanover: L. Ehlermann, 1859.

Goethe, Johann Wolfgang. *Goethes Werke.* Weimar: Hermann Böhlaus Nachfolger, 1887–1919. Cited as WA.

——. *Goethes Briefe.* Edited by Karl Robert Mandelkow. Hamburg: Christian Wegner, 1964.

——. *Werke.* Edited by Erich Trunz. Munich: C. H. Beck, 1982. Cited as HA.

——. *Sämtliche Werke. Briefe, Tagebücher und Gespräche.* Edited by Karl Eibl. Frankfurt: Deutscher Klassiker Verlag, 1987. Cited as FA.

——. *West-östlicher Divan.* Edited by Hendrik Birus. Berlin: Deutscher Klassiker Verlag, 2010.

Goeze, Johann Melchior. *Kurze aber nothwendige Erinnerungen über die Leiden des jungen Werthers.* Hamburg: Schröders Wittwer, 1775.

Goitein, S. D., and Mordechai Akiva Friedman. *Indian Traders of the Middle Ages, Documents from the Cairo Geniza.* Leiden: Brill, 2008.

Golvers, Noël. *Building Humanistic Libraries in Late Imperial China: Circulation of Books, Prints and Letters between Europe and China.* Rome: Edizioni Nuova Cultura, 2011.

Goodman, Dana. *The Republic of Letters: A Cultural History of the French Enlightenment.* Ithaca, NY: Cornell University Press, 1996.

Goodrich, L. Carrington, and Chaoying Fang, eds. *Dictionary of Ming Biography, 1368–1644.* New York: Columbia University Press, 1976.

Görres, Joseph. *Die teutschen Volksbüchern.* Heidelberg: Mohr und Zimmer, 1807.

Grimm, Jacob and Wilhelm. *Deutsches Wörterbuch.* Leipzig: Hirzel, 1854. http://woerterbuchnetz.de/cgi-bin/WBNetz/call_wbgui_py_from_form?sigle=DWB&mode=Volltextsuche&lemid=GM06319#XGM06319.

Guggisberg, Kurt. "Johann Caspar Lavater und die Idee der 'Imitatio Christi.'" *Zwingliana* 7.5 (1941): 337–66.

Guthke, Karl S. *Goethes Weimar und "Die große Öffnung in die weite Welt."* Wiesbaden: Harrassowitz, 2001.

Hadot, Pierre. *Philosophy as a Way of Life.* Translated by Michael Chase. Oxford: Blackwell, 1995.

Hagdorn, Christian. *Aeyquan, oder der Große Mogol. Das ist Chinesische und Indische Stahts-Kriegs- und Liebes-geschichte.* Amsterdam: Jacob von Mörs, 1670.

Halde, Johann Baptista du. *Description géographique, historique, chronologique, politique, et physique de l'empire de la chine et de la tartarie chinoise*, vol. 1. Paris: Henri Scheurleer, 1736.

Hamburger, Käte. *Das Mitleid.* Stuttgart: Klett-Cotta, 1986.

Hamm, Heinz. *Goethe und die französische Zeitschrift Le Globe: Eine Lektüre im Zeichen der Weltliteratur.* Weimar: Hermann Böhlaus Nachfolger, 1998.

Hanser, Jessica. *Mr. Smith Goes to China: Three Scots in the Making of Britain's Global Empire.* New Haven, CT: Yale University Press, 2019.

Harloe, Katherine. "Sympathy, Tragedy, and the Morality of Sentiment in Lessing's Laocoon." In *Rethinking Lessing's Laocoon: Antiquity, Enlightenment, and the 'Limits' of Painting a Poem*, edited by Avi Lifschitz and Michael Squire, 158–78. Oxford: Oxford University Press, 2017.

Harris, Steven J. "Confession-Building, Long-Distance Networks, and the Organization of Jesuit Science." *Early Science and Medicine* 1.3 (1996): 287–318.

——. "Long-Distance Corporations, Big Sciences, and the Geography of Knowledge." *Configurations* 6.2 (1998): 269–304.

Harst, Joachim. *Heilstheater: Figur des barocken Trauerspiels zwischen Gryphius und Kleist.* Munich: Wilhelm Fink, 2012.

Hart, Henry H. *Marco Polo: Venetian Adventurer*. Norman: Oklahoma University Press, 1967.

Hawhee, Debra. "Looking into Aristotle's Eyes: Toward a Theory of Rhetorical Vision." *Advances in the History of Rhetoric* 14.2 (2011): 139–65.

Hau Kiou Choaan, or The Pleasing History. A Translation from the Chinese Language in Four Volumes with Notes. London: Dodsley, 1761.

Hayot, Eric. *The Hypothetical Mandarin: Sympathy, Modernity, and Chinese Pain*. Oxford: Oxford University Press, 2009.

Healey, Patsy. "Relational Complexity and the Imaginative Power of Strategic Spatial Planning." *European Planning Studies* 14.4 (May 2006): 525–46.

Hegel, Georg Wilhelm Friedrich. *The Philosophy of History*. Translated by J. Sibree. New York: Dover, 1956.

——. *Vorlesungen über die Geschichte der Philosophie*. Edited by Eva Moldenhauer and Karl Markus Michel. Frankfurt: Suhrkamp, 1986.

——. *Vorlesungen über die Philosophie der Geschichte*. Edited by Eva Moldenhauer and Karl Markus Michel. Frankfurt: Suhrkamp, 1986.

Hegel, Robert. *Reading Illustrated Fiction in Late Imperial China*. Stanford, CA: Stanford University Press, 1998.

Heidsieck, Arnold. "Adam Smith's Influence on Lessing's View of Man and Society." *Lessing Yearbook* 15 (1983): 125–44.

Heine, Heinrich. *Historisch-Kritische Gesamtausgabe der Werke*. Edited by Manfred Windfuhr. Hamburg: Hoffmann and Campe, 1987.

Hesselink, Reinier H. "Memorable Embassies: The Secret History of Arnoldus Montanus' *Gedenkwaerdige Gesantschappen*." *Quaerando* 32.1 (2002): 99–123.

Hintze, Hans-Jörg. "Christian Missionaries and Their Perceptions of Hinduism: Intercultural Exchange." In *Halle and the Beginning of Protestant Christianity in India*, edited by Andreas Gross, Y. Vincent Kumaradoss, and Heike Liebau, 2:885–902. Halle: Verlag der Franckeschen Stiftungen, 2006.

Hoffman, E. T. A. "Der goldne Topf." *Fantasie- und Nachtstücke*. Darmstadt: Wissenschaftliche Buchgesellschaft, 1985.

Hohendahl, Peter Uwe. "Zum Erzählproblem des utopischen Romans im 18. Jahrhundert." In *Gestaltungsgeschichte und Gesellschaftsgeschichte*, edited by Helmut Kreuzer and Katie Hamburger, 79–114. Stuttgart: Metzler, 1969.

Hosne, Ana Caroline. *The Jesuit Missions to China and Peru, 1570–1610: Expectations and Appraisals of Expansionism*. London: Routledge, 2013.

Hsia, Adrian. *Chinesia: The European Construction of China in the Literature of the 17th and 18th Centuries*. Berlin: De Gruyter, 1998.

——. "The Jesuit Plays on China and Their Relation to the Profane Literature." In *Mission und Theater, Japan und China auf den Bühnen der Gesellschaft Jesu*, edited by Adrian Hsia and Ruprecht Wimmer. 209–39. Regensburg: Schnell and Steiner, 2005.

Hsia, Adrian, and Ruprecht Wimmer, eds. *Mission und Theater: Japan und China auf den Bühnen der Gesellschaft Jesu*. Regensburg: Schnell and Steiner, 2005.

Hsia, Florence. *Sojourners in a Strange Land: Jesuits and Their Scientific Missions in Late Imperial China.* Chicago: University of Chicago Press, 2009.

Hsia, Ronnie Po-chia. "Twilight in the Imperial City: The China Mission, 1748–60." In *The Jesuits II: Cultures, Sciences, and the Arts, 1540–1173,* edited by John W. O'Malley, SJ, Gauvin Alexander Bailey, Steven J. Harris, and T. Frank Kennedy, SJ, 725–37. Toronto: University of Toronto Press, 2006.

——. *A Jesuit in the Forbidden City: Matteo Ricci 1552–1610.* Oxford: Oxford University Press, 2010.

——. "Imperial China and the Christian Mission." In *A Companion to the Early Modern Catholic Global Missions,* edited by Ronnie Po-chia Hsia, 344–64. Leiden: Brill, 2018.

Hume, David. *Enquiries Concerning Human Understanding and Concerning the Principals of Morals.* Edited by P. H. Nidditch. Oxford: Clarendon Press, 1975.

——. *A Treatise of Human Nature.* New York: Barnes and Noble, 2005.

Ibbett, Katherine. "Fellow-Feeling," In *Early Modern Emotions: An Introduction,* edited by Susan Broomhall, 61–64. London: Routledge, 2017.

Imhof, Dirk. "Between Philip II and William of Orange: The Correspondence of Christopher Plantin (ca. 1520–1589)." In *Between Scylla and Charybdis: Learned Letter Writers Navigating the Reefs of Religious and Political Controversy in Early Modern Europe,* edited by Jeanine De Landtsheer and Henk Nellen, 218–32. Leiden: Brill, 2011.

Israel, Jonathan I. *Radical Enlightenment: Philosophy and the Making of Modernity (1650–1750).* Oxford: Oxford University Press, 2001.

Iu-Kiao-Li, ou Les deux cousines. Translated by Abel Rémusat. Paris: Libraire Moutarde, 1826.

Iu-Kiao-Li: or, the Two Fair Cousins, from the French Version of M. Abel-Remusat. London: Hunt and Clark, 1827.

Jantz, Harold, ed. *Fortitudo christiana in Tito Japone exhibita—Obsigende Glauben-Lieb Titi Eines Edlen Japonesers, Vorgestellt auf der Schau-Bühne von der Studierenden Jugend des Chur-Fürstlichen Gymnasii Societatis JESU zu Mindelheim, den 4. Und 6. Tag Herbstmonats 1724.* Middelheim: Adolph Joseph Ebel, 1724.

Jaspers, Karl. *Vom Ursprung und Ziel der Geschichte.* Frankfurt: Fischer, 1955.

Jauß, Hans Robert. *Ästhetische Erfahrung und literarische Hermeneutik.* Frankfurt: Suhrkamp, 1982.

Jayne, Sears Reynolds. *Marsilio Ficino's Commentary on Plato's 'Symposium.'* Columbia: University of Missouri Press, 1944.

Jeyaraj, Daniel. *Genealogy of the South Indian Deities: An English Translation of Bartholomäus Ziegenbalg's Original German Manuscript with a Textual Analysis and Glossary.* London: Routledge, 2005.

——. "Mission Reports from South India and Their Impact on the Western Mind: The Tranquebar Mission of the Eighteenth Century." In *Converting Colonialism: Visions and Realities in Mission History, 1706–1914,* edited by Dana L. Robert, 21–42. Grand Rapids, MI: William B. Eerdmans, 2008.

Johnson, W. R. Review of *Virgil's Aeneid: Cosmos and Imperium* by Philip Hardie. *Classical Journal* 83.3 (1988): 269–271.

Ju-Kiao-Li, oder die beyden Basen, Ein Chinesischer Roman übersetzt von Abel Rémusat. Vienna: Schade, 1827.

Juneja, Monica. "'Malabarian' Dialogues: The Encounter between German Pietists and the Tamilian Populace during the Early Eighteenth Century." *Medieval History Journal* 5.2 (2002): 333–46.

Jürgens, Hanco. "On the Crossroads: Pietist, Orthodox and Enlightened Views on Mission in the Eighteenth Century." In *Halle and the Beginnings of Protestant Christianity in India*, edited by Andreas Gross, Y. Vincent Kumaradoss, and Heike Liebau, 1:7–36. Halle: Verlag des Franckeschen Stiftungen, 2006.

Kaempfer, Engelbert. *Geschichte und Beschreibung von Japan*. Edited by Christian Wilhelm von Dohm. Lemgo: Meyer, 1977.

Kaiser, Gerhard. *Pietismus und Patriotismus im literarischen Deutschland: Ein Beitrag zum Problem der Säkularistion*, 2nd ed. Frankfurt: Athenäum, 1973.

Kant, Immanuel. *Critique of Pure Reason*. Translated by Norman Kemp Smith. New York: St. Martin's Press, 1965.

——. "Perpetual Peace: A Philosophical Sketch." In *Kant's Political Writings*, translated by H. B. Nesbit, edited by Hans Reiss, 93–130. Cambridge: Cambridge University Press, 1970.

——. *Schriften zur Anthropologie, Geschichtsphilosophie, Politik und Pädagogik*. Vol. 11 of *Werkausgabe*, edited by Wilhelm Weischedel. Frankfurt: Suhrkamp, 1981.

Kern, Iso. "Matteo Riccis Verhältnis zum Buddhismus." *Monumenta Serica* 36 (1984–1985): 65–126.

Kircher, Athanasius. *China Illustra with Sacred and Secular Monuments, Various Spectacles of Nature and Art and Other Memoriabilia*. Translated by Charles Van Tuyl. Bloomington: Indiana University Press, 1987.

Kittler, Friedrich A. *Discourse Networks 1800/1900*. Translated by Michael Meteer and Chris Cullens. Stanford, CA: Stanford University Press, 1990.

——. *Optische Medien, Berliner Vorlesung 1999*. Berlin: Merve, 2002.

Kittler, Wolf. *Der Turmbau zu Babel und das Schweigen der Sirenen, Über das Reden, das Schweigen, die Stimme und die Schrift in vier Texten von Franz Kafka*. Erlangen: Palm und Enke, 1985.

Klawitter, Arne. *Ästhetische Resonanz, Zeichen und Schriftästhetik in der deutschsprachigen Literatur und Geistesgeschichte*. Göttingen: V and Runipress, 2015.

Klein, Johannes. *Geschichte der deutschen Lyrik*. Wiesbaden: Frank Steiner, 1960.

Kleingeld, Pauline. "Six Varieties of Cosmopolitanism in Late Eighteenth-Century Germany." *Journal of the History of Ideas* 60.3 (1999): 505–24.

Kommerell, Max. *Gedanken über Gedichte*, 4th ed. Frankfurt: Klostermann, 1985.

Kopper, John M. "Building Walls and Jumping over Them: Constructions in Franz Kafka's 'Beim Bau der chinesischen Mauer.'" *MLN* 98.3 (1983): 351–65.

Koschorke, Albrecht. *Körperströme und Schriftverkehr: Mediologies des 18. Jahrhunderts*. Munich: Wilhlem Fink, 1999.

——. "Selbststeuerung: David Hartley's Assoziationstheorie, Adam Smith's Sympathielehre und die Dampfmachine von James Watt." In *Das Laokoon-Paradigma, Zeichenregime im 18. Jahrhundert*, edited by Inge Baxmann, Michael Franz and Wolfgang Schäffner, 179–90. Berlin: Akademie Verlag, 2000.

Kracauer, Siegfried. *The Mass Ornament: Weimar Essays*. Translated by Thomas Y. Levin. Cambridge, MA: Harvard University Press, 1995.

Krämer, Sybille. *Medium, Messenger, Transmission: An Approach to Media Philosophy*. Translated by Anthony Enns. Amsterdam: University of Amsterdam Press, 2015.

Kurtz, Joachim. "Framing European Technology in Seventeenth-Century China; Rhetorical Strategies in Jesuit Paratexts." In *Cultures of Knowledge; Technology in Chinese History*, edited by Dagmar Schäfer, 209–32. Leiden: Brill, 2011.

Kutcher, Norman. "The Fifth Relationship: Dangerous Friendships in the Confucian Context." *American Historical Review* 105.5 (2000): 1615–29.

Kutcher, Norman, and Edwin J. Van Kley. *Asia in the Making of Europe*, vols. 6–9. Chicago: University of Chicago Press, 1965–1993.

La Croze, Maturin Veyssiere. *Abbildung des Indianischen Christenstaates*, Translated by G. Chr. Bohnstedt. Leipzig: Samuel Benjamin Walther, 1739.

Lach, Donald. "The Chinese Studies of Andreas Müller." *Journal of the American Oriental Society* 60.4 (1940): 564–75.

——. *Asia in the Making of Europe*, vols. 1–2. Chicago: University of Chicago Press, 1965–1993.

Lach, Donald, and Edwin J. Van Kley. *Asia in the Making of Europe*, vol. 3. Chicago: University of Chicago Press, 1993.

Lange, Horst. "Goethe and Spinoza: A Reconsideration." *Goethe Yearbook* 17 (2011): 11–33.

Langen, August. *Der Wortschatz des deutschen Pietismus*. Tübingen: Max Niemeyer, 1954.

Larner, John. *Marco Polo and the Discovery of the World*. New Haven, CT: Yale University Press, 1999.

Latour, Bruno. *Science in Action: How to Follow Scientists and Engineers through Society*. Cambridge, MA: Harvard University Press, 1987.

Law, John. "On the Methods of Long-Distance Control: Vessels, Navigation, and the Portuguese Route to India." In *Power, Action and Belief: A New Sociology of Knowledge?*, edited by John Law, 234–63. Henley: Routledge, 1986.

Lee, Meredith. "Goethes Chinesisch-Deutsche Jahres- und Tageszeiten." In *Goethe und China—China und Goethe*, edited by Günther Debon and Adrian Hsia, 37–50. Bern: Peter Lang, 1985.

Le Globe, Journal Philosophique et Littéraire 4.57 (December 23, 1826).

Lehmann, Arno. *Es began in Tranquebar: die Geschichte der ersten evangelischen Kirche in Indien*. Berlin: Evangelische Verlagsanstalt, 1956.

Leibniz, Gottfried Wilhelm. *Sämtliche Schriften und Briefe*. Edited by Deutsche Akademie der Wissenschaften zu Berlin. Darmstadt: O. Reichl, 1923.

——.*The Preface to Leibniz' Novissima Sinica*. Translated by Donald Lach. Honolulu: University of Hawaii Press, 1957.

Leitmeir, Christian Thomas and Bernard Klingenstein. "Catholic Music in the Diocese of Augsburg c. 1600: A Reconstructed Tricinium Anthology and Its Confessional Implications." *Early Music History* 21 (2002): 117–73.

Lenz, Jakob Michael Reinhold. *Werke und Schriften*. Stuttgart: Gouverts 1966.

Lessing, Gotthold. "Marco Polo, aus einer Handschrift ergänzt, und au seiner andern sehr zu verbessern." In *Zur Geschichte und Litteratur, aus den Schätzen der herzoglichen Bibliothek zu Wolfenbüttel, Zweyter Beytrag*, edited by Gotthold Lessing, 259–98. Braunschweig: Waysenhaus, 1773.

——. *Lessings Werke*, edited by Paul Stapf. Berlin: Deutsche Buch Gemeinschaft, 1957.

——. *Werke*, edited by Herbert Georg Göpfert and Karl Eibl. Munich: C. Hanser, 1970.

Leung, K. C. "Chinese Courtship: The Huajian Ji in English Translation." *CHINOPERL: Journal of Chinese Oral and Performing Literature* 20.1 (1997): 269–88.

Levy, Evonne. "Early Modern Jesuit Arts and Jesuit Visual Culture: A View from the Twenty-First Century." *Journal of Jesuit Studies* 1 (2014): 66–87.

Li, Menjun. "Master of Heavenly Flowers Scripture: Constructing Tianhua zang zhuren's—Three Personae as Publisher, Commentator, and Writer of Scholar-Beauty Fiction." MA thesis, Ohio State University, 2009.

Li-bing, Bai. "On *Yijing* in Chinese and English Nature Poetry: The Case Study of Wordsworth and Wang Wei" *US-China Foreign Language* 12.5 (2014): 415–21.

Lillo, George. "The London Merchant." In *Eighteenth-Century Plays*, edited by Ricardo Quintana. New York: Modern Library, 1952.

Liu, Yu. "The Jesuits and the Anti-Jesuits: The Two Different Connections of Leibniz with China." *Eighteenth Century* 43.2 (2002): 161–74.

Locke, John. *The Works of John Locke*. London: Thomas Davison, 1823.

Lodenstein, Jodocus van. "Jesus Geboren." *Uyt-spanningen, behelsende eenige stigtelyke liederen*. Utrecht: Willem Clerck, 1676. http://www.dbnl.org/tekst/lode002uyt_01_01/lode002uyt_01_01_0077.php.

Logan, Anne-Marie, and Liam M. Brockey. "Nicolas Trigault, SJ: A Portrait by Peter Paul Rubens." *Metropolitan Museum Journal* 38 (2003): 157–67.

Longo, Lucia. "Martino Martinis *Traktat über die Freundschaft (1661)*." In *Martini Martini (1614–1661) und die Chinamission im 17. Jahrhundert*, edited by Roman Malek and Arnold Zingerle, 184–99. Sankt Augustin: Institut Monumenta Sinica, 2000.

Longxi, Zhang. "The Myth of the Other: China in the Eyes of the West." *Critical Inquiry* 15.1 (1988):108–31.

Lovejoy, Arthur O. *Essays in the History of Ideas*. Westport, CT: Greenwood Press, 1978.

Loyola, Ignatius. *The Spiritual Exercises of St. Ignatius Loyola*. Translated by Elisabeth Meier Tetlow. Lanham, MD: University Press of America, 1987.

——. *The Spiritual Exercises and Selected Works*. Edited by George E. Ganss, SJ. New York: Paulist Press, 1991.

Ludolph of Saxony, Carthusian. *The Life of Jesus Christ*. Translated by Milton T. Walsh. Collegeville, MN: Liturgical Press, 2018.

Ma, Ning. *The Age of Silver: The Rise of the Novel East and West*. New York: Oxford University Press, 2016.

Macfie A. L. *The Individual in Society: Papers on Adam Smith*. London: George Allen and Unwin, 1967.

Mandeville, Bernard. *The Fable of the Bees*. London: Penguin 1970.

Manger, Klaus. "Wielands Kosmopoliten." In *Europäische Sozietätsbewegung und demokratische Tradition: Die europäischen Akademien der Frühen Neuzeit zwischen Frührenaissance und Spätaufklärung*, edited by Klaus Garber, Heinz Wismann, and Winfried Siebers, 1637–1667. Tübingen: Niemeyer, 1996.

Mani, B. Venkat. *Recoding World Literature: Libraries, Print Culture, and Germany's Pact with Books*. New York: Fordham University Press, 2017.

Marin, Louis. *Utopics: The Semiological Play of Textual Spaces*. Translated by Robert A. Vollrath. Amherst, NY: Humanity Books, 1984.

Marinetti, Filippo. "Technical Manifesto of Futurist Literature." In *Futurism: An Anthology*, edited by Lawrence Rainey, Christine Poggi, and Laura Wittman, 119–24. New Haven, CT: Yale University Press, 2009.

Martin, A. Lynn. *The Jesuit Mind: The Mentality of an Elite in Early Modern France*. Ithaca, NY: Cornell University Press, 1988.

Martinec, Thomas. "Übersetzung und Adaption, Lessings Verhältnis zu Francis Hutcheson." In *'ihrem Originale nachzudenken': Zu Lessings Übersetzungen*, edited by Helmut Berthold, 95–114. Tübingen: Niemeyer, 2008.

Martini, Fritz. "Nachwort." In Christoph Martin Wieland, *Werke*, vol. 3, edited by Fritz Martini and Reinhard Döhl, Munich: Carl Hanser, 1967.

Martini, Martino. *Bellum Tartaricum, or the Conquest of the Great and Most Renowned Empire of China, by the Invasion of the Tartars*. London: John Crook, 1654.

——. *Historische Beschreibung deß Tartarischen Kriegs in Sina*. Munich: Lucas Straub, 1654.

Marx, Karianne J. *The Usefulness of the Kantian Philosophy: How Karl Leonhard Reinhold's Commitment to Enlightenment Influenced His Reception of Kant*. Berlin: De Gruyter 2011.

Marx, Karl. "Revolution in China and in Europe." In *On Colonialism*, 15–23. Moscow: Foreign Languages Publishing, 1960.

McKenna, Antony. "Klandestine Philosophie." Translated by Astrid Finke and Gloria Buschor-Kotzor. In *Radikalaufklärung*, edited by Jonathan I. Israel and Martin Mulsow, 149–86. Berlin: Suhrkamp, 2014.

McLuhan, Marshall. *Understanding Media: The Extensions of Man*. Cambridge, MA: MIT Press, 1994.

McMahon, Keith. "The Institution of Polygamy in the Chinese Imperial Palace." *Journal of Asian Studies* 72.4 (2013): 917–36.

Medick, Hans, and Pamela Selwyn. "Historical Event and Contemporary Experience: The Capture and Destruction of Magdeburg in 1631." *History Workshop Journal* 52 (Autumn 2001): 23–48.

Meng, Weiyan. *Kafka und China*. Munich: iudicum verlag, 1986.

Meng, Louis Luixi. "Idea-scape (*yijing*): Understanding Imagery in the Chinese Poetic Tradition." *Comparative Literature: East & West* 23.1 (2015): 29–48.

Merkel, R. F. "Herder und Hegel über China." *Sinica* 17 (1942): 5–26.

Meyer-Kalkus, Reinhart. *Wollust und Grausamkeit: Affektenlehre und Affektdarstellung in Lohensteins Dramatik*. Göttingen: Vandenhoeck and Ruprecht, 1986.

——. *Geschichte der literarischen Vortragskunst*. Berlin: Metzlar, 2020.

Meyer-Sickendiek, Burkhard. "Die Stimmung einer Stadt. Urbane Atmosphären in der Lyrik des 20. Jahrhunderts." *Weimarer Beiträge* 59.4 (2013): 558–79.

Miazek-Mecynska, Monika. "Polish Jesuits and Their Dreams about Missions in China, According to the *Litterae indipetae*." *Journal of Jesuit Studies* 5.3 (2018): 404–20.

Milne, Roderick R. "Line of Desire: The Body and the Spirit in the Pre-Erotic Texts of Christoph Martin Wieland." PhD dissertation, University of Toronto, 1998.

Mittmann, Jörg-Peter. "Das Prinzip der Selbstgewissheit. Fichte und die Entwicklung der nachkantischen Grundsatzphilosophie." PhD dissertation, University of Munich, 1992.

Molina, J. Michelle. *To Overcome Oneself: The Jesuit Self and Spirit of Global Expansion*. Berkeley: University of California Press, 2013.

Montanus, Arnold. *Denckwürdige Gesandtschafften der Ost-Indischen Gesellschaft in den Vereinigten Niederländern an unterschiedliche Keyser von Japan*. Amsterdam: Jacob Meurs, 1669.

Moritz, Karl Philipp. *Anton Reiser, Ein psychologischer Roman*. Frankfurt: Insel, 1979.

Mücke, Dorothea von. *Virtue and the Veil of Illusion: Generic Innovation and the Pedagogical Project in Eighteenth-Century Literature*. Stanford, CA: Stanford University Press, 1991.

Müller, Johannes, SJ. *Das Jesuitendrama in den Ländern deutscher Zunge vom Anfang (1555) bis zum Hochbarock (1665)*. Augsburg: Benno Filser, 1930.

Müller, Marion. *Zwischen Intertextualität und Interpretation: Friedrich Schillers dramaturgische Arbeiten 1796–1805*. Karlsruhe: KIT Publishing, 2004.

Müller-Bongard, Kristina. "Konzepte zur Konsolidierung einer jesuitischen Identität. Die Märtyrerzyklem der jesuitischen Kollegien in Rom." In *Le monde est une peinture. Jesuitische Identität und die Rolle der Bilder*, edited by Elisabeth Oy-Marra and Volker Remmert, 153–75. Berlin: Akademie, 2011.

Mulsow, Martin. "Socinianism, Islam and the Radical Uses of Arabic Scholarship." *Al-Qantara* 31.2 (2010): 549–86.

Mungello, David. "Die Quellen für das Chinabild Leibnizens." *Studia Leibnitiana* 14.2 (1982): 233–43.

——. *Curious Land: Jesuit Accommodation and the Origins of Sinology.* Honolulu: University of Hawaii Press, 1989.

Münkler, Marina. *Erfahrung des Fremden, Die Beschreibung Ostasiens in den Augenzeugenberichten des 13. Und 14. Jahrhunderts.* Berlin: Akademie Verlag, 2000.

Murr, Christoph Gottlieb von. *Haoh Kjöh Tschwen, d.i. Die angenehme Geschichte des Haoh Kjöh, Ein chinesischer Roman in vier Büchern, Aus dem Chinesischen in das Englische, und aus diesem in das Deutsche übersetzt.* Leipzig: Johann Friedrich Junius, 1766.

Muslim, Zahim Mohammed. "Lessing unter Islam: Eine Studie zu Lessings Auseinandersetzung mit dem Islam." PhD dissertation, Humboldt University, 2010.

Nassar, Dalia. "Spinoza in Schelling's Early Conception of Intellectual Intuition." In *Spinoza and German Idealism,* edited by Eckart Förster and Yitzhak Y. Melamed, 136–55. Cambridge: Cambridge University Press, 2012.

Navarette, Dominick Fernandez. *An Account of the Empire of China, Historical, Political, Moral and Religious.* London: Lintot, 1732.

Nebgen, Christoph. *Missionarsberufungen nach Übersee in drei Deutschen Provinzen der Gesellschaft Jesu im 17. und 18. Jahrhundert.* Regensburg: Schnell Steiner, 2007.

Nelles, Paul. "Seeing and Writing: The Art of Observation in the Early Jesuit Missions." *Intellectual History Review* 20.3 (2010): 317–33.

——. "*Casas y cartas*: Scribal Production and Material Pathways in Jesuit Global Communication (1547–1573)." *Journal of Jesuit Studies* 2.3 (2015): 421–50.

Niekerk, Carl. "Der Orient-Diskurs in Lessings *Hamburgische Dramaturgie.*" *Lessing Yearbook/Jahrbuch* 41 (2014):175–87.

Nietzsche, Friedrich. *On the Genealogy of Morals.* Translated by Walter Kaufmann. New York: Random House, 1967.

——. *Beyond Good and Evil.* Translated by R. J. Hollingdale. London: Penguin, 1973.

Nieuhof, John. *Het Gezantschap der Neêrlandtsche Oost-Indische Compagnie aan den Grooten Taratarischen Cham, den tegenwoordigen Keizer van China.* Amsterdam: Jacob van Meurs, 1665.

——. *Die Gesantschaft der Ost-Indischen Gesellschaft in den Vereinigten Niederländern und den Tartarischen Cham/und nunmehr auch Sinischen Keyser.* Amsterdam: Jacob Mörs, 1669.

——. *An Embassy from the East-India Company of the United Provinces, to the Grand Tartar Cham, Emperor of China . . . Englished and Set Forth with Their Several Sculptures by John Ogilby.* London: Ogilby, 1673.

Norden, Eduard. *Die antike Kunstprosa, vom VI. Jahrhundert v. Chr. bis in die Zeit der Renaissance,* vol. 2. Leipzig: B. G. Teubner, 1923.

Nouveaux Advis du Grand Royaume de la Chine, escrits par le P. Nicolas Lombard de la Compagnie de Iesus. Au T. R. P. Claude Aquaviua General de la mesme Compagnie; Et traduits en Francois par le P. Jean de Bordes. Paris: Rolin Thierry, 1602.

Noyes, John. "The World Map and the World of Goethe's *Weltliteratur.*" *Acta Germanica* 38 (2010): 128–45.

——. "Eradicating the Orientalist: Goethe's 'Chinesisch-deutsche Jahres- und Tageszeiten.'" In *China in the German Enlightenment*, edited by Bettina Brandt and Daniel L. Purdy, 142–64. Toronto: Toronto University Press, 2016.

Ohler, Norbert. *The Medieval Traveller*. Translated by Caroline Hillier. Woodbridge, Suffolk: Boydell, 1989.

Olbricht, Peter. *Das Postwesen in China unter der Mongolenherrschaft im 13. Und 14. Jahrhundert*. Wiesbaden: Harrassowitz, 1954.

O'Malley, John. *The First Jesuits*. Cambridge, MA: Harvard University Press, 1993.

"On Translation of Chinese Poetry." *Asiatic Journal* 2 (May 1830): 37.

Osbeck, Peter. *A Voyage to China and the East Indies*. Translated by John Reinhold Forster. London: Benjamin White, 1771.

Osinski, Jutta. "Eichendorffs Kulturkritik." *Aurora: Jahrbuch der Eichendorff-Gesellschaft* 61 (2001): 83–96.

Osterhammel, Jürgen. *Unfabling the East: The Enlightenment's Encounter with Asia*. Translated by Robert Savage. Princeton, NJ: Princeton University Press, 2018.

Pao, Lea. "Informational Practices in German Poetry: Ernst Meister, Oswald Egger, Friedrich Gottlieb Klopstock." PhD dissertation, Pennsylvania State University, 2017.

Parente, James. *Religious Drama and the Humanist Tradition: Christian Theater in Germany and in the Netherlands, 1500–1680*. Leiden: Brill, 1987.

Park, Peter. *Africa, Asia, and the History of Philosophy: Racism in the Formation of the Philosophical Canon, 1750–1830*. Albany: State University of New York Press, 2013.

Peters, John Durham. *The Marvelous Clouds: Toward a Philosophy of Elemental Media*. Chicago: University of Chicago Press, 2015.

Phillips, Kim A. *Before Orientalism: Asian Peoples and Cultures in European Travel Writing, 1245–1510*. Philadelphia: University of Pennsylvania Press, 2014.

Pizer, John. *The Idea of World Literature: History and Pedagogical Practice*. Baton Rouge: Louisiana State University Press, 2006.

Polo, Marco. *Devisement du monde ou Livre des Merveilles Récit de voyage* (1410–1412). Paris: Bibliotheque national de France, Manuscripts, Fr. 2810 fol. 1. https://gallica.bnf.fr/ark:/12148/btv1b52000858n/f9.planchecontact.

——. *The Travels of Marco Polo*. Translated by Ronald Latham. London: Penguin, 1958.

Porter, David. *Ideographia: The Chinese Cipher in Early Modern Europe*. Stanford, CA: Stanford University Press, 2001.

Proot, Goran, and Johan Verbercknoes. "Japonica in the Jesuit Drama of the Southern Netherlands." *Bulletin of Portuguese-Japanese Studies* 5 (December 2002): 27–47.

Pufendorf, Samuel von. *Ueber die Verfassung des deutschen Reiches.* Translated by Harry Breßlau. Berlin: Heimann, 1870.

Purdy, Daniel. *The Tyranny of Elegance: Consumer Cosmopolitanism in the Era of Goethe.* Baltimore: Johns Hopkins University Press, 1997.

——. "Chinese Ethics within the Radical Enlightenment: Christian Wolff." In *Radical Enlightenment*, edited by Carl Niekerk, 112–30. Amsterdam: Ropodi, 2018.

Rabbow, Paul. *Seelenführung, Methodie der Exerzitien in der Antike.* Munich: Kösel, 1954.

Rebhorn, Wayne. "Baldesar Castiglione, Thomas Wilson and the Courtly Body of Renaissance Rhetoric." *Rhetorica* 11.3 (1993): 241–78.

Reichert, Folker E. "Marco Polos Buch. Lesarten des Fremden." In *Fiktion des Fremden. Erkundung kultureller Grenzen in Literatur und Publizistik*, edited by Dietrich Harth. 180–202. Frankfurt: Fischer, 1994.

Reichwein, Adolf. *China und Europa: Geistige und Künstlerische Beziehungen im 18. Jahrhundert.* Berlin: Oesterheld, 1923.

Reinhold, Ernst. *Karl Leonhard Reinhold's Leben und litterarisches Wirken.* Jena: Friedrich Frommann, 1825.

Reinhold, Karl Leonhard. *Versuch einer neuen Theorie des menschlichen Vorstellungsvermögens*, 2nd ed. Prague: C. Widtmann and J. M. Mauke, 1795.

——. *Auswahl vermischter Schriften.* Jena: Mauke, 1797.

Rétif, Andre. "Breve histoire des Lettres édifiantes et curieuses." *Neue Zeitschrift für Missionswissenschaft = Nouvelle revue de science missionaire* 7 (1951): 37–50.

Ricci, Matteo, SJ. *China in the Sixteenth Century: The Journals of Matthew Ricci (1583–1610).* Translated by Louis J. Gallagher. New York: Random House, 1953.

——. *The True Meaning of the Lord in Heaven.* Translated by Douglas Lancashire and Peter Hu Kuo-chon, SJ. St. Louis, MO: Institute of Jesuit Sources, 1985.

Ringer, Fritz K. *The Decline of the German Mandarins: The German Academic Community, 1890–1933.* Cambridge, MA: Harvard University Press,1969.

Robertson, Ritchie. "*Weltliteratur* from Voltaire to Goethe." *Comparative Critical Studies* 12.2 (2015): 163–81.

Rochemonteix, Camille de, SJ, *Les Jésuites de la Nouvelle France au XVIIe siècle.* Paris: Letouzey et Ané, 1895.

Roeber, Anthony Gregg. *Hopes for Better Spouses: Protestant Marriage and Church Renewal in Early Modern Europe, India, and North America.* Grand Rapids, MI: William B. Eerdsmann, 2013.

Rubiés, Joan-Pau, "Real and Imaginary Dialogues in the Jesuit Mission of Sixteenth-Century Japan." *Journal of the Economic and Social History of the Orient* 55 (2012): 447–94.

Said, Edward. *Orientalism*. New York: Vintage, 1979.

Sauerländer, Willibald. *The Catholic Rubens, Saints and Martyrs*. Translated by David Dollenmayer. Los Angeles: Getty Research Institute, 2014.

Saussy, Haun. *Great Walls of Discourse and Other Adventures in Cultural China*. Cambridge, MA: Harvard University Press, 2001.

Schelling, Friedrich Wilhelm Joseph. *Ideen zu einer Philosophie der Natur*, 1st ed. Leipzig: Breitkopf and Härtel, 1797.

Scherpe, Klaus R. *Werther und Wertherwirkung, Zum Syndrom bürgerlicher Gesellschaftsordnung im 18. Jahrhundert*. Bad Homburg: Gehlein, 1970.

Schiller, Friedrich. *Geschäftsbriefe Schillers*. Edited by Karl Goedeke. Leipzig: Veit and Co. 1875.

——. *Werke: Nationalausgabe*. Weimar: Verlag Hermann Böhlaus Nachfolger, 1943– (ongoing).

Schmidt, Jochen. *Goethes Faust Erster und Zweiter Teil Grundlagen-Werk-Wirkung*. Munich: Beck, 1999.

Schmitz, Hermann. *Goethes Altersdenken im problemgeschichtlichen Zusammenhang*. Bonn: Bouvier, 1959.

Schneider, Helmut J. "Empathy, Imagination, and Dramaturgy—A Means of Society in Eighteenth-Century Theory," In *Empathy*, edited by Vanessa Lux and Sigrid Weigel, 203–21. London: Palgrave MacMillan, 2017.

Schneider, Ulrich Johannes. "Der Aufbau der Wissenswelt. Eine phänotypische Beschreibung enzyklopädischer Literatur." In *Kulturen des Wissens im 18. Jahrhunderts*, edited by Ulrich Johannes Schneider, 95–114. Berlin: De Gruyter, 2008.

Schöffler, Herbert. *Deutscher Geist im 18. Jahrhundert: Essays zur Geistes- und Religionsgeschichte*, 2nd ed. Göttingen: Vandenhoeck and Ruprecht, 1967.

Schuster, Ingrid. *Vorbilder und Zerrbilder: China und Japan im Spiegel der deutschen Literatur, 1773–1890*. Bern: Peter Lang, 1988.

Schurhammer, Georg, SJ. *Japan and China, 1549–1552*. Vol. 4 of *Francis Xavier: His Life, His Times*. Rome: Jesuit Historical Institute, 1982.

Seidel, Siegfried, ed. *Der Briefwechsel zwischen Schiller und Goethe*. Leipzig: Insel, 1984.

Seigworth, Gregory J. and Melissa Gregg, eds. *The Affect Theory Reader*. Durham, NC: Duke University Press, 2010.

Semedo, Alvarez. *The History of the Great and Renowned Monarchy of China*. London: E. Tyler for John Crook, 1655.

Sendtschreiben auß den weit berhümpten Landschafften China, Japon un India . . . Sampe Angehenecker erzehlung eines mercklichen Schiffbruchs wie in andern schreiben des P. Petri Martonez an den Ehrwürdigen P. General der Soceitet Jesu. Dillingen: Johannem Meyer, 1589.

Seneca, Lucius Annaeus. *Natural Questions*. Translated by Harry M. Hine. Chicago: University of Chicago Press, 2010.

Serres, Michel. "Platonic Dialogue." In *Hermes: Literature, Science, Philosophy*, edited by Josué Harari and David Bell, 65–71. Baltimore, MD: Johns Hopkins University Press, 1992.

Shaftesbury, Anthony, Earl of. *Characteristics of Men, Manners, Opinions, Times*. Indianapolis: Bobbs-Merril, 1964.

Sibau, Maria Franca. *Reading for the Moral: Exemplarity and the Confucian Moral Imagination in Seventeenth-Century Chinese Short Fiction*. Albany: State University of New York Press, 2018.

Sieber, Patricia. "The Imprint of the Imprints: Sojourners, *Xiaoshuo* Translations, and the Transcultural Canon of Early Chinese Fiction in Europe, 1697–1826." *East Asian Publishing and Society* 3 (2013): 31–70.

——. "Translation as Self-Invention: Jin Shengtan (1608–1661), Arcade Houange (1679–1716), and the Fashioning of a Transcultural Discourse of Scholar-Beauty Ideals." In *Towards a History of Translating: In Celebration of the Fortieth Anniversary of the Research Centre for Translation*, edited by Lawrence Wang-chi Wong, 3:229–276. Hong Kong: Chinese University of Hong Kong, 2013.

——. "Location, Location, Location: Peter Perring Thoms (1790–1855), Cantonese Localism, and the Genesis of Literary Translation from the Chinese." In *Sinologists as Translators in the Seventeenth to Nineteenth Centuries*, edited by Lawrence Wang-chi Wong and Bernhard Fuehrer, 127–68. Hong Kong: Chinese University of Hong Kong, 2015.

Siegert, Bernhard. *Relays: Literature as an Epoch of the Postal System*. Translated by Kevin Repp. Stanford, CA: Stanford University Press, 1999.

——. *Passage des Digitalen: Zeichenpraktiken der neuzeitlichen Wissenschaften, 1500–1900*. Berlin: Brinkmann and Bose, 2003.

——. "Cacophony or Communication? Cultural Techniques in German Media Studies." Translated by Geoffrey Winthrop-Young. *Grey Room* 29 (Winter 2008): 26–47.

Simmel, Georg. "The Problem of Style." Translated by Mark Ritter. *Theory, Culture, and Society* 8.3 (1991): 63–71.

Sindemann, Kerstin-Katja. "Japanese Buddhism in the 16th Century: Letters of the Jesuit Missionaries." *Bulletin of Portuguese Japanese Studies* 2 (2001): 111–33.

Singh, Brijraj. *The First Protestant Missionary to India: Bartholomaeus Ziegenbalg (1683–1719)*. Oxford: Oxford University Press, 1999.

Sloterdijk, Peter. "*Rules for the Human Zoo*: A Response to the *Letter on Humanism*." Translated by Mary Varney Rorty. *Environment and Planning D: Society and Space* 27.1 (2009): 12–28.

Smith, Adam. *Adam Smiths Theorie der sittlichen Gefühle*. Translated by Ludwig Theobul Kosegarten. Leipzig: Graff, 1791.

——. *An Inquiry into the Nature and Causes of the Wealth of Nations*. Edited by R. H. Campbell, A. S. Skinner, and W. B. Todd. Oxford: Oxford University Press, 1976.

——. *The Theory of Moral Sentiments*. Indianapolis: Liberty, 1976.

Southern, R. W. *The Making of the Middle Ages.* New Haven, CT: Yale University Press, 1953.

Spence, Jonathan D. *The Memory Palace of Matteo Ricci.* New York: Penguin, 1985.

———. "The Paris Years of Arcadio Huang." *Granta* 32 (1992): 123–32.

Spitzer, Leo. "Classical and Christian Ideas of World Harmony: Prolegomena to an Interpretation of the Word 'Stimmung.'" *Traditio* 2 (1944): 409–64 and 3 (1945): 307–65.

Staiger, Emil. *Johann Wolfgang Goethe Sämtliche Gedichte.* Zürich: Artemis Verlag, 1953.

———. *Basic Concepts of Poetics.* Translated by Janette C. Hudson and Luanne T. Frank. University Park: Pennsylvania State University Press, 1991.

Standaert, Nicolas. *Yang Tingyuan, Confucian and Christian in Late Ming China.* Leiden: Brill, 1988.

———. "Jesuits in China." In *The Cambridge Companion to the Jesuits*, edited by Thomas Worcester, 169–85. Cambridge: Cambridge University Press, 2015.

Starr, Chloe. *Red-Light Novels in the Late Qing.* Leiden: Brill, 2007.

Stempfle, Lorenz. *Bericht über die königlichen Studien-Anstalten zu Dillingen am Ober-Donau Kreise.* Dillingen: Roßnagel, 1832.

Stoler, Ann Laura, and Carole McGranahan, eds. *Imperial Formations.* Santa Fe, NM: School for Advanced Research Press, 2007.

Strasser, Gerhard. "The Impact on the European Humanities of the Early Reports from Catholic Missionaries in China, Tibet and Japan between 1600 and 1700." In *The Making of the Humanities*, vol. 2 of *From Early Modern to Modern Disciplines*, edited by Rens Bod, Jaap Maat, and Theijs Weststeijn, 185–208. Amsterdam: Amsterdam University Press, 2012.

Strasser, Ulrike. "Copies with Souls: The Late Seventeenth-Century Marianas Martyrs, Francis Xavier, and the Question of Clerical Reproduction." *Journal of Jesuit Studies* 2.4 (2015): 558–85.

Streit, Robert. *Asiatischer Missionsliteratur 1600–1699.* Vol. 5 of *Bibliotheca Missionum.* Aachen: Franziskus Xaverius Missionsverein, 1929.

Subrahmanyam, Sanjay. "Holding the World in Balance: The Connected Histories of the Iberian Overseas Empires, 1500–1640." *American Historical Review* 112.5 (2007): 1359–85.

Sucquet, Antoine. *Weeg zum ewigen Leben.* Translated by Carl Stengel. Augsburg: Langenwalder, 1627.

Sulieri, Sara. *The Rhetoric of English India.* Chicago: University of Chicago Press, 1992.

Szarota, Elida Maria. *Künstler, Grübler und Rebellen, Studien zum europäischen Märtyrdrma des 17. Jahrhunderts.* Bern: Francke, 1967.

———. "Die Jesuitendrama als Vorläufer der modernen Massenmedien." *Daphnis* 4 (1975): 129–143.

———. *Das Jesuitendrama im deutschen Sprachgebiet: Texte und Kommentare.* Munich: Wilhelm Fink, 1983.

Szondi, Peter. *Die Theorie des bürgerlichen Trauerspiels im 18. Jahrhundert.* Frankfurt: Suhrkamp, 1973.

Takenaka, Masahiro. "Jesuit Plays on Japan in the Baroque Era." In *Mission und Theater: Japan und China auf den Bühnen der Gesellschaft Jesu,* edited by Adrian Hsia and Ruprecht Wimmer, 379–410. Regensburg: Schnell and Steiner, 2005.

Talbot, Michael. *The Vivaldi Compendium.* Woodbridge, UK: Boydell Press, 2011.

Tan, Yuan. *Der Chinese in der deutschen Literatur, Unter besonderer Berücksichtugung chinesischer Figuren in den Werken von Schiller, Döblin und Brecht.* Göttingen: Cuvier, 2007.

Tang, Yanfang. "Translating across Cultures: *Yi Jing* and Understanding Chinese Poetry." *Intercultural Communication Studies* 23.1 (2014): 197–202.

Tantillo, Astrida. "The Catholicism of Werther." *German Quarterly* 81.4 (2008): 408–23.

Tautz, Birgit. *Reading and Seeing Ethnic Differences in the Enlightenment from China to Africa.* New York: Palgrave, 2007.

——. *Translating the World: Toward a New History of German Literature around 1800.* University Park: Pennsylvania State University Press, 2018.

Taylor, Charles. *Sources of the Self: The Making of Modern Identity.* Cambridge: Cambridge University Press, 1989.

Thielking, Sigrid. *Weltbürgertum: Kosmopolitische Ideen in Literatur und politischer Publizistik seit dem achtzehnten Jahrhundert.* Munich: Fink, 2000.

Tscharner, Horst von. "China in der deutschen Dichtung des Mittelalters und der Renaissance." *Sinica* 9 (1934): 8–31.

Trigault, Nicholas, SJ. *De Christiana Expeditione apud Sinas Suscepta ab Societate Iesu ex. P. Matthaei Riccii.* Augsburg: Christoph Mangius, 1615.

——. *De Christiana Expeditione apud Sinas Suscepta ab Societate Iesu ex. P. Mattaei Riccii.* Cologne: Bernardi Gualteri, 1617.

——. *Historia von der Einführung der christlichen Religion in das große Königreich China durch die Societet Jesu.* Augsburg: Antony Hierat, 1617.

——. *De Christianis apud Iaponios Triumphis.* Munich: Sadeler, 1623.

——. *The Christian Expedition Undertaken among the Chinese by the Society of Jesus, from the Commentaries of Father Matteo Ricci.* In *Jesuit Writings of the Early Modern Period, 1540–1640,* edited by John Patrick Donnelly, SJ, 90–95. Indianapolis: Hackett, 2006.

Tucker, Robert C., ed. *The Marx-Engels Reader,* 2nd ed. New York: Norton, 1972.

Väth, Alfons, SJ. "Nicht in den Missionen, und doch Missionär." *Die Katholischen Missionen* 45.7 (April 1917): 145–47.

——. *Johann Adam Schall von Bell S.J. Missionar in China, kaiserlicher Astronom und Ratgeber am Hofe von Peking 1592–1666 Ein Lebens- und Zeitbild,* new ed. China-Zentrum und Instituts Monumenta Serica. Sankt Augustin: Steyer, 1991.

Valignano, Alessandro, SJ. *Historia del principle y progresso de la Campañia de Jesus en las Indias Orientates (1542–1564)*. Edited by Josef Wicki. Rome: Institutum Historicum S. I., 1944.

Verhofstadt, Edward. "Vondel und Gryphius: Versuch einer literarischen Topographie." *Neophilologus* 53 (1969): 290–99.

Virgil. *The Aeneid*. Translated by Robert Fitzgerald. New York: Vintage, 1981.

Vogel, Hans Ulrich. *Marco Polo Was in China: New Evidence from Currencies, Salts and Revenues*. Leiden: Brill, 2013.

Voss, Steffan. "Die Partitur von Vivaldis Oper 'Motezuma' (1733)." *Studi Vivaldiani* 4 (2004): 52–72.

Wagner-Dittmar, Christine. "Goethe und die chinesischer Literatur." In *Studien zu Goethes Alterswerken*, edited by Erich Trunz, 122–228. Frankfurt: Athenäum, 1971.

Walravens, Hartmut. *China Illustrata: Das europäische Chinaverständnis im Spiegel des 16. bis 18. Jahrhunderts*. Wolfenbüttel: Herzon August Bibliothek, 1987.

Walsh, Milton. " 'To Always Be Thinking Somehow about Jesus': The Prologue of Ludolph's *Vita Christi*." *Studies in the Spirituality of Jesuits* 43.1 (Spring 2011): 1–39.

Wang, Hung-tai. "Information Media, Social Imagination, and Public Society during the Ming and Qing Dynasties." *Frontiers of History in China* 5.2 (2010) 169–216.

Waszek, Norbert. *The Scottish Enlightenment and Hegel's Account of 'Civil Society.'* Dordrecht: Kluwer, 1988.

——. "The Scottish Enlightenment in Germany." In *Scotland in Europe*, edited by Tom Hubbard and R. D. S. Jack, 55–72. Amsterdam: Rodopi, 2006.

Weber, Max. *Economy and Society*. Edited by Guenther Roth and Claus Wittich. Berkeley: University of California Press, 1978.

——. *The Protestant Ethic and the "Spirit" of Capitalism*. Translated by Peter Baehr and Gordon Wells. New York: Penguin, 2002.

Weber, Samuel. *Benjamin's -abilities*. Cambridge, MA: Harvard University Press, 2008.

Wedderburn, David. "The Two Fair Cousins, A Chinese Romance." *The Fortnightly* 24 (1878): 493–508.

Weerdt, Hilde de. *Information, Territory, and Networks: The Crisis and Maintenance of Empire in Song China*. Cambridge, MA: Harvard University Press, 2015.

Weerdt, Hilde de, Chu Ming-Kin, and Ho Hou-leong. "Chinese Empires in Comparative Perspective: A Digital Approach." *Verge: Studies in Global Asias* 2.2 (Fall 2016): 58–69.

Wegner, Irene. " 'China' in der Fest- und Theaterkulturs Bayerns." In *Die Wittelsbacher und das Reich der Mitte, 400 Jahre China und Bayern*, edited by Renate Eikelmann, 342–47. Munich: Hirmer, 2009.

Weigel, Sigrid. "The Heterogeneity of Empathy: An Archeology of Multiple Meanings and Epistemic Implications." In *Empathy*, edited by Vanessa Lux and Sigrid Weigel, 1–23. London: Palgrave MacMillan, 2017.

Weinberg, Kurt. *The Figure of Faust in Valery and Goethe*. Princeton, NJ: Princeton University Press, 1976.

Weiß, Wilhelm. *Chronik von Dilligen im Regierungsbezirke Schwaben und Neuburg des Königreichs Bayern*. Dillingen: Kränzle, 1861.

Weitz, Hans-Juergen. "'Weltliteratur' zuerst bei Wieland." *Arcadia* 22.2 (1987): 206–8.

Wellbery, David. *The Specular Moment: Goethe's Early Lyric and the Beginnings of Romanticism*. Stanford, CA: Stanford University Press, 1996.

——. "Stimmung," In *Historisches Wörterbuch Ästhetischer Grundbegriffe*, edited by Karlheinz Barck, Martin Fontius, Dieter Schlenstedt, Burkhard Steinwachs, and Friedrich Wolfzettel. 5:703–33. Stuttgart/Weimar: Metzler, 2003.

Wetzel, Hermann H. "Marco Polos *Milione* zwischen Beschreibung und Erzählen." In *Beiträge zur sprachlichen, literarischem und kulturellen Vielfalt in den Philologien: Festschrift für Rupprecht Rohr*, edited by Gabriele Birken-Silveman and Gerda Rössler, 523–40. Stuttgart: Franz Steiner Verlag, 1992.

Wheelan, Frederick. *Enlightenment Political Thought and Non-Western Societies: Sultans and Savages*. London: Routledge, 2012.

Wieland, Christoph Martin. *Sämmtliche Werke*. Leipzig: Göschen, 1796.

——. *Sämmtliche Werke*. Leipzig: Göschen, 1853–1858.

Wiesinger, Liselotte, and Eva Kraft. "Die chinesische Bibliothek des Großen Kurfursten und ihre Bibliothekare." In *China und Europa: Chinaverständnis und Chinamode im 17. Und 18. Jahrhundert*, 166–73. Berlin: Staatlicher Schlösser und Gärten, 1973.

Wiggins, Ellwood. "Pity Play: Sympathy and Spectatorship in Lessing's *Miss Sara Sampson* and Adam Smith's *Theory of Moral Sentiments*." In *Performing Knowledge: 1750–1850*, edited by Mary Helen Dupree and Sean B. Franzel, 85–111. Berlin: De Gruyter, 2015.

Wilhelm, Richard. *Chinesische Volksmärchen, Die Märchen der Weltliteratur, Märchen des Orients*. Edited by Friedrich von der Leyen. Jena: Eugen Diedrich, 1914.

Will, Georg Andreas. *Nürnbergisches Gelehrten-Lexikon oder Beschreibung aller Nürnbergischen Gelehrten beyderley Geschlechtes*. Nürnberg: Lorenz Schüpfel, 1755.

Wilson, W. Daniel. "Intellekt und Herrschaft. Wielands Goldner Spiegel, Joseph II, und das Ideal eines kritischen Mäzenats im aufgeklärten Absolutismus." *MLN* 99.3 (1984): 479–502.

Wimmer, Ruprecht. "Japan und China auf den Jesuitenbühnen des deutschen Sprachgebietes." In *Mission und Theater: Japan und China auf den Bühnen der Gesellschaft Jesu*, edited by Adrian Hsia and Ruprecht Wimmer, 17–58. Regensburg: Schnell and Steiner, 2005.

Witek, John W., SJ. "Johann Adam Schall von Bell and the Transition from Ming to Ch'ing." In *Western Learning and Christianity in China: The Contribution and Impact of Johann Adam Schall von Bell, S.J. (1592–1666)*, edited by Roman Malek, SVD, 109–24. Sankt Augustin: China-Zentrum and Monumenta Serica Institute, 1998.

Wolf, Peter. "Protestantischer 'Jesuitismus' im Zeitalter der Aufklärung: Christoph Gottlieb Murr (1733–1811) und die Jesuiten." *Zeitschrift für bayerische Landesgeschichte* 62 (1999): 99–137.

Wood, Michael. "Kafka's China and the Parable of Parables." *Philosophy and Literature* 20.2 (1996): 325–37.

Wu, Yulian. *Luxurious Networks: Salt Merchants, Status, and Statecraft in Eighteenth-Century China.* Stanford, CA: Stanford University Press, 2017.

Yule, Henry, and A. C. Burnell. *Hobson-Jobson: A Glossary of Anglo-Indian Colloquial Words and Phrases and of Kindred Terms.* London: John Murray, 1903.

Xavier, Francis. *Letters and Instructions of Francis Xavier.* Translated by M. Joseph Costelloe, SJ. St. Louis: Institute of Jesuit Sources, 1992.

Xu, Dongfeng. "The Concept of Friendship and the Culture of Hospitality: The Encounter between the Jesuits and Late Ming China." PhD dissertation, University of Chicago, 2011.

Zanker, G. "Enargeia in the Ancient Criticism of Poetry." *Rheinische Museum für Philologie*, N.F. 124 (1981): 297–311.

Zedler, Johann Heinrich. *Grosses vollständiges Universal-Lexicon aller Wissenschaften und Künste.* Leipzig: Zedler, 1732–1754.

Zhang, Chunjie. "Goethe's *Chinesisch-deutsche Jahres- und Tageszeitung*: Vernacular Universal, *Erotica Sinica*, and the Temporality of *Nachträglichkeit*." In *Receptions: Reading the Past across Space and Time*, edited by Brenda Schildgen and Ralph Hexter, 245–64. New York: Palgrave Macmillan, 2017.

——. *Transculturality and German Discourse in the Age of European Colonialism.* Evanston, IL: Northwestern University Press, 2017.

Zhaoguang, Ge. *What Is China? Territory, Ethnicity, Culture and History.* Translated by Michael Gibbs Hill. Cambridge, MA: Harvard University Press, 2018.

Ziegenbalg, Bartholomäus. *Beschreibung der Religion und heiligen Gebräuche der Malabarischen Hindous.* Berlin: Königl Preußischen akademischen Kunst und Buchhandlung, 1791.

——. *Genealogy of the Malabar Gods.* Edited by Wilhelm Germann. Madras: Christian Knowledge Society Press, 1867.

Zilcosky, John. *Kafka's Travels: Exoticism, Colonialism, and the Traffic Writing.* New York: Palgrave, 2003.

INDEX

Page numbers with *fig* appended indicate a figure.

Abraham, 172
accommodation: administrative elite
and, 76, 162, 175, 254; analogies
and, 7, 122; Buddhism and, 162,
254, 270, 288; Chinese literature
and, 332; Chinese sympathies and,
254; colonialism and, 187; cosmopolitanism and, 114, 122–23, 165,
209; criticism of, 87, 209, 286, 291,
293; development of, 76–77, 88;
Enlightenment and, 116, 209, 278;
friendship and, 204; heresy and,
161–62, 192, 254; idolatry and, 165,
192; influence of, 7, 116, 152, 154,
288, 293; information networks and,
88, 162; letter writing and, 88;
literati and, 181, 254; martyrdom
and, 160, 163, 165; overview of, 7,
10, 76; philosophy and, 7, 270;
resemblances and, 10; risk of culture
loss from, 254; rulers and, 162, 329;
scholarship on, 164–65, 291–92;
sympathy and, 140; theater and,
175, 181; translation and, 94; world
literature and, 122–23, 298. *See also*
Confucianism; Jesuits
Achsenzeit (Axial Age), 243–44
actor-network theory, 59, 88, 90
Ad Christiana (Ricci and Trigault),
191–92
administrative elite: accommodation
and, 76, 162, 175, 254; analogies
and, 349n126; Chinese literature and,
45, 307n24; Chinese sympathies and,
7, 17, 32, 205; Confucianism and, 9,
261; corruption within, 191, 338;

administrative elite (*continued*)
Enlightenment and, 271; fables and, 48; friendship and, 331; idealization of, 271; information networks and, 43, 45; Jesuits and, 7–8, 20, 22, 35, 42, 91, 175, 245, 306; poetry and, 271, 345, 349; postal systems and, 39, 43, 48; print culture used by, 169, 327; rebellion prompted by, 191; reforms to selection of, 191, 338; travel literature and, 30. *See also* rulers
Adnotationes et meditationes (Nadal), 134
Aeneid, The (Virgil), 183n14, 184
aesthetic autonomy, 14, 263, 331
Aeyquan, oder der Große Mogol (Hagdorn), 63, 169
affect theory, 3–5
Aigenier, Adam, 186n23
Albrecht V (duke of Bavaria), 104–5
Aleni, Guilo, 134
Alexander the Great, 72
Alexander VII (pope), 55–56
Algonquin Club, 292
Almeida, Antonio, 21–22, 108–13
Amalia, Anna, 54
Amrhyn, Beatus, 186n23
Analects (Confucius), 204
analogies: accommodation and, 7, 122; administrative elite and, 349n126; Chinese literature and, 7; Chinese sympathies and, 7, 10, 15; Christianity and, 121–22; Confucianism and, 7, 269; Enlightenment and, 157; European literature and, 157–58, 324, 331; imagination and, 125–26; information networks and, 6, 302; Jesuits and, 7, 157, 192, 269, 312; literary theory of, 302–3; philosophy and, 157–58, 286, 302–3; political use of, 50–51, 171, 190, 194, 229, 302; sympathy and, 122, 232; translation and, 311; world literature and, 302–3
androgyny, 334
Angelet, Andreas, 349

Anton Reiser (Moritz), 132n36
apatheia, 128, 238–40, 329
Aravamudan, Srinivas, 66
Aristotle, 23, 99, 126, 166, 205, 232, 288
Asian despotism trope, 19, 51, 54, 137–38, 159, 173, 179–80, 195, 227, 283
Asian literature, 14, 266, 303, 322
astrology, 304–5, 329, 352–53, 352n132
astronomy, 91, 257, 304–5, 352–53
atheism, 25, 208–9, 245–46, 272–73, 279, 281, 288–90
Atlas (Martini), 167, 170
atmosphere. *See* mood
attentiveness, 22, 126, 128, 244
August the Strong (duke), 7
Austria critiqued through China comparison, 49–53
autonomy aesthetics, 147, 263, 331

Bachelard, Gaston, 49
baroque style: Chinese sympathies and, 2, 18, 20–21, 162, 165, 224; colonialism and, 18, 156, 249; compilations in, 2, 14, 162, 246; development of, 263, 268; European literature and, 9, 12, 64, 124, 145, 173, 176, 195, 248–49, 263–64, 268; influence of, 20; Jesuits and, 124, 143, 249; knowledge and, 2, 14, 249; letter writing and, 143; martyrdom and, 9, 139, 163, 182; rulers and, 60, 138, 145, 173, 182; scholarship on, 189; sympathy and, 223; theater and, 19–20, 124, 138–40, 145, 165, 173, 175–78, 182, 185, 188–91, 223, 235–36; *Trauerspiele* in, 140, 175, 177–78, 189–90
Barthes, Roland, 124, 126
Bauer, Wolfgang, 249n13, 350, 353
Baumgartner, Alexander, 185
"Bekenntnisse einer schönen Seele" (Goethe), 152
Benjamin, Walter, 19–21, 158, 173, 182, 186, 189, 264, 271–72, 299

Berensmeyer, Ingo, 240n58
Berman, Russell, 67, 229
Bernard of Clairvaux, 150
Bertuch, Friedrich, 277
Berze, Gaspar, 83
Bhatti, Anil, 300
Biedermann, Woldemar von, 284, 318n57
Bildung, 108
Blaeu, Jan/Joan, 167, 185
Blondheim, Menahem, 95–96
Bonaventura, 150
Book of 25 Paragraphs, The (Ricci), 205–6
book printing, 105–7, 112–13, 134, 166, 322
Börne, Ludwig, 50–51
Botero, Giovanni, 29
Boxer, C. A., 86
Braudel, Ferdinand, 158
Breze, Gaspar, 102
British Empire, 227
British Society for Promoting Christian Knowledge, 151
Buddhism: accommodation and, 162, 254, 270, 288; Christianity and, 25, 187, 256; Confucianism and, 6, 77, 253–54, 253n23, 288; consciousness and, 274–75; God and, 187, 253, 272, 285; heresy and, 77, 162, 259, 288; idolatry and, 253, 270, 293; imagination and, 273; Jesuits and, 6, 77, 162, 245–46, 247n7, 252–53, 257–58, 283–84, 288, 293; pantheism of, 270, 284; philosophy and, 257–58, 261–62, 270, 272–75, 279, 284, 286
bureaucracy. *See* administrative elite
Bürger, Peter, 264
Burke, Edmund, 139, 176, 227–30
Burschel, Peter, 160, 164
Bush, Christopher, 51

Calvinism, 149, 212
Cameron, Nigel, 59n68
Candide (Voltaire), 280
Canisius, Peter, 97, 104–5

Canton, 13, 43, 107, 112, 225
Carruthers, Mary, 136n46
Carvalhal, George de, 90
Catharina von Georgien (Gryphius), 138, 161
Catholic Church: Chinese sympathies and, 9; conversion mission of, 8–9, 21–22; cosmopolitanism and, 123, 137, 207, 210–11; Counter-Reformation and, 115; Enlightenment and, 23, 122; global mission of, 8–9, 22, 26, 95–96, 120, 137, 196–97, 208–9, 211; heresy and, 106; information networks and, 22, 96; laity and, 79, 91, 95–97, 101, 124–25, 127, 161–62, 169, 178, 198, 206, 208; letter writing and, 79, 122, 144; martyrdom and, 8–9, 17, 97, 119, 161; missionary networks of, 85, 92–93, 122, 208, 210; philosophy and, 22; Reformation and, 74, 105, 207; sense of calling and, 97; spiritual circuit and, 22, 79, 213; sympathy and, 119; theater and, 237; world literature and, 26. *See also* Christianity; Jesuits
Chandler, James, 115, 233
channels. *See* information networks and communication channels
Chaocungus (martyr), 175
Charlemagne (Charles the Great), 34, 89–90
China: admiration for, 3, 13–15, 34–36, 41, 63, 76, 177; antiquity of, 35, 45, 58, 183–84, 322, 347; civilization of, 46, 76, 78, 177, 243, 347; fables, as land of, 55–56, 59–61, 70, 297, 342; history of, 170, 173, 195; as ideal moral society and, 23, 35, 56, 60, 77–78; inaccessibility of, 41, 225–26, 249; vastness of, 34–36. *See also specific topics, persons, and works*
China Illustrata (Kircher), 57, 84, 166–67
Chinese Courtship. In Verse (Thoms), 306–7, 316–20, 318n57, 324, 341, 353

Chinese literati. *See* literati
Chinese literature: accommodation
and, 332; administrative elite and,
45, 307n24; analogies and, 7;
antiquity of, 320, 322, 347; benefits
for Europeans of, 309, 311–12;
Chinese sympathies and, 14, 17, 25,
206, 282; Christianity and, 13–14;
cosmopolitanism and, 297–98;
Enlightenment and, 61; etiquette
and, 330; European literature and, 7,
14–15, 52, 243–44, 309, 339; fables
and, 61, 72–73; foreigners in,
329–30; friendship and, 330–31;
idolatry and, 316–17; imperial court
in, 328; information networks and,
13–14, 309; internal character of,
14, 312–13; Jesuits and, 7–8, 13, 91,
309–10, 313–14, 317, 332, 338;
knowledge and, 8, 14, 69, 309–12,
330; letter writing and, 339; literati
and, 328–32, 334, 339; mood and,
14, 339–41, 343–44; pantheism and,
298; poetry and, 316–17, 327;
polygamy in, 324–25; postal systems
and, 307; romances in, 15, 52,
306–7, 307n24, 323–24; rulers and,
52; space and, 326–27, 327n81;
subjectivity in, 327; themes in, 14,
297, 312–13, 319n57, 320–21, 323,
327, 330; trade and, 13–14;
translation and, 7–8, 11, 13–14, 25,
52, 68–69, 72–73, 309–11, 313–16,
331–32; travel literature and, 28, 69,
317; world literature and, 12–15, 21,
297–98, 306–7. *See also specific
works*
Chinese philosophy. *See* philosophy
Chinese poetry. *See* poetry
Chinese sympathies: accommodation
and, 254; administrative elite and, 7,
17, 32, 205; aesthetic experience
and, 16–17; analogies and, 7, 10, 15;
baroque style and, 2, 18, 20–21,
162, 165, 224; Chinese literature
and, 14, 17, 25, 206, 282; Christianity and, 6; colonialism and, 18–19,

249; Confucianism and, 17, 138;
contemporary context and, 5–6;
cosmopolitanism and, 6, 17, 26,
114–15, 123, 159, 196–97; development of, 4–7, 16–17, 20–21, 114–15,
124, 129, 134, 137–38, 159, 224,
243–44; Enlightenment and, 2, 6, 9,
12, 66–67, 77–78, 115–16, 138, 140,
177, 196; European literature and,
119, 156–57; friendship and, 206;
imagination and, 17–18, 129, 131,
134, 158; information networks and,
5–6, 17, 24, 114, 123–24, 141, 158,
231, 251–52; Jesuits and, 1–2, 6,
8–9, 22, 25–26, 115–16, 124,
137–39, 140, 254; knowledge and,
261; letter writing and, 97, 124;
literati and, 244, 249, 348–49;
martyrdom and, 17, 116, 120–22,
137–40, 162–63, 165; media and, 5,
17–18, 41, 230–31; mobilization
and circulation of, 9–10, 16–18,
25–26; orientalism and, 18–20, 61;
overview of, 1–7, 20, 25–26; postal
systems and, 51–52; psychology
required for, 2–6, 16, 21; reading
practices and, 114, 123–24; rulers
and, 7, 17, 20, 129, 137, 138, 165,
224; scholarship on, 3–4, 18,
123–24; secularization and, 196–97,
251; space and, 36, 251; theater and,
137, 158, 159–60, 174, 179, 181,
194–95, 226; translation and, 2;
transportation and, 6, 21; travel
literature and, 28–32, 65, 124;
utopianism and, 7; world literature
and, 140. *See also* sympathy
"Chinesisch-Deutsche Jahres-und
Tageszeiten" (Goethe), 10, 271, 304,
308, 311
chinoiserie, 61, 181, 282, 312, 341,
344, 347–48, 3128
Chongzhen (emperor), 182–84
Christ. *See* Jesus Christ
Christianity: analogies and, 121–22;
Buddhism and, 25, 187, 256;
Chinese literature and, 13–14;

Chinese sympathies and, 6; Confucianism and, 7, 23, 77, 122, 168, 187, 193, 254, 269; cosmopolitanism and, 6, 123, 159, 196; Enlightenment and, 196; imagination and, 130; philosophy and, 255, 271, 278–79, 286–87; revelation and, 278; rulers and, 180–82; secularization of, 219; sentimentalism and, 197n1; sympathy and, 115, 117, 119–22, 125–28; world literature and, 119. *See also* Catholic Church; Jesuits; Protestantism

Cicero, 71–72, 99–100, 129, 143, 146, 166, 204, 205, 260

Le Cinesi (Metastasio), 175

circuits. *See* information networks and communication channels

Codacio, Pietro, 101

Coleridge, Samuel Taylor, 129

colonialism: accommodation and, 187; arguments against, 227–30; baroque style and, 18, 156, 249; Chinese sympathies and, 18–19, 249; cosmopolitanism and, 211; development of, 197; Enlightenment and, 18, 202; European literature and, 157, 202; ideology of, 249, 304; information networks and, 231; Jesuits and, 197; knowledge and, 249; martyrdom and, 237; orientalism and, 19; rulers and, 227; sympathy and, 227–30, 231, 237; technical form of, 19; theater and, 181, 186–87, 237; trade and, 19, 249; utopianism and, 63; world literature and, 202, 297

communication channels. *See* information networks and communication channels

Communist Manifesto (Marx and Engels), 201

compassion. *See* sympathy

Confucianism: administrative elite and, 9, 261; analogies and, 7, 269; Buddhism and, 6, 77, 253–54, 253n23, 288; Chinese sympathies

and, 17, 138; Christianity and, 7, 23, 77, 122, 168, 187, 193, 254, 269; cosmopolitanism and, 122; Enlightenment and, 140, 209; Figuralism interpretation of, 161; friendship and, 204–6; God and, 77, 187, 259; heresy and, 254; idolatry and, 261–62; imagination and, 135, 136*fig*; literati and, 162, 253, 255; martyrdom and, 9, 165; natural theology and, 77; neo-Confucianism in, 255, 293; philosophy and, 77, 138, 157–58, 161, 205, 244, 271, 278, 280, 284–86, 293; revelation and, 278; rulers and, 31; sympathy and, 115; theater and, 181; travel literature and, 31, 65. *See also* accommodation

Confucius Sinarum philosophus (Couplet), 135–36, 136*fig*, 186

Conquest of China by the Tartars, The (Settle), 165–66

consciousness, 49, 128, 256–57, 274–76

Constantine, 35, 182, 192

Constitutions (Ignatius Loyola), 78–79

Conversations with Goethe (Eckermann), 199, 297, 306, 323, 340

converts in Asia, 8–9, 21–22, 116, 120, 137–40, 156, 160–61, 171–72, 179, 182, 185n17

Correia-Afonso, John, 83, 86, 100n62

Cosma, Nicola, 165

cosmopolitanism: accommodation and, 114, 122–23, 165, 209; ancient precursors to, 198, 208, 218, 219; Chinese literature and, 297–98; Chinese sympathies and, 6, 17, 26, 114–15, 123, 159, 196–97; Christianity and, 6, 123, 159, 196; colonialism and, 211; Confucianism and, 122; contemporary application of, 6, 114, 137, 159, 208; critics of, 123, 216, 218; development of, 6, 114, 116, 202, 207–8, 211, 218–19; distance and, 123, 199; Enlightenment and, 6, 26, 160, 198, 202,

cosmopolitanism (*continued*)
207–11, 269; friendship and, 23,
196, 203, 215; imagination and,
130, 208; information networks and,
8, 17, 24–25, 114, 207–8, 231;
Jesuits and, 8, 20, 116, 196–97, 208,
215n35, 293; love of country and,
218; martyrdom and, 116, 137, 140,
159, 210; media and, 137, 199;
postal systems and, 198–99;
psychology and, 196–97; scholarship
on, 216; secret history of, 144, 211,
216–17, 219; secularization of, 6,
196, 208, 210–11; sentimentalism
and, 24, 197, 202, 220; space and,
218; sympathy and, 6, 114–17, 123,
196, 207–8, 218, 222–23, 241;
theater and, 159–60, 175; trade and,
159, 202; world literature and, 123,
196, 199, 207, 297
Council of Trent (1545–1563), 119,
127, 164
Counter-Reformation, 115
Couplet, Philipp, 136, 185–86
Critique of Pure Reason (Kant), 125,
275–77
Cronegk, Johann Friedrich von, 118
cultured language (*Kultursprache*), 303

Damrosch, David, 10, 299n5
Dante Alighieri, 186
Debon, Günther, 249, 270n1, 314,
350n129
De Christiana Expeditione apud Sinas
(Ricci), 252, 287
*De Christianis apud Iaponios
Triumphis* (Trigault), 120, 179–80
Dekonick, Ralph, 135
Democritus, 208, 215
De Oratore (Cicero), 129
De Pauw, Cornelius, 280
Descartes, René, 189, 234
despotism, 19, 51, 54, 137–38, 159,
173, 177, 179–80, 195, 227, 283
*Les deux cousines. See Two Fair
Cousins, The*
Dharampal-Frick, Gita, 151–52

Dibao (administrative gazettes), 45
Dichtung und Wahrheit (Goethe), 142,
142n50, 250, 285, 299
Diderot, Denis, 209
Diez, Heinrich Friedrich von, 281
Dillinger press, 106
Discipline and Punish (Foucault), 235
disputations. *See* Nanjing disputation
distance effect on sympathy, 17–18,
27, 121, 123, 176, 199, 212–13,
218, 223–24, 227, 231–34, 242
divine revelation, 47, 77, 122, 186–87
Dodds, Phil, 225
Doody, Margaret Ann, 145
drama. *See* theater
Dryden, John, 139, 145, 175–76,
186–87
Du Halde, Jean-Baptiste, 58, 65, 85,
102, 115, 161, 175n43, 225, 308–9,
317
Dulcitus (von Gandersheim), 145
Dutch East India Company, 43, 75,
150, 167, 202
Dutch embassy in China, 19, 43, 44*fig*
Dutch rebellion (1566–1648), 177–78

earthquake thought experiment
(Smith), 9–10, 24, 176, 222–23, 230,
235, 237–40
East India Company (Dutch), 43, 150,
167, 202
East India Company (English), 176,
202, 227, 308, 316
Eckermann, Johann Peter: Chinese
literature and, 297, 316, 321n65,
322, 341–42, 344; cosmopolitanism
and, 298, 306; *Gespräche mit
Goethe* (Conversations with
Goethe), 199, 297, 306, 323, 340;
Goethe and, 25, 296–99, 306, 310,
316, 318, 321–23, 321n65, 324–25,
341–42, 344, 346; Greek antiquity
and, 298; mood and, 340; poetry
and, 298–99, 322–23, 346; on
rewriting established stories, 266;
Schiller and, 207; world literature
and, 199, 207, 299n5, 310

education, 74–75, 105–8, 115, 124–25,
178, 204, 255, 257, 258, 261n35,
289–90
Eichendorff, Joseph von, 210–11, 219
Einfühlung (empathy), 18, 133, 282
Elective Affinities (Goethe), 146, 264,
299
elites. *See* administrative elite
Emilia Galotti (Lessing), 118, 194
emperors. *See* rulers
Endter, Johannes, 248
English East India Company, 176, 202,
227, 308, 316
Enlightenment: accommodation and,
116, 209, 278; administrative elite
and, 271; analogies and, 157;
atheism and, 290; Chinese literature
and, 61; Chinese sympathies and, 2,
6, 9, 12, 66–67, 77–78, 115–16, 138,
140, 177, 196; Christianity and,
196; colonialism and, 18, 202;
Confucianism and, 140, 209;
cosmopolitanism and, 6, 26, 160,
198, 202, 207–11, 269; enthusiasm
in, 121; European literature and, 66,
221; fables and, 12, 57, 65–67, 69,
73; friendship and, 24; German
Enlightenment, 18, 69, 220–21,
223n9, 278; God and, 140;
information networks and, 12;
Jesuits and, 12, 23, 77–78, 84–85,
95, 115, 124, 162, 181, 209, 210,
217; knowledge and, 67, 73, 95;
letter writing and, 92, 143, 339;
literati and, 269; martyrdom and, 9,
23, 116, 121, 165; orientalism and,
66, 73; pantheism in, 270; *philosophes* in, 339; philosophy and, 2, 9,
66–67, 73, 140–41, 188, 211, 221,
270, 280; reading practices and,
146; religion critiqued in, 23–25,
209, 280–81, 290; rulers and, 9,
165; salons during, 201–2, 207,
301–2, 323; scholarship on, 12, 18;
Scottish Enlightenment, 121, 225;
secret societies and, 216–17;
sentimentalism and, 196, 202, 221;

superstition in, 67; sympathy and,
2–4, 9, 23–25, 115–16, 121; theater
and, 23–24, 188; trade and, 67;
travel literature and, 65–67, 72;
utopianism and, 67; world literature
and, 12–13, 26, 207
enthusiasm, 3, 121, 185
L'eroe Cinese (Gluck), 175
eschatology, 171, 195
Ethics (Spinoza), 286
ethnography, 14, 28, 65, 68–69, 89,
151–52, 262, 310–11, 314
ethnology, 151, 152n80
Euripides, 227
European literature: analogies and,
157–58, 324, 331; ancient influence
on, 157; baroque style and, 9, 12,
64, 124, 145, 173, 176, 195,
248–49, 263–64, 268; Chinese
literature and, 7, 14–15, 52, 243–44,
309, 339; Chinese sympathies and,
119, 156–57; colonialism and, 157,
202; Enlightenment and, 66, 221;
fables and, 66–68, 70–71; imagination and, 126, 135, 147; information
networks and, 63–64; Jesuits and,
23, 63–64, 124; knowledge and, 10,
47, 68, 244, 267; martyrdom and,
117–18; philosophy and, 66–67;
psychology and, 118; rulers and,
52–53; sympathy and, 115, 117–19;
theater and, 23, 117–18; trade and,
67; translation and, 69; travel
literature and, 68; utopianism and,
60–61; wars and, 156–57. *See also
specific works*
European philosophy. *See* philosophy
Evangelicae historiae imagines
(Nadal), 133–34

fables: administrative elite and, 48;
China as land of, 55–56, 59–61, 70,
297, 342; Chinese literature and, 61,
72–73; Enlightenment and, 12, 57,
61, 65–67, 69, 73; European
literature and, 66–68, 70–71;
imagination and, 66; information

fables (*continued*)
  networks and, 28; Jesuits and, 65;
  persistence of, 65–73; philosophy
  and, 66–67, 69; psychology and,
  70–71; space and, 36; travel
  literature and, 21, 28, 32, 36, 55–57,
  59, 60, 66–68, 71; truth opposed to,
  61, 66, 69; utopianism and, 342
Fang Xiaoru, 163
Faust (Goethe), 246–48, 251, 263–64,
  266–68, 290
Feder, Johann Heinrich Georg, 222
fencing metaphor, 260–61, 281
Festa, Lynn, 241
Fichte, Johann Gottlieb, 25, 247, 253,
  270, 272–79, 284, 290–91
Ficino, Marsilio, 292
fictionality, 27–28, 64–65, 71
Fletcher, Joseph, 244
Forbidden City, 43, 77, 178
Fortitudo Japonica, 180–81
Fortunate Union, The (Davis), 315
fortune, 191–92, 329
Foucault, Michel, 6, 20, 36–37, 235
Fourmont, Étienne, 313
Franciscans, 79, 127, 127n22, 285
Francisci, Erasmus: compilation of
  stories by, 247–49, 251, 267, 287;
  fencing metaphor of, 281; Goethe
  and, 249, 249n13, 263, 267, 270,
  284; Jesuits and, 258, 260–62, 284,
  315; knowledge and, 261; Nanjing
  disputation and, 258–59, 261, 270,
  286–87; the Other and, 261; "Die
  ungeschickte Schluß-Künstler," 260
Francke, August, 151–54, 153n83
Francken, Christian, 92
Fräulein von Sternheim (Laroche), 332
Frederick II the Great (Prussian ruler),
  72, 176, 181–82, 271, 280
Frederick IV (Danish king), 151
Freedberg, David, 131n33
Free Masons, 215n35, 218, 277
French Revolution, 216–17, 267, 322
Friedrich, Markus, 81, 88–90, 108
friendship: accommodation and, 204;
  administrative elite and, 331;

Chinese literature and, 330–31;
  Chinese sympathies and, 206;
  Confucianism and, 204–6; cosmopolitanism and, 23, 196, 203, 215;
  Enlightenment and, 24; humanism
  and, 205; Jesuits and, 101, 204–6,
  330; letter writing and, 101, 202–4,
  206; literati and, 204–6; martyrdom
  and, 23, 206; media and, 203;
  philosophy and, 204–5; sentimentalism and, 203, 206; space and, 203;
  world literature and, 203, 207

Garve, Christian, 72
"Das Geheimniß des Kosmopoliten-
  Ordens" (Wieland), 216
Gellert, Christian, 141–43
gender, 117, 188, 203, 237–38, 283, 324
Genealogie der malabarischen Götter
  (Ziegenbalg), 153–54
Genghis Khan, 38
German Enlightenment, 18, 69,
  220–21, 223n9, 278
German Idealism, 253, 260
German literature, 63, 141–44,
  142n50, 263, 268
Germann, Wilhelm, 153–54n85
German poetry, 32, 268
German tragic drama. *See* theater
Geschichte der Abderiten (Wieland),
  215–16, 215n35
"Gesicht von einer Welt unschuldiger
  Menschen" (Wieland), 215
Gespräche mit Goethe (Eckermann),
  199, 297, 306, 323, 340
global history, 171, 184
"Glorious Martyrdom and Blessed Life
  of Jacobi Macaximi, The" (Jesuit
  school drama), 180
Göchhausen, Ernst August Anton, 218
God: Buddhism and, 187, 253, 272,
  285; Confucianism and, 77, 187,
  259; Enlightenment and, 140;
  imagination and, 128; Jesuits and,
  12, 22, 83, 109, 120; knowledge
  and, 261; letter writing and, 79;
  philosophy and, 259

Goes, Joannes Antonides van der, 181
Goethe, Johann Wolfgang: accommodation and, 7, 10, 122, 254, 270,
283; administrative elite and,
348–49; analogies and, 10, 15, 25,
122, 244–45, 249, 273, 275, 302–3,
302n14, 324, 348; atheism and, 245,
279, 288, 290–91; baroque style
and, 263–64; Buddhism and, 25,
246, 249–50, 256–57, 270, 272–75,
279, 282–83, 286–87, 295; Chinese
literature and, 10, 15, 43, 52, 201,
207, 263–66, 296–307, 311–18,
321–25, 339–46, 350–54; Chinese
sympathies of, 11, 25, 244, 251, 260,
279–83, 296–97, 354; Christianity
and, 250–51, 272; colonialism and,
216, 300–301; Confucianism and,
122; cosmopolitanism and, 6,
197–98, 216, 283, 298; critical
reception of, 68, 142, 263, 271, 289,
303–4; Eckermann and, 25, 296–99,
306, 310, 316, 318, 321–23,
321n65, 324–25, 341–42, 344, 346;
education and, 257, 289–90; fables
and, 59, 68, 71, 297; Fichte and,
279, 290; Francisci and, 249,
249n13, 263, 267, 270, 284; God
and, 272, 285; heresy and, 250–51,
284; humanity and, 244, 246,
299–301, 305–6, 340, 353–54;
imagination and, 147–48; influences
on, 6, 14, 25, 59–60, 70, 142, 145,
152–53, 245–49, 249n13, 251,
263–66; information networks and,
11, 251–52, 288–89, 304; Islam and,
70, 254, 288, 299–300; Jesuits and,
25, 124, 245–50, 256–57, 260, 273,
276, 278, 283, 306; knowledge and,
10, 244, 301, 303; literati and, 271,
347–48; martyrdom and, 145–46;
media and, 11, 25, 142, 304, 322;
mood and, 308, 325, 339–40,
342–45; Nanjing disputation and,
246–51, 256–60, 262–63, 269–71,
273, 275–82, 287–90, 297, 304,
314, 345, 348; Persia studied by, 8,

59, 68, 216, 263–64, 266, 299,
344–45; philosophy and, 25,
245–46, 257–58, 260, 269–76,
272n5, 277–79, 284–86, 299,
304–5, 352–54, 352n132; Pietism
and, 148, 154, 207, 244, 250–51;
poetry and, 216, 265–71, 279–80,
288, 299, 304, 308, 311, 319,
324–25, 339–46, 348; reading
practices and, 6, 145–47, 244; rulers
and, 51, 271, 283; Schiller correspondences of, 245–51, 262,
265–75, 279–82, 284, 287–90,
294–95, 314, 343, 349; sentimentalism and, 244; sympathy and, 299,
340, 352; translation and, 11, 14,
15, 209, 339–40; wars and, 36, 63;
world literature theory of, 10–11,
14–15, 24–25, 122–23, 198, 216–19,
263, 291–92, 296–304, 310,
321–22, 347; writing style of,
263–65, 267, 305–6. *See also specific
works*
Goeze, Johann Melchior, 145
*Der goldne Spiegel, oder Die Könige
von Schechian* (Wieland), 53, 197
Golius, Jacobus, 162, 167–68
Goodman, Dena, 261n35
Görres, Joseph, 72
Gospels, 117, 132–34, 145, 151
Gozzi, Carlo, 70, 118, 282–83
Great Wall of China, 52, 58, 166
"Great Wall of China, The" (Kafka),
52
Greek antiquity, 128, 137, 173,
183–84, 201, 298
Gregory XIII (pope), 164
Gryphius, Andreas, 138, 189
Guigues, Joseph de, 62

Habermas, Jürgen, 202
Habsburg Empire, 21, 50–51, 90,
229n26
Hadot, Pierre, 128, 239
Hafez (Persian poet), 60, 69, 198, 207,
214, 216, 219, 263–64, 299
Hagdorn, Christian, 63–65, 169

Hallesche Berichte (Halle reports), 151–52, 154, 250
Hamburger, Käte, 224
Hamburgische Dramaturgie (Lessing), 117–18
Hammer-Purgstall, Joseph von, 69, 263, 281
Hamm, Heinz, 322n69
Harloe, Katherine, 221
harmony, 95, 215, 225, 342, 350
Harris, Steven J., 87–88, 91–92, 99
"Harzreise im Winter" (Goethe), 265–66, 352
Hausen, Wolfgang von, 106
Hayot, Eric, 160
heathens, 21, 96, 151, 153, 187, 237
Hegel, Georg Wilhelm Friedrich, 32, 63, 239, 251, 264, 277, 284, 286, 303–4, 341, 345
Heine, Heinrich, 187, 264–65
Herder, Johann Gottfried, 18, 263, 280–81
heresy, 77, 161–62, 192, 251, 254, 259, 261, 284, 288, 293–94
"Hermann und Dorothea" (Goethe), 267
Hinduism and Hindus, 150–54, 152n80
Hippocrates, 215
History of the Abderites, The (Wieland), 215–16
Hoffmann, E. T. A., 71–72, 345
Holy Roman Empire, 7, 34, 36, 50, 53, 63, 97, 189, 228–29, 348–49
Homer, 119, 157
Horace, 199–201, 332
hospitality, 1, 20, 286, 292
Hsia, Adrian, 175, 175n43, 189n26
Hsia, Florence, 75
Huang Arcade, 313, 323
Huang Zuo, 163
humanism, 11–12, 35, 42, 75, 104, 137–38, 143, 166, 171, 203–5, 244, 282
Humboldt, Wilhelm von, 300
Hume, David, 2, 207, 220, 224–25
Hutcheson, Francis, 220–21

Idealism, 21, 245–46, 251, 253, 257, 260, 270–75, 277–79, 284, 286–87, 304
Ideas on the Philosophy of Human History (Herder), 18
Ideen zu einer Philosophie der Natur (Schelling), 273
identificatory reading, 6, 115, 146
idolatry, 30, 160–61, 165, 192, 253–56, 261–62, 270, 293, 312
Ignatius Loyola: *Constitutions*, 78–79; cosmopolitanism and, 78; curiosity types distinguished by, 102; directives of, 78, 100; imagination and, 129–31; information networks and, 81–92; Jesuits founded by, 74, 131–32; letter writing by, 78, 100, 102, 143; reading practices and, 148; sentimentalism and, 148; *Spiritual Exercises*, 124–26, 128, 130–31, 131n33, 148–49; spiritual exercises of, 125, 127–28, 148–49; vision experienced by, 131–32
Illuminati Order, 218
imagination: analogies and, 125–26; ancient conception of, 130, 135–36, 148; Buddhism and, 273; Chinese sympathies and, 17–18, 129, 131, 134, 158; Christianity and, 130; Confucianism and, 135, 136fig; cosmopolitanism and, 130, 208; development of, 127–31; European literature and, 126, 135, 147; expansion of, 130–31; fables and, 66; God and, 128; hermeneutics and, 137; illustrations in devotional books and, 135; information networks and, 49; Jesuits and, 127–34, 131n32; martyrdom and, 164, 241; monastic practices and, 128–31, 136–37, 136n46, 150; philosophy and, 125–26; poetry and, 5, 135–36, 176, 341; postal systems and, 49; religious dimensions of, 127–31; scripture and, 133–34; sentimentalism and, 146–47, 150, 197n1; sympathy and, 115, 125–29,

134, 176, 232, 235; theater and, 148; travel literature and, 33, 148–49; visualization and, 82, 126, 131, 134, 136n46

Imitation of Christ (Kempis), 132, 144–45

imperial administrators. *See* administrative elite

imperial court, 35, 43, 45, 52, 55, 61, 178, 226, 253n23, 271, 327–29, 338

"An Imperial Message" (Kafka), 47–48, 50–53, 213

India: accommodation and, 152, 154; analogies and, 228–30; China compared to, 230; colonialism and, 227–30; Europe compared to, 228–30; fables about, 64, 66, 72; geography of, 228; Germany compared to, 228–30; God and, 153–54; information networks and, 95; Jesuit mission in, 75, 82, 95, 97, 102–4, 151; letter writing and, 79, 82–83, 90, 96–98, 102–3; literature in, 14; Pietism in, 150–53; stereotypes about, 151; sympathy for, 227–30; travel literature on, 37, 64, 66, 72

India Bill (1783), 227–29

Indian Emperour, The (Dryden), 139, 186–87

Indian Queen, The (Dryden), 175–76

information networks and communication channels: accommodation and, 88, 162; actor-network theory and, 59, 88, 90; administrative elite and, 43, 45; analogies and, 6, 302; Chinese literature and, 13–14, 309; Chinese sympathies and, 5–6, 17, 24, 114, 123–24, 141, 158, 231, 251–52; colonialism and, 231; communication theory and, 93–94, 94n43; cosmopolitanism and, 8, 17, 24–25, 114, 207–8, 231; Enlightenment and, 12; European literature and, 63–64; fables and, 28; imagination and, 49; Jesuits and, 6, 8, 21–22, 35, 42, 74, 78–80, 88, 89,

90–91; knowledge and, 30, 68, 80, 91, 162; letter writing and, 57–58, 80–88, 91–94, 96–97, 99, 143, 203, 294–85; martyrdom and, 24; media and, 11, 18, 46, 47, 87, 94, 203, 230–31, 253, 301, 304; noise in, 87–88; poetry and, 304; postal systems and, 40, 43, 46, 49, 155; reciprocal exchange in, 304; sender and receiver in, 8, 46–48, 80, 93–94, 107, 199–200, 253, 295; space and, 36; spiritualization of, 80, 95–96, 207; sympathy and, 5–6, 24, 114, 121, 158, 234; trade and, 1–2; world literature and, 25, 199–200, 298–99. *See also* knowledge; media

Instituio oratoria (Quintilian), 129

Intorcettaand, Prospero, 186n23

Iphigenia auf Tauris (Goethe), 71n83, 266–67, 283

Islam and Muslims, 22, 30, 82, 118, 176, 251, 288, 305

Israel, Jonathan, 217, 285, 290

Italian Journey (Goethe), 344

Japan: converts in, 21–22, 116, 120, 138–39, 160, 171–72, 179, 182, 192–93; European portrayals of, 160, 180; foreign trade and, 226; Jesuits mission in, 21, 108, 174, 179; martyrdom in, 17, 98, 116, 120, 139, 156, 164, 174–75, 179–80, 192; sympathy and, 17, 116, 120, 137, 165, 190; theater and, 120, 137, 174–75, 178, 182

Jaspers, Karl, 243–44, 254

Jauß, Hans Robert, 16, 144

Jesuits: administrative elite and, 7–8, 20, 22, 35, 42, 91, 175, 245, 306; analogies and, 7, 157, 192, 269, 312; Asia mission of, 75, 79, 102–3, 109–10, 192; baroque style and, 124, 143, 249; book printing and, 105–6; Buddhism and, 6, 77, 162, 245–46, 247n7, 252–53, 257–58, 283–84, 288, 293; China as ideal moral society and, 23, 35, 56, 60,

Jesuits (*continued*)
77–78; China mission of, 42, 76–77, 97, 105, 108–9, 110, 161–62, 208–9, 262, 287; Chinese literature and, 7–8, 13, 91, 309–10, 313–14, 317, 332, 338; Chinese sympathies and, 1–2, 6, 8–9, 22, 25–26, 115–16, 124, 137–39, 140, 254; colonialism and, 197; conspiracy theories about, 216–18; cosmopolitanism and, 8, 20, 116, 196–97, 208, 215n35, 293; critical reception of accounts by, 23, 35, 55–58, 65, 69, 110, 312; Enlightenment and, 12, 23, 77–78, 84–85, 95, 115, 124, 162, 181, 209, 210, 217; European literature and, 23, 63–64, 124; fables and, 65; founding of, 74, 131; friendship and, 101, 204–6, 330; goals of, 12, 20–21, 23, 26, 35, 55, 74–75, 98, 161, 162, 213; God and, 12, 22, 83, 109, 120; imagination and, 127–34, 131n32; India mission of, 75, 82, 95, 97, 102–4, 151; influence of, 15, 115–16, 124, 280; information networks and, 6, 8, 21–22, 35, 42, 74, 78–80, 88, 89, 90–91; Japan mission of, 21, 108, 174, 179; Jesus and, 109, 126–27, 134; knowledge and, 8, 12–15, 63–65, 76, 80, 84–85, 91–92, 96, 162, 168–70, 245, 312; literati and, 91–92, 140, 255, 270–71, 317, 347–48; local culture adopted by, 7, 21–22, 75, 80, 108–13, 306; martyrdom and, 9, 24, 116, 120–21, 160–64, 164n17; media strategies of, 42, 65, 80–82, 84, 87, 160, 162–63; medieval meditative practices and, 126–27, 127n22; organization of, 81, 89–90, 105; pedagogy of, 74–75, 105–6, 115, 124–25, 178, 204, 255, 258, 261n35; philosophy and, 259–60; poetry and, 13; postal systems and, 42, 84, 123, 338; reading practices and, 115, 124, 126–27, 154; rulers and, 20, 23, 192; scholarship on, 13,

86–87, 90–91, 100, 122, 162, 293; school dramas of, 12, 81, 120–21, 137–38, 161, 172–75, 175n43, 178–81, 185n17, 190; sentimentalism and, 141, 148, 154; space and, 81, 115, 130–31, 134–35; spiritual circuit and, 22, 79–80; spiritual exercises of, 82–84, 124–28, 130–31, 131n33, 148–49; suppression of, 15, 23, 57, 76, 116, 262, 276; sympathy and, 8, 75, 115, 124–25; trade and, 1–2, 20, 85; translation and, 7–8, 13, 42, 94, 104–5, 107, 205, 306, 317; transportation and, 6, 75; travel literature and, 30, 91; wars and, 95; world literature and, 13, 24. *See also* accommodation; Catholic Church; Christianity; letter writing
Jesus Christ: Confucianism and, 158; God and, 120; imagination and, 126–27; Jesuits and, 109, 126–27, 134; letter writing and, 109–10; martyrdom and, 119–20, 125, 181; model of, 110, 119–20, 125, 132, 144; monastic practices and, 22, 109, 132–33, 144; sympathy and, 119–22, 126–27, 144, 241; world literature and, 119
Job, 172, 266
Josef, Franz, 50
Joseph II (Holy Roman emperor), 53–54, 277
Journeymanship (Goethe), 308
Judaism and Jews, 22, 259, 287, 289
Juneja, Monica, 152

Kaempfer, Engelbert, 62n74
Kafka, Franz: administrative elites in, 55, 269; analogies and, 50–52, 269; Austria critiqued through comparison by, 50–52; Chinese sympathies and, 49–51; emperors and, 48, 50, 52, 55; fables and, 47–49; "The Great Wall of China," 52; "An Imperial Message," 47–48, 50–53, 213; information networks and, 48–49; letter writing and, 47–48;

media and, 47–49, 47n39; political context of writings by, 50–52; Polo's influence on, 21, 48, 51–52; postal systems and, 47–49, 52; rulers and, 55, 269; space and, 49; writing style of, 52

"Der Kampf mit Dem Drachen" (Schiller), 267

Kangxi (emperor), 20, 35–36

Kantianism: analogies and, 125; categorical imperative in, 231; colonialism and, 231; consciousness and, 275; cosmopolitanism and, 216, 231; Idealist debates with, 25, 245, 270–71; imagination and, 125–26; impartial spectator and, 222; information networks and, 231; knowledge and, 25, 257, 277; media and, 231; rational subject and, 351–52; sympathy and, 222, 231; thing in itself in, 273–75

Kant, Immanuel, 16, 20, 25, 125–26, 142n50, 159, 202, 222, 231, 234, 352

Karl August (duke), 54

Kern, Iso, 247n7

Kino, Eusebio, 98, 186n23

Kircher, Athansius, 57–58, 84, 166–67, 267

Kittler, Friedrich, 48, 94–95, 263, 268

Kittler, Wolf, 47

Klawitter, Arne, 347

Kleingeld, Pauline, 198, 202

Klettenberg, Susanne von, 250

knowledge: baroque style and, 2, 14, 249; Chinese literature and, 8, 14, 69, 309–12, 330; Chinese sympathies and, 261; colonialism and, 249; Enlightenment and, 67, 73, 95; European literature and, 10, 47, 68, 244, 267; God and, 261; information networks and, 30, 68, 80, 91, 162; Jesuits and, 8, 12–15, 63–65, 76, 80, 84–85, 91–92, 96, 162, 168–70, 245, 312; letter writing and, 80, 85, 93, 99, 102, 107–10; postal systems and, 39–40, 47; rulers and,

30–32; scientific knowledge, 13, 99, 342; self-examination and, 87, 149, 233, 261; self-knowledge, 261; sentimentalism and, 149–50, 220; sympathy and, 119; translation and, 107, 309–10; transportation and, 42; travel literature and, 42, 68; world literature and, 12–13, 15, 201, 310. *See also* information networks and communication channels

Kommerell, Max, 353–54

Körner, Christian Gottfried, 283

Koschorke, Albrecht, 143, 240n58

Koselleck, Reinhold, 217, 290

Kracauer, Siegfried, 67

Krämer, Sybille, 46

Kublai Khan, 30–32, 38–39, 46, 48, 62

Kuo Mo-jo, 353

Kurtz, Joachim, 259

Lach, Donald, 95

laity, 79, 91, 95–97, 101, 124–25, 127, 161–62, 169, 178, 198, 206, 208

Laokoon oder Über die Grenzen der Malerei und Poesie (Lessing), 221, 236

Latour, Bruno, 59, 83, 91–93

Lavater, Johann Caspar, 144

Law, John, 87–88, 91–92

Lee, Meredith, 350

"Die Lehrlinge von Sais" (Wieland), 214

Leibniz, Gottfried: accommodation and, 7, 18, 278; Chinese sympathies and, 3, 35, 69, 77–78, 78n9, 243, 245–46, 285; Confucianism and, 77–78; cosmopolitanism and, 197; Jesuits and, 77–78, 91, 94, 162, 185, 243, 293, 324; *Novissima Sinica*, 243; pantheism and, 285–86; philosophy and, 69, 197, 278, 280; polygamy and, 324; sympathy and, 213

Lenz, Jakob Michael Reinhold, 145–46

Lessing, Gotthold, 18, 61–62, 69–71, 117–19, 187, 221, 236, 236n47, 241, 280, 291

letter writing: accommodation and, 88; annual letters and, 88–89, 180; audience of, 99, 100, 112–13; baroque style and, 143; Chinese literature and, 339; Chinese sympathies and, 97, 124; compilations of, 84–85; cultural transformation through, 108–13; development of, 102, 123; directions for, 90, 93, 99, 100, 100n62; distance and, 294, 295; editorial decisions in, 88–89, 101; education and, 107–8; Enlightenment and, 92, 143, 339; friendship and, 101, 202–4, 206; information networks and, 57–58, 80–88, 91–94, 96–97, 99, 143, 203, 294–85; knowledge and, 80, 85, 93, 99, 102, 107–10; local letters and, 88–89; martyrdom and, 98, 107, 109; media and, 84, 142–43, 203; postal systems and, 102–3, 122–23, 294–95; psychology and, 109–10; publication of, 102, 104–7, 112–13, 144, 180; purposes of, 78–79, 81–84, 86, 92–93, 95–97, 99, 102–3, 107–10, 112, 143, 295; rewriting in, 88–89; scholarship on, 92, 99, 111, 122; scriptural citations in, 101, 104; sender and receiver in, 93–94, 295; sentimentalism and, 122, 141, 199; space and, 195, 203; spiritual circuit established by, 22, 79, 95–96, 98, 106–8, 112–13; strategic dimensions of, 107; style of, 90, 101, 106, 123, 143–44, 170, 200; sympathy and, 122; theater and, 125, 173, 178, 180; translation and, 104–7, 112, 144; transportation and, 111; types of, 99–101; world literature and, 199–200. *See also* postal systems
Lettres édifiantes et curieuses (Du Halde), 84–85, 102, 115, 308–9
Levy, Evonne, 131n32
Linnaeus, Carl, 148–49
Li-Po, 353
literati: accommodation and, 181, 254; ancient sources and, 205; Chinese

literature and, 328–32, 334, 339; Chinese sympathies and, 244, 249, 348–49; Confucianism and, 162, 253, 255; Enlightenment and, 269; friendship and, 204–6; Jesuits and, 91–92, 140, 255, 270–71, 317, 347–48; martyrdom and, 162; theater and, 181
literature. *See* Asian literature; Chinese literature; European literature; German literature; travel literature; world literature
Livre des merveilles du monde (Polo), 38
Livy (Titus Livius), 194
Li Zicheng, 190–91, 194
Locke, John, 57, 148–49
logical argumentation, 259–60, 278
London Merchant, The (Lillo), 158, 223–24
Longobardo, Nicoló, 12, 133
Loos, Adolf, 229n26
Louis XIV (King of France), 51
Lovejoy, Arthur O., 76
Ludolph of Saxony, 132–34

Macao, 107, 112, 191
Macartney expedition, 110, 115, 180, 249, 262, 307, 315
Magdeburg siege (1631), 155
Malabarische Correspondenz (Francke), 153
Manchu invasion: baroque style and, 177; implications for Europe of, 35, 171, 177–78; Ming dynasty conquest by, 12, 22, 156, 165–67, 177–78; postal systems and, 43; theater and, 174, 182
mandarins. *See* administrative elite
Mandeville, Bernard, 16, 232
Mandeville, John, 11, 30, 38, 57, 61–62, 72
Ma Ning, 307n24, 323
Marco Polo. *See* Polo, Marco
Martin, A. Lynn, 100
Martini, Martino: *Atlas*, 167, 170; friendship and, 205–6; God and, 12,

171, 192; history written by, 171–75, 195; illustrations in works by, 173; influence of, 22–23, 172, 185, 192, 195; information network and, 170–71; justification for writing by, 169; knowledge and, 169; martyr plays and, 171; Ming dynasty writings of, 12, 22, 165–66, 171, 182–83, 191; motivations for writings of, 185; Polo's influence on, 57; publications by, 205–6; translations by, 205

martyrdom: accommodation and, 160, 163, 165; baroque style and, 9, 139, 163, 182; Chinese sympathies and, 17, 116, 120–22, 137–40, 162–63, 165; colonialism and, 237; Confucianism and, 9, 165; cosmopolitanism and, 116, 137, 140, 159, 210; differing modes of, 160–61; education and, 107–8; Enlightenment and, 9, 23, 116, 121, 165; European literature and, 117–18; false and true forms of, 118; friendship and, 23, 206; heresy and, 161; imagination and, 164, 241; information networks and, 24; Jesuits and, 9, 24, 116, 120–21, 160–64, 164n17; letter writing and, 98, 107, 109; literati and, 162; psychology and, 164; reading practices and, 164; rulers and, 165, 173, 179–82, 186; scholarship on, 164–65; sentimentalism and, 145; space and, 126; sympathy and, 24, 117, 119–20, 140, 158, 164; theater and, 9, 17, 117–18, 137, 139, 159–61, 165, 174, 179–82, 188, 235–37; world literature and, 119

Martyrologium Romanum (Gregory XIII), 164

Marx, Karl, 51, 201

Mary, 125, 127

masculinity, 117, 188, 203, 237–38

Maximillian II (emperor), 104

Mayer, Johannes, 105–6

Mayer, Sebald, 106–7

McLuhan, Marshall, 39, 54, 93–95

McMahon, Keith, 324, 337

media: Chinese sympathies and, 5, 17–18, 41, 230–31; cosmopolitanism and, 137, 199; friendship and, 203; information networks and, 11, 18, 46, 47, 87, 94, 203, 230–31, 253, 301, 304; Jesuit strategies using, 42, 65, 80–82, 84, 87, 160, 162–63; letter writing and, 84, 142–43, 203; philosophy and, 160; poetry and, 304; postal systems and, 41, 46–47, 55; prayer and, 94, 96; space and, 41, 47n39, 251; sympathy and, 2, 5, 17–18, 25, 223, 231; technologies of, 37, 95, 142; theater and, 137; theory of, 6, 46, 81, 96, 122, 141–42, 240n58; time and, 41; wars and, 155–57; world literature and, 304. *See also* information networks and communication channels

medieval meditative practices, 126–27, 127n22, 131–33, 131n33, 150

medieval travelogues, 57, 89

Meister, Wilhelm, 307, 334

merchants. *See* trade

metaphysics. *See* philosophy

Meurs, Jacob de, 63

Milton, John, 189n30, 215, 290

Milvian Bridge Battle (312), 192

Ming dynasty: administrative gazettes in, 45; baroque style and, 162, 165, 182; Chinese sympathies and, 157; Christianity during, 165–66; Confucianism in, 162; God and, 171; implications for Europe of, 35, 165, 171, 177–78; Jesuit reports on, 156; Manchu conquest of, 12, 22, 35, 155–56, 165–67, 177–78; martyrdom in, 156, 162–63; media and, 155–56; ruler as figure of sympathy in, 162–63, 165–66, 172, 181–82, 188, 194–95; theatrical representation of, 155, 181–82; travel literature on, 156; Troy compared to, 183–84

missionaries. *See* Jesuits; Pietism;
  Protestantism
Mitleid (pity), 221, 224
mitteilen (sharing), 93–94
Mittmann, Jörg-Peter, 278
mnemonics, 129–30, 129n26
Molina, J. Michelle, 79, 127n23
Mongol empire, 30, 32–34, 37–41, 43,
  45–49, 93, 339
Montanus, Arnold, 29
Montesquieu (Charles-Louis de
  Secondat), 54, 339
Montezuma, 139, 175–76, 181–82,
  186–88
Montezuma (Vivaldi), 176, 182
mood: Chinese literature and, 14,
  339–41, 343–44; poetry and,
  340–41, 343–45; *Stimmung* and, 5,
  325, 339–41, 343–45; subjectivity
  and, 344; sympathy and, 9
moral psychology, 2–6, 16, 21, 141,
  221, 231, 244
Moritz, Karl Phillip, 132, 144
Müller, Andreas, 59
Müller, Johannes, 174
Mulsow, Martin, 251
Mungello, David, 173, 252
Murr, Christian Gottlieb von, 262,
  262n38, 313–14
Muslims and Islam, 22, 30, 82, 118,
  176, 251, 288, 305
mysticism, 126, 132, 144

Nadal, Jerónimo, 97, 104, 133–34
Nanjing disputation: accommodation
  and, 288; accuracy of, 291; administrative elite and, 288; analogies and,
  25; audience of, 291; Buddhist voice
  in, 250, 292; cosmopolitanism and,
  292; Enlightenment and, 280–81;
  function of disputations and, 281,
  287–88, 291, 294; God in, 285;
  heresy and, 251; importance of, 288;
  influence of, 256, 258, 287, 289,
  291, 294; information networks and,
  288–89, 294; knowledge and, 249,
  256, 281, 294; literati and, 249;

media and, 253; philosophy and,
  278, 287; scholarship on, 292;
  Weimar debates and, 25, 245–46,
  249, 253, 269–71, 273, 304
Napoleon Bonaparte, 25, 36, 63
"Nathan the Wise" (Lessing), 69–70,
  71n83
natural reason, 186–88, 257–60
Navarrete, Domingo, 172
Navigationi et Viaggi (Rumusio), 84
networks. *See* information networks
  and communication channels
Der Neue Weltbott (Stöcklein), 115
newspapers, 45, 223, 241, 304, 322
New Testament, 79, 151
New World, 156, 164n17, 181
Niekerk, Carl, 118
Nietzsche, Friedrich, 16, 198, 231,
  289
Nieuhof, Jan, 43, 148–49, 156,
  184n15
Noah's Ark, 57
Nobelaer, Cornelius von, 186
Novalis (Georg Philipp Friedrich
  Freiherr von Hardenberg), 71, 214
Novissima Sinica (Leibniz), 243
Novus Atlas Sinensis (Blaeu), 185
Noyes, John, 301n13, 348, 348n125

"Of Other Spaces" (Foucault), 36
Olbricht, Peter, 46
Opium Wars, 20, 51
Order of Things, The (Foucault), 36
Le Orfano della Cina (Gluck), 175
orientalism, 18–20, 36, 61, 66, 73
Orphan (Voltaire), 175n43, 178, 226
Osterhammel, Jürgen, 11–12, 66–69,
  73
Ottomans, 281

pantheism, 258, 270, 281, 284–85,
  289
Paradise Lost (Milton), 290
Parente, James, 161
Passions of the Soul, The (Descartes),
  234
Paul, 79

Percy, Thomas, 308–13, 317

"Perpetual Peace" (Kant), 231

Persia: colonialism and, 301; European literature and, 66; imagination and, 66; poetry and, 68, 216, 281, 345; rulers and, 129; world literature and, 8, 14, 59, 68, 266, 344

Persian Letters (Montesquieu), 339

perspectivism, 351

Petzold, Christian Friedrich, 277

philosophy: accommodation and, 7, 270; analogies and, 157–58, 286, 302–3; Buddhism and, 257–58, 261–62, 270, 272–75, 279, 284, 286; charges of atheism in, 25; Chinese ethics in, 228, 273; Chinese philosophy and, 135, 160, 270, 278–79, 280, 284–86, 291, 293–94; Christianity and, 255, 271, 278–79, 286, 287; Confucianism and, 77, 138, 157–58, 161, 205, 244, 271, 278, 280, 293, 284286; consciousness and, 49, 128, 256–57, 274–76; debates in, 25; Enlightenment and, 2, 9, 66–67, 73, 140–41, 188, 211, 221, 270, 280; European literature and, 66–67; fables and, 66–67, 69; friendship and, 204–5; God and, 259; Greek philosophy and, 22, 208, 219; Idealism in, 21, 245–46, 251, 253, 257, 260, 270–75, 277–79, 284, 286–87, 304; idolatry and, 270; imagination and, 125–26; Jesuits and, 259–60; logical argumentation in, 259–60, 278; media and, 160; metaphysics and, 255, 271, 275–76, 278–79, 284–86, 287, 299; moral philosophy, 9, 121, 128, 138, 222, 226, 228, 236, 240, 273; moral psychology and, 2–6, 16, 21, 141, 221, 231, 244; natural philosophy, 2, 21, 285; natural reason and, 186–88, 257–60; rationalism and, 66–67, 71, 73, 269, 278–79, 280, 286–87, 293; rulers and, 31; similarities between approaches of, 25, 78–79, 78n9, 245–46, 249, 253, 269–71, 273,

304; sympathy and, 2–3, 15–16, 121, 231, 233, 235–36. *See also* Kantianism; Stoicism

Pietism: accommodation and, 150, 152, 154; Confucianism and, 293; cosmopolitanism and, 197, 214; Halle group of, 150–51, 293; heresy and, 152; influence of, 142, 144; Jesuits and, 150, 154; letter writing and, 143, 152–53; literature and, 142; media and, 151; missionary work of, 150–54, 278; philosophy and, 278, 291; reading practices and, 244; scholarship on, 141; sentimentalism and, 141–42, 144, 154; subjectivity and, 141; transportation and, 150; travel reports of, 123, 151

Pinto, Fernão Mendes, 57

Pipinus, Franciscus, 59

Pizarro, Francisco, 186–87

Pizer, John, 199

Plantin, Christophe, 113

Plantin press, 133

Plato, 78n9, 205, 288, 292

Pleasing History, The (Hau Kiou Choaan), 262, 306–8, 313–14, 321n65

Plütschau, Henry, 151

Poe, Edgar Allan, 264

Poetics (Aristotle), 126

poetry: administrative elite and, 271, 345, 349; Chinese literature and, 316–17, 327; Chinese poetry and, 5, 68, 311, 316–18, 320, 320n62, 346; German poetry, 32, 268; imagination and, 5, 135–36, 176, 341; information networks and, 304; Jesuits and, 13; media and, 304; mood and, 340–41, 343–45; Persian poetry, 68, 216, 281, 345; rulers and, 271; space and, 295, 341, 344; sympathy and, 352; translation and, 69, 320–21; world literature and, 301; *yi jing* in, 5, 341

Poetry and Truth (Goethe), 142, 142n50, 250, 285, 299

Polanco, Juan Alfonso de, 101

Polo, Marco: administrative elite and, 30; authority of, 29–30; Chinese sympathies and, 21; Christianity and, 30; credibility of, 32–33, 42, 48, 58–60, 61–62; critical reception of, 11, 29, 32, 57–59, 61, 65–66; Enlightenment and, 62, 66; fables and, 21, 29, 32–33, 59–60, 66; first journey of, 21, 33, 38, 40; imprisonment of, 33; influence of, 21, 28–30, 35, 51, 59–60, 62, 66, 70, 74, 84, 166; information networks and, 21, 28, 34, 37, 43; Jesuits and, 55–58; *Livre des merveilles du monde*, 38; as mediator, 31, 62; missionary purpose of, 30, 57; postal systems and, 34, 38–42, 48–49, 338; rulers and, 21, 30, 31–33; scholarship on, 34, 60, 62, 62n74; space and, 36–37, 40–41; trade and, 30, 31, 34; translation of, 59; transportation and, 33–34, 37, 39, 41–42; travel literature and, 21, 28–29; *Travels*, 21, 28–30, 32–33, 35–37, 38–42, 57, 59, 61–62, 65–66, 84, 166; writing style of, 29, 34, 38, 40, 74
polygamy, 324–25, 337
Porter, David, 177
Posevino, Antonio, 100
postal systems: administrative elite and, 39, 43, 48; Chinese literature and, 307; Chinese sympathies and, 51–52; cosmopolitanism and, 198–99; horse use in, 43, 44*fig*; imagination and, 49; information networks and, 40, 43, 46, 49, 155; Jesuits and, 42, 84, 123, 338; knowledge and, 39–40, 47; letter writing and, 102–3, 122–23, 294–95; media and, 41, 46–47, 55; rulers and, 39, 45–46; scholarship on, 122–23, 142; sentimentalism and, 141, 144, 199; space and, 38–39, 41, 295; travel literature and, 34, 38, 48; world literature and, 24, 123. *See also* letter writing
prayer, 12, 22, 79, 92, 94, 96–100, 131, 162, 195, 198, 208, 215

Prester John, 38
Priam, 157, 184, 194
prosoche (attention over self), 128
Protestantism: colonialism and, 156, 237; cosmopolitanism and, 211; Enlightenment and, 211; imagination and, 241; information networks and, 94; Jesuits and, 13, 92, 94–95, 162, 258; knowledge and, 13, 15; letter writing and, 92, 94–95, 98; martyrdom and, 120, 138–39, 161; media and, 156; missionary work of, 153, 254; sympathy and, 241; trade and, 20, 94, 95
Pro theologia mystica Clavis (Sandaeus), 150
psychological factors, 2–6, 16, 21, 70–71, 108–10, 118, 141, 196–97, 221–25, 235–36, 244, 303
Pufendorf, Samuel von, 229

Qianlong (emperor), 20
Qing dynasty, 36, 43, 50, 193, 308, 323, 339
queerness, 334
Quintilian, 129, 183n14

Rabbow, Paul, 131
Rameau's Nephew (Diderot), 209
Ramusio, Giovanni Battista, 32
rationalism, 66–67, 71, 73, 269, 278–79, 280, 286–87, 293
Die Räuber (Schiller), 315
reading practices, 6, 11, 115, 122–24, 141–47, 148–49, 154, 164, 207, 244, 297
reason (natural), 186–88, 257–60
reception theory, 146
Reformation, 35, 60–61, 63, 74, 104–5, 115, 131n33, 173, 177, 207, 254, 258
Reinhold, Karl Leonhard, 270, 274–79, 287, 290
religious wars of Europe, 156, 165, 171, 173, 177
Rémusat, Abel, 52, 271, 310, 316, 321–24, 331–32, 339–40, 345

Renaissance, 4, 6, 75, 292
resemblances, 3, 10–11, 224, 230, 244, 301
Rétif, Andre, 100n62
rhetoric, 123–24, 126, 129, 131, 135, 141, 158, 207, 236, 255, 257, 289–90
Rhetorica ad Herenium (anonymous), 129
Ricci, Matteo: accommodation and, 76–78, 87, 165, 175, 193, 252, 254, 259, 271, 278, 288, 291; administrative elite and, 77, 205, 255, 288, 327, 329–30, 338; Buddhism and, 77, 252–62, 253n23, 288; China mission travels of, 77, 103–4; Chinese culture adopted by, 77, 107; Chinese language skills of, 107; Confucianism and, 78, 161, 204, 252–55, 258–59, 271, 288; cosmopolitanism and, 219; as first Westerner to enter Forbidden City, 77; friendship and, 204–5, 330–31; God and, 253, 255–56, 258–59, 261–62, 285; influence of, 76, 115–16, 245–46; information networks and, 251–52; letter writing by, 42, 87, 92, 103; literati and, 91, 227, 271, 329–31, 338, 348; media strategies of, 42, 92; Nanjing disputation and, 254–55, 273, 286–88, 292, 297, 348; philosophy and, 258, 261–62, 278–79; politeness and, 292, 330–31; rhetoric and, 255; translations by, 204–5. *See also specific works*
Richardson, Samuel, 145, 221, 240, 297, 332
Ringer, Fritz K., 349n126
Rites Controversy, 115–16, 161, 167, 181, 209, 312
rococo style, 176, 262–63, 282, 349
Rodriguez, Gonçalo, 83
Roman Catholic Church. *See* Catholic Church
Roman Empire, 31, 35, 183, 203
Romanticism: Buddhism and, 273; Chinese literature and, 298, 324;

critiques of, 341, 345; fables and, 72; German Romanticism, 5, 21, 129; imagination and, 115, 273; Jesuits and, 83; mood and, 5, 341, 345; orientalism and, 71; poetry and, 72, 298, 341; sympathy and, 115; travel literature and, 72; world literature and, 68
Roser, Isabel, 79
Rowlandson, Thomas, 240n58
Rubiés, Joan-Pau, 281, 292
Rückert, Friedrich, 68
Rudolf I (King of the Romans), 50
Ruggieri, Michele, 76–77, 108, 110, 112, 309–10
rulers: accommodation and, 162, 329; baroque style and, 60, 138, 145, 173, 182; Chinese literature and, 52; Chinese sympathies and, 7, 17, 20, 129, 137, 138, 165, 224; Christianity and, 180–82; colonialism and, 227; Confucianism and, 31; conversion attempts of, 13–14, 23; despotism of, 19, 50–51, 54, 67, 72, 137–38, 159, 173, 177–82, 195, 227, 283; Enlightenment and, 9, 165; European literature and, 52–53; imperial court and, 35, 43, 45, 52, 55, 61, 178, 226, 253n23, 271, 327–29, 338; Jesuits and, 20, 23, 192; knowledge and, 30–32; mandate from heaven and, 269; martyrdom and, 165, 173, 179–82, 186; philosophy and, 31; poetry and, 271; postal systems and, 39, 45–46; similarities between, 31, 35, 51–53, 60, 173, 181, 192, 269; sympathy and, 158, 172–73, 175, 181–82, 195; theater and, 138, 160, 175, 178–84, 186–87, 195; threat of weakened power of, 182; trade and, 19–20, 31, 138; travel literature and, 30, 40. *See also* administrative elite; *specific rulers*

Sacchini, Francesco, 81
Said, Edward, 18–19

St. Anselm, 259
St. Paul's College (India), 75
saints, veneration of, 9, 120, 164
salons, 201–2, 207, 301–2, 323
Sandaeus, Maximilian, 150
Sande, Eduardo de, 108
Sanhoi (Buddhist scholar), 246,
    256–57, 278–81, 329
Saussy, Haun, 253n23
Schall, Adam, 167, 182–83, 185,
    190–91, 193
Schelling, Friedrich Wilhelm Joseph,
    273–74, 284
Schiller, Friedrich: baroque style and,
    283; Buddhism and, 281, 283;
    Chinese literature and, 14, 266–67,
    282, 314–15, 322; Christianity
    rejected by, 272; death of, 296, 315;
    Goethe correspondences of, 245–51,
    262, 265–75, 279–82, 284, 287–90,
    294–95, 314, 343, 349; Jesuits and,
    283, 315; mood and, 343; theater
    and, 70, 71n83, 118, 282–83, 314;
    translations and, 314–15; travel
    literature and, 40; world literature
    and, 207, 267; writing style of, 263,
    266–67. *See also specific works*
Schleger, Friedrich, 18, 301
Schneider, Theodor, 98–99
Scholasticism, 75, 91, 100, 138, 166
Schopenhauer, Johanna, 301–2
Scottish Enlightenment, 121, 225
secularization, 6, 21, 119, 121,
    144–46, 197–98, 208, 210, 219,
    235–39, 251
self-examination, 87, 149, 233, 261
Seneca, 238–39
sentimentalism: Christianity and,
    197n1; cosmopolitanism and, 24,
    197, 202, 220; emergence of, 220;
    Enlightenment and, 196, 202, 221;
    friendship and, 203, 206; humanitar-
    ian feelings and, 241; imagination
    and, 146–47, 150, 197n1; Jesuits
    and, 141, 148, 154; knowledge and,
    149–50, 220; letter writing and, 122,
    143, 199; martyrdom and, 145;

postal systems and, 141, 144, 199;
    reading techniques and, 144–45,
    148, 154; scholarship on, 197n1;
    secularization and, 122, 144–46,
    148, 150; sympathy and, 4, 241;
    world literature and, 24
Serres, Michel, 253, 298
Shaftesbury, Anthony Ashley Cooper,
    earl of, 121, 198, 207, 211–12, 220,
    233
Shakespeare, William, 147, 266
Shannon, Claude, 47
Siegert, Bernhard, 84, 122–23
Simmel, Georg, 347
Sinomania, 76
Sinophilia, 3–4, 65, 76, 304
Sinophobia, 3–4, 65, 76, 304
Sloterdijk, Peter, 204
Smith, Adam: Chinese sympathies and,
    139, 225–26, 230–31, 238; Chris-
    tianity and, 128, 235, 237; con-
    science and, 233–34, 237–38;
    cosmopolitanism and, 24, 116, 197,
    226, 233, 239; distance and, 224,
    227, 231, 234; earthquake thought
    experiment of, 24, 222–23, 230,
    235, 237–40; Enlightenment and,
    24; imagination and, 240–41;
    impartial spectator and, 16, 222,
    233, 238; influence of, 220–22,
    240n58, 241; information networks
    and, 24, 223, 225, 231–32; Jesuits
    and, 225, 237; Jesus and, 235;
    martyrdom and, 235; media and,
    222–23, 231; moral views of, 16,
    207–8, 230, 238, 240–41; philoso-
    phy of, 234, 237–38; psychology
    and, 24, 221–22, 224–25, 235–36,
    236n47; scholarship on, 221;
    self-interest and, 234–35, 237;
    sentimentalism and, 239–40;
    Stoicism and, 128, 207, 236,
    238–41; sympathy and, 16, 24–25,
    116–17, 121, 221–25, 230–42;
    Theory of Moral Sentiments, 24,
    116, 220–22, 233, 239; trade and,
    158–59, 225–26; *Wealth of Nations*,

221–22, 225–26; world literature and, 24–25
Society for the Propagation of the Gospel in Foreign Parts, 151
Society of Jesus. *See* Jesuits
soliloquy (practice), 233
Song dynasty, 43
soothsayers, 193
Sorrows of Young Werther, The (Goethe), 142, 144–47, 152, 257, 305, 349
Southern, R. W., 127n22
space: Chinese literature and, 326–27, 327n81; Chinese sympathies and, 36, 251; cosmopolitanism and, 218; fables and, 36; friendship and, 203; information networks and, 36; Jesuits and, 81, 115, 130–31, 134–35; letter writing and, 195, 203; martyrdom and, 126; media and, 41, 47n39, 251; poetry and, 295, 341, 344; postal systems and, 38–39, 41, 295; spatial terms, 327n81; sympathy and, 5–6, 15, 98; time and, 36, 41, 304; trade and, 41; world literature and, 201
Spanish colonialism, 156, 181, 187, 237
spectatorship, 126, 221, 233, 236
Spinola, Karel, 186
Spinoza, Buruch, 16, 258, 260, 272–73, 284–86, 290–91, 299
spiritual circuit, 22, 79–80, 95–96, 98, 106–8, 112–13
Spiritual Exercises (Ignatius Loyola), 124–26, 128, 130–31, 131n33, 148–49
Staiger, Emil, 340, 350, 352
Starr, Chloe, 336
state administrators. *See* administrative elite
Staunton, George, 320n62
Stella (Goethe), 324
Sterne, Lawrence, 240n58
Stimmung (mood), 5, 325, 339–41, 343–45
Stöcklein, Joseph, 115

Stoicism: accommodation and, 173; *apatheia* in, 128, 238–40, 329; baroque style and, 235, 238; cosmopolitanism and, 198, 207–8, 218–19, 239–40; Enlightenment and, 198; friendship and, 204; imagination and, 131; martyrdom and, 139, 175; neo-Stoicism and, 234; rulers and, 187; self-command in, 237–38, 240; sentimentalism and, 146; sympathy disavowed by, 115, 117, 224; theater and, 160, 187, 235
Die Studelhofstiege (von Doderer), 332
Sturm-und-Drang (literary movement), 142, 144, 256, 303, 315
subjectivity, 17, 141, 152, 240n58, 242, 303, 327
Subrahmanyam, Sanjay, 31
Sucquet, Antoine, 134–35
suffering of strangers. *See* sympathy
Suleri, Sara, 228
superstitions, 66–67, 97, 149, 193, 277, 329
Sympathien (Wieland), 216
sympathy: accommodation and, 140; analogies and, 122, 232; ancient approaches to, 115, 128, 352; baroque style and, 223; Christianity and, 115, 117, 119–22, 125–28; colonialism and, 227–30, 231, 237; Confucianism and, 115; cosmopolitanism and, 6, 114–17, 123, 196, 207–8, 218, 222–23, 241; development of, 2–4, 115–17, 242; distance effect on, 17–18, 27, 121, 123, 176, 199, 212–13, 218, 223–24, 227, 231–34, 242; *Einfühlung* and, 18, 133, 282; emotions and, 230–31, 233, 242; Enlightenment and, 2–4, 9, 23–25, 115–16, 121; European literature and, 115, 117–19; extension of, 121, 176, 240; identificatory reading and, 6, 115, 146; imagination and, 115, 125–29, 134, 176, 232, 235; information networks and, 5–6, 24, 114, 121, 158, 234; Jesuits and, 8, 75, 115,

sympathy (*continued*)
124–25; knowledge and, 119; letter writing and, 122; limitations of, 15–16, 121, 242; martyrdom and, 24, 117, 119–20, 140, 158, 164; medieval meditative practices and, 126–28, 127n22; *Mitleid* and, 221, 224; mood and, 9; naturalness of, 2–3, 5; philosophy and, 2–3, 15–16, 121, 231, 233, 235–36; poetry and, 352; reading practices and, 115, 122; requirements for, 5, 224; rulers and, 158, 172–73, 175, 181–82, 195; secularization of, 119, 121, 235–36, 239; sentimentalism and, 4, 241; sequence of, 233–34, 236; shared emotions and, 230–31; space and, 5–6, 15, 98; strangers and, 1, 5, 114, 137, 207, 224, 242; theater and, 125–26, 179, 232, 234, 236–37; trade and, 159; wars and, 159; world literature and, 119, 140, 241. *See also* Chinese sympathies
Symposium (Plato), 292
A System of Moral Philosophy (Hutcheson), 221
Szarota, Elida Maria, 81, 180–81
Szondi, Peter, 158

Tacitus, 156–57
Tag-und Jahres Hefte als Ergänzung meiner sonstigen Bekenntnisse (Goethe), 346
Takenaka, Masahiro, 172
Talbot, Michael, 176
Tamil culture, 152
Tartars, 165–66, 191, 226
"Der Taucher" (Schiller), 267
Tautz, Birgit, 202–3, 207
Taylor, Charles, 340–41
Der Teutsche Merkur (Wieland), 215–16, 277
theater: accommodation and, 175, 181; audiences of, 179–80, 181, 232, 236–37; baroque style and, 19–20, 124, 138–40, 145, 165, 173, 175–78, 182, 185, 188–91, 223,

235–36; Chinese sympathies and, 137, 158, 159–60, 174, 179, 181, 194–95, 226; colonialism and, 181, 186–87, 237; Confucianism and, 181; conversion mission of, 179–80; cosmopolitanism and, 159–60, 175; Enlightenment and, 23–24, 188; European literature and, 23, 117–18; Greek drama and, 117; imagination and, 148; Jesuit school dramas and, 12, 81, 120, 137–38, 161, 172–75, 175n43, 178–81, 185n17, 190; letter writing and, 125, 173, 178, 180; literati and, 181; martyrdom and, 9, 17, 117–18, 137, 139, 159–61, 165, 174, 179–82, 188, 235–37; media and, 137; rulers and, 138, 160, 175, 178–84, 186–87, 195; sympathy and, 125–26, 179, 232, 234, 236–37; theatricality in, 125, 148; themes in, 174, 235–37; trade and, 159; *Trauerspiele* in, 140, 175, 177–78, 189–90; travel literature and, 234; wars and, 159
Theory of Moral Sentiments (Smith), 24, 116, 220–22, 233, 239
Thirty Years' War (1618–1648), 155, 177–78, 258
Thomas Aquinas, 150, 166
Thomism, 166, 188
Thoms, Peter Perring, 316–17, 320n62, 341, 353
A Thousand and One Nights, 53–54, 67, 69, 283
Thucydides, 12, 171, 227
time, 36, 41, 304
Titus (Japanese convert), 171–72, 179
To the Lighthouse (Woolf), 157
trade: China's refusal to engage in, 225–26, 249; Chinese literature and, 13–14; colonialism and, 19, 249; cosmopolitanism and, 159, 202; Enlightenment and, 67; European literature and, 67; free trade, 19–20, 24; information networks and, 1–2; Jesuits and, 1–2, 20, 85; rulers and, 19–20, 31, 138; space and, 41;

sympathy and, 159; theater and, 159; translation and, 13–14; wars and, 158–59; world literature and, 201–2
tragic drama. *See* theater
translation: accommodation and, 94; analogies and, 311; Chinese literature and, 7–8, 11, 13–14, 25, 52, 68–69, 72–73, 309–11, 313–16, 331–32; Chinese sympathies and, 2; European literature and, 69; Jesuits and, 7–8, 13, 42, 94, 104–5, 107, 205, 306, 317; knowledge and, 107, 309–10; letter writing and, 104–7, 112, 144; poetry and, 69, 320–21; trade and, 13–14; world literature and, 199, 310
transportation, 6, 33–34, 37, 39, 40–42, 75, 148
Trauerspiele, 140, 175, 177–78, 189–90
travel literature: administrative elite and, 30; ancient forms of, 157; authenticity of, 27–29, 37, 40–41, 57, 65, 72; Chinese literature and, 28, 69, 317; Chinese sympathies and, 28–32, 65, 124; Confucianism and, 31, 65; development of, 27, 29–30; Enlightenment and, 65–67, 72; European literature and, 68; fables and, 21, 28, 32, 36, 55–57, 59, 60, 66–68, 71; imagination and, 33, 148–49; Jesuits and, 30, 91; knowledge and, 42, 68; medieval travelogues in, 57, 89; postal systems and, 34, 38, 48; reception of, 65, 157; rulers and, 30, 40; scholarship on, 65–66; theater and, 234; transportation and, 37, 40–42, 148; travelogues in, 16, 40, 42, 57, 63, 68, 89, 234, 262, 310–12, 317; utopianism and, 56, 67; wars and, 156–57; world literature and, 68; writing style of, 27–28, 29, 65–68, 73, 111
Travels (Mandeville), 30
Travels (Polo), 21, 28–30, 32–33, 35–37, 38–42, 57, 59, 61–62, 65–66, 84, 166

A Treatise on Friendship (Ricci), 169n28, 331
Treaty of Westphalia (1648), 229
Trent, Council of (1545–1563), 119, 127, 164
Trigault, Nicholas, 76, 120, 170–72, 192, 252, 261, 287, 309
Troy, 184, 193
True Meaning of the Lord in Heaven, The (Ricci), 252
Turandot (Schiller), 62–63, 70, 71n83, 118, 282–83
Turmgesellschaft (Society of the tower), 334
Two Fair Cousins, The (Les deux cousines): administrative elite in, 326, 333–34, 338–39; analogies and, 324, 331, 342; autonomy aesthetics and, 331; gender in, 324, 334–36; information networks in, 338; literati in, 271, 334; poetry in, 307, 320, 334–36, 337, 339–40, 342–45; polygamy in, 337; postal systems in, 338–39; reception of, 45, 52, 308, 310, 321–22, 324, 332, 342–43, 345, 348; space in, 327; translation of, 306, 321, 331–32; writing style of, 308

"Über den Grund unseres Glaubens an eine göttliche Weltregierung" (Fichte), 290
Unger, Jacob Friedrich, 314
"Die ungeschickte Schluß-Künstler" (Francisci), 260
utopianism, 7, 10, 56, 60–61, 63, 65, 67, 76–77, 176, 342

Valignano, Alessandro, 90, 106–7
Väth, Alfons, 185
veneration of saints, 9, 120, 164
Verhofstadt, Edward, 189
Vicar of Wakefield, The (Goldsmith), 305
Virgil, 157, 183–84, 186
visualization. *See* imagination
Vita Christi (Ludolph of Saxony), 132

Voltaire (François-Marie Arouet), 124, 175n43, 226, 240, 271, 280–81
Vondel, Joost van den: accommodation and, 192–93; ancient references by, 183–84; Chinese sympathies and, 193–94, 224; Christianity and, 188, 193; Confucianism and, 193; conversion of, 185; influences on, 183–85; Jesuits and, 171, 178, 185–86, 195; Manchu conquest and, 177, 182–83; martyrdom and, 175, 182, 186; political stability and, 183–85, 190–91, 192, 194; rulers and, 173, 182–85, 186, 190–93; scholarship on, 189; sympathy and, 173
Vorstellungsvermögen (Reinhold), 277
Voyage to China and the East Indies (Osbeck), 148

Die Wahlverwandtschaften (Goethe), 264
Waldburg, Otto Truchseß von, 105
Walravens, Hartmut, 41n30
Wang Hung-tai, 339
wars, 20, 51, 95, 155–59, 165, 171, 173, 177–79
Watt, Ian, 233
Wealth of Nations (Smith), 221–22, 225–26
Weber, Max, 97, 149–50, 212n24, 349n126
Weber, Samuel, 94n43
Wedderburn, David, 45–46
Weimar and Nanjing disputation, 25, 245–46, 249, 253, 269–71, 273, 304
Weimar classicism, 70, 264, 267
Weinberg, Kurt, 148
Weitz, Hans-Jürgen, 199
Wellbery, David, 265, 343n114
Weltliteratur (world literature), 24–25, 197, 199–201, 303
West-Eastern Divan (Goethe): administrative elite and, 348–50; audience of, 70, 306; Chinese literature and, 346–47, 350, 354; colonialism and, 300–301; inspira-
tion for, 60, 68–70, 299, 305, 348–49; Islam and, 70, 254; literati and, 347; opening of, 70, 349; Persian poetry and, 346; perspectivism in, 351; reception of, 264; scholarship on, 346–48, 352–54; subjectivity in, 268, 351–52; world literature actualized by, 347
Westphalia Treaty (1648), 229
Wieland, Christoph: administrative elite and, 55; Chinese sympathies and, 160, 216; cosmopolitan sentimentalism and, 24, 196–200, 209–18; distance and, 212–13, 218; Enlightenment and, 197, 202–3, 215–18; fables and, 71; friendship and, 23, 214–16; God and, 213; influences on, 21, 198, 200–201, 215, 277; Jesuits and, 198, 212–13; letter writing and, 199–200; martyrdom and, 23; meditative practices and, 197–98; philosophy and, 197, 197n2, 217; Pietism and, 197, 207, 212, 214–15; postal systems and, 198; rulers and, 53–55; secularization and, 197–98, 219; Stoicism and, 218–19; sympathy and, 4, 197, 212–16, 218–19; translation and, 53–55, 199–201; world literature and, 24, 197–201; writing style of, 53–55, 213, 214, 215. *See also specific works*
Wiggins, Ellwood, 221
Wilhelm Meister's Apprenticeship (Goethe), 250, 308
Wilhelm, Richard, 72–73
Wilkerson, James, 308
Wissenschaftslehre (Fichte), 272, 275–76
Wolff, Christian, 7, 18, 197, 202, 228, 272–73, 278, 280, 291, 293
world literature: accommodation and, 122–23, 298; analogies and, 302–3; ancient sources of, 198–201; Chinese literature and, 12–15, 21, 297–98, 306–7; Chinese sympathies and, 140; Christianity and, 119; colonialism and, 202, 297; cosmology and,

257, 303; cosmopolitanism and, 123, 196, 199, 207, 297; development of, 14–15, 196, 199–200, 206–7, 301, 307; Enlightenment and, 12–13, 26, 207; friendship and, 203, 207; information networks and, 25, 199–200, 298–99; Jesuits and, 13, 24; knowledge and, 12–13, 15, 201, 310; letter writing and, 199–200; martyrdom and, 119; media and, 304; narrative and information in, 11–15; otherness in, 297; poetry and, 301; postal systems and, 24, 123; reading practices and, 11, 123, 207, 297; resemblances required for, 301; scholarship on, 298, 307; sentimentalism and, 24; space and, 201; sympathy and, 119, 140, 241; trade and, 201–2; translation and, 199, 310; travel literature and, 68; *Weltliteratur* and, 24–25, 197, 199–201, 303

Xavier, Francis: Asia mission of, 75, 79, 102–3, 109–10, 192; biography of, 110; canonization of, 21; diplomacy of, 178; imagination and, 109, 127; influence of, 8, 21, 75, 79, 98, 102, 110–11, 185–86; Japan mission of, 83, 102, 108, 110, 180, 186, 192; letter writing and, 21, 82–83, 83n24, 101, 103–4, 108, 143; martyrdom and, 98, 109–10; scriptural citations by, 82–83; theater and, 174, 180, 185; translation and, 104

Xuelang Hong'en (Sanhoi), 246, 256–57, 278–81, 329

yi jing, 5, 341
Yongle usurpation (1402), 162–63
Yu Jiao Li, 323–24

Zedler, Johann Heinrich, 2
Zhang Chunjie, 347
Ziegenbalg, Bartholomaeus, 150–54, 254
Zungchin (van den Vondel), 12, 23, 165, 175–76, 178, 186, 188, 195

CPSIA information can be obtained
at www.ICGtesting.com
Printed in the USA
LVHW090224201121
703843LV00010BA/836

9 781501 759741